INTRODUCTION TO EQUITY INVESTMENT
FUND ACCOUNTING

INTRODUCTION TO EQUITY INVESTMENT FUND ACCOUNTING

John Casey

BLACKHALL
PUBLISHING

Published by Blackhall Publishing
Lonsdale House
Avoca Avenue
Blackrock
Co. Dublin
Ireland

e-mail: info@blackhallpublishing.com
www.blackhallpublishing.com

ISBN: 978-1-84218-193-5

A catalogue record for this book is available from the British Library.

Printed and bound in Great Britain by CPI Antony Rowe, Chippenham, Wiltshire.

To Bríd, Liam and Eimear

Foreword

Over the past twenty years, as Ireland has established itself as a leading global jurisdiction for internationally distributed investment funds, many people have developed and are enjoying successful careers in the investment funds industry in Ireland. The industry offers many opportunities for those who demonstrate the appropriate skills and knowledge; skills and knowledge which will be enhanced and developed throughout your career. A textbook that addresses the fundamentals of investment fund accounting is both a welcome and an overdue development which will aid that career commencement. The Irish Funds Industry Association (IFIA) is committed to supporting the development of those in the industry and we view this book as an important element of that commitment. Many new entrants to the industry begin their careers in the fund accounting area and a book that assists in acquiring this skill set, using clear and comprehensive examples, is invaluable.

The IFIA represents the custodians, administrators, managers, transfer agents, fund promoters and professional advisory firms involved in the international fund services industry in Ireland. Since the members of the Association include the companies involved in all aspects of the industry, the Association is well placed to support and compliment the continued development of the industry in Ireland. The Association plays an active role in supporting the professional development of the industry's most valuable resource, its people, and this is achieved through the certificate and diploma in Investment Fund Services (a joint programme with the Institute of Bankers), a schedule of training programmes, and industry-specific seminars and briefings. The Association is also to the fore and leads the defining of practice in complex areas such as compliance, valuation, accounting, corporate governance, share dealing and registration.

It is my expressed wish that you enjoy a rewarding and challenging career in the industry and I hope this book will be the start of that journey.

Gary Palmer
CEO, Irish Funds Industry Association
www.irishfunds.ie

About the Author

John Casey lectures at Waterford Institute of Technology (WIT), where he is programme director for the MBS in Accounting. He has a B.Comm., FCA and M.Sc. in Finance and previously worked as an auditor with Price Waterhouse. He is also an examination moderator for the professional accounting institutes, a former committee member of the Irish Accounting and Finance Association and a member of the AIB Centre for Finance and Business Research at WIT.

Acknowledgements

I would like to express my gratitude to a number of people who provided invaluable feedback and support throughout the development of this book.

Dr Tom O'Toole, Head of the School of Business at Waterford Institute of Technology, was an unwavering supporter and motivator of the book – without him you would not be reading these words. Sincere thanks are due to Pat Quinn, who laboured through a very rough draft and provided me with a series of insightful and informed suggestions. Gary Palmer, Chief Executive of the Irish Funds Industry Association, kindly wrote the foreword but, more importantly, supported this project.

I am grateful to all of the various organisations, many of whom are participants in the investment/mutual fund industry, for permission to reproduce their original material. It is testimony to the support that the industry offers to development and education that in no instance did any organisation refuse permission for the use of their material. In a small number of cases it was not possible, after considerable effort, to make contact with the owners of copyright material. The material was used in good faith and I would appreciate any information to enable me to resolve any outstanding permissions.

I would like to thank all the people in Blackhall Publishing, in particular Eileen O'Brien and Elizabeth Brennan. Writing a book can be a chastening process and my poor grammar and syntax probably didn't help. This must have been infuriating for Eileen but she maintained a professional and thorough approach right to the very end. The editing process is unseen; however, without Eileen's input, this book would have been significantly harder to read and comprehend. She was unflappable, particularly in the face of criminal levels of poor expression and missed deadlines. I sincerely appreciate the work that Eileen put into this book. I can really only hold one person responsible for any remaining errors and mistakes – me.

An apology and a word of thanks is due to all the past students who studied Introduction to Fund Accounting at Waterford Institute of Technology. The apology is because you were unwitting participants in the development of the book and the thanks are because your comments contributed to the book, in particular, the pedagogical style used. While you do not get the benefit of your input, your successors will.

I would like to express my appreciation to all my colleagues at Waterford Institute of Technology, especially Tom Egan and Sheila O'Donohoe, who share an office with me, and Jackie Deise Murphy. They ensured that I stayed positive and provided advice whenever it was requested on any issue.

Finally to my family – Mam, Dad, Edel, Lisa and Pony, but, in particular, Bríd, Liam and Eimear – you ensured that I did not go investment-fund crazy, although you may have a different opinion.

Preface

This book is intended for students of investment fund accounting. It assumes very little prior knowledge – even beginning with the discussion 'What is an Investment Fund?' It will also be of benefit to those beginning their careers in investment fund auditing, as it explains how a basic investment fund operates from an accounting perspective.

There is no need for a detailed knowledge of accounting (i.e. debits and credits); this is explained in Chapter 2. In fact, if the debit/credit concept frightens you, it is possible to bypass it by adopting the spreadsheet approach used in this book. For the die-hards, the full accounting treatment for any transaction is also addressed, using the simple logic of double entry bookkeeping (i.e. the debit/credit system).

At the end of each major chapter, there is a 'Bringing It All Together' section. This does exactly what it says but also includes elements from previous chapters. In this way, it is possible to develop an understanding of investment fund accounting in stages, while learning how all of the different elements fit together. If you can master this part of a chapter then you have achieved a lot and are more than ready to move to the challenge of the next chapter.

Another important feature of the book is that the solution to each example is explained in detail. This should allow the reader to understand the logic behind the recording of any transaction, instead of being presented with the answer as a *fait accompli*. Repeat transactions from earlier sections may be outlined without much discussion; in these cases you should refer to the previous sections for a more complete explanation.

In an age when information technology (IT) systems can eliminate the drudgery of many investment fund processing operations, it also has a negative effect – the need to understand the underlying transaction is reduced. Over the past two decades the investment fund industry has utilised the benefit of technology extensively but there is a price. It is more difficult to appreciate the impact of the transactions being processed. This is particularly true when errors are made, since correcting any errors is more complex and time-consuming. It is hoped that this book, by taking a step back to basic accounting, will help to alleviate some of these issues.

In this way, it will allow those starting out in the industry to develop a greater understanding of what they are doing and act as a springboard for their future development.

This book concentrates on equity fund accounting; the next stage is fixed income fund accounting followed by hedge fund accounting. Once you have completed this book, you will have overcome many of the hurdles associated with accounting for investment funds. While there is certainly more to learn, you will have achieved a great deal. This book should provide you with a good grounding and an understanding that will allow you to advance to the more complex aspects of investment fund accounting. Difficulties will be encountered; this is common to any learning process. This book should help to allow you to resolve these difficulties for yourself. Stick with it and you will have a sound understanding that will give you the foundation to move to the next level.

It is my desire that the book explains each topic in simple language. In addition, the examples and associated solutions should act as a means of testing your understanding. However, if I have failed in some areas then please let me know and future versions can be improved for those students that follow you. Remember, if you can't understand a topic, it is probably because it wasn't explained very well. Any comments will be gratefully accepted so please email me at jcasey@wit.ie.

Thank you for using this book. I hope you find it helpful. Any errors are, of course, my own and my responsibility. If you do disagree with any item in this book then please let me know. Good luck with your studies and subsequent careers. For downloadable copies of the work tables for the further comprehensive questions please visit www.blackhallpublishing.com/index.php/business-and-management/introduction-to-equity-investment-fund-accounting.html.

John Casey
January 2010

Contents

Contents

Chapter 1

Introduction

- Introduction
- A little context
- Investment funds
- Why invest in an investment fund?
- Types of investment funds
- Workings of a typical investment fund
- Why establish an investment fund?
- Conclusion
- Additional questions

LEARNING OUTCOMES

At the end of this chapter you should:

- Be able to explain what an investment fund is.
- Be able to describe why an investor might invest their money in an investment fund product.
- Be familiar with the different types of investment fund.
- Be able to describe how an investment fund works.
- Be able to discuss why a financial institution might set up an investment fund.

1.1: INTRODUCTION

In this chapter we will consider the workings of the investment fund industry. An attempt will be made to answer some fundamental questions about the industry. This will be done from the point of view of someone who has no real exposure to the sector. Section 1.2 puts the industry within its context and addresses some of the issues that will arise again and again throughout this book. In Section 1.3 we will consider investment funds in a little more detail and this will lead into a discussion, in Section 1.4, on the benefits of investing in investment funds.

The investment fund industry has developed significantly over the past two decades and there is a wide range of products available to suit the requirements of nearly any potential investor. This range of different products is addressed in Section 1.5. Before we can move to accounting for investment funds it is important to have an understanding of how an investment fund works and the different parties involved – this is the subject of Section 1.6. Finally, Section 1.7 considers why a financial institution goes to the trouble (and expense) of setting up an investment fund.

After studying this chapter you will have a much deeper understanding of how the investment fund industry works. It will also provide you with the base level of knowledge that you will require when, later, we move on to accounting for investment funds.

1.2: A LITTLE CONTEXT

It may surprise you that the author of this book does have a social life. Inevitably at parties I am asked what I do and I proudly explain my connection to the investment fund industry. At this point, I can often see eyes glaze over and the conversation moves to centre on the helicopter rescue pilot who used to live next door (this is true, it was hard to compete). However, there are always some who will persevere and the next question is often to do with stocks and shares.[1] These questions I generally try to avoid as my own track record in this matter isn't that great. As the conversation continues, the main questions that I tend to be asked can be summarised into the four set out below. These questions act as a good starting point for a discussion on investment funds. Perhaps the real lesson is to avoid me at any party!

1. What, in very simple terms, is an investment fund?
2. What is so unusual about accounting for investment funds?
3. What is 'regulation'?
4. What does an investment fund look like?

1.2.1: What Is an Investment Fund?

Consider this example – you and your friends wish to buy a new gaming console but do not have enough cash individually to purchase the console. Instead, you decide to pool your money and buy the console between you, agreeing to share its usage.

---

[1] The helicopter rescue pilot and his family moved away and a jockey/racehorse trainer moved in with his family. People are usually more interested in horse racing tips than share tips; I can't win.

An investment fund is no different. You want to buy shares in a company (e.g. Microsoft) but you do not have enough money to make a meaningful purchase. So you pool your money with some others. However, there is a problem – you do not know the 'others'. In the console example, above, the group is self-regulating – you all know one another and are so involved in the purchase that, as a group, you are able to come to an agreement over who gets to use the console and for how long. In the case of an investment fund, there needs to be a legal agreement, structure and regulations to protect the various investors.

So an investment fund is a legal arrangement that allows individuals to pool their cash to make investments in shares (also called equities) or bonds or commodities or property or any asset – even horses. Individuals often cannot afford to buy a horse so they get together with their friends to buy the horse as a group – in the horsey world this is called a syndicate, but it is also a type of investment fund. What do you think of this as a form of investing?

One of the problems with the gaming console purchase or the horse syndicate is that the 'investment' can be illiquid.[2] What if one of the 'investors' wishes to sell out? Can you see any problems and how can they be resolved? Most equity investment funds do not suffer from this liquidity problem – the funds are valued regularly (often daily) and this provides a price at which new investors can buy into the fund and existing investors can sell out. Calculating this price is a key role of the investment fund accountant.

Another benefit of an investment fund is that individuals do not have to put in equal amounts. If you put more money in, you get a greater percentage share of the assets of the fund. Consider the console example from earlier – what if one of your friends did not have the same amount of money as the rest of the group? How would you deal with this? You need his or her cash to buy the console but should that person get the same rights over the use of the console? Assuming that you put no value on friendship, you would probably insist on two things:

1. That person would get less usage time with the console.
2. If the console is sold on, then that person would get less of the ultimate sales proceeds.

---

[2] 'Illiquid' is a technical term meaning there are very few buyers and sellers in the market. Thus, it can be difficult to convert the investment or asset into cash. Some assets are more illiquid than others – houses can be more difficult to sell than shares. In addition, in times of uncertainty markets generally tend to become more illiquid as buyers are afraid to invest.

Investment funds are no different: they contain a mechanism to ensure that those investors who put in the most money get the greatest benefits (assuming that the fund is making money).

1.2.2: What Is so Unusual about Accounting for Investment Funds?

Much of the accounting for investment funds is very similar to accounting for any business. However, the main difference is the requirement to value the assets and liabilities of the fund on a regular basis, often daily.

The reason for this has been alluded to in the previous section. Frequently, investors will want to buy into and exit from the investment fund. Thus they will need to have a price that they can trust. Let's go back to the horse example. You and your nine friends each paid €10,000 to buy a share in a horse. Let's assume that the horse had a strong lineage and you were confident that the horse would be a winner. Two years later you have been proved right: the horse has won a number of top races, generating significant prize money. However, now one of the friends wishes to leave the syndicate (investment fund). How do you manage this transaction? There could also be further complications if some of the 'friends' had not been contributing to the upkeep of the horse. An investment fund is no different except that there could be thousands of investors who want to buy into or sell out of the fund (consider having to value the horse on a daily basis).

Most of the issues in accounting for investment funds arise when the valuation process is undertaken. There are reasonably straightforward accounting entries to be made but, often, arriving at the valuation is the most complicated part (as in the example of the race horse syndicate).

1.2.3: What Is 'Regulation'?

In recent times, financial regulation (or the lack of it) has come into a central position in the public consciousness. It is a complex area with many different parties involved. In addition, it can be difficult to identify the authority and priority of each of these parties. The explanation that follows attempts to consider regulation from a broader perspective. However, there is another course that could be purely devoted to the detail of all of the regulations.

In a general sense 'regulation' is the name given to the rules that the parties involved in the funds industry must play by. The rules have a number of sources: they can be legally defined by statute, they can be defined by the 'Regulator', they can be defined by the industry (best practice guidelines), they can be defined by accounting bodies (accounting standards) and they can be defined by the fund itself (in its prospectus).

These rules are important because they protect investors, give certainty to those involved and provide a code that investors can refer to if they feel that their rights have not been upheld. Without these rules (regulations) it is unlikely that any investor would give their money to an investment manager who they do not know or have never met.

While often the regulations are self-policing, it is the Regulator who has overall responsibility to ensure that everyone plays by the rules. The Regulator is a body that is independent of the parties involved in the industry, is often government appointed and receives its authority through statute. The regulator for the Irish investment fund industry is the Irish Financial Services Regulatory Authority (IFSRA) (see www.ifsra.ie). In addition, those funds that are quoted on the Irish Stock Exchange are bound by its regulations (see www.ise.ie). The Regulator has wide-ranging powers to investigate those involved in a fund and can initiate a court action that may, in serious cases, end with imprisonment. In the United States (US), Bernard Madoff was sentenced to 150 years in jail, but this is an extreme example − he stole $50 billion by using his hedge fund as a Ponzi scheme.

While investors are the beneficiaries of any rules, the extent of regulation can be resented by the industry. The reasons for this are twofold:

1. Regulation is perceived as placing a cost on the parties involved. Producing reports, getting financial statements audited and setting up systems to ensure compliance costs a significant amount of money. This cost must either be borne by the service provider (the investment fund manager, the custodian of the fund, etc.) or passed on to the investor. Often, the opportunity to pass the cost on to the investor can be difficult as it may result in many investors withdrawing from the fund and investing in other products that are not subject to such high regulatory costs.

2. Regulation reduces the freedom of the participants in the industry. For example, some funds are not allowed to borrow or speculate on derivatives.[3] This constrains the investment managers from exploiting some opportunities that may exist in the market. The other side of the argument is that it prevents investment managers from taking large risks with other people's money, thus protecting investors.

---

[3] Derivatives are complex financial products. An example of a derivative is a share option. Derivatives tend to have much a higher risk than equities or bonds. It is because of the risk characteristics of derivatives that some funds may be precluded from investing in them.

What happens if the rules are weak or fail? This will often result in lengthy legal battles. Take, as an example, lotto syndicates. These are informal arrangements where individuals pool their cash when buying lotto tickets on the understanding that any prizes will also be shared (not too dissimilar to an investment fund). As you can imagine there is little regulation around lotto syndicates (it does not come within the remit of IFSRA), so it is not difficult to see what can potentially occur. Most lotto syndicates operate without dispute – why do you think this is the case? It is probably because most lotto syndicates rarely win any big prizes worth arguing over. However, when there are big winnings, there is also potential for big disputes. See the article, Figure 1.1, from the *Western People* on 25 January 2005 describing a lotto syndicate dispute.

Figure 1.1: The Need for Regulation?

Lotto syndicate opts to appeal court decision

THE battle for a share in the infamous Ballyvary Lotto jackpot is set to continue for another two years following the decision by the men involved to appeal last month's High Court verdict which awarded a share of the jackpot to a fifth member of the syndicate.

Bohola man, Martin Horan, had been told that he was entitled to a one-fifth share of the €2 million Lotto jackpot after he instituted the High Court proceedings against the four other members of the syndicate – Frank O'Reilly, a publican, of O'Reilly's pub, Ballyvary; Michael McHale, a farmer from Currane; John Joyce a taxi driver of Keelogue; and Seamus O'Brien, also a taxi driver from Ballyvary.

It had been expected that the case would go no further than the High Court but the *Western People* understands that an appeal is now pending in the Supreme Court. When contacted by this newspaper, the members of the syndicate refused to confirm if they had lodged an appeal, claiming they had been told by their legal team not to discuss the matter with the media.

"I can't talk to you about the case, you'll have to talk to my solicitor," Mr Frank O'Reilly told the *Western People*.

However, Mr O'Reilly acknowledged that he and the other members of the syndicate had not yet collected their shares of the €2 million jackpot. Under the High Court ruling each member of the syndicate – including Martin Horan – is entitled to around €400,000 each. Both sides in the dispute had 21 days to appeal the High Court judgement which was delivered by Justice Frederick Clarke on December 3rd last.

If an appeal had not been lodged the men would have been entitled to pick up their earnings on Christmas Eve. However, the *Western People* understands that an extension was sought to the appeal period – to cover the Christmas holidays – and the appeal was then lodged last week.

News of the Supreme Court appeal comes almost four years to the day that the syndicate won the €2 million jackpot. When the case came before the High Court, it was claimed that Mr Horan had been 'removed' from the syndicate because he was constantly in arrears.

Figure 1.1: *(Continued)*

Throughout the proceedings Mr Horan, a plant operator, with an address of Carragowan, Bohola, has claimed that he was a member of the Lotto syndicate, which won the massive prize on January 6, 2001. He said that in 1999 he and the four men agreed to contribute equally to the Lotto syndicate each week and to share any winnings equally. While the men agreed that Mr Horan was part of the syndicate for a short time, they claimed that he failed to make the payments and therefore was not entitled to any of the winnings.

However, Justice Clarke ruled in favour of Mr Horan on the basis that the syndicate had accepted arrears from him in the past. Crucially, the Judge also ruled that Mr Horan was entitled to his costs, which were estimated to be in the region of €100,000.

After the High Court decision the four Ballyvary men had 21 days to appeal the result, bringing them up to Christmas Eve. But only days before Mr Horan was to pick up €400,000 from the National Lottery Headquarters in Dublin he was notified of an appeal.

The four-year battle for a share in the jackpot now looks set to continue for another two years leaving the five men involved unsure what money they will receive and creating further bad feeling in the village of Ballyvary, where the five men had participated in regular card games in O'Reilly's pub. An appeal to the Supreme Court will inevitably mean further substantial costs.

This has now become such an issue for both the UK and Irish lotteries that they have issued guidelines for anyone starting up a lotto syndicate. See www.national-lottery.co.uk/player/p/help/syndicates.ftl for an example. In essence, the guidelines state that there should be a syndicate agreement to set the rules and then a systematic approach to record keeping. A systematic approach to record keeping and transaction processing is one of the key purposes of investment fund accounting. Much of this book is about ensuring that all of the funds' transactions are properly recorded.

If the example of a horse syndicate (Section 1.2.2) whetted your appetite, have a look at this site: www.ownaracehorse.co.uk. It raises some interesting questions on the nature of investment and regulation:

- What do you think of this site?
- Is buying a racehorse being portrayed as an investment?
- How is a return generated? Is there an impression that the return will exceed the investment made?
- Can you see any financial statements (for either the management company or for the individual horses)?
- Should this type of 'product' be regulated by the UK Financial Regulator (FSA)?

1.2.4: What Does an Investment Fund Look Like?

Unfortunately, an investment fund is not like any other business. Generally, there are no buildings, production machinery or delivery trucks. The investments (in shares and bonds) are held in paper or electronic format in a secure location. If you would like to see an investment fund's financial statements have a look at the next chapter or try any internet search engine; most funds publish their annual reports on their websites. It is in the annual report that you will be able to see the most tangible manifestation of an investment fund.

Investment funds do not have any employees. The fund contracts all of its services to third parties. The investment manager is employed by an investment advisory company that charges the funds for its services, similarly for the fund accountant, the auditor, etc. The advantage of this arrangement is that the fund itself is very flexible: if the investment manager is not doing a good job then the agreement can be terminated and a different advisor appointed. In addition, by hiring an investment management company the fund can benefit from the expertise of the investment team, research division and experience of a large organisation rather than place its trust in the judgement of just a single individual.

1.3: INVESTMENT FUNDS

We have had a broad discussion on investment funds; now we need to consider them in more detail. Investment funds are also known as Collective Investment Schemes, Undertakings for Investments in Transferrable Securities (UCITS),[4] Mutual Funds, Unit Trusts or Managed Funds. These have some very slight differences but the underlying principle is the same.

According to Investopedia.com, an investment fund or mutual fund is

> An investment vehicle that is made up of a pool of funds collected from many investors for the purpose of investing in securities such as stocks, bonds, money market instruments and similar assets. Mutual funds are operated by money mangers, who invest the fund's capital and attempt to produce capital gains and income for the fund's investors. A mutual fund's portfolio is structured and maintained to match the investment objectives stated in its prospectus.[5]

---

[4] This is a bit of a mouthful but it is an important legal term. Its abbreviation is more commonly used: UCITS, pronounced 'yoo-sits'. UCITS is the name given to the EU directive that regulates a particular type of investment fund that is sold to the public across the EU.

[5] *Source*: www.investopedia.com, © Investopedia.com. All rights reserved. www.investopedia.com is an excellent website with lots of articles and help on all matters investment related. It has a handy dictionary function; if there is any term that you do not understand there is probably help on www.investopedia.com/dictionary/default.asp.

An investment fund is where investors pool their money in return for shares in the fund. Using the expertise of professional investment management advice, the fund then uses the investors' money to buy shares, bonds, commodities, property or any other asset you can think of. If the value of the shares, bonds, etc. increase then the investors in the fund are better off. However, if the value decreases then the investors end up with less cash than they originally invested. Remember the voice on the radio that says (albeit very quickly), 'This is an investment product, its value can go up as well as down, past performance is not an indicator of future performance….' For most funds there is a lower limit; investors cannot lose more than they invested in the fund. This is known as limited liability, which also exists in the same format outside the funds industry. While an investor might not be happy with this outcome, the alternative is much worse – losing more than the cash you initially invested in the fund.

Consider a scenario where, as an investor, you decide to put €10,000 into a fund. This is done in the expectation that the €10,000 will increase in value over time. However, stock markets can be volatile and the €10,000 could lose value and after a year could become just €4,500. Things could get worse (more poor investments by the investment manager) and the investment could fall further, to, say, €2,400. But that might not be the end of it; the value might decrease again to €600, just when you thought things couldn't get worse. The pattern is evident. The value of your investment can fall down to zero but that's the limit and it will go no further. This is the benefit of limited liability. If this did not exist and the value of the fund became negative then you would have to put more and more money into the fund to return it to a positive position. You could ultimately have to sell your house or car to do this. So, while losing €10,000 is a bitter pill, it is not as unpalatable as the possibility of losing a lot more. In addition, the benefit of the protection of limited liability means that you also know where the bottom is. If this did not exist then it is unlikely that anyone would invest in an investment fund.

There have been examples of investment funds that have gone out of business. When investment funds go bankrupt, the amounts involved tend to be large (sometimes billions of euro).[6] While bankrupt investment funds are rare events, the possibility always exists. Thus, the protection of limited liability for investors is a key foundation stone for the investment fund industry.

---

[6] The credit crisis of 2008–2009 has resulted in many investment funds getting into difficulty. The media like to report the numbers, but these are often overstated. So far, the record holders are Madoff Securities (a fraud/Ponzi scheme) – with supposedly in excess of $50 billion under management – and the Reserve Primary Fund (not a fraud but some legal cases are pending) – with over $64 billion under management on 31 May 2008, but the final loss will be significantly less.

Here is what we know so far – investors pool their cash into the fund and the fund then uses that cash to make investments; this is shown diagrammatically in Figure 1.2.

In Figure 1.2, 'Inv 1', 'Inv 2', 'Inv 3', etc. represent the individual investors in an investment fund. There can be tens of thousands of these investors, each putting varying amounts into the fund. The fund then uses the money received from the investors to buy shares in AIB, Ryanair, Vodafone or other companies. There can be hundreds of different investments. In this book we will be concentrating on equities (i.e. shares) but the fund could purchase any asset – corporate bonds, government bonds, derivatives, property, etc.

Figure 1.2: A Simplified Representation of an Investment Fund

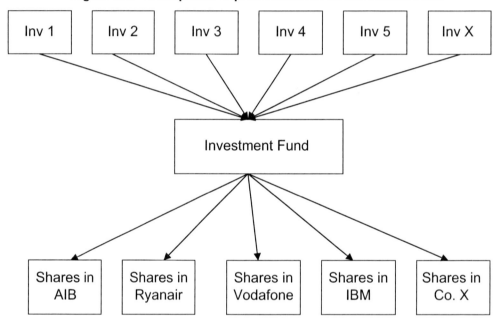

1.4: WHY INVEST IN AN INVESTMENT FUND?

Now that we know the basic structure of investment funds we should consider why ordinary investors put their own money into investment funds.

1.4.1: Diversification

One of the first rules of investing is that you shouldn't put all your eggs in one basket. Thus, if you have €10,000 of available funds, you would be taking a huge risk if you invested it all into the shares of just one company (Ryanair, for example). It should be possible to determine why: if Ryanair shares fell, your investment would suffer quite dramatically. Or, worse again, if Ryanair went bankrupt (an unlikely but not impossible outcome), your investment would be worth zero.

A better solution would be to spread your funds across a number of shares. Studies have shown that, on average and over time, stock markets increase in value.[7] However, hidden in the averages are numerous companies that do badly. It can be very difficult to determine which company is likely to perform poorly, but the number of companies that perform well outweigh the number of companies that perform badly. Thus, a means of protecting your investment is to play the averages and invest in many different companies.

Remember, the stock market is not a gamble like a horse race. If you bet on every horse in a race, you will lose money over time because the odds are such that the bookies make a return. However, with the stock market it is possible to invest in every share on the market and still (over time) make a positive return. This might appear to be a strange approach to investing but there is a complete sector of the investment fund industry devoted to it – the Tracker Fund/Index Fund (it is probably the sector with the most cash invested).

Going back to the Ryanair example – it might make more sense to put €5,000 into Ryanair and €5,000 into BP (the oil company British Petroleum). Why might this be a good investment strategy?[8] However, it is still possible that both BP and Ryanair could buck the stock market trend and fall in value. So, perhaps, we should spread our funds over three or four or five shares? The act of buying a number of different shares is called 'diversification'. The question then becomes how many different shares should we purchase so that we get the benefit of diversification? There is a lack of agreement here but many studies have put the number at twenty;[9] others put it higher. Investment funds would purchase numerous different shares, often in excess of 100.

The difficulty for the individual investor is that it is hard to diversify. If you 'only' have €10,000 to invest then spreading that across twenty shares results in €500 in

---

[7] According to Ibbotson and Chen (2003), depending on which measure is used the average return on the stock market is 12.56 per cent per annum for the period 1926–2000.

[8] As the price of jet fuel (and oil) increases, the share price of Ryanair tends to fall whereas the opposite is true of BP. A matched pair of this nature can act as a hedge against oil price volatility.

[9] See Malkiel (2007), *A Random Walk Down Wall Street*, for a good discussion on the benefits of diversification and portfolio theory. This is a famous book on investing that was first published in 1973 and is now into its ninth edition.

each share. It makes much more sense to pool your money with others – if a fund has €10 million to invest this means the average investment is €500,000, which is a much more meaningful investment.

1.4.2: Professional Management and Administration

When someone invests in a fund they generally leave the investment decisions to professional investment managers. If the investment managers are not very good then they can be replaced. This is similar to hiring football managers – the top premiership sides do not hire unknown rookie managers. Instead they go for qualified, experienced managers with a strong track record. If football managers were investment managers then Alex Ferguson and the like would attract the most investors. However, if performance begins to falter then the manager can be replaced with someone new. It is no different for investment managers.

Investment managers have considerable investing experience. Ideally, they understand the risks (and expected returns) of the investments that they are making. They are in a position to ensure that the assets purchased are suited to the requirements of the fund. Selecting and making investments can be a daunting and time-consuming exercise – an investment manager will do this on behalf of investors.

Furthermore, an investment manager should carry out a significant amount of research in advance of deciding which shares/bonds, etc. to purchase. Much of this research is beyond the average investor and, even if it was possible, is a lengthy process. Many investors are prepared to leave share selection to the experts.

There is a downside: investment managers charge for their services and advice. For example, the T. Rowe Price Equity Income Fund was charged over $105 million in investment management fees for the year ended 31 May 2008.[10] However, if the fund is large then these fees tend to become less significant as the cost of the advice is spread over a larger asset base. In the example used above, the net asset value of the T. Rowe Price Equity Income Fund was $14.1 billion; the investment management fee represents just 0.75 per cent of the value of the fund.

There has been a lot of debate as to whether investment managers are any good at their job, i.e. selecting shares that will beat the market for their funds. It is impossible to predict the future and investment managers do not have a crystal ball; they can also make poor decisions. In fact many studies would point to the fact that investment managers, on average, fail to beat the market.[11] Even tracker fund

---

[10] T. Rowe Price Equity Income Fund annual report for year ended 31 May 2008, available at www.troweprice.com.

[11] See Malkiel, *A Random Walk Down Wall Street*, for a good discussion on the performance of investment managers.

managers often fail to track the index they are supposed to be following due to a problem known as tracking error.[12]

Investment funds also offer the benefit of professional administration. If you buy shares and other investments on your own account on a regular basis, there is a degree of administration that needs to be undertaken. This is necessary for a number of reasons: you would need to keep track of what you own, there are tax and possibly other statutory returns that you need to complete whenever you transact in the shares, and it might be handy to be able to value your investments from time to time. This all takes time and some knowledge. Many smaller investors may not want to do this. If your money is invested in a fund then this is part of the service. It costs money but if it is spread over a large number of investors (a large asset base) then the percentage cost becomes small.

1.4.3: Economies of Scale

This has already been indirectly referred to in the two previous sections. An economy of scale is where there is a benefit to being large. It doesn't imply that costs are lower – in fact the costs are often higher but they are spread across a much larger number of investors. The resulting effect is that the cost per investor is greatly reduced.

For example, if an investor with €10,000 to invest obtains independent investment advice, he or she will be charged a fee; €500 would not be unreasonable. This represents 5 per cent of their available cash. A fund with €100 million may be charged €1.5 million (depending on the nature of the fund but this level of fees would not be unusual), or 1.5 per cent of the available funds. So the cost per investor is much less.

There are numerous other savings also. For example, it can cost an Irish retail investor a flat fee of €32 plus 1.25 per cent of the value of the shares to purchase equities.[13] Thus, an individual buying €5,000 worth of shares will be charged €94.50, nearly 2 per cent of the value of the shares purchased. However, investment funds purchase shares in much larger blocks (often in excess of €1 million per transaction). The size of the transaction does not significantly impact on the cost to the stockbroker and funds can bargain for a much reduced dealing cost. The Sprott Canadian Equity Fund paid nearly $1.6 million CAD in brokerage

---

[12] See Section 1.5.8 for a discussion on tracker funds.

[13] Rates as per Goodbodys on 1 June 2008 (available on www.goodbody.ie/products/ costs.html). This does not include other additional charges such as stamp duty of 1 per cent, account maintenance fees and third party fees. The above fees relate to the purchase of Irish shares; overseas shares will cost more.

commissions on total purchases and sales of shares of $748 million CAD, a broker-age cost of 0.2 per cent.[14]

In general, the larger the fund the lower the cost per investor share. One of the largest funds in the world, the Vanguard 500 Index Fund, had total net assets on 31 December 2007 of over $121 billion USD. It paid total expenses of $142 million USD. This is a large amount of expenses but is only 0.12 per cent of total net assets.[15] Remember, this includes all of the expenses of the fund: investment advice, administration costs, trustee fees, etc. No matter how efficient an individual investor is, it is unlikely that they would get close to this level of cost.

1.4.4: Regulatory and Other Safeguards

There have been numerous instances where individuals have given their cash to a 'trusted' financial advisor only to find later that the advisor gambled/spent/ran off with their money.[16] Over the years there has been a raft of rules and laws put in place to help protect investors.

When a retail investor (ordinary person) decides to invest in a fund, they get the benefit of a wide range of investor protection regulations. Some of these protections will depend on the nature of the fund and its legal structure but the effect of the rules is to ensure that:

- The possibility of an investor losing their money due to fraud is minimised
- The possibility of the fund making investments that it isn't authorised to make is minimised
- Investors are provided with information to allow them to evaluate the performance of their fund and the fees and expenses that they are charged
- Those involved in the operation of the fund (investment managers, trustees, administrators, etc.) have a duty to act in the interests of the investors

The regulations come from a number of sources. The Financial Regulator (www.ifsra.ie) issues new regulations from time to time. All investment funds that are registered in Ireland are required to abide by these regulations. In addition,

---

[14] Sprott Canadian Equity Fund details from annual report for year ended 31 December 2004. CAD = Canadian Dollar.

[15] Vanguard 500 Index Fund data from annual report for year ended 31 December 2007. USD = US Dollar.

[16] One of the most famous Irish cases is where accountant Russell Murphy defrauded broadcaster Gay Byrne of his life savings in 1986.

there are legal (statutory) requirements that funds may be required to respect – the Companies Acts and the Unit Trusts Act 1990, for example.

Often, an even greater safeguard is the reputation of the financial institution offering the investment fund. As an example, Citi is one of the largest financial services organisations in the world and it offers a wide range of investment fund products. These large organisations trade on their reputation. If investors lose confidence in these companies then they will be seriously undermined. Thus, it is in their best interests to ensure that their own in-house controls and procedures are even more stringent than the legal and regulatory rules. In addition, the resources of these large businesses are so vast that if there is a problem, it is likely that they will have the ability to make good any loss caused by their negligence (although this can be a slow and protracted process). In January 2009, Banco Santander offered its private clients some compensation (€1.4 billion) to cover their losses on the Madoff Securities Ponzi scheme. Santander did this to allow the bank to maintain 'its business relationships with those clients'.[17]

1.4.5: Tax Minimisation

Possibly the main benefit of investing in a fund is the tax benefit that accrues (if the fund is a pension fund, the tax benefits are even greater). The tax benefits can vary from country to country and from fund to fund. For most Irish-based funds, the fund is effectively a tax free zone.

When a fund generates an income from its investments (generally dividends or interest) it does not pay any tax and when a fund sells its investments it is not subject to any tax. Contrast that with an individual – if an individual buys shares themselves, instead of through a fund, they will pay income tax at 41 per cent plus levies of at least 2 per cent[18] on their dividend income. In addition, when the shares are sold they will pay capital gains tax of 25 per cent on any gain.

The real benefit of this is not just the tax saving, but that a fund has much more money available to make gains than an individual. This reinvestment effect gets larger and larger the more often a fund buys and sells shares.

---

[17] Banco Santander is one of the largest banks in Europe. It had facilitated some of its clients to invest in Madoff Securities via an intermediate fund (Optimal Strategic US Equity Fund). At the time of writing the complete settlement had not been arrived at. For more information see www.santander.com.

[18] Assume that the individual is taxed at the higher rate of tax, currently 41 per cent plus 2 per cent income levy. PRSI is ignored. Rates applicable from 1 May 2009. Irish tax rates used.

When an investor exits a fund then they may be subject to a tax liability. Irish residents will have to pay tax of up to 28 per cent[19] on the gain. Non-resident investors may not be subject to any Irish tax but may be subject to tax in the country they are resident in.

These tax benefits have a significant impact on the funds industry in Ireland. In addition, all those companies that service the investment funds – administration companies, custodian companies, etc. – only pay 12.5 per cent corporation tax on their profits.

Consider the following example; this will give you an insight into the tax benefit of investment funds.

Example 1.1: Tax Effect of Funds

A fund has €100,000 which it invests in shares that give an annual return (share price gain) of 15 per cent and a dividend yield of 5 per cent. At the end of each year it sells its shares and reinvests the proceeds and dividends in different shares. The new shares now give a return of 15 per cent and a dividend yield of 5 per cent. The fund repeats this process for five years. At the end of the five years what is the fund worth?

Now an individual has €100,000 which he or she invests personally in shares that give the same annual return of 15 per cent and a dividend yield of 5 per cent. The dividend is subject to income tax and levies of 43 per cent. At the end of the year, the individual sells the shares. However, the gain on the sale of the shares is subject to capital gains tax of 25 per cent. The proceeds of the sale of the shares less any capital gains tax and the dividend less income tax is reinvested in new shares. The new shares will give a return of 15 per cent and a dividend yield of 5 per cent subject to the same tax rates. The individual repeats this for five years. At the end of the five years what is the individual worth?

What is the difference between the fund and the individual after five years?

This is a good opportunity to utilise your Excel skills – this type of problem can be solved much faster using Excel. Use the value of shares at the start of the year to calculate the dividend yield (see Table 1.1).

Note, in Table 1.1, that after five years the fund is worth €55,000 more than the individual. This needs to be considered in the context of an original investment of €100,000; the return of the fund is nearly 150 per cent over five years, whereas the individual has generated just 93 per cent in the same period.

---

[19] Rates applicable from 1 May 2009. The final tax liability will depend on the nature of the fund. Pension fund payments are subject to different tax rates. Irish tax rates used.

Table 1.1:   The Tax Benefit of Investment Funds

Year 1	Fund	Individual	
Buy Shares	€100,000	€100,000	
Price Gain	€15,000	€15,000	
Dividend Income	€5,000	€5,000	
Tax on Gain		(€3,750)	
Tax on Dividends		(€2,150)	
Value at End of Year	€120,000	€114,100	
Year 2	**Fund**	**Individual**	
Buy Shares	€120,000	€114,100	(using previous year's proceeds)
Price Gain	€18,000	€17,115	
Dividend Income	€6,000	€5,705	
Tax on Gain		(€4,279)	
Tax on Dividends		(€2,453)	
Value at End of Year	€144,000	€130,188	
Year 3	**Fund**	**Individual**	
Buy Shares	€144,000	€130,188	(using previous year's proceeds)
Price Gain	€21,600	€19,528	
Dividend Income	€7,200	€6,509	
Tax on Gain		(€4,882)	
Tax on Dividends		(€2,799)	
Value at End of Year	€172,800	€148,545	
Year 4	**Fund**	**Individual**	
Buy Shares	€172,800	€148,545	(using previous year's proceeds)
Price Gain	€25,920	€22,282	
Dividend Income	€8,640	€7,427	
Tax on Gain		(€5,570)	
Tax on Dividends		(€3,194)	
Value at End of Year	€207,360	€169,489	
Year 5	**Fund**	**Individual**	
Buy Shares	€207,360	€169,489	(using previous year's proceeds)
Price Gain	€31,104	€25,423	
Dividend Income	€10,368	€8,474	
Tax on Gain		(€6,356)	
Tax on Dividends		(€3,644)	
Value at End of Year	€248,832	€193,387	

1.4.6: Range of Product Types

A significant feature of investing in funds is the vast range of fund products available to suit any potential investor. In Section 1.5 we will take a look at some of these types of funds. While some investors find the extent of the choice bewildering, there are benefits. The most important is that this variety offers small investors a cheap and easy means of investing in complicated investments. In addition, there are a number of investments that are difficult for ordinary individuals to participate in. It is difficult to participate in the corporate bond market directly (minimum investments are quite high), the commodities market (no real tradition of small investors), overseas investing (difficult to access information and markets) and property (minimum investment is significant).

For example, consider you are an investor with €50,000 to invest. You have always liked the notion of having foreign property. There is a choice that you can make – you could buy a property in Spain and manage it yourself or you could invest in a Property Investment Fund. If you buy a property yourself in Spain then you have to go to the trouble of finding out all about the Spanish property market and how to buy property in Spain, and you will have to find tenants. Ultimately, you will have just one property and if anything goes wrong with that individual property or the Spanish property market[20] then you could be exposed to significant loss.

The other option is to invest in a property fund. This fund is likely to have a wide range of properties in different countries. There will be a professional property management company charged with the task of generating an income from the property. If one property does badly, there are numerous other properties in the fund to make up for it. This level of professional advice and management will cost money but if the fund is large then the cost per investor will be quite small.

Furthermore, you 'only' had €50,000 to invest – this would not buy much property in Spain (in fact it would probably not permit you to purchase anything other than a caravan). So a property fund will allow you to participate in the property market with just small amounts of money invested.

There are numerous other examples of products that fill various niches in the investment market. It is possible to invest in a number of investment funds that only purchase shares in alternative energy companies. Even through the recession of 2008–2009 this was a growth area. Why? Can you think of any other growth sectors?

---

[20]   This is what actually occurred in 2008–2009. The Spanish property market collapsed and many who had invested in holiday homes were left nursing large losses. Furthermore, a significant number of investors had borrowed to finance their foreign investment leaving them exposed to a much higher level of risk. According to *The* (London) *Times* the Spanish property market could fall by up to 40 per cent (Emmett, 2009).

Funds that only invest in socially responsible companies are also proving to be popular. How would you define a socially responsible company? Who do you think would be likely to invest in such a fund? How do you think these funds perform relative to funds that invest in any type of company? (A little research on the internet will provide you with a lot of the answers – try www.socialinvest.org as a starting point.)

1.5: Types of Investment Funds

In the last section (1.4.6) the range of different types of funds was discussed. We will now consider some of the more common types in more detail. The list below is not exhaustive but it should cover some of the more usual fund types.

- Equity funds
- Bond funds
- Money market funds
- High yield funds
- Emerging market funds
- Income funds
- Growth funds
- Umbrella funds
- Tracker funds
- Actively versus passively managed funds
- Single share class versus multi-share class funds
- Hedge funds/alternative investment funds

1.5.1: Equity Funds

An equity fund is a fund that restricts itself to investing in the shares or common stock of companies. This is the most common type of investment fund. Generally, these funds will only invest in publicly quoted companies or companies that are large enough to be quoted on a stock exchange: CRH, Diageo, HSBC, etc. Often these funds will specialise in certain types of shares, for example, many funds only invest in the equities of companies that are quoted on the London Stock Exchange or the Dublin Stock Exchange or the Far Eastern Stock Exchanges. Other funds may decide to concentrate on different sectors (telecommunications, biotechnology, alternative energy), buying shares in those companies that operate in that particular sector. Other funds again may decide to buy shares in the largest companies (more stable and secure), whereas some funds could specialise in smaller companies (less stable but with a greater potential for high returns).

1.5.2: Bond Funds/Fixed Income Funds

A bond fund is a fund that restricts its investing to bonds or debt instruments of companies and governments. A bond is where an investor lends money to a company or government and in return the investor gets an annual interest payment (this is called a coupon payment). At the end of the loan period the company or government must return the principal amount to the investor. Bonds are a safer investment than shares because the investors get their principal back at the end of the term and, in the event of a company getting into financial difficulty, the bond-investors get paid before the shareholders. As the investment is safer than equities then the expected return is generally less.

There are two broad categories of bond fund: government bond funds and corporate bond funds. Government bond funds are where the fund only invests in bonds issued by governments (a government will issue a bond when it is looking to borrow cash – if tax revenues are less than government spending). In return for lending the government money, an investor will receive an interest payment and their money back at the end of the term. These kinds of funds are very safe as the chances of a government defaulting[21] is extremely low. There are funds that only invest in US government bonds, other funds invest in European government bonds, other funds are worldwide; again there is a wide variety of choice depending on your preferences and attitude to risk.

Corporate bond funds invest in the bonds of companies. These bonds operate on a similar basis to government bonds except that there is a greater level of risk attached to them. The chances of a company not being able to repay a bond are higher than the chances of a government default. Again, there are different types of corporate bond funds, depending on factors such as industry sector, region/country, credit rating of company, size of company and type of bond issue.

It is also worth noting that the bond market is much larger than the stock market.[22] This is unusual because the media (print and broadcast) devote much more time to the stock market. It may be indicative of the lower levels of volatility in the bond market. If prices are not fluctuating by large amounts then there is little to report on.

---

[21] It is low because a government can either pass laws to generate more tax revenue or print money. The latter is one of the risks of holding bonds: as governments print more money the risk of inflation increases significantly. Inflation causes the value of the principal invested to decrease in real terms. This is exactly the approach taken by the US government in response to the credit crisis of 2008–2009, except that they called it 'quantitative easing'.

[22] According to IFSL Research the size of the global bond market in December 2008 was $83 trillion USD. According to the World Federation of Exchanges the size of the global stock market was $37 USD trillion in June 2009.

1.5.3: Money Market Fund

A money market fund lends money for very short periods of time (generally less than nine months and often less than one month) to banks, financial institutions, governments and large corporations. In return, the fund receives an interest payment and the principal is repaid at the end of the term. This is considered to be one of the safest investments an individual can make but the return also tends to be very small. These funds operate on the basis that if a large number of small investors pool together then it is possible to get a much higher rate of interest. Consider the example given in Table 1.2, which illustrates how the rate of interest on offer can increase as the size of the deposit increases.

Table 1.2: Bank of Scotland Instant Access Savings Account Reward

Balance	A.E.R.	Gross p.a.	Net p.a.
£500,000+	3.15%	3.11%	2.49%
£2,500+	2.60%	2.57%	2.06%

Source: © Bank of Scotland, 31 July 2009, www.bankofscotlandhalifax.co.uk. All rights reserved.

If more money is put on deposit (i.e. lent to the bank) then a much better rate is obtained. So if 100 investors with €5,000 each got together they would get a much greater level of return than as individuals. As long as the cost of operating the fund is less than 0.55 per cent then the investors are better off. This is the difference between the two A.E.R.[23] percentages in Table 1.2. The above example is simplified. Consider a fund that has €100 million available; it can bargain for a much higher rate of interest.

One of the largest money market funds in the world is J.P. Morgan Prime Money Market Fund. On 28 February 2009, it had $165 billion USD worth of net assets and generated a return of approx 2 per cent with net expenses of $305 million USD (0.2 per cent of net assets).[24] With such a large amount of money available to it, this fund is in a very strong position to obtain high interest rates.

1.5.4: High Yield Funds

This is a category of bond fund. These types of bond funds tend to invest in the bonds of riskier companies. The risk of a company is generally determined by its

---

[23] A.E.R. is the annual equivalent rate; it takes into account the number of times that interest is paid in a year and the compounding effect of that interest.

[24] J.P. Morgan Prime Money Market Fund Annual Report for year ended 28 February 2009. While the annual return of 2 per cent appears low, for most of the period base interest rates were close to 0 per cent.

credit rating. This is assigned by an independent credit rating agency (such as Standard and Poor's or Moody's). The bonds of companies with weaker credit ratings will generate a higher level of interest than those of stronger companies. The downside is that weaker companies have a much greater chance of not repaying the principal amount. However, if investments are spread across a large number of companies, if one or two default it shouldn't have a serious long-term impact on the value of the fund. These types of funds are also known as junk bond funds.

An extreme version is the distressed debt fund – a fund that buys the debt of companies that are in or near bankruptcy. The debt of near bankrupt companies can be purchased at a large discount (i.e. cheaply). This is extremely high risk but the rewards can also be significant.

The Vanguard High-Yield Corporate Fund is an example of such a fund. It has nearly $7.8 billion USD of net assets (on 31 January 2009). While its performance for the year ended 31 January 2009 was not stellar due to the poor market conditions, it did manage to pay a dividend of almost 10 per cent.[25]

1.5.5: Emerging Markets Funds

This is a category of equity fund that specialises in the equities of companies that are quoted on the stock exchanges of the emerging market economies. An emerging market country is one that is undergoing a transition from a developing to a developed country. As a result, these countries are in the throes of massive expansion and their stock markets tend to mirror this activity. However, regulation can be weak and governments and institutional structures may be subject to corruptive influences (to varying degrees). Furthermore, the markets can suffer from wild speculation and boom–bust cycles, making them very volatile and risky. The potential for gains is significant but so too is the potential for loss.

The emerging market economies change over time. However, the main emerging market countries are Russia, China, India, Brazil and Argentina (among others).[26] In the year to 30 July 2009, the MSCI Emerging Markets Index lost almost 20 per cent; this gives an indication of the extent of the risks inherent in this type

---

[25] Details from the annual report of Vanguard High-Yield Corporate Fund for the year ended 31 January 2009.

[26] As of July 2009 the MSCI Emerging Markets Index consisted of the following 22 emerging market country indices: Brazil, Chile, China, Colombia, Czech Republic, Egypt, Hungary, India, Indonesia, Israel, South Korea, Malaysia, Mexico, Morocco, Peru, Philippines, Poland, Russia, South Africa, Taiwan, Thailand and Turkey. See www.mscibarra.com/products/indices/equity/em.html for details.

of investing. The year to 30 July 2009 is probably a poor time period to use for examples of stock market performance. This is the period that experienced the worst of the credit crisis and recession. In that time period the Dow Jones Industrial Average lost 18 per cent of its value.[27]

1.5.6: Income Funds

An income fund is a fund that attempts to pay an ongoing return to its investors (on a monthly, quarterly, semi-annual or annual basis). With these types of funds, price gains are not as important as income generation. As a result, they tend to concentrate on investing in the equities of companies with large dividend payout histories and bonds (both corporate and government).

These types of funds can be attractive to certain investors – those who prefer a steady income stream rather than a capital gain on redemption at the end. Depending on the tax status of the investor, there can be tax implications. This is because the investor is generating an income from the fund.

1.5.7: Growth Funds

This is the opposite of an income fund. These types of funds do not tend to make regular payments (distributions) to investors. Instead, all the income and gains are reinvested back into the fund in the hope of generating an even higher capital gain. Growth funds can invest in any type of asset but many limit themselves to equities with strong growth prospects (and low/no dividend histories). The type of equities that are characterised as growth companies are those with high earnings growth and that reinvest most, if not all, of their earnings in the business to fund future growth.

Investors who put their money into growth funds should be prepared to leave their investment in place for an extended period to generate its full potential. These types of funds tend to suit those investors who have no need for a regular income from their investment and are prepared to wait for a long period before they get their return. An example of such a fund is the Growth Fund of America by American Funds. The fund description is reproduced in Table 1.3; notice the emphasis on growth rather than income. As of 30 June 2009, its top five investments were in Microsoft, Apple, Google, Oracle and Cisco Systems: five high potential companies operating in an expanding sector of the economy.

---

[27] The Dow Jones Industrial Average is an index made up of the 30 largest most widely held companies in the US. The word 'industrial' is an anachronism – most of the companies in the index are not 'industrial': they include Bank of America, McDonalds and Microsoft, for example. Index price data is from www.marketwatch.com.

Table 1.3: Fund Description of American Funds' Growth Fund of America

Fund Objective	Seeks to provide long-term growth of capital through a diversified portfolio of common stocks.
Distinguishing Characteristics	Has the flexibility to invest wherever the best growth opportunities may be. The fund emphasizes companies that appear to offer opportunities for long-term growth, and may invest in cyclical companies, turnarounds and value situations.
Types of Investments	Invests primarily in common stocks, convertibles, preferred stocks, U.S. government securities, bonds and cash.
Non-U.S. Holdings	May invest up to 15% of assets in securities of issuers domiciled outside the United States and Canada and not included in the S&P 500.
Portfolio Restrictions	May invest up to 10% of assets in debt securities rated below investment grade.

Source: © American Funds, 2005, www.americanfunds.com/funds/details.htm?fundNumber=5. All rights reserved.

1.5.8: Tracker Funds

Tracker funds have been one of the most popular types of funds over the past number of years. A tracker fund is a fund that 'tracks' the returns of a particular index or stock market. For example, a fund that is required to track the Irish stock market would need to purchase all of the shares that make up the ISEQ index.[28] It would probably need to weight its portfolio; it should invest more money in Ryanair, which is so large that it accounts for 13 per cent of the index, than in Aer Lingus, which accounts for just 0.24 per cent.[29] These weights can be determined quite easily as the information is publicly available on www.ise.ie. If you wished to follow the UK stock market what would you do?

There are now stock market indices to track a range of different variables; some concentrate on large companies only (large caps), some concentrate on specific sectors, and so on. The benefit of investing in trackers is that investment management fees (the largest of all of the expenses of operating a fund) are very low. In addition, because the fund follows an index they can be less risky.

An example of a tracker fund is the Legal and General UK Index Trust, a tracker fund that follows the UK stock market. This fund is worth over £3 billion and had expenses of £15 million or 0.5 per cent for the year ended 6 October 2008.[30] At year end this fund had invested in 652 of the 655 companies that made up the

---

[28] ISEQ stands for Irish Stock Exchange Quotient. It measures the overall performance of the Irish stock market. It began at 1,000 on 4 January 1988.

[29] Irish Stock Exchange Monthly Report for June 2009.

[30] Legal & General UK Index Trust – data as per annual report for year ended 6 October 2007.

UK FTSE All Share Index. The missing three companies are probably very small or new to the stock market; in any case, their effect is likely to be immaterial.

1.5.9: Umbrella Funds

An umbrella fund (also referred to as a fund of funds) is a legal structure used by financial institutions when setting up a group of funds. The umbrella fund will have a number of sub-funds within it. Each sub-fund will operate as if it were a separate and individual fund. So, what is the benefit?

The main benefit is from a regulation cost perspective: when setting up a fund there is an amount of legal and regulatory documentation required. The production of this has a significant cost. Much of the documentation is very similar so by having this umbrella fund structure much of the duplication can be eliminated.

A benefit from the investor perspective is that these umbrella funds will often allow the investor to switch from one sub-fund to another without attracting a cost penalty. Normally, when an investor takes their money out of a fund they are charged a fee (this can vary but could be as high as 5 per cent); this cost is waived when investors are moving between sub-funds. It is an incentive to encourage investors to keep their funds with the same fund family or financial institution.

1.5.10: Actively versus Passively Managed Funds

This is not a fund type as such, but rather a fund investment strategy. Some funds are actively managed by the investment manager who continually monitors the markets and the performance of the fund, buying and selling equities and bonds, etc. as appropriate. This type of fund gets the benefit of professional investment management advice in real time but it can also be expensive. A passively managed fund is where the investment strategy of the fund is dictated by outside events. An example of a passively managed fund is a tracker fund; here the investment managers have very little to do except to purchase the shares that make up the particular index. Consequently, investment management fees are low but returns may not be stellar.

1.5.11: Single Share Class versus Multi-Share Class Funds

When an investor decides to invest in a fund they are given shares in the fund. As more money is invested, more shares are received by the investor. In some funds there is just one share class and all investors are treated equally.

However, in many funds there are different classes of shares depending on the type of investor. A share class is another name for a share type. The holders of different share classes or types would be entitled to different rights although the investor's money would be invested in the same fund. For example, larger investors can often be given different class shares than smaller investors; generally the share class given to a larger investor attracts lower fees and charges. This is because it is more efficient for a fund administrator to transact with large investors than with small investors.

Often, these shares can be differentiated based on sales charge; most funds charge a fee when an investor invests in the fund. Some funds issue a share class that levies the charge at the time the investor buys into the fund and have a second class that defers the charge until the investor sells out. Thus the investor has a choice: pay the sales charge up front or defer the charge until they leave the fund (the size of the charge can differ).

The example in Table 1.4 shows the different classes of shares from the Reserve Primary Fund.[31] There are eleven share classes in total. The class depends on the amount of money invested in the fund: the more money invested the smaller the fee. As can be seen, the Institutional Class investor only pays annual fees totalling 0.13 per cent of the investment, whereas a Class R investor pays 1.06 per cent of fees. To be categorised as an Institutional Class investor you must invest $35 million USD in the fund; a Class R investor needs only to invest $5 (although, in reality, the real minimum is probably $1,000).

1.5.12: Hedge Funds/Alternative Investment Funds

Over the past decade much of the growth in investment funds took place in this area. Hedge funds tend to be less regulated than other funds and as a result are generally only available to professional investors.

Hedge funds invest in a wide variety of assets including equities, bonds, commodities and property. They also use derivative[32] products extensively. As a result, they can be subject to greater levels of risk than other types of funds (i.e. the non-hedge fund variety). In addition, hedge funds use leverage as a means of increasing potential returns.

Leverage increases the amount of money that a fund has available to it. Say, for example, a fund has received €100 million from its investors. It can use this to

---

[31] These share classes have now become part of a major legal case. The Reserve Fund was suspended on 16 September 2008 and now a class action lawsuit is pending on behalf of many investors who lost money in the fund.

[32] A derivative includes products such as futures, options, forwards and swaps. A derivative is a contract between two parties: the value of the contact is derived from another asset. For example, the value of a futures contract on oil is derived from the current price of oil (plus other influences). For a more extensive discussion on derivatives see www.investopedia.com.

Table 1.4: The Different Classes of Shares from The Reserve Primary Fund

Primary Fund

Shareholder Fees

(Fees paid directly from your investment)	Class R	Investor Class III	Investor Class II	Investor Class I	Class Treasurer's Trust	Liquidity Class V
Shareholder Transaction Fees	None	None	None	None	None	None
Redemption Fees	None	None	None	None	None	None

Annual Fund Operating Expenses

(Expenses that are deducted from Fund assets)						
Management Fee	0.81%	0.76%	0.56%	0.51%	0.61%	0.46%
Distribution and Service (12b-1 fee)	0.25%	0.25%	0.25%	0.25%	None	None
Other Expenses	None	None	None	None	None	None
Total Annual Fund Operating Expenses	1.06%	1.01%	0.81%	0.76%	0.61%	0.46%

Primary Fund (continued)

Shareholder Fees

(Fees paid directly from your investment)	Liquidity Class IV	Liquidity Class III	Liquidity Class II	Liquidity Class I	Class Institutional
Shareholder Transaction Fees	None	None	None	None	None
Redemption Fees	None	None	None	None	None

Annual Fund Operating Expenses

(Expenses that are deducted from Fund assets)					
Management Fee	0.36%	0.26%	0.21%	0.16%	0.13%
Distribution and Service (12b-1 fee)	None	None	None	None	None
Other Expenses	None	None	None	None	None
Total Annual Fund Operating Expenses	0.36%	0.26%	0.21%	0.16%	0.13%

The minimum investment for each category is given below:

Share Class	Initial Minimum
Class Institutional	$35 million
Liquidity Class I	$20 million
Liquidity Class II	$15 million
Liquidity Class III	$10 million

(Continued)

Table 1.4: *(Continued)*

Share Class	Initial Minimum
Liquidity Class IV	$7 million
Liquidity Class V	$5 million
Class Treasurer's Trust	None
Investor Class I	$2 million
Investor Class II	$1 million
Investor Class III	$50,000
Class R	None

Source: © The Reserve Primary Fund Prospectus, September 2007, www.ther.com/pdfs/rsvPGTprospectus.pdf.

borrow (or lever) more money from financial institutions – say, another €50 million. Now the fund has €150 million to invest. As long as the investments that the fund make generate a greater return than the interest on the funds borrowed then the investors can do very well. However, if the fund is in trouble and loses value then the shareholders can see their investment evaporate very quickly.

An example can illustrate easily the benefits and risks of investing in a levered fund. A fund has attracted €100 million from its investors. It then uses leverage to maximise potential returns for investors by borrowing €50 million at an interest rate of 8 per cent; thus after one year €54 million will have to be repaid to the bank before the investors can take any return. As long as the fund can generate a return in excess of 8 per cent then the investors will do very well. However, as returns fall then the losses that investors make can be magnified (see Table 1.5). It presents three different scenarios, assuming that the fund generates returns of 15 per cent, 3 per cent and –20 per cent. When the fund generates 15 per cent then the investors get a return of 19 per cent but when the fund loses 20 per cent the investors lose 34 per cent. Investment losses of 20 per cent have not been unusual in the credit crisis of 2008–2009. It is clearly evident how investors in hedge funds lost even larger amounts in 2008–2009. This is even more extreme where the fund is even more highly levered; try the example again but allow the fund to borrow €80 million at 8 per cent.[33] These effects exist because the bank is repaid irrespective of the performance of the fund.

---

[33] You should get investor returns of 20.6 per cent, −1.0 per cent and −42.4 per cent for each of the scenarios respectively.

Table 1.5: Hedge Fund Leverage Illustration

Scenario	15.00%	3.00%	−20.00%	
Investors	€100m	€100m	€100m	
Bank Loan	€50m	€50m	€50m	
Total Funds Available	*€150m*	*€150m*	*€150m*	
Investment Gains/(Losses)	€23m	€5m	−€30m	(15%, 3% and −20% of €150m)
Value of Fund	*€173m*	*€155m*	*€120m*	
Repay Bank Loan + Interest	−€54m	−€54m	−€54m	(€50m + 8% interest)
Remaining for Investors	*€119m*	*€101m*	*€66m*	*(rounded)*
Percentage Return for Investors	*19%*	*1%*	*−34%*	

Hedge funds also have the ability to make profits when the market is declining. This is because they can short sell. Short selling involves selling equities (or other assets) that are not owned by the fund so that they can be repurchased later. If the share price has fallen then the fund will make a profit. However, the fund loses if the share price increases in the interim. This does give hedge funds a huge degree of flexibility but it can also increase the risk of the fund.

Non-hedge funds are not permitted to engage in these types of activities and as a result are less risky than hedge funds. Indeed, some of the more notable recent fund failures (Amaranth, Long Term Capital Management, Madoff Securities) were almost all hedge funds. This is not unexpected given the extra risk involved in these funds.

1.6: WORKINGS OF A TYPICAL INVESTMENT FUND

The funds that we will be accounting for will not have any direct employees. So how can a fund with no employees operate? Each of the service providers will have a contractual arrangement with the fund, often called subcontracting. This is similar to building a house using direct labour: there is an agreement with a block-layer to build the house, a roofer to do the roof, a plumber to do the plumbing, an electrician to do the electrics, etc. A fund works on a similar principle. The investment management and advice is subcontracted to an investment management company, the administration to a fund administration company, legal issues to a law firm, shareholder services to a company that specialises in this area and so on.

Most of these contractual arrangements are set out in the fund's prospectus so investors in the fund will know in advance what the expenses are likely to be. The various parties to a fund typically are

- The investment manager
- The custodian

- The fund accountant/administrator/corporate secretarial services
- The transfer agent/shareholder services
- The trustees/directors
- The fund sponsor/promoter
- The auditor
- The legal advisors
- The distributor

1.6.1: The Investment Manager

Investment managers make the decisions on the securities (shares, bonds, etc.) that the fund buys and sells. They also ensure that any investment-related regulatory provisions are adhered to and that the fund remains within the bounds as laid out in its prospectus.[34] They will advise the directors or trustees on investment strategy and on the level of dividends to declare.

They are the best paid of all the parties, generally getting a percentage of the net assets of the fund with a further payment based on the increase in the value of the fund relative to a benchmark. This is because the performance of the fund will depend on the decisions made by the investment managers. Often, the investment managers are the fund's sponsor/promoter; they use the fund as a means of generating fees for their business. The better known investment managers in Ireland are AIBIM (Allied Irish Banks Investment Mangers) and BIAM (Bank of Ireland Asset Management).

1.6.2: The Custodian

The custodian is the company that holds the assets of the fund on behalf of the fund. When a fund purchases shares and bonds then someone has to ensure that these are held in an appropriate form. In bygone days, the custodian was effectively a big safe; it was the custodian's responsibility to ensure that all share certificates, etc. were kept securely in this safe. Electronic means of communication have changed the role somewhat but the basic principles remain the same.

The custodian also controls the flow of cash in and out of the fund's bank account (paying expenses when authorised, ensuring interest and dividends are received, and so on). Often, the responsibility for the settlement of transactions involving the purchase and sale of securities rests with the custodian.

---

[34] Often a fund will have a requirement not to invest more than 10 per cent of their funds into the shares of one company, otherwise the fund will not be fully diversified. It is up to the investment manager to abide by this.

All of the major financial institutions have custody departments. The larger financial institutions have an advantage as they have more global reach. Funds can purchase securities in a number of different countries, thus the larger financial institutions can use their local operations to act as a sub-custodian. For example, a UK fund buys shares in an Indian company; rather than the shares being held in London it might make more sense to hold the shares in India, which could facilitate a quicker sale at a later stage.

The custodian should remain in contact with the fund accountant and investment managers. Regular controls should be in place to ensure that the fund has ownership and access to the assets that it is supposed to hold.

1.6.3: The Fund Accountant/Administrator/Corporate Secretary

It is this part of the industry that has a large presence in Ireland. Also, it is the activity that concerns us most; much of this book concentrates on the technical work of the fund accountant. The fund accountant ensures compliance with the appropriate regulatory framework (e.g. the Central Bank of Ireland, Insitiute Monetaire de Luxembourg (IML), Financial Services Authority (FSA)), prices the investments held by the fund, keeps the accounts and publishes the NAV per share.[35] The role also involves the preparation of the annual and semi-annual report, and liaising with auditors. Sometimes, there can be a blurring of roles between the fund accountant and the custodian, as the fund accountant can also be involved in the settlement of transactions, the payment of expenses, ensuring that the fund receives any interest and dividend it is properly entitled to, and reconciliations of the fund's holdings.

The fund accountant can be a branch of the sponsoring institution. Many of the larger financial institutions have significant fund administration departments. Thus, when a financial institution sets up a fund, the fund administration department gets the role of fund accountant for that fund.

1.6.4: Transfer Agent/Shareholder Services

The transfer agent deals with the individual investors in the fund. Generally, the transfer agent is not involved in recruiting investors (this is done by the distributor or fund sponsor). However, all subsequent correspondence with investors is carried out by the transfer agent. This will involve the issuing of share certificates, the redemption of share certificates, dealing with investor queries and ensuring

---

[35] NAV per share is short for Net Asset Value per share. This is the price at which new investors buy into the fund and exiting investors sell out of the fund. It is a term that you will become very familiar with by the end of this book; a significant objective of the work of a fund accountant is to calculate the NAV per share of a fund.

anti–money laundering regulations are adhered to. There will be a significant degree of interaction between the transfer agent, the fund accountant and the investment manager; if an investor redeems their shares then the fund may have to sell some assets to generate the cash to repay the investor.

The transfer agent will also have to manage situations where investors have lost their documentation and where investors have died and passed on their holdings to their beneficiaries. Other duties include the payment of any distributions out of the fund to investors and the distribution of annual and semi–annual reports, along with other updates on fund performance.

1.6.5: Trustees/Directors

The trustees/directors are the individuals with the overall responsibility for the fund operating in the investors' interests. It is their duty to ensure that the fund's money is invested appropriately and the assets of the fund are protected. They generally discharge this responsibility by engaging the services of an investment manager, custodian, fund accountant and so on. When there is a fall in fund performance then it is their duty to investigate and take any appropriate action (up to and including replacing the investment managers). If there is a failure by any of the other service providers, it is the responsibility of the trustees to manage that scenario in a timely manner.

Being a fund trustee is an onerous task. The trustees have numerous legal responsibilities; if they fail in their duties they may be held personally liable. The majority of the trustees should be independent of the investment managers and other interested parties. Remember the abiding principle: trustees/directors should act in the best interests of the investors in the fund. They should not profit by virtue of their position at the expense of the investor; this does not preclude them from taking a reasonable fee for the work that they do on behalf of the fund. The payment that the directors/trustees are entitled to should be set out in the prospectus.

Initially, the trustees/directors will be senior executives in the sponsoring financial institution along with a number of outside independent individuals who should have significant expertise in the industry. Take a look at the financial statements of the Reserve Primary Fund.[36] Each of the trustees is listed, along with their affiliations and experience. In the year to 31 May 2007, the fund had ten trustees, eight of whom it classified as independent. It was evident that all of the trustees had industry experience. This, however, did not prevent the failure of the fund in September 2008.

---

[36] Available from: www.ther.com/pdfs/pgtannual.pdf.

1.6.6: The Fund Sponsor/Promoter

The fund sponsor is the individual or institution that establishes the fund. The sponsor will often be a financial institution and may use its own investment management arm as investment advisors, custodian division as custodians, and so on. The fund sponsor ensures that all the regulatory permissions are in place before the fund is offered to investors. The fund sponsor may have to provide some seed capital to get the fund going; this need not be a significant amount.

In Ireland, the fund sponsor is often one of the large retail banks that identifies an investment fund as an additional product it can offer to its customers. In return, the bank is able to generate a significant fee income for managing the fund. There is often a blurring between the roles of the investment manager, the fund sponsor and the distributor, particularly from the individual investor's perspective.

1.6.7: The Auditor

The auditor must be independent of the other parties. It is their role to provide an independent opinion on the financial statements of the fund and of the controls in place. The auditor will also ensure compliance with the regulatory authorities and the provisions of the prospectus.

The auditor is generally one of the big four audit firms: PricewaterhouseCoopers, KPMG, Deloitte and Ernst & Young. The audit is an additional control to protect the investors but it is not a guaranteed check against fraud. In addition, the auditors do not have a role in evaluating the performance of the investment managers – this is the job of the trustees/directors.

1.6.8: The Legal Advisors

The role of the legal advisor is to advise on legal issues pertaining to the establishment and the ongoing operation of the fund. Some of the documentation relating to a fund has significant legal implications; as a result, it is vital that they are subject to legal review. The legal advisors may represent the trustees/directors at fund meetings and give advice on legal issues as they arise.

1.6.9: The Distributor

The distributors are the sales people of the fund. They are often a branch or division of the sponsoring institution. For example, the branch network of the Irish retail banks (AIB, Bank of Ireland) often act as distributors for investment products that are managed by the investment management division of the bank (AIBIM and BIAM respectively). The distributor makes contact with the potential investor and offers the investment fund to them (having due regard for consumer and IFSRA regulations). Once the initial investment is made then the handling of investor communications is passed over to the transfer agent.

Some funds now market directly without the use of a distributor; this has become more commonplace as the use of the internet by individuals to conduct their banking and other investing arrangements is now considered normal.

1.7: WHY ESTABLISH AN INVESTMENT FUND?

The discussion earlier (in Section 1.4) considered why someone should invest in a fund. However, what are the motivations behind someone establishing an investment fund?

The main reason why financial institutions establish investment funds is to provide a broad range of financial products to their customers. Banks traditionally only offered savings products to customers and these were mainly just variations on the deposit account. As a result, their products tended to be very safe (low risk) but also gave a low return. Many customers would consider accepting some element of risk for the prospect of generating a higher level of return. Investment funds are an extremely efficient means of offering customers a range of risk-related products, with an expectation of a higher level of returns.

While the demand for these types of products is customer-led, where is the benefit from the banks' perspective? The other significant reason why financial institutions establish investment funds is to generate fee income. When an investment fund is set up by a bank the various departments of the bank supply services to the fund, for which they charge a fee. For example, the distributor (an arm of the financial institution) charges fees, the investment manager (an arm of the financial institution) charges fees, the administrator, transfer agent and custodian (again departments or subsidiaries of the sponsoring financial institutions) all charge fees.

Investment fund expenses are probably the most contentious aspect of the investment fund sector. Many funds go to great lengths to set out their expense ratio (expenses of the fund as a percentage of total net assets) and it is often used as a selling point. There are two broad categories of fees charged:

- Shareholder fees: these are the fees charged when a shareholder initially invests in the fund or withdraws from the fund. They vary from fund to fund but can be as high as 5 per cent of the money being invested or withdrawn.
- Fund operation fees: these are the fees charged for operating the fund and include such items as investment management fees and administration fees. These also vary quite considerably from fund to fund but annual expenses in the order of 2.5 per cent are not unusual.

Fees are contentious because of the impact that they have on the investor. Consider a fund that generates an annual return of 12 per cent per annum before fees. Now assume that fees are equal to 2 per cent of the value of the fund, giving an after-fee return to investors of 10 per cent. An investor has €20,000 to invest. After twenty years what is the investment worth? You should get €134,550 (this is €20,000$(1 + 10\%)^{20}$, taking annual compounding into account). Now consider the same scenario where the fund has an expense ratio of 1 per cent. You should get €161,246 (this is €20,000$(1 + 11\%)^{20}$). The total difference as a result of a 1 per cent change in the expense ratio is €26,696 over twenty years; this is greater than the amount originally invested.[37]

Consider the Sprott Canadian Equity Fund. In 2007, the fund had expenses of $60 million CAD on total net assets of $2 billion CAD, an expense ratio of 3 per cent.[38] This does not take into account any of the shareholder fees mentioned earlier. It is for this fee income (much of which goes to Sprott companies) that the Sprott management decided to set up the fund. This may appear to be an extremely high fee; however, investors in this fund have generated an annual return of 23 per cent (after expenses) in the five years to 2007. Not many funds would have matched that level of consistency.

With trillions of dollars and euro of money invested in investment funds, a small percentage of fees generate quite a healthy revenue stream for the financial institutions. An expense ratio of 1 per cent on $1 trillion of net assets represents a revenue stream of $10 billion annually. This is probably the most significant reason why the investment fund industry exists. It still represents good value for money; the alternatives are potentially much more expensive.

1.8: CONCLUSION

The purpose of this chapter was to introduce some of the basics of the investment fund industry. At this stage you should be able to describe what an investment fund is, set out the various benefits of investing in these products, explain the various types of investment funds and outline the parties involved in the workings of a typical investment fund.

Some of the issues discussed in the preceding sections cut to the core of the investment fund industry. Issues such as the tax benefit of funds, the diversification effect, the benefit of professional investment management and the debate on expense ratios are often discussed within the industry. However, remember that, in

---

[37] For a more extensive discussion of investment fund fees see www.sec.gov/answers/mffees.htm.

[38] See www.sprott.com/docs/FinancialReports/Mgmt_Report/2007Dec_CEq_EN.pdf for the full annual report.

simple terms, an investment fund is a vehicle that allows many smaller investors to pool their cash so that the money can be invested in accordance with the objective of the particular fund.

In the next chapter, the accounting will begin. In the meantime, you should try some of the additional questions that follow as these will help to cement the learning to date.

1.9: ADDITIONAL QUESTIONS

Question 1.9.1

Why would an investor give their money to someone that they do not know (i.e. an investment manager)?

Question 1.9.2

If an investment fund can go down in value as well as up in value then why do people invest their money in them?

Question 1.9.3

Recall the example of Ryanair and BP in Section 1.4.1. Why might this be a smart investment strategy? Can you think of any other companies outside of the airline and oil industries that could display similar effects?

Question 1.9.4

Recall Example 1.1. Recalculate the tax effect in a situation where an investor has €200,000 to invest. The annual share price increase is 20 per cent and the dividend yield is 3 per cent. The capital gains tax rate is 30 per cent and the income tax rate is 45 per cent. After ten years what is the difference between the fund's value and the individual's value? This exercise is much easier if you design your own Excel spreadsheet.

Question 1.9.5

Go though some of the funds that have been highlighted in the chapter and calculate the expense ratio of the funds.

Question 1.9.6

Consider an investment fund that generates a return of 9 per cent per annum before expenses. How much would an investor with a €14,000 initial investment be worth after twenty years if the expenses ratio (as a percentage of net assets) was:

1. 3 per cent of net assets
2. 1.5 per cent of net assets
3. 0.5 per cent of net assets

Chapter 2

Review of Double Entry Bookkeeping

- Introduction
- The accounting identity
- The balance sheet
- Recording transactions – initial steps
- Recording transactions – double entry system and 'T' accounts
- The spreadsheet approach for recording transactions
- The income statement (the statement of operations and the statement of changes in net assets)
- Conclusion
- Additional questions

LEARNING OUTCOMES

At the end of this chapter you should:

- Be able to describe the financial statements of an investment fund.
- Be able to prepare basic financial statements using the accounting identity (review of prior studies).
- Be able to record transactions (review of prior studies).
- Be comfortable with the terminology used.
- Be able to describe the interaction between the balance sheet, the statement of operations and the statement of changes in net assets.
- Be able to record some basic investment fund transactions and prepare a balance sheet, statement of operations and statement of changes in net assets.

2.1: INTRODUCTION

This chapter will review some of the fundamentals of accounting. Accounting for an investment fund is similar to accounting for a 'normal' business but there are some important differences. It might be a good strategy at this point to retrieve your old financial accounting textbook as this will help to refresh your memory.

A review of the accounting identity is the starting point for the chapter; this will lead to a discussion of the balance sheet and its components (assets, liabilities and capital). Then the process of recording transactions will be explored, which will be done using two approaches: the traditional debit and credit approach and the spreadsheet system that this book utilises throughout. Finally, some rudimentary financial statements will be prepared: a balance sheet, an income statement and a statement of changes in equity.

Some of the material may appear to be heavy going. However, once you understand how a particular transaction is recorded then you will know how to approach similar transactions that will undoubtedly recur in the future. In fact, if you know how to record the top twenty different transactions in investment fund accounting then you are probably able to account for over 80 per cent of the volume of fund transactions. So while it may be difficult to begin with, it will get easier over time as the transactions begin to repeat themselves.

2.2: THE ACCOUNTING IDENTITY/EQUATION

This chapter is a review of some basic accounting principles. If you have already studied a course in financial accounting there should be enough here to refresh your memory. If not (or your memory is not still refreshed) then you should have a look at the initial chapters in any introductory accounting textbook. You may recall the idea of a balance sheet and an income statement; these will also be quite important in the world of investment fund accounting.[1]

We will start with the balance sheet. A balance sheet, in its simplest form, is a list of assets and liabilities. It is not called a balance sheet for no reason: it must balance, i.e. the total on one side must equal the total on the other side. Or, more correctly, the total of all of the assets that a company (or investment fund) has must equal the total of all the liabilities that the same company (or investment fund) owes.

This can be represented below as an equation; this equation is called the accounting identity or the accounting equation:

$$\textbf{Assets = Liabilities} \qquad \qquad \text{(eqn 1)}$$

---

[1] In investment fund accounting the balance sheet will be called the statement of net assets while the income statement (profit and loss account) will be called the statement of operations. This is a minor point but later in the chapter this is the terminology that we will use. Also, to make matters more complex, the terminology is changing: a balance sheet will soon become known as a statement of financial position.

So far, so good, but we need to be more precise in our definition of 'an asset' and 'a liability'.

2.2.1: An Asset

An asset:

- Is something that is owned by the business (or fund)
- In more complicated terms, an asset is 'a resource controlled by an entity as a result of past events and from which future economic benefits are expected to flow to an entity'.[2]

From a theoretical perspective the second definition is more correct. For example, the equities/shares that a fund purchases (or buildings that a company purchases) are assets of the fund. The following are characteristics of these items:

- They are controlled by the fund – the fund can decide to do whatever it wishes with these equities, when to sell them, when to lend them to others and so on.
- They result from past events – the fund purchased the equities some time ago by entering into an agreement with the previous owner for which cash was paid.
- Future economic benefits are expected to flow from them – the fund hopes to generate dividends and capital gains in the future as a result of owning the equities. $\Rightarrow$ Equities purchased are assets of the fund.

A similar line of reasoning can be applied to the buildings, vehicles and inventory of a 'normal' company.

What about some more unusual (or intangible) assets; do you think that employees or brand names or reputation could be considered to be assets?[3] Can you think of any examples in the context of an investment fund? Consider this example: a fund has a ten-year contract with a top investment manager who has always generated excellent returns. This has already resulted in a large number of new investors entering the fund. Should the value of the contract with the investment manager be included as an asset of the fund? This is a difficult scenario; clearly, there is some benefit to having such a good investment manager signed to the fund, similar to having a top football player signed to a football club. However, the practice is to exclude the contract with

---

[2] International Accounting Standards Board (2001).

[3] There may be 'ownership' issues over employees; thus it might be difficult to consider employees as assets. But brand names and reputation are different. However, these are a special kind of asset: an intangible asset. This makes them very difficult to value; hence, in a lot of cases their value is not included in the accountant's balance sheet.

the investment manager as an asset of the fund. This is because the future benefits (over and above any 'normal' investment manager) are difficult to measure and very uncertain. Indeed, finance theory would indicate that it is difficult for any investment manager to remain on top for an extended period of time.[4]

2.2.2: A Liability

A liability:

- Is something that is owed by the business (or fund)
- Or, in more complicated terms, is 'a present obligation as a result of past events, the settlement of which is expected to result in the outflow of resources' (cash, for example).[5]

Again, from a theoretical perspective, the second definition is more correct but the first definition should cover most situations. For example, consider a fund that has just purchased some equities but has not yet paid for them. The fund has an asset: the equities just purchased (see previous section on assets). However, it also has a liability because it owes cash to the previous owner for the equities just purchased. Can you think of any other examples of a liability from a 'normal' company and then from a fund?

For a normal company, possible liabilities include bank loans, money owed to suppliers and taxes owed. A fund's liabilities could be money owed to investors wishing to withdraw from the fund and money owed to the investment manager for advice given to the fund.

2.2.3: Capital

The next stage in our analysis considers liabilities in more detail. There are different categories of liabilities, but for the moment we will split them in two:

1. Liabilities to the owner/shareholder
2. Liabilities to outsiders/everyone else

We will use the term 'capital' for 'liabilities to the owner/shareholder' and the term 'liabilities' for 'liabilities to outsiders'. As a result, the accounting identity from earlier changes to become:

---

[4]   This effect (called 'mean reversion') has been known of since the 1960s and has been explored many times since. For example, see Malkiel (1995). He showed that the top performing funds of the 1970s were not the top performing funds of the 1980s.

[5]   International Accounting Standards Board (2001).

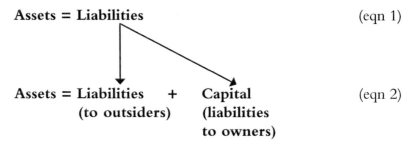

$$\text{Assets} = \text{Liabilities} \qquad\qquad (\text{eqn } 1)$$

$$\text{Assets} = \text{Liabilities} \;+\; \text{Capital} \qquad (\text{eqn } 2)$$
$$\text{(to outsiders)} \quad \text{(liabilities}$$
$$\text{to owners)}$$

Reflect on this for a moment and consider these questions:

1. How can there be a liability to the owner/shareholders?
2. Why do we differentiate between liabilities and capital?

The answers to these questions are connected. A business (and an investment fund) is generally a separate legal entity from the owners; this comes from the notion of limited liability. A business or fund, once it is properly constituted,[6] operates independently from its owners. This means that the owners can lose any money invested but their personal assets are not at risk.[7] Thus, if someone invests in a business (or investment fund), money is transferred from the owner to the business – the business now has an asset (cash) and a liability, which in this case is capital (the amount owed back to the owners). If the business is wound up, anything that remains is owed back to the owners; this is often called the residual interest that the owners have in the business. The owners/shareholders receive whatever is left once all the other liabilities have been paid. If the business has operated profitably then the shareholders will receive more cash than they invested. However, if the business has made losses then the owners will get less than their original investment. Capital is a liability of the business because ultimately the cash invested plus any profits (or less any losses) must be paid back to the owners.

A distinction is made between capital and liabilities (to everyone else) because a liability is, generally, a contractual or constructive obligation of the business to make a payment to a third party. For example, if an investment fund purchases equities without making a payment, it is legally bound to pay for these equities within a specified number of days. With capital, the likelihood of repaying the full amount to investors is remote. In fact, often an investment fund doesn't have to pay a regular dividend to its shareholders. In addition, if an investment fund does badly then the liability for the equities purchased remains unchanged, but less will be owed to the shareholders/investors as they bear the brunt of any losses.

---

[6] A lawyer or accountant will be able to do this for you but there are many self-help guides, particularly for companies (see www.cro.ie). However, it is probably a good idea to get professional help in the case of investment funds.

[7] This assumes that the owners/directors have acted responsibly.

In summary, liabilities to third parties are very different to liabilities to share-holders in terms of the obligation to make the payment and the specification of the amount due (generally, this amount is fixed for a liability but varies with gains and losses for capital). Hence, it is best practice to distinguish between the two:

- Capital is another name for liabilities to the owner and investors.
- Capital is the resources invested by the owner and investors.

In an investment fund, capital is also called shareholders' funds, capital stock or unit holders' equity. If an investment fund does well then capital will increase, but if it does badly then capital will decrease.

2.3: THE BALANCE SHEET

We now have enough information to prepare a balance sheet. A balance sheet is a list of assets, liabilities and capital at a point in time (a list of what the business owns and owes).

Recall our equation:

$$\textbf{Assets = Liabilities} \quad + \quad \textbf{Capital} \qquad \text{(eqn 2)}$$

A balance sheet is this equation, just presented in a different format.

$$
\begin{array}{lll}
\textbf{Assets} & \underline{\underline{\textbf{X}}} & \text{(eqn 3)} \\[1em]
\textbf{Capital} & \textbf{Y} & \\
\textbf{Liabilities} & \underline{\underline{\textbf{Z}}} &
\end{array}
$$

In the case of investment funds, items are just presented in a different order:

Assets − Liabilities = Capital Stock   (liabilities have just moved to the other side of the '=', hence, the '+' sign has changed to a '−'.)   (eqn 4)

A simple balance sheet for an investment fund now reads:

$$
\begin{array}{lll}
\textbf{Assets} & \textbf{X} & \text{(eqn 5)} \\
\textbf{Less Liabilities} & \underline{\textbf{(Z)}} & \\
\textbf{Net Assets} & \underline{\textbf{Y}} & \\[1em]
\textbf{Capital Stock} & \underline{\underline{\textbf{Y}}} &
\end{array}
$$

Example 2.1: Identifying Assets, Liabilities and Capital, and Preparing the Balance Sheet

An investment fund has the following items, as shown in Table 2.1 (all items in thousands of euro).

Table 2.1:   The Typical Items of an Investment Fund

Investments at Cost	€140,000
Unrealised Gains on Investments	€10,000
Investments Purchased Payable	€12,000
Investments Sold Receivable	€5,000
Fund Shares Sold Receivable	€7,500
Fund Shares Redeemed Payable	€6,750
Dividends Receivable	€4,500
Cash	€2,500
Owners' Equity/Capital Stock	€150,750

A: For each item in Table 2.1, state whether it is an asset, a liability or capital.
B: Prepare the balance sheet of the fund (also called the statement of net assets).
C: If the fund has 1,000,000 shares issued to shareholders what is the value of each share (also known as the net asset value per share)?

Note: unrealised gains on investments represent the gains made on all of the investments in the funds portfolio. For example, if 10,000 AIB shares are purchased at €13 and two months later they are worth €14 then the unrealised gain is €10,000 (the gain is unrealised as the shares have not been sold yet).

Solution 2.1: Identifying Assets, Liabilities and Capital, and Preparing the Balance Sheet

Part A: State whether each item is an asset, liability or capital.

Some of the terminology here is new. They will be explained in more detail in Chapter 3. However, considering each item in turn:

- Investments at cost (€140,000) and unrealised gains on investments (€10,000) represent the value of the investments owned by the fund. They are split into the original cost of the investments and the gains made since. The investments are now worth a total of €150,000. These items are owned by the fund and the fund has control over them; therefore they are **assets** of the fund.

- Investments purchased payable (€12,000) means that the fund owes money for investments that it has purchased. Thus, in the recent past, the fund purchased investments (that it now owns) but has yet to pay for these investments. Soon (generally in less than one week) this will have to be paid to the previous owner of the shares. This is an amount owed by the fund; therefore, it is a **liability** of the fund.
- Investments sold receivable (€5,000) means that the fund is due to receive money for investments that it has sold. Thus, in the recent past the fund sold investments; it no longer owns the investments but has yet to receive the cash. This money will be received soon from the new owner of the shares. This is an amount due to the fund; therefore, it is an **asset** of the fund.
- Fund shares sold receivable (€7,500): following a similar logic to the previous receivable, this is money due to the fund; therefore, it is an **asset** of the fund.
- Fund shares redeemed payable (€6,750): following a similar logic to the previous payable, this is money owed by the fund; therefore, it is a **liability** of the fund.
- Dividends receivable (€4,500): following a similar logic to the previous receivable, this is money due to the fund; therefore, it is an **asset** of the fund.
- Cash (€2,500): this is the money that the fund has in its bank account. It owns this money and has control over it; therefore it is an **asset** of the fund.
- Owners' equity (€150,750): this is the shareholders' interest in the fund. If the fund was wound up now, €150,750 would be due to the owners of the fund. However, this is an unlikely event. So while the amount is owed, it is not likely to be called upon. Therefore, this is the **owner's capital** of the fund.

Note: many of the terms used above will be explained in detail in Chapter 3.

Part B: Prepare the balance sheet of the fund (see Table 2.2).

Table 2.2: The Balance Sheet of a Typical Investment Fund

Assets	(Thousands)
Investments at Cost	€140,000
Unrealised Gains on Investments	€10,000
Investments Sold Receivable	€5,000
Fund Shares Sold Receivable	€7,500
Dividends Receivable	€4,500
Cash	€2,500
Total Assets	*€169,500*

(Continued)

Table 2.2: *(Continued)*

Liabilities	
Investments Purchased Payable	€12,000
Fund Shares Redeemed Payable	€6,750
Total Liabilities	€18,750
Net Assets (Total Assets less Liabilities)	**€150,750**
Owners' Equity	€150,750

Part C: If the fund has 1,000,000 shares issued to shareholders, what is the value of each share?

> The total value of the owners' equity is €150,750,000. There are 1,000,000 shareholders. Therefore, each share is worth €150.75 (€150,750,000 divided by 1,000,000). This is called the net asset value per share. It is a simple calculation. Don't worry about it at this stage as it will be explained in more detail later.

Try Questions 2.9.1–2.9.3. You will need to determine if something is an asset or a liability. If you are unsure of any of the items (particularly in Questions 2.9.2 and 2.9.3) then jump forward to the next chapter where the terminology is discussed in more detail.

2.4: RECORDING TRANSACTIONS – INITIAL STEPS

Now that we are familiar with the balance sheet and its components (described in Section 2.3), the next stage is to identify and record transactions. If you have already taken a course in financial accounting then this section should be a review of your previous studies. If not, then all of the basics will be explained. This is where the simple and powerful logic of double entry bookkeeping (the debit and credit system) is outlined. Later, we will develop a spreadsheet approach to recording transactions that will mirror the debit and credit approach. Many find it more intuitive to follow this type of methodology and we will use it extensively in subsequent chapters.

2.4.1: Identifying Transactions

A transaction is any event that a fund enters into which changes the composition of the balance sheet. For the purposes of fund accounting, recognising that a transaction has taken place is generally not the difficult part; calculating the amounts and recording the transaction is where the issues arise. An example of a transaction is:

- A business purchases a machine for €500,000 on credit
- A business sells stock for €12,000 on credit
- An investment fund receives a dividend of €15,000 from one of its investments
- An investment fund sells investments (that it owned) for €12,000 to settle in five days' time

2.4.2: Recording Transactions

Golden Rule #1:

- A transaction always affects at least two items (these are called accounts).
- This needs to be the case to ensure that the balance sheet continues to balance (remember the accounting identity).

An account is any item for which a fund would like to group all of the transactions relating to that item. It might be a good idea to keep track of all of the dividends that a fund receives from its investments over the course of the year. Thus, a dividend income account is created. It is also a good idea to keep track of any money that we are owed from investments that we have sold, thus we will operate an investments sold receivable account.

Example 2.2a: Recording Transactions

Set out the accounts that are involved for each of the items below:

A small business:

1. Owner invests €100,000 cash in the business.
2. Business purchases goods on credit for €10,000.
3. Business pays for the goods just purchased: €10,000.
4. Business purchases motor vehicle for €25,000 cash.

An investment fund:

1. Investors invest €100,000 into the fund (in return they receive 100,000 shares).
2. Fund buys shares in Bank of Ireland for €55,000 to settle in three days.
3. Fund pays for the Bank of Ireland shares.

Solution 2.2a: Recording Transactions

1. Owner invests €100,000 cash in the business:

After this transaction, the business has more cash in its bank account but it also owes that money back to the owner. Thus, the bank account and the owners' equity account are involved.

2. Business purchases goods on credit (€10,000):

After this transaction, the business has more goods in its warehouse (this is called inventory) while it also owes its supplier for the goods as they were purchased on credit (this is called trade payables). Thus, the inventory account and the trade payable account are involved.

Note: for those of you who may have studied financial accounting there is also another method of recording this transaction using a purchases account.

3. Business pays for the goods just purchased (€10,000):

After this transaction, the business has less cash in its bank account and no longer owes any money to the supplier (now called trade payable). Thus, the bank account and the trade payable account are involved.

4. Business purchases motor vehicle for €25,000 cash:

After this transaction, the business now has a motor vehicle but it also has €25,000 less in its bank account. Thus, the motor vehicles account and the bank account are involved.

5. Investors invest €100,000 cash into the fund (in return they receive 100,000 shares):

After this transaction, the fund has €100,000 cash in its bank account but it owes that money back to the investors. Thus, the bank account and the owners' equity account are involved.

Note: although this is a fund, the transaction is almost the same as the first transaction. The accounting treatment is the same.

6. Fund buys shares in Bank of Ireland for €55,000 to settle in three days:

After this transaction, the fund has shares in Bank of Ireland that cost €55,000. The 'investments at cost account' is used to keep track of the cost of all the investments that a fund owns. The shares were not paid for (to settle in three days means that the fund will not pay for the shares for another three days). The €55,000 is still owed to the previous owner; this is called an 'investment purchased payable'. Thus, the investments at cost account and the investments purchased payable account are involved.

7. Fund pays for the Bank of Ireland shares:

After this transaction, the fund has €55,000 less in its bank account but it no longer owes the previous owner for the shares. Thus, the bank account and the investments purchased payable account are involved.

Golden Rule #2:

- Identify whether each account is increasing or decreasing

At this stage, stop and think – it is generally obvious if the accounts are increasing or decreasing. In the case of transaction 5, above, the two accounts are the owners' equity (capital) account and the bank account. As a result of the transaction, does the fund have more cash or less cash? Also, following the same logic, is there more investors' equity in the fund or less?

Example 2.2b: Recording Transactions

For each of the transactions in Example 2.2, identify whether the accounts involved are increasing or decreasing.

Solution 2.2b: Recording Transactions

1. Owner invests €100,000 cash in the business:
   The bank account and the owners' equity account are involved.
   The bank account is increasing by €100,000.
   The owners' equity account is increasing by €100,000.

2. Business purchases goods on credit (€10,000):
   The inventory account and the trade payable account are involved.
   The inventory account is increasing by €10,000.
   The trade payables account is increasing by €10,000.
   Note: for those of you who may have studied financial accounting there is also another method of recording this transaction using a purchases account.

3. Business pays for the goods just purchased (€10,000):
   The bank account and the trade payable account are involved.
   The bank account is decreasing by €10,000.
   The trade payable account is decreasing by €10,000.

4. Business purchases motor vehicle for €25,000 cash:
   The motor vehicles account and the bank account are involved.
   The motor vehicles account is increasing by €25,000.
   The bank account is decreasing by €25,000.

5. Investors invest €100,000 cash into the fund (in return they receive 100,000 shares):
   The bank account and the owners' equity account are involved.
   The bank account is increasing by €100,000.
   The owners' equity account is increasing by €100,000.
   Note: although this is a fund, the transaction is almost the same as the first transaction. The accounting treatment is the same.

6. Fund buys shares in Bank of Ireland for €55,000 to settle in three days:
   The investments at cost account and the investments purchased payable account are involved.
   The investments at cost account is increasing by €55,000.
   The investments purchased payable account is increasing by €55,000.

7. Fund pays for the Bank of Ireland shares (€55,000):
   The bank account and the investments purchased payable account are involved.
   The bank account is decreasing by €55,000.
   The investments purchased payable account is decreasing by €55,000.

We are now almost at a stage when the debit and credit for each transaction can be assigned. 'Debits and credits' is the language of accounting so it is important that you become familiar with it. The real benefit of the debit and credit system is that when a particular transaction type is done once then every similar transaction will be recorded in the same way, just the numbers will change. For example, a fund purchases €10,000 worth of shares in AIB to settle in three days. This is the same as Transaction 6 in Example 2.2a and Example 2.2b. You should now be able to assign the accounts and determine whether they are increasing or decreasing for this new transaction. As you practice more, recording transactions becomes relatively straightforward; the transactions repeat themselves over and over.

2.5: RECORDING TRANSACTIONS – THE DOUBLE ENTRY SYSTEM & 'T' ACCOUNTS

The example that we have just completed (Example 2.2) was for a very small business (the first four transactions) and a very small fund (the last three transactions). As a result, it is relatively easy to determine how much remains in each account for the business and for the fund.

Example 2.2c: Recording Transactions

For the transactions related to the investment fund (Transactions 5, 6 and 7), calculate the amount remaining in each account after all of the transactions. The amount remaining in the account is called 'the balance' in the account.

Solution 2.2c: Recording Transactions

Here is a recap of the final three transactions:

5. Investors invest €100,000 cash into the fund (in return they receive 100,000 shares).
    The bank account is increasing by €100,000.
    The owners' equity account is increasing by €100,000.

6. Fund buys shares in Bank of Ireland for €55,000 to settle in three days:
    The investments at cost account is increasing by €55,000.
    The investments purchased payable account is increasing by €55,000.

7. Fund pays for the Bank of Ireland shares (€55,000):
    The bank account is decreasing by €55,000.
    The investments purchased payable account is decreasing by €55,000.

Thus, at the end of the three transactions:

- The owners' equity account has a balance of €100,000 (from Transaction 5).
- The bank account has a balance of €45,000 (add €100,000 from Transaction 5 and less €55,000 from Transaction 7).
- The investments purchased payable account has a balance of €0 (add €55,000 from Transaction 6 and less €55,000 from Transaction 7).
- The investments at cost account has a balance of €55,000 (from Transaction 6).

In practice, the average fund would have many more transactions, making it very difficult to determine the amount that remains in the bank account. If there were thousands of transactions, this would be a laborious and error-strewn process. So another mechanism for recording transactions is required.

The approach that is used is the double entry system. When a transaction occurs, the double entry system gives guidance on how to record the transaction (this is known as bookkeeping). The double entry system works on the basis of four items:

1. 'T' accounts (Section 2.5.1)
2. The debit and credit (Section 2.5.2 and 2.5.3)
3. Balancing accounts (Section 2.5.4)
4. Extracting a trial balance (Section 2.5.5)

2.5.1: 'T' Accounts

These are similar to the accounts that were identified as part of Example 2.2a. The 'T' element is new; it represents a format of laying out an account, making it easier to determine the balance on the account. There is an account for every item in an investment fund that the fund wishes to keep track of. For example, it is often necessary to keep track of how much a fund has paid for investments, hence an 'investments at cost account (a/c)'. It is also a good idea to know how much is owed for investments that have been purchased but not yet paid for, hence an 'investments purchased payable account'. There will be an account for every item on the balance sheet (and also for every item on the income statement, which will be addressed later).

Accounts are given a 'T' shape (see Figure 2.1). This is so all the increases can be put on one side and all the decreases on the other. The name of the account is on the top. On each side, there is a column to record the date a particular transaction took place, a column to record a description of the transaction (this will normally just state the other account involved) and a column for the amount. Other columns can also be added; often there is a column for codes so that it is easy to trace back to the source of a transaction. This leads on to the next important item: the debit and credit. Notice that the debits are on the left of the account and the credits on the right.

Figure 2.1: Example of a 'T' Account

dr	Investments at Cost Account		cr
Date	Description	€	Date	Description	€
	All debits on this side			All credits on this side	

2.5.2: The Debit and Credit

The left-hand side of an account is called the debit (dr) side while the right-hand side is called the credit (cr) side. When a transaction occurs, the following should be done:

1. Identify which accounts are affected (there will always be at least 2). This is Golden Rule #1.
2. Determine whether the account is increasing or decreasing. This is Golden Rule #2.
3. Determine whether the account is an asset type account, a liability type account, an income type account or an expense type account. This is now Golden Rule #3.

4. Assign the debit or credit using the following rule:
   a) **debit asset and expense accounts with increases**
   b) **credit asset and expense accounts with decreases**
   c) **credit liability, capital and income accounts with increases**
   d) **debit liability, capital and income accounts with decreases**

   This is now Golden Rule #4.
5. It is now possible to put the amount into the appropriate side of the relevant 'T' account: the left-hand side for debits and the right-hand side for credits.

This may be a difficult concept to remember. The various items sound so alike that it is easy to get confused. But it is not that convoluted; it is a rule based on opposites. For example, recall that the rule is 'debit assets with increases' and the transaction that we would like to record results in an increase in a liability. An increase in a liability is the opposite of an increase in an asset. So the recording is the opposite (a credit).

A final aspect of the debit and credit system is that with every transaction there will be at least two accounts involved. The total of all the debits must equal the total of all the credits for a transaction. Thus, if we can identify the account to debit then by default the corresponding account should be a credit.

2.5.3: Debit v Credit – Summary

1. Identify the accounts involved (there will be at least two).
2. Determine whether the account is increasing or decreasing.
3. Determine whether the account is an asset, liability, capital, income or expense.
4. Assign the debit (dr) or credit (cr) using Table 2.3. The total of all the debits should equal the total of all the credits.
5. Enter the transaction in the account.

Table 2.3: Assigning Debits and Credits

Account Type	To Record	Entry	Side of Account
Asset and Expense	An increase	Debit	Left-hand side (LHS)
	A decrease	Credit	Right-hand side (RHS)
Liability, Capital and Income	An increase	Credit	Right-hand side (RHS)
	A decrease	Debit	Left-hand side (LHS)

This might appear longwinded but after a while it will be possible to short–circuit elements of this as you become more familiar with its workings. The best way to become familiar with this is to practice. Two examples will be used to illustrate the double entry system. The first is a continuation of Example 2.2 and is relatively short. The second, Example 2.3, is longer and more comprehensive. These should allow you to understand how the system operates.

Example 2.2d: Recording Transactions

Recall Example 2.2a and, using the solutions to Examples 2.2a, 2.2b and 2.2c, identify the debit and credit for each transaction.

Small business:

1. Owner invests €100,000 cash in the business.
2. Business purchases goods on credit (€10,000).
3. Business pays for the good just purchased (€10,000).
4. Business purchases motor vehicle for €25,000 cash.

Investment fund:

5. Investors invest €100,000 into the fund (in return they receive 100,000 shares).
6. Fund buys shares in Bank of Ireland for €55,000 to settle in three days.
7. Fund pays for the Bank of Ireland shares (€55,000).

Solution 2.2d: Recording Transactions

From the solutions to Examples 2.2a and 2.2b above, the accounts involved and whether they are increasing or decreasing are already known. If it can be determined whether the accounts are assets, liabilities, income or expenses then it should be possible to assign the debit or credit. Example 2.1 might help you to determine whether an item is an asset, liability, capital, income or expense.

Table 2.4a: Transaction 1 – Owner Invests €100,000 Cash in the Business

Account Name	Increasing or Decreasing?	Asset, Liability, Capital, Income or Expense?	Debit or Credit?	Amount
Bank a/c	Increasing	Asset	Debit (LHS)	€100,000
Owners' equity a/c	Increasing	Capital	Credit (RHS)	€100,000

Table 2.4a shows the first transaction of Example 2.2d. The bank account is an asset as the money is owned by the business. The owners' equity account is that special liability called capital or equity. The debit or credit is assigned based on Table 2.3 above.

Table 2.4b: Transaction 2 – Business Purchases Goods on Credit (€10,000)

Account Name	Increasing or Decreasing?	Asset, Liability, Capital, Income or Expense?	Debit or Credit?	Amount
Inventory a/c	Increasing	Asset	Debit (LHS)	€10,000
Trade payables a/c	Increasing	Liability	Credit (RHS)	€10,000

Transaction 2 is shown in Table 2.4b. The inventory account is an asset as the goods are now owned by the business. The trade payables account is a liability as the €10,000 is owed to the supplier of the goods. The debit or credit is assigned based on Table 2.3 above.

Table 2.4c: Transaction 3 – Business Pays for the Goods Just Purchased (€10,000)

Account Name	Increasing or Decreasing?	Asset, Liability, Capital, Income or Expense?	Debit or Credit?	Amount
Bank a/c	Decreasing	Asset	Credit (RHS)	€10,000
Trade payables a/c	Decreasing	Liability	Debit (LHS)	€10,000

Table 2.4d: Transaction 4 – Business Purchases Motor Vehicle for €25,000 Cash

Account Name	Increasing or Decreasing?	Asset, Liability, Capital, Income or Expense?	Debit or Credit?	Amount
Bank a/c	Decreasing	Asset	Credit (RHS)	€25,000
Motor vehicles a/c	Increasing	Asset	Debit (LHS)	€25,000

Table 2.4e: Transaction 5 – Investors Invest €100,000 in the Investment Fund

Account Name	Increasing or Decreasing?	Asset, Liability, Capital, Income or Expense?	Debit or Credit?	Amount
Bank a/c	Increasing	Asset	Debit (LHS)	€100,000
Owners' equity a/c	Increasing	Capital	Credit (RHS)	€100,000

Tables 2.4c, 2.4d and 2.4e show Transactions 3, 4 and 5 respectively. The bank account is an asset as the money is owned by the fund. The fund owes the money in the owners' equity account back to the investors. The debit or credit is assigned based on Table 2.3 above. You may notice that the debit and credit is the same as in Transaction 1 as the two transactions are very similar.

Table 2.4f: Transaction 6 – The Investment Fund Buys Shares in Bank of Ireland for €55,000 to Settle in Three Days

Account Name	Increasing or Decreasing?	Asset, Liability, Capital, Income or Expense?	Debit or Credit?	Amount
Investments at cost a/c	Increasing	Asset	Debit (LHS)	€55,000
Investments purchased payable a/c	Increasing	Liability	Credit (RHS)	€55,000

Transaction 6 is shown in Table 2.4f. The investments at cost account is an asset as the investments in Bank of Ireland are owned by the fund. The investments purchased payable account is a liability as €55,000 is owed to the previous owner of the shares; the shares were purchased on three days' credit.

Table 2.4g: Transaction 7 – The Investment Fund Pays for the Bank of Ireland Shares (€55,000)

Account Name	Increasing or Decreasing?	Asset, Liability, Capital, Income or Expense?	Debit or Credit?	Amount
Bank a/c	Decreasing	Asset	Credit (RHS)	€55,000
Investments purchased payable a/c	Decreasing	Liability	Debit (LHS)	€55,000

Finally, Transaction 7 is shown in Table 2.4g.

Summary of Solution

Small business transactions:

1. Dr bank account €100,000; credit owners' equity account €100,000.
2. Dr inventory account €10,000; credit trade payables account €10,000.
3. Dr trade payables account €10,000; credit bank account €10,000.
4. Dr motor vehicles account €25,000; credit bank account €25,000.

Investment fund transactions:

5. Dr bank account €100,000; credit owners' equity account €100,000.
6. Dr investments at cost account €55,000; credit investments purchased payable account €55,000.
7. Dr investments purchased payable account €55,000; credit bank account €55,000.

If you can follow this solution and the logic behind it, then you should try Example 2.3. It is a little longer and more difficult.

Example 2.3: The Equity Growth Fund

The Equity Growth Fund has the following transactions:

1. Investors invest €12,000 into the fund (amount lodged in bank account).
2. The fund buys (but doesn't pay for) 1,000 shares in Ryanair at €5.00 per share.
3. The fund pays for the shares purchased in Transaction 2.
4. The shares in Ryanair are now worth €5.50.
5. The shares in Ryanair now fall to €4.70.

Requirement:

1. For each transaction identify which account should be credited and debited.
2. Enter the transaction in the 'T' style account.

Solution 2.3: The Equity Growth Fund – Requirement 1 (Debit vs Credit)

The accounts to debit or credit will be determined first and then the items will be entered in the 'T' accounts that follow.

1. Investors invest €12,000 into the fund (amount lodged in bank account) (see Table 2.5a).

Table 2.5a: Transaction 1 – Investors Invest €12,000 in the Fund

Account Name	Increasing or Decreasing?	Asset, Liability, Capital, Income or Expense?	Debit or Credit?	Amount
Bank a/c	Increasing	Asset	Debit (LHS)	€12,000
Owners' equity a/c	Increasing	Capital	Credit (RHS)	€12,000

We have already observed this type of transaction in the previous example (Example 2.2). The fund's bank account is increasing (as there is now more cash in the fund's bank account) and the fund also owes more money back to the investors.

The next step will be to record this in a 'T' style account. This is Requirement 2 of this example. A full solution is presented later in Figure 2.2.

2. The fund buys (but doesn't pay for) 1,000 shares in Ryanair at €5.00 per share (see Table 2.5b).

We have also had a transaction very similar to this previously. The fund now has investments (shares in Ryanair) that it owns (i.e. an asset). These shares have not yet been paid for, so the fund owes for the shares (i.e. a liability). The accounts affected are investments at cost and investments purchased payable.

Table 2.5b: Transaction 2 – The Fund Buys 1,000 Shares in Ryanair at €5.00 per Share

Account Name	Increasing or Decreasing?	Asset, Liability, Capital, Income or Expense?	Debit or Credit?	Amount
Investments at cost a/c	Increasing	Asset	Debit (LHS)	€5,000
Investments purchased payable a/c	Increasing	Liability	Credit (RHS)	€5,000

Now enter these two items in the appropriate account using a suitable description (see Figure 2.2).

3. The fund pays for the shares purchased.

In this transaction €5,000 leaves the fund's bank account and the fund no longer owes for the shares purchased. We have also come across this transaction before. The table will be skipped at this point as it may be possible to record the transaction quicker.

- Cash, an asset, is decreasing ⇒ a credit of €5,000
- Investments purchased payable, a liability, is decreasing ⇒ a debit of €5,000

Now enter these two items in the appropriate account using a suitable description (see Figure 2.2).

4. The shares in Ryanair are now worth €5.50 (see Table 2.5c).

This is a new transaction. A short calculation should be performed to determine the amount of the gain on the Ryanair shares. The last time we checked, the shares in Ryanair were worth €5.00 (this is the price the fund paid for the shares). The shares are now worth €5.50; this is a gain of €0.50 per share, or €500 in total. How is this gain accounted for?

It might be a good suggestion to establish a separate account to track the gains (or losses) on the investments made by the fund. This will allow investors to see, at a glance, if the investment managers have made a good decision in purchasing the shares in Ryanair. This account will be called the unrealised appreciation/ depreciation account. It is a mouthful but 'unrealised' means that the gains (or losses) have not yet been converted into cash. This will only happen when the shares are sold. 'Appreciation' is another word for gains and 'depreciation' is another word for losses. Thus, this account keeps track of the gains (or losses) that the fund has made on its investments but these gains (or losses) have not yet been converted into cash.

The unrealised appreciation/depreciation account is an asset account that is closely linked to the investments at cost account. If these two accounts are added together, the resulting total is the market (current) value of the investments in the fund.

Where does the other side of the transaction go to? If the investments in a fund increase in value, the gain normally goes to the investors in the fund. The opposite is also true: if the investments in a fund fall in value then the investors must bear any loss. In this instance we will increase the owners' equity by €500.

As you can imagine, this is a very common transaction for an investment fund.

Table 2.5c: Transaction 4 – The Shares in Ryanair are Now Worth €5.50

Account Name	Increasing or Decreasing?	Asset, Liability, Capital, Income or Expense?	Debit or Credit?	Amount
Unrealised appreciation/ depreciation a/c	Increasing	Asset	Debit (LHS)	€500
Owners' equity a/c	Increasing	Capital	Credit (RHS)	€500

Now enter these two items in the appropriate account using a suitable description (see Figure 2.2).

5. The shares in Ryanair now fall to €4.70.

This is nearly the same transaction as the previous transaction. The previous time we checked (Transaction 4) the shares in Ryanair were worth €5.50. This is a loss of €0.80 per share, or €800 in total.

The fund's investments are decreasing in value. The same accounts are involved but the amount will be in reverse. The investors in the fund are now worth less and the unrealised appreciation/depreciation account is worth less:

- Unrealised appreciation/depreciation, an asset, is decreasing ⇒ a credit of €800
- Owners' equity (capital) is decreasing ⇒ a debit of €800

Solution 2.3 – The Equity Growth Fund – Requirement 2 – The 'T' Accounts

The complete solution is presented in Figure 2.2. However, it is a sequential process. Each transaction is recorded in turn. Thus, we start with Transaction 1. We know that this was:

- Dr bank account €12,000 and cr owners' equity account €12,000.

In the bank account on the debit (left-hand side) side, enter €12,000 under the amount column, the name of the other account involved under the description column (i.e. owners' equity account) and 'Transaction 1' under the date column (we do not have the actual date).

In the owners' equity account on the credit (right-hand side) side, enter €12,000 under the amount column, the name of the other account involved under the description column (i.e. bank account) and 'Transaction 1' under the date column (we do not have the actual date).

This is repeated for all of the other transactions to give the solution as shown in Figure 2.2.[8] The best approach is to do each transaction in turn, record the debit and credit of each transaction into the appropriate account and then move on to the next transaction. (The alternative of recording all of the bank account transactions into the bank account, all the owners' equity account transactions into the owners' equity account, etc. is a recipe for error as it is more likely that something will be left out.)

Figure 2.2: The 'T' Accounts

dr			Bank A/c		cr
Date	**Description**	**€**	**Date**	**Description**	**€**
Trans. 1	Owners' Equity A/c	12,000	Trans. 3	Investments Purchased Payable A/c	5,000

(Continued)

---

[8] You should try this yourself using a blank sheet of paper and then check to see if your answer is correct.

Figure 2.2: *(Continued)*

dr	Owners' Equity A/c		cr		
Date	**Description**	**€**	**Date**	**Description**	**€**
Trans. 5	Unrealised Appreciation/ Depreciation A/c	800	Trans. 1	Bank A/c	12,000
			Trans. 4	Unrealised Appreciation/ Depreciation A/c	500

dr	Investments at Cost A/c		cr		
Date	**Description**	**€**	**Date**	**Description**	**€**
Trans. 2	Investments Purchased Payable A/c	5,000			

dr	Investments Purchased Payable A/c		cr		
Date	**Description**	**€**	**Date**	**Description**	**€**
Trans. 3	Bank A/c	5,000	Trans. 2	Investments at Cost A/c	5,000

dr	Unrealised Appreciation/Depreciation A/c		cr		
Date	**Description**	**€**	**Date**	**Description**	**€**
Trans. 4	Owners' Equity A/c	500	Trans. 5	Owners' Equity A/c	800

Well done on getting this far. But what does this information tell us about the fund after these five transactions? To put the data into a more meaningful format, it is necessary to 'balance' the accounts. 'Balancing' an account is a mechanical procedure that will tell us the current position with regard to that account.

2.5.4: Balancing an Account

This is a mechanical process. Just follow the steps given in Figure 2.3. The bank account from the last example (Example 2.3: The Equity Growth Fund) will be used. Then try to balance the remaining accounts.

Figure 2.3:   The 'T' Accounts – Balancing an Account

1. At the end of each side of the account draw a total line (with the double underline):

dr			Bank A/c		cr
Date	**Description**	**€**	**Date**	**Description**	**€**
Trans. 1	Owners' Equity A/c	12,000	Trans. 3	Investments Purchased Payable A/c	5,000
		——			——
		══			══

2. Total both sides and put the higher amount in the space just created.

dr			Bank A/c		cr
Date	**Description**	**€**	**Date**	**Description**	**€**
Trans. 1	Owners' Equity A/c	12,000	Trans. 3	Investments Purchased Payable A/c	5,000
		——			——
		12,000			12,000
		══			══

3. On the smaller of the two sides add in an amount to ensure that the side adds to the total in the space. In the bank account example, the credit side only adds to €5,000 at the moment but the total entered is €12,000. Thus, another €7,000 needs to be added. This is called the 'balance'.

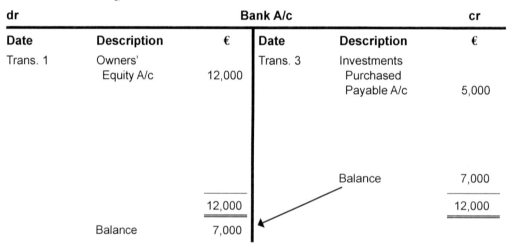

dr			Bank A/c		cr
Date	**Description**	**€**	**Date**	**Description**	**€**
Trans. 1	Owners' Equity A/c	12,000	Trans. 3	Investments Purchased Payable A/c	5,000
				Balance	7,000
		12,000			12,000

4. Then bring this total across to the other side and below the total line.

dr			Bank A/c		cr
Date	**Description**	**€**	**Date**	**Description**	**€**
Trans. 1	Owners' Equity A/c	12,000	Trans. 3	Investments Purchased Payable A/c	5,000
				Balance	7,000
		12,000			12,000
	Balance	7,000			

The balance below the total is on the debit side, so it is called a debit balance. Typically, assets tend to have debit balances and liabilities have credit balances.

In this instance, the information is telling investors that the fund has a cash balance of €7,000. The balance is on the debit side, so it is an asset. The fund has cash in its bank account (as opposed to an overdraft if the balance was on the credit side). We knew this anyway since investors gave the fund €12,000 to start with and the fund spent €5,000 purchasing investments, giving a remaining balance of €7,000. If the fund was bigger, with many transactions, then this would be an efficient method of determining how much was in the bank account of the fund.

Example 2.4a: The Equity Growth Fund

The Equity Growth Fund had the following transactions:

1. Investors invest €12,000 into a fund (amount lodged in bank account).
2. The fund buys (but doesn't pay for) 1000 shares in Ryanair at €5.00 per share.
3. The fund pays for the shares purchased in Transaction 2.
4. The shares in Ryanair are now worth €5.50.
5. The shares in Ryanair now fall to €4.70.

Previously, as part of Example 2.3, you were required to identify which account should be credited and debited and enter the transaction in the 'T' style account. The solution has been provided and explained. The next stage in the process is to balance the accounts.

Requirement:

Balance the remaining accounts (the bank account has been done):
1. Investments at cost account
2. Owners' equity account
3. Investments purchased payable account
4. Unrealised appreciation/depreciation account

Solution 2.4a – Equity Growth Fund – Calculating the Balance

Figure 2.4 shows how to calculate the balance for Example 2.4a using the 'T' accounts.

Figure 2.4:   The 'T' Accounts – Calculating the Balance for the Equity Growth Fund

dr			Bank A/c			cr
Date	**Description**	**€**	**Date**	**Description**		**€**
Trans. 1	Owners' Equity A/c	12,000	Trans. 3	Investments Purchased Payable A/c		5,000
				Balance		7,000
		12,000				12,000
	Balance	7,000				

(Continued)

63

Figure 2.4: *(Continued)*

dr			Owners' Equity A/c		cr
Date	**Description**	**€**	**Date**	**Description**	**€**
Trans. 5	Unrealised Appreciation/ Depreciation A/c	800	Trans. 1	Bank A/c	12,000
			Trans. 4	Unrealised Appreciation/ Depreciation A/c	500
	Balance	11,700			
		12,500			12,500
				Balance	11,700

dr			Investments at Cost A/c		cr
Date	**Description**	**€**	**Date**	**Description**	**€**
Trans. 2	Investments Purchased Payable A/c	5,000			
				Balance	5,000
		5,000			5,000
	Balance	5,000			

dr			Investments Purchased Payable A/c		cr
Date	**Description**	**€**	**Date**	**Description**	**€**
Trans. 3	Bank A/c	5,000	Trans. 2	Investments at Cost A/c	5,000
		5,000			5,000

Note: in this account there is no balance as both sides are equal.

(Continued)

Figure 2.4: *(Continued)*

dr	Unrealised Appreciation/Depreciation A/c		cr		
Date	**Description**	**€**	**Date**	**Description**	**€**
Trans. 4	Owners' Equity A/c	500	Trans. 5	Owners' Equity A/c	800
	Balance	300			
		800			800
				Balance	300

2.5.5: The Trial Balance

Now that all the accounts are balanced, the next step is to arrive at a format that facilitates the interpretation of this information. The approach used is to prepare a report called a trial balance. A trial balance is a list of the balances on the individual accounts. It is also a useful check on arithmetic as the trial balance should balance (or both sides should equal). If this does not occur then a mistake has been made. The trial balance is also the intermediate step before a set of financial statements is produced.

Similar to balancing individual accounts, drawing up a trial balance is a mechanical exercise. Take the balance for each account. For a debit balance, put it into the debit column (dr) and for a credit balance, put it into the credit column (cr). Then add up each column and the totals should be equal.

Example 2.4b: The Equity Growth Fund

Requirement:

Using the balances calculated from the solution to Example 2.4a (the Equity Growth Fund), prepare the trial balance (see Table 2.6a).

Solution 2.4b: The Equity Growth Fund – Preparing the Trial Balance

This trial balance informs users that the equity growth fund has €7,000 cash in its bank account. It has investments that originally cost the fund €5,000 (investments at cost) but it has lost €300 on these investments. This is because the balance on the unrealised appreciation/depreciation account is €300 credit (had this been on the debit side then the investments would have gained in value). Finally, the investors

Table 2.6a: Solution 2.4b – Equity Growth Fund Trial Balance

Equity Growth Fund: Trial Balance – Transactions 1 to 5	Dr	Cr
Bank A/c	7,000	
Owners' Equity A/c		11,700
Investments at Cost A/c	5,000	
Investments Purchased Payable A/c		0
Unrealised Appreciation/Depreciation A/c		300
	12,000	12,000

are worth €11,700, which is less than their original investment, on account of the fall in the value of Ryanair shares.

The final stage in the process is to convert this trial balance into something that an investor would be able to read more easily – a balance sheet. To prepare the balance sheet, all that needs to be done is to re-arrange the items in the trial balance. Have a look back at a previous example of a balance sheet (Example 2.1) and see if you can prepare the balance sheet for the Equity Growth Fund. The solution follows. Remember, the figures are as provided in the trial balance; all that is changing is the presentation.

Example 2.4c: The Equity Growth Fund

Using the trial balance as prepared in Table 2.6a (the solution to Example 2.4b), prepare a balance sheet (also known as a statement of net assets) for the Equity Growth Fund (see Table 2.6b).

Solution 2.4c – Equity Growth Fund – Balance Sheet

Table 2.6b: Equity Growth Fund – Balance Sheet (Transactions 1–5)

Assets	
Investments at Cost	5,000
Unrealised Appreciation/(Depreciation)	(300)
Market Value of Investments (Note 1)	4,700
Bank	7,000
Total Assets	*11,700*

(Continued)

Table 2.6b: *(Continued)*

Liabilities

Investments Purchased Payable	0
Total Liabilities	*0*

Total Net Assets	**11,700**

Capital

Owners' Equity	11,700

Note: the 'market value of investments' is investments at cost plus unrealised appreciation (or less any unrealised depreciation, as in this instance). It should equal the current value of the shares in the portfolio: 1,000 Ryanair shares @ €4.70 each = €4,700.

2.6: THE SPREADSHEET APPROACH FOR RECORDING TRANSACTIONS

2.6.1: A Word of Warning

The spreadsheet approach is an alternative to the debit/credit system. It is a useful mechanism to help understand the fundamentals of accounting for investment funds. However, if you wish to progress in this sector there is no escaping the debit and credit system. The spreadsheet approach mirrors the debit and credit system, without explicitly mentioning it. If you follow the spreadsheet approach, making the jump to formal double entry accounting should be much more straightforward.

All investment funds are accounted for using the principles of double entry accounting. You will eventually have to convert to this. Also, the debit and credit system is the language of accounting; it is a simple and logical system and all participants understand how it operates, which leaves little opportunity for communication errors or misunderstandings. Modern computerised accounting systems have, to some extent, removed the need to understand the double entry system. However, when mistakes and errors are made or when unusual transactions occur, an understanding of double entry accounting is essential.

The spreadsheet system used in this book is an excellent tool for learning how to account for investment funds. It gets over the mental block that many have with double entry accounting. In addition, a difficulty with using the formal double entry system (with 'T' accounts and debits/credits) is that it is very time-consuming for the learning environment where there are limited numbers of transactions within any question. The spreadsheet permits funds with a small number of transactions to be solved relatively quickly. Thus, it is possible to see the bigger picture much more easily. In addition, the use of this method will help to improve your Excel skills. Microsoft Excel is one of the main software packages used by accountants.

> In conclusion, the spreadsheet approach is a good tool to learn about accounting for investment funds. You will eventually have to become comfortable with formal double entry accounting. As a result, every example is explained using the spreadsheet system, but the debit and credit is also set out. This should make the transition to formal double entry easier.

2.6.2: The Spreadsheet Approach Explained

The spreadsheet approach uses a column- and row-based system just as in Excel (or its equivalent Open Office version, Calc). Under this approach, each item (or account) on the balance sheet is given a row. The columns represent each of the transactions (see Table 2.7a). The items in the balance sheet (statement of net assets) should be familiar from the previous chapter.

Table 2.7a: The Spreadsheet Approach to a Balance Sheet

An Investment Fund – Balance Sheet (Statement of Net Assets) (Empty)

	Opening	Trans. 1	Trans. 2	Trans. 3	Trans. X	Closing
Assets						
Investments at Cost	0					
Unrealised Appreciation/ Depreciation	0					
Cash	0					
Investments Sold Receivable	0					
Total Assets	*0*					
Liabilities						
Investments Purchased Payable	0					
Total Liabilities	*0*					
Total Net Assets	**0**					
Capital						
Investors' Equity	0					

This system should remove some of the mystique around debit and credits; effectively the debit/credit can be bypassed for the majority of transactions. Let's consider the layout of the balance sheet. Remember from earlier the accounting identity (Assets – Liabilities = Investors' Equity) – here it is again. The balance sheet is the list of assets less liabilities, which should equal the investors' equity.

At the moment, everything is zero as the fund has not started. Many of these titles should not be new (see previous sections) but a there is a brief recap below. This list will be added to over time.

The assets are divided into:

- Investments at cost – this represents the investments that a fund owns at their original cost to the fund.
- Unrealised appreciation/depreciation – this represents any subsequent gains or losses on the investments that the fund owns.

Why is a distinction made between investments at cost and unrealised appreciation/ depreciation?

Investors would like to know if the investments of the fund have gained or lost value since purchase. If the value of the investments was reported as just one number then this would not be apparent. For example, a fund has 10,000 shares in Ryanair that it purchased for €5 each. These shares are now worth €4.25 each. There is much more information content in the following:

Investments at Cost	€50,000
Unrealised Appreciation/Depreciation	–€7,500

Rather than

Value of Investments	€42,500

Why is the first version better than the second version (from the perspective of the investors in the fund)?[9]

- Investments sold receivable – this represents the amount that the fund is owed by third parties for investments sold but where the cash has not yet been received. When a fund sells shares or investments, it will have to wait a few days before it receives the money. This is normal practice; it is called the 'settlement period'. Investments sold receivable is the opposite of investments purchased payable (see liabilities below).
- Cash – this represents the money in the fund's bank accounts; most funds only hold very small amounts in their bank accounts.

---

[9] Under the first scenario, the investors in the fund can now more easily judge the skill (or otherwise) of the investment manager at selecting profitable investments.

Liabilities are divided into:

- Investments purchased payable – this represents the amount that the fund owes to third parties for investments purchased but not yet paid for. There is generally a lag of a few days before the previous owner of the shares/investment is paid (the settlement period).
- Investors' equity – this represents the value of the investors' interest in the fund. If the fund has performed well then this will increase but if it has performed badly then this will decrease. Later, this will be divided by the number of shares in the fund to give a NAV per share (Net asset value per share).

Now that we know what each of the items relates to, the next step is to consider the columns (Transaction 1, Transaction 2, etc.). When it comes to a transaction, just identify the items (or accounts) that are affected, the amounts involved and whether the accounts are increasing or decreasing.

For example: the investors in a fund put €100,000 into a new fund by opening a bank account for the fund and lodging the money there.

- Which accounts are affected?
  - the fund now has money in a bank account ⇒ cash
    the investors have put money into the fund, so if the fund ceases then this money would have to be returned to the investors ⇒ investors' equity
- What is the amount involved?
  - this is easy: €100,000
- Are the accounts increasing or decreasing?
  - the fund has more cash than before this transaction; thus, the cash account is increasing
    - or cash is an asset as it is increasing ⇒ debit
  - the business 'owes' more money back to its investors than before this transaction; thus, the investors' equity is increasing
    - or investors' equity or capital; it is increasing ⇒ credit
- Fill in the spreadsheet:
  - opposite cash, under column 'Trans. 1', enter +€100,000
  - opposite investors' equity, under column 'Trans. 1', enter +€100,000

After this transaction the balance sheet should look like Table 2.7b.

Each transaction is recorded in the appropriate column and at the end of the day (or week or month) the rows are totalled across. Once the rows have been totalled then the final column (i.e. 'Closing') is totalled to make sure that the balance sheet continues to balance.

Table 2.7b: An Investment Fund – Balance Sheet (Statement of Net Assets) (Opening Transaction)

	Opening	Trans. 1	Trans. 2	Trans. 3	Trans. X	Closing
Assets						
Investments at Cost	0					
Unrealised Appreciation/ Depreciation	0					
Cash	0	100,000				
Investments Sold Receivable	0					
Total Assets	*0*					
Liabilities						
Investments Purchased Payable	0					
Total Liabilities	*0*					
Total Net Assets	**0**					
Capital						
Investors' Equity	0	100,000				

This may appear a little convoluted but once you become familiar it will get much easier and faster. Try the next example, for which a solution is provided.

Example 2.5a: Spreadsheet Approach

This fund is just starting (so all the 'Opening' column numbers will be zeros). The Equity Growth Fund had the following transactions:

1. Investors invest €12,000 into a fund (amount lodged in bank account).
2. The fund buys (but doesn't pay for) 1,000 shares in Ryanair at €5.00 per share.
3. The fund pays for the shares purchased in Transaction 2.
4. The shares in Ryanair are now worth €5.50.
5. The shares in Ryanair now fall to €4.70.

Fill in the blank spreadsheet in Table 2.8a, record Transactions 1 to 5 and complete the closing balance sheet.

Table 2.8a: The Equity Growth Fund – Balance Sheet (Statement of Net Assets) (Blank)

	Opening	Trans. 1	Trans. 2	Trans. 3	Trans. 4	Trans. 5	Closing
Assets							
Investments at Cost	0						
Unrealised Appreciation/ Depreciation	0						
Cash	0						
Investments Sold Receivable	0						
Total Assets	*0*						
Liabilities							
Investments Purchased Payable	0						
Total Liabilities	*0*						
Total Net Assets	**0**						
Capital							
Investors' Equity	0						

Solution 2.5: The Spreadsheet Approach

Transaction 1:

Investors invest €12,000 into a fund (amount lodged in bank account).
This is the same as the transaction given in the last example, only the amount has changed (it is now €12,000). The recording of this transaction will be the same; use the same logic but with a different amount. After Transaction 1 the spreadsheet will look like Table 2.8b.

Transaction 2:

The fund buys (but doesn't pay for) 1,000 shares in Ryanair at €5.00 per share.
Follow the system (much of this can be short circuited after a while).
Which accounts are affected?

- The fund now has investments (shares in Ryanair) in its portfolio; this is recorded in the investments at cost account.
- The fund has not paid for the shares; the previous owner is still owed for the shares. This is called a 'payable', i.e. where the fund owes money for investments purchased ⇒ investments purchased payable.

Table 2.8b: Equity Growth Fund – Balance Sheet (Statement of Net Assets) (Transaction 1)

	Opening	Trans. 1	Trans. 2	Trans. 3	Trans. 4	Trans. 5	Closing
Assets							
Investments at Cost	0						
Unrealised Appreciation/ Depreciation	0						
Cash	0	12,000					
Investments Sold Receivable	0						
Total Assets	*0*						
Liabilities							
Investments Purchased Payable	0						
Total Liabilities	*0*						
Total Net Assets	**0**						
Capital							
Investors' Equity	0	12,000					

What is the amount involved?

- This is easy: €5,000.

Are the accounts increasing or decreasing?

- The fund has more investments than before this transaction; thus, the investments at cost account is increasing.
  - o or investments at cost is an asset; it is increasing ⇒ debit
- The fund owes more to the previous owner than before this transaction (going from €0 to €5,000); thus, investments purchased payable is increasing.
  - o or investments purchased payable is a liability; it is increasing ⇒ credit

Fill in the spreadsheet (Table 2.8c):

- Opposite investments at cost, under column 'Trans. 2', enter +€5,000.
- Opposite investments purchased payable, under column 'Trans. 2', enter +€5,000.

Table 2.8c: Equity Growth Fund – Balance Sheet (Statement of Net Assets) (Transactions 1–2)

	Opening	Trans. 1	Trans. 2	Trans. 3	Trans. 4	Trans. 5	Closing
Assets							
Investments at Cost	0		5,000				
Unrealised Appreciation/ Depreciation	0						
Cash	0	12,000					
Investments Sold Receivable	0						
Total Assets	*0*						
Liabilities							
Investments Purchased Payable	0		5,000				
Total Liabilities	*0*						
Total Net Assets	**0**						
Capital							
Investors' Equity	0	12,000					

Transaction 3:

The fund pays for the shares purchased in Transaction 2.
Which accounts are affected?

- The fund has less cash in its bank account, so cash is affected.
- The fund no longer owes money to the previous owner of the shares, so investments purchased payable is affected.

What is the amount involved?

- €5,000, from the previous transaction.

Are the accounts increasing or decreasing?

- The fund has less cash than before this transaction, thus the cash account is decreasing.
  - o or cash is an asset, it is decreasing ⇒ credit
- The business no longer owes money for the shares it purchased, thus investments purchased payables is decreasing.
  - o or investments purchased payable is a liability, it is decreasing ⇒ debit

Review of Double Entry Bookkeeping

Table 2.8d: Equity Growth Fund – Balance Sheet (Statement of Net Assets) (Transactions 1–3)

	Opening	Trans. 1	Trans. 2	Trans. 3	Trans. 4	Trans. 5	Closing
Assets							
Investments at Cost	0		5,000				
Unrealised Appreciation/ Depreciation	0						
Cash	0	12,000		−5,000			
Investments Sold Receivable	0						
Total Assets	*0*						
Liabilities							
Investments Purchased Payable	0		5,000	−5,000			
Total Liabilities	*0*						
Total Net Assets	**0**						
Capital							
Investors' Equity	0	12,000					

Fill in the spreadsheet (see Table 2.8d):

- Opposite cash, under column 'Trans. 3', enter −€5,000.
- Opposite investments purchased payable, under column 'Trans. 3', enter −€5,000.

Transaction 4:

The shares in Ryanair are now worth €5.50.
Which accounts are affected?

- The investments have increased in value. In these instances the unrealised appreciation/depreciation account is used to track any changes of this nature
- Any increases or decreases in the value of the investments in the fund usually accrue to the investors ⇒ investors' equity.

What is the amount involved?

- Previously the shares were worth €5.00 each; now they are worth €5.50. This gives an increase of €0.50 over 1,000 shares ⇒ €500.

Are the accounts increasing or decreasing?

- The shares have increased in value; thus the unrealised appreciation/depreciation account is increasing
  - o or the unrealised appreciation/depreciation account, an asset, is increasing ⇒ debit
- The fund now owes more to the investors, thus investors' equity is increasing
  - o or investors' equity, a capital account, is increasing ⇒ credit

Fill in the spreadsheet (see Table 2.8e):

- Opposite unrealised appreciation/depreciation, under column 'Trans. 4', enter +€500.
- Opposite investors' equity, under column 'Trans. 4', enter +€500.

Table 2.8e: Equity Growth Fund – Balance Sheet (Statement of Net Assets)
(Transactions 1–4)

	Opening	Trans. 1	Trans. 2	Trans. 3	Trans. 4	Trans. 5	Closing
Assets							
Investments at Cost	0		5,000				
Unrealised Appreciation/ Depreciation	0				500		
Cash	0	12,000		–5,000			
Investments Sold Receivable	0						
Total Assets	*0*						
Liabilities							
Investments Purchased Payable	0		5,000	–5,000			
Total Liabilities	*0*						
Total Net Assets	**0**						
Capital							
Investors' Equity	0	12,000			500		

Transaction 5:

The shares in Ryanair now fall to €4.70.
This transaction is the same as Transaction 4, but the figures are different.
Which accounts are affected?

- The investments have decreased in value. The unrealised appreciation/depreciation account is used to track these changes.
- Any increases or decreases in the value of the investments in the fund usually accrue to the investors ⇒ investors' equity.

What is the amount involved?

- Previously the shares were worth €5.50 each; now they are worth €4.70. This gives a decrease of €0.80 over 1,000 shares ⇒ €800.

Are the accounts increasing or decreasing?

- The shares have decreased in value, so the unrealised appreciation/depreciation account is decreasing
  - o or the unrealised appreciation/depreciation account is an asset; it is decreasing ⇒ credit
- The fund now owes less to the investors, so investor equity is decreasing.
  - o or investors' equity, a capital account; it is decreasing ⇒ debit

Fill in the spreadsheet (Table 2.8f):

- Opposite unrealised appreciation/depreciation, under column 'Trans. 5', enter −€800.
- Opposite investors' equity, under column 'Trans. 5', enter −€800.

As Transaction 5 was the last item then the final task is to complete the 'Closing' column. Add the rows across, beginning with the first row:

- Investments at cost is €0 (opening) + €5,000 (Trans. 2), which gives €5,000. This represents the original cost of the investments that the fund has made.
- Unrealised appreciation/depreciation is €0 (opening) + €500 (Trans. 4) − €800 (Trans. 5), which gives − €300. This means that the fund has lost €300 on the investments that it currently holds.
- Cash is €0 (opening) + €12,000 (Trans. 1) − €5,000 (Trans. 3), which gives €7,000. This means that the fund, after five transactions, has €7,000 in its bank account.

- There was no movement on the investments sold receivable account, so it is still €0.
- Investments purchased payable is €0 (opening) + €5,000 (Trans. 2) − €5,000 (Trans. 3), which gives €0. This means that the fund does not owe any money for shares that it has purchased.
- Investors' equity is €0 (opening) + €12,000 (Trans. 1) + €500 (Trans. 4) − €800 (Trans. 5), which gives €11,700. This means that the investors' interest in the fund is worth €11,700. As this is less than the €12,000 invested, the investors have lost money over the period.
- Then add up all the assets on the 'Closing' column: €5,000 (investments at cost) − €300 (unrealised appreciation/depreciation) + €7,000 (cash) + €0 (investments sold receivable) gives €11,700. This represents the total assets of the fund after the five transactions.
- Add up the liabilities of the fund. These come to zero.
- Subtract the total liabilities from the total assets, i.e. total assets (€11,700) less total liabilities (€0) = €11,700. This is the total net assets of the fund.
- This should equal the investors' equity, €11,700. Thus, the balance sheet (statement of net assets) balances (see Table 2.8f). If these two items are not equal then a mistake has been made; it would be essential go back to isolate and correct the mistake.

Table 2.8f: Equity Growth Fund – Balance Sheet (Statement of Net Assets) (Transactions 1–5 and Closing Balance)

	Opening	Trans. 1	Trans. 2	Trans. 3	Trans. 4	Trans. 5	Closing
Assets							
Investments at Cost	0		5,000				5,000
Unrealised Appreciation/ Depreciation	0				500	−800	−300
Cash	0	12,000		−5,000			7,000
Investments Sold Receivable	0						0
Total Assets	*0*						*11,700*
Liabilities							
Investments Purchased Payable	0		5,000	−5,000			0
Total Liabilities	*0*						*0*
Total Net Assets	**0**						**11,700**
Capital							
Investors' Equity	0	12,000			500	−800	11,700

Note: this example is the same as Examples 2.4a, 2.4b and 2.4c. You should notice that the figures in the 'Closing' column equal the figures in the balance sheet (statement of net assets) as per Solution 2.4c. Whether the spreadsheet approach or the formal double entry system is used, the end result should be the same.

Example 2.6a: The Irish Opportunity Fund

This is a more complex example than Example 2.5a. However, you should, even at this stage, notice that some transactions are starting to repeat themselves. This will make the accounting quicker as the approach will be the same. The transactions are:

1. A group of investors invest €100,000 into a new fund, the 'Irish Opportunity Fund'; the money is put into the fund's bank account.
2. The fund buys 2,500 shares in AIB for €20 each (but does not pay for them yet).
3. The shares in AIB are now worth €21 each.
4. The fund pays for the shares in AIB that it bought in Transaction 2.
5. The shares in AIB are now worth €22 each.
6. The fund sells 1,400 shares in AIB for €23 each but does not receive any money yet, while the remaining shares are worth €23.
7. The fund receives the cash due from the sale of the AIB shares; the shares in AIB are now worth €24.
8. The fund pays a dividend/distribution to its investors of €2,700.

Fill in the blank spreadsheet (Table 2.9a), record Transactions 1 to 8 and complete the closing balance sheet.

Solution 2.6a: Irish Opportunity Fund

Transaction 1:

A group of investors invest €100,000 into a new fund, the Irish Opportunity Fund; the money is put into the fund's bank account.
This is a repeat transaction. Cash has increased by €100,000 and the fund now owes €100,000 back to the investors (this would be payable in the unlikely event that the fund was wound up immediately).
Which accounts are affected?

- Cash account
- Investors' equity account

What is the amount involved?

- This is easy: €100,000.

Table 2.9a: Irish Opportunity Fund – Balance Sheet (Opening Balance)

	Opening	Trans. 1	Trans. 2	Trans. 3	Trans. 4	Trans. 5	Trans. 6	Trans. 7	Trans. 8	Closing
Assets										
Investments at Cost	0									
Unrealised Appreciation/Depreciation	0									
Cash	0									
Investments Sold Receivable	0									
Total Assets	*0*									
Liabilities										
Investments Purchased Payable	0									
Total Liabilities	*0*									
Total Net Assets	**0**									
Capital										
Investors' Equity	0									

Are the accounts increasing or decreasing?

- Cash is increasing.
- Investors' equity is increasing.

Fill in the spreadsheet (Table 2.9b):

- Opposite cash, under column 'Trans. 1', enter +€100,000.
- Opposite investors' equity, under column 'Trans. 1', enter +€100,000.

The debit and credit equivalent:

- Cash, an asset, is increasing ⇒ dr cash €100,000.
- Investors' equity, capital, is increasing ⇒ cr investors' equity €100,000.

We will do Transactions 2, 3 and 4 together in Table 2.9c.

Transaction 2:

The fund buys 2,500 shares in AIB for €20 each (but does not pay for them yet).
This is also a repeat transaction. In total, €50,000 is invested in AIB shares. The fund now has some investments of its own that cost €50,000. Thus 'investments at cost' is increasing; this is an asset as the fund owns the investments. On the other side, the fund has not yet paid for the shares; it still owes money for them so this is a liability that we will put into the 'investments purchased payable' account – remember, this is the account to keep track of the money that the fund owes for investments that it has purchased.
Which accounts are affected?

- Investments at cost
- Investments purchased payable

What is the amount involved?

- €50,000

Are the accounts increasing or decreasing?

- Investments at cost is increasing.
- Investments purchased payable is increasing.

Fill in the spreadsheet (Table 2.9c):

- Opposite investments at cost, under column 'Trans. 2', enter +€50,000.
- Opposite investments purchased payable, under column 'Trans. 2', enter +€50,000.

Table 2.9b: Irish Opportunity Fund – Balance Sheet (Transaction 1)

	Opening	Trans. 1	Trans. 2	Trans. 3	Trans. 4	Trans. 5	Trans. 6	Trans. 7	Trans. 8	Closing
Assets										
Investments at Cost	0									
Unrealised Appreciation/Depreciation	0									
Cash	0	100,000								
Investments Sold Receivable	0									
Total Assets	*0*									
Liabilities										
Investments Purchased Payable	0									
Total Liabilities	*0*									
Total Net Assets	**0**									
Capital										
Investors' Equity	0	100,000								

The debit and credit equivalent:

- Investments at cost, an asset, is increasing ⇒ dr investments at cost €50,000.
- Investments purchased payable, a liability, is increasing ⇒ cr investments purchased payable €50,000.

Transaction 3:

The shares in AIB are now worth €21.

This is a repeat transaction. The shares were worth €20; they are now worth €21. This is a gain of €1 per share over the last price or a total gain of €2,500 (the fund owns 2,500 shares). The unrealised appreciation/depreciation account is used to track these changes. In addition, if the investments in a fund increase in value then that gain normally goes to the investors in the fund. At this stage, the process will be short-circuited a little.

Which accounts are affected, what is the amount and are the accounts increasing or decreasing?

- Unrealised appreciation/depreciation: €2,500 (increasing)
- Investors' equity: €2,500 (increasing)

Fill in the spreadsheet (Table 2.9c):

- Opposite unrealised appreciation/depreciation, under column 'Trans. 3', enter +€2,500.
- Opposite investors' equity, under column 'Trans. 3', enter +€2,500.

The debit and credit equivalent:

- Unrealised appreciation/depreciation, an asset, is increasing ⇒ dr unrealised appreciation/depreciation €2,500.
- Investors' equity, capital, is increasing ⇒ cr investors' equity €2,500.

Transaction 4:

The fund pays for the shares in AIB that it bought in Transaction 2.

This is also a repeat transaction from an earlier example. The fund owed €50,000 for the shares it purchased in Transaction 2. There is less money in the fund's bank account. At the same time the fund now no longer owes anyone for its investments (as that person has now been paid).

Which accounts are affected, what is the amount and are the accounts increasing or decreasing?

- Cash: €50,000 (decreasing)
- Investments purchased payable: €50,000 (decreasing)

Table 2.9c: Irish Opportunity Fund – Balance Sheet (Transactions 1–4)

	Opening	Trans. 1	Trans. 2	Trans. 3	Trans. 4	Trans. 5	Trans. 6	Trans. 7	Trans. 8	Closing
Assets										
Investments at Cost	0		50,000							
Unrealised Appreciation/Depreciation	0			2,500						
Cash	0	100,000			–50,000					
Investments Sold Receivable	0									
Total Assets	*0*									
Liabilities										
Investments Purchased Payable	0		50,000		–50,000					
Total Liabilities	*0*									
Total Net Assets	**0**									
Capital										
Investors' Equity	0	100,000		2,500						

Fill in the spreadsheet (Table 2.9c):

- Opposite cash, under column 'Trans. 4', enter −€50,000.
- Opposite investments purchased payable, under column 'Trans. 4', enter −€50,000.

The debit and credit equivalent:

- Cash, an asset, is decreasing ⇒ cr cash €50,000.
- Investments purchased payable, a liability, is decreasing ⇒ dr investments purchased payable €50,000.

Now try the next two transactions.

Transaction 5:

The shares in AIB are now worth €22 each.
This transaction is similar to Transaction 2. Therefore, once the amount is determined then the recording of the transaction should be very similar. The previous time it was recorded, the shares in AIB were worth €21 each, they are now worth €22 each. The fund has made another gain of €1 per share or €2,500 in total (the fund owns 2,500 shares in AIB).
Which accounts are affected, what is the amount and are the accounts increasing or decreasing?

- Unrealised appreciation/depreciation: €2,500 (increasing)
- Investors' equity: €2,500 (increasing)

Fill in the spreadsheet (Table 2.9d):

- Opposite unrealised appreciation/depreciation, under column 'Trans. 5', enter +€2,500.
- Opposite investors' equity, under column 'Trans. 5', enter +€2,500.

The debit and credit equivalent:

- Unrealised appreciation/depreciation, an asset, is increasing ⇒ dr unrealised appreciation/depreciation €2,500.
- Investors' equity, capital, is increasing ⇒ cr investors' equity €2,500.

Transaction 6:

The fund sells 1,400 shares in AIB for €23 each but does not receive any money yet, while the remaining shares are worth €23 each.

This is the most difficult transaction to date, but think about it logically. There are two elements to the transaction: one element has already been addressed and the second is new.

1. The shares in AIB are now worth €23 each.
2. The fund sells 1,400 shares in AIB for €23 each.

<u>Transaction 6A</u>:   *The shares in AIB are now worth €23 each.*
All the shares, including the ones we sold, are €23 each. The previous time it was recorded the shares in AIB were worth €22; they are now worth €23. The fund has made another gain of €1 per share or €2,500 in total.
Which accounts are affected, what is the amount and are the accounts increasing or decreasing?

- Unrealised appreciation/depreciation: €2,500 (increasing)
- Investors' equity: €2,500 (increasing)

Fill in the spreadsheet (see Table 2.9d):

- Opposite unrealised appreciation/depreciation, under column 'Trans. 6', enter +€2,500.
- Opposite investors' equity, under column 'Trans. 6', enter +€2,500.

The debit and credit equivalent:

- Unrealised appreciation/depreciation, an asset, is increasing ⇒ dr unrealised appreciation/depreciation €2,500.
- Investors' equity, capital, is increasing ⇒ cr investors' equity €2,500.

<u>Transaction 6B</u>:   *The fund sells 1,400 shares in AIB for €23 each.*
The fund is due to receive €32,200 for the shares sold; this amount has not yet been received so the fund is owed €32,200 by the new owner of the shares. The account that represents amounts for investments sold that the fund is due to receive is called 'investments sold receivable'.

The fund now holds less investments (the fund holds 1,400 shares fewer in AIB), so the investments at cost account will need to decrease. These shares originally cost €20 each, or €28,000 in total.

This leaves a difference of €4,200, which represents the gains on the AIB shares that the fund is now selling. The fund sold 1,400 shares on which it had gained €3 per share, €4,200 in total. These gains are also leaving the unrealised appreciation/depreciation account (to be ultimately converted into cash), so we need to reduce the unrealised appreciation/depreciation account by €4,200. Remember that this account only keeps track of the gains and losses on the shares that the investment fund continues to own. Since the fund no longer owns the 1,400 shares, the associated gains must also leave the unrealised appreciation/depreciation account. Which accounts are affected, what is the amount and are the accounts increasing or decreasing?

- Investments at cost: €28,000 (decreasing)
- Unrealised appreciation/depreciation: €4,200 (decreasing)
- Investments sold receivable: €32,200 (increasing)

Fill in the spreadsheet (see Table 2.9d):

- Opposite investments at cost, under column 'Trans. 6', enter −€28,000.
- Opposite unrealised appreciation/depreciation, under column 'Trans. 6', enter −€4,200.
- Opposite investments sold receivable, under column 'Trans. 6', enter +€32,200.

The debit and credit equivalent:

- Investments at cost, an asset, is decreasing ⇒ cr investments at cost €28,000.
- Unrealised appreciation/depreciation, an asset, is decreasing ⇒ cr unrealised appreciation/depreciation €4,200.
- Investments sold receivable, an asset, is increasing ⇒ dr investments sold receivable €32,200.

Note: the net amount entered into the unrealised appreciation/depreciation account is +€2,500 and −€4,200, giving −€1,700.

Only two transactions remain.

Transaction 7:

The fund receives the cash due from the sale of the AIB shares; the shares in AIB are now worth €24 each.

This is another double transaction:

1. The shares in AIB are now worth €24 each.
2. The fund receives the cash due from the sale of the shares in Transaction 6.

Transaction 7A: *The shares in AIB are now worth €24 each.*

The previous time it was recorded, the shares in AIB were worth €23 each; they are now worth €24 each. The fund has made another gain of €1 per share or €1,100 in total (just 1,100 AIB shares remain).

Table 2.9d: Irish Opportunity Fund – Balance Sheet (Transactions 1–7)

	Opening	Trans. 1	Trans. 2	Trans. 3	Trans. 4	Trans. 5	Trans. 6	Trans. 7	Trans. 8	Closing
Assets										
Investments at Cost	0		50,000				−28,000			
Unrealised Appreciation/Depreciation	0			2,500		2,500	−1,700			
Cash	0	100,000			−50,000					
Investments Sold Receivable	0						32,200			
Total Assets	*0*									
Liabilities										
Investments Purchased Payable	0		50,000		−50,000					
Total Liabilities	*0*									
Total Net Assets	**0**									
Capital										
Investors' Equity	0	100,000		2,500		2,500	2,500			

Which accounts are affected, what is the amount and are the accounts increasing or decreasing?

- Unrealised appreciation/depreciation: €1,100 (increasing)
- Investors' equity: €1,100 (increasing)

Fill in the spreadsheet (see Table 2.9e):

- Opposite unrealised appreciation/depreciation, under column 'Trans. 7', enter +€1,100.
- Opposite investors' equity, under column 'Trans. 7', enter +€1,100.

The debit and credit equivalent:

- Unrealised appreciation/depreciation, an asset, is increasing ⇒ dr unrealised appreciation/depreciation €1,100.
- Investors' equity, capital, is increasing ⇒ cr investors' equity €1,100.

<u>Transaction 7B:</u>   *The fund receives the cash due from the sale of the shares in Transaction 6.* The fund now has more money in its bank account, so cash increases by €32,200 (this is the amount for which the shares were sold). However, the fund is no longer owed any money from the party that the shares were sold to, so investments sold receivable is reduced by €32,200.

Which accounts are affected, what is the amount and are the accounts increasing or decreasing?

- Cash: €32,200 (increasing)
- Investments sold receivable: €32,200 (decreasing)

Fill in the spreadsheet (see Table 2.9e):

- Opposite cash, under column 'Trans. 7', enter +€32,200.
- Opposite investments sold receivable, under column 'Trans. 7', enter −€32,200.

The debit and credit equivalent:

- Cash, an asset, is increasing ⇒ dr cash €32,200.
- Investments sold receivable, an asset, is decreasing ⇒ cr investments sold receivable €32,200.

Transaction 8:

The fund pays a dividend/distribution to its investors of €2,700.
An investment fund returns cash to its investors from time to time (particularly if the fund is increasing in value). This is done to provide the investors with a tangible return on their investment and to manage investor sentiment (i.e. keep investors happy). This is called a dividend or a distribution (in the funds business it is more often called a distribution).

When this occurs, the fund has less cash (in this instance the distribution was paid) and now the fund owes less money back to its investors (in the event of a cessation of the fund). This is the opposite transaction to investors putting money into the fund: the investors are taking money out of the fund.

Which accounts are affected, what is the amount and are the accounts increasing or decreasing?

- Cash: €2,700 (decreasing)
- Investors' equity: €2,700 (decreasing)

Fill in the spreadsheet (see Table 2.9e):

- Opposite cash, under column 'Trans. 8', enter –€2,700.
- Opposite investors' equity, under column 'Trans. 8', enter –€2,700.

The debit and credit equivalent:

- Cash, an asset, is decreasing ⇒ cr cash €2,700.
- Investors' equity, capital, is decreasing ⇒ dr investors' equity €2,700.

Now that all the hard work is done, all that remains is to do some simple arithmetic – see Table 2.9f.

- Add across each of the rows and put that total in the 'closing' column.
- Total all of the assets (total assets) in the 'closing' column; this results in a total of €105,900.
- Total all the liabilities (total liabilities) in the 'closing' column (there is only one); these come to €0.
- Subtract the total liabilities from the total assets and put the resulting figure in for total net assets in the 'closing' column, giving €105,900.
- This figure should equal the investors' equity figure; if not, then a mistake has been made.

Table 2.9e: Irish Opportunity Fund – Balance Sheet (Transactions 1–8)

	Opening	Trans. 1	Trans. 2	Trans. 3	Trans. 4	Trans. 5	Trans. 6	Trans. 7	Trans. 8	Closing
Assets										
Investments at Cost	0		50,000				−28,000			
Unrealised Appreciation/Depreciation	0			2,500		2,500	−1,700	1,100		
Cash	0	100,000			−50,000		32,200	32,200	−2,700	
Investments Sold Receivable	0						32,200	−32,200		
Total Assets	*0*									
Liabilities										
Investments Purchased Payable	0		50,000		−50,000					
Total Liabilities	*0*									
Total Net Assets	**0**									
Capital										
Investors' Equity	0	100,000		2,500		2,500	2,500	1,100	−2,700	

Table 2.9f: Irish Opportunity Fund – Balance Sheet (Closing Balance)

	Opening	Trans. 1	Trans. 2	Trans. 3	Trans. 4	Trans. 5	Trans. 6	Trans. 7	Trans. 8	Closing
Assets										
Investments at Cost	0		50,000				−28,000			22,000
Unrealised Appreciation/Depreciation	0			2,500		2,500	−1,700	1,100		4,400
Cash	0	100,000			−50,000		32,200	32,200	−2,700	79,500
Investments Sold Receivable	0						32,200	−32,200		0
Total Assets	0									105,900
Liabilities										
Investments Purchased Payable	0		50,000		−50,000					0
Total Liabilities	0									0
Total Net Assets	**0**									**105,900**
Capital										
Investors' Equity	0	100,000		2,500		2,500	2,500	1,100	−2,700	105,900

There are a couple of checks to ensure that our numbers are correct:

1. The balance sheet should balance; both sides add to €105,900.
2. The balance on the cash account (€79,500) should equal the statements provided to the fund by its bankers.
3. It should be possible to reconcile the investments at cost account and the unrealised appreciation/depreciation account. Performing these reconciliations will become more common in later chapters.

The fund's portfolio is 1,100 AIB shares (should reconcile to the custodian's records)
Market value: $1,100 \times €24 = €26,400$ (using most recent share price)
According to the accounting records:

Cost: $1,100 \times €20 =$	€22,000
Unrealised appreciation/depreciation	€4,400
Total	€26,400

(reconciles to the market value above)

Well done for getting this far. A lot of new techniques and transactions have been addressed in the last few pages. If you can master the last example then you will have given yourself a good grounding for what is about to follow. If you have any difficulty with a later section of this book it might be an idea to return to this point to see if you can figure it out using the logic that we have just employed.

2.6.3: Summary: Spreadsheet Approach – Some Common Investment Fund Transactions

Table 2.10 gives a summary of the most common investment fund transactions.

Table 2.10: A Summary of the Spreadsheet Approach – Some Common Investment Fund Transactions

Transaction Type	Accounting – Spreadsheet Approach	
Buy investments on credit	Increase asset: Investments at Cost	Increase liability: Investments Purchased Payable
Investments increase (decrease) in value	Increase (decrease) asset: Unrealised Appreciation/ Depreciation	Increase (decrease) capital: Investors' Equity
Pay for the investments previously purchased	Decrease asset: Cash	Decrease liability: Investments Purchased Payable

(Continued)

Table 2.10: *(Continued)*

Transaction Type	Accounting – Spreadsheet Approach		
Investors pay in extra money to fund	Increase asset: Cash	Increase capital: Investors' Equity	
Investors take out money from fund in the form of a dividend/distribution	Decrease asset: Cash	Decrease capital: Investors' Equity	
Investments sold on credit	Increase asset: Investments Sold Receivable (full amount)	Decrease asset: Investments at Cost (original cost)	Decrease asset: Unrealised Appreciation/ Depreciation* (profit on sale/balance figure)

* Assumes that the shares were sold for more than they were purchased; if sold at a loss then decrease asset: Unrealised Appreciation/Depreciation (loss on sale/balancing figure).

2.7: The Income Statement (The Statement of Operations and the Statement of Changes in Net Assets)

So far, only the balance sheet has been considered. Now it is time to take a look at the income statement (also known as the statement of operations); this used to be called the profit and loss account.

The income statement (statement of operations) is a report that shows the profit (or loss) made by an investment fund over a defined period (generally yearly intervals). In essence, it just gives the detail on the movement of the investors' equity account. In the recent example (Example 2.6a: Irish Opportunity Fund) the investors' equity went from €0 to €105,900. The income statement will allow investors to identify how that movement occurred.

In the two previous examples it was straightforward to explain the movement in investors' equity. However, in a more complex fund with many more transactions, it is not as easy to identify the key drivers of the increase or decrease in investors' equity. Hence the need for a separate report on this.

The income statement follows a generic format. In the case of investment funds it is subdivided into two documents:[10]

- The statement of operations (often called the income statement)
- The statement of changes in net assets

---

[10] This also happens in the case of general companies; however, for a general company the main focus of attention is the income statement, which reports on the annual profit figure.

2.7.1: The Statement of Operations

The statement of operations is a report that informs shareholders of the returns that the fund's investments have generated and the expenses or cost of running the fund. This is the report that is used to judge the performance of the investment manager. Investors will also pay particular attention to the level of expenses in the fund to ensure that the returns from the investments are not being absorbed by abnormally high expenses. The statement of operations has two sections: the first is where all the investment gains (or losses) of the fund are detailed and the second is where all the expenses are itemised.

An example of a statement of operations is shown in Table 2.11.

Don't worry at the moment about some of the terminology, but it should be possible to follow the broad layout of the report. Would investors be satisfied with the performance of the investment manager of this fund? What other information would be helpful before a definitive conclusion is reached?

The investment manager made investments that generated an income of €416,686. This could be considered to be a good result (at least it wasn't a loss). To draw a more reliable conclusion it might be helpful to know how much money the investment managers had at their disposal; if the investment managers only had €1 million to invest then this is an excellent return for a one-year period. If, however, the investment managers had €100 million to invest then an investor

Table 2.11:   Statement of Operations for the Year Ended 31/12/20X8

Gains/(Losses) on Investments	158,698
Dividend Income	155,488
Appreciation/(Depreciation) on Forward Contracts	20,000
Gain/(Loss) on Future Contracts	25,000
Foreign Exchange Gain/(Loss)	17,000
Interest Income	2,500
Bond Discount/(Premium)	38,000
Total Investment Income/(Loss)	*416,686*
Administration Fee	3,000
Management Fee	6,000
Management Fee Waived	−4,000
Other Fees	4,000
Auditing Fee	1,000
Total Fund Expenses	*10,000*
Increase/(Decrease) in Net Assets from Operations	**406,686**

might have to come to a different conclusion. An additional piece of information that would help in the analysis is the state of the markets and what other investment managers in similar funds were achieving. If, for example, the markets have being losing value over the past twelve months and all other investment managers in similar funds have been unable to generate a positive return, then the net increase reported by this fund would look quite healthy (even if the investment managers had large sums of money to invest).

As regards the expenses, they appear to be quite low. However, investors would need to be aware of the size of the fund and the expense levels of similar funds before definitive conclusions can be arrived at. Even if this fund had only a net asset value of €1 million, the expenses would represent just 1 per cent of net assets; this is low for many funds.

The statement of operations does, indeed, provide a lot of information on the performance of the fund over a specific period. However, it is not the full picture; this is why a second report, the statement of changes in net assets, is required.

2.7.2: The Statement of Changes in Net Assets

There are two key elements responsible for increases in the total value of an investment fund. The first is that the investment managers have made good investment decisions and this resulted in an 'increase in net assets as a result of operations'; the statement of operations will give information on this. The second is that investors have put more money into the fund; this will be evident from the statement of changes in net assets.

The corollary also works. An investment fund can decrease in value if the investment manager makes poor investment decisions resulting in a decrease in net assets. Again, the statement of operations will provide the detail on this. A fund can also decrease in value if large dividends or distributions are paid to the investors or if a number of investors decided to exit the fund during the year.

An example of the statement of changes in net assets is shown in Table 2.12.

This report provides additional valuable information on the performance of the fund. Firstly, investors can determine how the value of the fund has increased from a little over €25 million to over €26.5 million in the year 20X8. The €26.5 million represents the value of the investor's interest in the fund at 31 December 20X8; if the fund ceased now, the investors would receive €26.5 million back (this would be split in proportion to the number of shares that each investor holds).

From the statement of operations, it is already known that one of the reasons for the increase in the value of the fund is due to the good work of the investment managers; they generated an extra €406,686 over the year. However, most of the increase in the value of the fund was as a result of new investors entering the fund.

Table 2.12: Statement of Changes in Net Assets for the Year Ended 31/12/X8

Investors' Equity at 01/01/X8	25,016,343
Distributions to Investors	–60,500
Capital Fund Share Transactions	
Proceeds from the sale of shares	1,556,221
Redemption of units	(398,500)
Dividend reinvestment	–
Total	*1,157,721*
Increase/Decrease in Net Assets from Operations	406,686
Investors' Equity at 31/12/X8	**26,520,250**

During the year, new investors put €1,556,221 into the fund, while existing investors withdrew (or left the fund) €398,500. This gives a net increase in the value of the fund of €1,157,721. Thus, most of the increase in the value of the fund is not due directly to the investment manager but because there is a large number of new investors who invested in the fund. This is an important distinction; perhaps it is the fund's distributors[11] who need to be rewarded for this result.

However, the investment managers may have had an indirect impact on this increase. It is unlikely that many investors would have invested in this fund had they not been convinced that the investment managers were capable of generating a good return. Investment fund promoters are always keen to highlight the performance of their investment managers as a means of attracting investment into a fund. Thus, the increase of money into the fund (the €1,157,721) can be taken as an indication that investors are satisfied with the past performance of the investment manager.

The final figure (which in Table 2.12 is the second figure) that needs to be considered is the distributions to investors (€60,500). This represents money that was paid to investors as a direct return on their investment. Generally, for most funds, this is low as most investors generate a return from the increase in the value of the fund. These payments will reduce the value of the fund. However, while investors are alarmed by large expense payments (as per the statement of operations), they are happier with distribution payments, even though both have the same effect on the value of the fund. This is down to self-interest. Expense payments are made to individuals who provide services to funds (investment managers and advisors, administrators, auditors, etc.), whereas distribution payments go directly to the investor.

---

[11] Don't feel sorry for the distributors; they will be well rewarded for any new investor that they bring to the fund.

Example 2.5b (Equity Growth Fund) and Example 2.6b (Irish Opportunity Fund)

Reconsider the solution to Example 2.5a, the Equity Growth Fund; see Table 2.8f.

Prepare a statement of operations and statement of changes in net assets for each of these examples. These will be rudimentary as there were only very few transactions, but they should give an indication of the workings of these reports.

Solution 2.5b – Equity Growth Fund

Table 2.13 shows the statement of operations for the Equity Growth Fund studied in Example 2.5a.

Table 2.13:   Equity Growth Fund – Statement of Operations for the Period Ended XX/XX/XX

Gains/(Losses) on Investments	(300)
Total Investment Income/(Loss)	*(300)*
Total Fund Expenses	*0*
Increase/(Decrease) in Net Assets From Operations	**(300)**

The net decrease in net assets from operations represents the loss in the value of the Ryanair shares (Transaction 4 − a gain of €500; and Transaction 5 − a loss of €800). There were no expenses.

Table 2.14 shows the statement of changes in net assets for the Equity Growth Fund studied in Example 2.5a.

Table 2.14:   Equity Growth Fund – Statement of Changes in Net Assets for the Period Ended XX/XX/XX

Investors' Equity at Start	0
Distributions to Investors	0
Capital Fund Share Transactions	
Proceeds from the sale of shares	12,000
Redemption of units	0
Dividend reinvestment	–
Total	*12,000*
Increase/Decrease in Net Assets from Operations	−300
Investors' Equity at End	**11,700**

In the statement of changes in net assets it is possible to determine how the value of the fund has increased from €0 to €11,700. There were no distributions to investors during the period. The sum of €12,000 was put into the fund by the investors (Transaction 1) and the fund lost €300 as a result of its operating activities (this is the figure at the end of the statement of operations). Therefore, it is evident that the increase in value occurred because of new money coming into the fund and not because of the performance of the fund's investments.

The €11,700, investors' equity at end (the last figure on the statement of changes in net assets), should equal the total net assets of the fund as stated on the balance sheet (statement of net assets). Reconsider the solution to Example 2.5 and you should notice that this is, indeed, the case.

Example 2.6b: The Irish Opportunity Fund

Reconsider the solution to Example 2.6a, the Irish Opportunity Fund; see Table 2.9f.

Prepare a statement of operations and statement of changes in net assets. These will be rudimentary as there were only very few transactions, but they should give an indication of the workings of these reports.

Solution 2.6b: The Irish Opportunity Fund

Table 2.15 shows the statement of operations for the Irish Opportunity Fund studied in Example 2.6a.

Table 2.15:   The Irish Opportunity Fund – Statement of Operations for the Period Ended XX/XX/XX

Gains/(Losses) on Investments	8,600
Total Investment Income/(Loss)	*8,600*
Total Fund Expenses	*0*
Increase/(Decrease) in Net Assets from Operations	**8,600**

The gains represent the increase in the investments previously recorded in investors' equity. It is made up of €2,500 (Transaction 3), €2,500 (Transaction 5), €2,500 (Transaction 6) and €1,100 (Transaction 7). There were no expenses in the fund for the period.

Table 2.16 shows the statement of changes in net assets for the Irish Opportunity Fund studied in Example 2.6a.

Table 2.16: The Irish Opportunity Fund – Statement of Changes in Net Assets for the Period Ended XX/XX/XX

Investors' Equity at Start	0
Distributions to Investors	−2,700
Capital Fund Share Transactions	
Proceeds from the sale of shares	100,000
Redemption of units	0
Dividend reinvestment	−
Total	*100,000*
Increase/Decrease in Net Assets from Operations	8,600
Investors' Equity at End	**105,900**

This is a new fund; hence the opening position is €0. During the period, €2,700 was paid back to the investors (Transaction 8). This will reduce the size of the fund; therefore it is a negative. The investors added €100,000 to the fund (Transaction 1) and there were no withdrawals. The investment managers increased the value of the fund by €8,600 (from the statement of operations) as a result of their investment decisions. The final value of the fund at the end of the period is €105,900, which equals the net assets of the fund as determined earlier (see the final balance sheet, the 'closing' column, as per the solution to Example 2.6a).

2.8: CONCLUSION

If you have never taken a course in financial accounting then it is quite an achievement to make it to this stage. There is probably a lot to take in. The best method to become familiar with the mechanics of investment fund accounting is to practice sample questions. Try the examples in this chapter again and then attempt the questions that follow in Section 2.9. Many of the transactions are repeated. With practice it is possible to become faster at recording the transactions (either using formal double entry or the spreadsheet approach). Much of the excessive detail presented in the solutions to the examples can be short-circuited. Indeed, eventually it should be possible to do a short calculation to explain the figures and then enter the figures directly into the spreadsheet.

In this chapter, the fundamentals of financial accounting were explained. Two systems were used: the traditional double entry system with its 'T' accounts and debits and credits; and an alternative spreadsheet model. The spreadsheet approach may be easier to use in the short style examples that will be employed throughout this book, but eventually becoming familiar with double entry cannot be avoided.

A summary for recording transactions is presented in Table 2.17.

In the next chapter the format of a complete set of financial statements for a fund will be outlined and the terminology therein will be explained in more detail.

Table 2.17:   A Summary of How to Record Transactions

	Double Entry	**Spreadsheet**
Step 1	Calculate the figures involved	
Step 2	Determine the accounts involved	
Step 3	Decide which accounts to debit and credit	Decide whether the accounts are increasing or decreasing
Step 4	Complete the 'T' accounts	Complete the spreadsheet
	Repeat steps 1 to 4 until all transactions have been recorded	
Step 5	Balance the accounts	
Step 6	Prepare a trial balance	Complete the 'closing' column in the spreadsheet
Step 7	Prepare the balance sheet	

2.9 ADDITIONAL QUESTIONS

Question 2.9.1: General Business

Classify the following items as assets or liabilities:

1. Office equipment
2. Plant
3. Trade payables (money owed to suppliers of raw materials)
4. Bank overdraft
5. Trade receivables (money owed by customers for goods sold)
6. Inventory
7. Loan from bank
8. Bank account
9. Funds invested by owners
10. Provision for likely litigation on court case the business is involved in (this amount represents the lawyers' estimate of the amount that the company may have to pay)

Question 2.9.2: Investment Funds

Outline what each of the following items represents. Classify the items as assets or liabilities of a fund:

1. Cost of investments in equities
2. Investments purchased payable
3. Fund shares redeemed payable
4. Investments sold receivable
5. Expenses payable
6. Fund shares sold receivable
7. Distributions to shareholders payable
8. Dividend receivable
9. Interest receivable

Question 2.9.3

An investment fund has the following items (all items in thousands of euro):

Investments at Cost	€15,000
Unrealised Gains on Investments	€5,000
Investments Purchased Payable	€3,000
Fund Shares Sold Receivable	€4,250
Investments Sold Receivable	€3,500
Fund Shares Redeemed Payable	€2,100
Dividends Receivable	€2,700
Cash	€1,200

A: Calculate the amount of shareholders' funds (capital) or net assets.
B: If the fund has 2,000,000 shares issued to shareholders, what is the value of each share (also known as the NAV per share)?

Note: unrealised gains on investments are the gains made on all of the investments in the funds portfolio. For example, if 10,000 AIB shares are purchased at €13 each and two months later they are worth €14.50 each then the unrealised gain is €15,000 (the gain is unrealised as the shares have not yet been sold).

Question 2.9.4

You are the accountant to the Irish Assets Leader Fund. A fund starts with €50,000 of net assets; this is invested: €5,000 in cash and €45,000 in Ryanair shares. The fund holds 5,000 Ryanair shares that were originally purchased for €6 each and are now worth €9 each.

1. Prepare the balance sheet as it now stands.
2. Draw up 'T' accounts with these opening balances.

During the next period the following transactions occurred:
   a) A group of investors invest €100,000 into the fund; the money is put into the fund's bank account.
   b) The fund buys 2,500 shares in AIB for €20 each (but does not pay for them yet). The Ryanair shares are worth €10 each.
   c) The shares in AIB are now worth €21 each; the Ryanair shares are worth €11 each.
   d) The fund pays for the shares in AIB that it bought in Transaction 2.
   e) The shares in AIB are now worth €22 each; the Ryanair shares are worth €11 each.
   f) The fund sells 1,400 shares in AIB for €23 each but does not receive any money yet, while the remaining shares are worth €23 each. The Ryanair shares are worth €10.50 each.
   g) The fund receives the cash due from the sale of the AIB shares; the shares in AIB are now worth €24 each. The Ryanair shares are worth €11.25 each.
   h) The fund pays a dividend/distribution to the shareholders of €2,700.
   i) The fund pays the investment manager €4,000.
   j) The Ryanair shares pay a dividend of €1.25 per share (€6,250 in total).
3. Record these transactions in the balance sheet using a spreadsheet approach (see Example 2.6) and draw up the balance sheet, having recorded Transactions 1 to 10.
4. Complete the following tasks:
   a) Record the transactions using the 'T' account approach (see Equity Growth Fund).
   b) Balance the 'T' accounts.
   c) Draw up a trial balance.
   d) Prepare the balance sheet based on the trial balance from Question 4c.
5. Prepare the statement of operations for the period.
6. Prepare the statement of changes in net assets for the period.

Question 2.9.5

A fund starts with €75,000 of net assets; this is invested: €15,000 in cash, €50,000 in Aer Lingus shares and €10,000 in investments sold receivable (the fund has just sold some shares for which it will receive the money in a few days time). The fund holds 20,000 Aer Lingus shares, which were originally purchased for €3 each and are now worth €2.50 each.

1. Prepare the balance sheet as it now stands.
2. Draw up 'T' accounts with these opening balances.

During the next period the following transactions occurred:

a) A group of investors invest €90,000 into the fund; the money is put into the fund's bank account.
b) The fund sells 3,000 shares in Aer Lingus for €2.60 each (but does not receive the money), while the remaining shares are worth €2.60 each.
c) The money for the investments sold in the last period is received.
d) The shares in Aer Lingus are worth €2.70 each.
e) The fund buys 20,000 shares in Blackrock Land (BL) for €3 each (but does not pay for them yet); the Aer Lingus shares are worth €2.65 each.
f) The shares in Aer Lingus are now worth €2.85 each, the BL shares are orth €2.25 each.
g) Some investors withdraw their cash from the fund; they withdraw a total of €30,000.
h) The auditors are paid €2,000.
i) BL pays a dividend of €0.10 per share and Aer Lingus announces that it will not be paying a dividend.
j) The fund pays a dividend or distribution to the shareholders of €3,700.
k) The fund pays the investment manager €3,000.
3. Record these transactions in the balance sheet using a spreadsheet approach (see Example 2.6) and draw up the balance sheet, having recorded Transactions 1 to 11.
4. Complete the following tasks:
   a) Record the transactions using the 'T' account approach (see equity growth fund).
   b) Balance the 'T' accounts.
   c) Draw up a trial balance.
   d) Prepare the balance sheet based on the trial balance from Question 4c.
5. Prepare the statement of operations for the period.
6. Prepare the statement of changes in net assets for the period.

Question 2.9.6

A fund starts with €75,000 of net assets; this is invested: €15,000 in cash, €25,000 in Abbey shares and €35,000 in Bank of Ireland (BoI) shares. The fund holds 5,000 Abbey shares, which were originally purchased for €6 each and are now worth €5 each and the fund holds 3,500 BoI shares, which were purchased for €8 each and are now worth €10 each.

1. Prepare the balance sheet as it now stands.
2. Draw up 'T' accounts with these opening balances.

During the next period the following transactions occurred:

   a) A group of investors invest €70,000 into the fund; the money is put into the fund's bank account.
   b) The fund sells 3,000 shares in Abbey for €4.50 each (but does not receive the money), while the remaining shares are worth €4.50 each. The BoI shares are worth €11 each.
   c) The shares in Abbey are worth €4 each, the shares in BoI are worth €11.50 each.
   d) The fund buys 2,500 shares in CRH for €30 each (but does not pay for them yet). The Abbey shares are worth €4.25 each and the BoI shares are worth €12 each.
   e) The fund receives the money for the shares that it sold and the fund pays for the shares that it has just purchased.
   f) The shares in Abbey are now worth €4.50 each, the BoI shares are worth €12.25 each and the CRH shares are worth €31 each.
   g) Some investors withdraw their cash from the fund; they withdraw a total of €20,000.
   h) The auditors are paid €2,000.
   i) Bank of Ireland pays a dividend of €1 per share and CRH pays a dividend of €2 per share.
   j) The fund pays a dividend or distribution to the shareholders of €5,700.
   k) The fund pays the investment manager €4,000.
3. Record these transactions in the balance sheet using a spreadsheet approach (see Example 2.6) and draw up the balance sheet having recorded Transactions 1 to 11.
4. Complete the following tasks:
   a) Record the transactions using the 'T' account approach (see Equity Growth Fund).
   b) Balance the 'T' accounts.
   c) Draw up a trial balance.
   d) Prepare the balance sheet based on the trial balance from Question 4c.
5. Prepare the statement of operations for the period.
6. Prepare the statement of changes in net assets for the period.

Chapter 3

Financial Statements of an Investment Fund

- Introduction
- The financial statements of a fund
- Terminology/jargon and glossary
- Template fund
- Conclusion
- Additional questions

LEARNING OUTCOMES

At the end of this chapter you should:

- Be able to prepare the financial statements of an investment fund from a trial balance.
- Be able to describe the various sections and items in the financial statements of an investment fund.
- Be familiar with much of the terminology used.

3.1: INTRODUCTION

In this chapter the financial statements of an investment fund will be reviewed in detail. This will be done from the point of view of a real investment fund (the Sprott Canadian Equity Fund) and then a general template will be presented. The template will be used for the remainder of this book. It will be added to as new topics are introduced. There will, inevitably, be an amount of jargon and new terminology throughout this chapter. This (while extensive) should not be overwhelming. Most of the terms represent straightforward items; often the hardest part is remembering them.

One of the difficulties with fund financial statements is that there can be some differences between them, particularly from the point of view of terminology.

There are some moves being made to standardise the layout and terminology used; however, a final agreement is some time off.[1] This may be confusing at the outset, but over time it will get easier. The terminology used in this book will be kept as consistent as possible.[2]

3.2: THE FINANCIAL STATEMENTS OF A FUND

As already established, the financial statements of a fund can be divided into three reports: the statement of net assets (balance sheet), the statement of operations and the statement of changes in net assets (see, in particular, Sections 2.3 and 2.7). Now, it is time to consider the financial statements of a real fund. These are relatively easy to find on the internet; most funds that are sold to the public tend to publish their financial statements on their websites.

The fund that will be used for illustration purposes is the Sprott Canadian Equity Fund for the year ended 31 December 2003. This fund was selected for a number of reasons. Firstly, it is a relatively straightforward fund; as the name suggests, it only invests in shares on the Canadian Stock Exchanges. In addition, the fund is quoted in Canadian Dollars (CAD) so there are no foreign exchange issues. Also, there is only one class of investor;[3] this makes many of the calculations much simpler. Finally, the financial statements are presented in a very clear manner, making them easier to follow. We will only show the basic financial statements here. If you wish to see the detail, why not take a look at the Sprott Asset Management website on www.sprott.com, and navigate to 'resources' and then to 'financial and management reports'. There you will find all of the financial statements for the Sprott managed funds.

---

[1] In November 2007, the International Investment Funds Association endorsed a motion advocating a transition towards a consistent global approach to investment fund financial reporting. Recently, however, the International Accounting Standards Board (IASB), the global body with responsibility for issuing accounting standards, has been preoccupied with the reporting implications of the credit crisis.

[2] This will mean that once an item is described then that terminology will be used throughout. For example, payments made to investors in a fund can be called 'dividends to investors' or 'distributions to investors'. This book will use the term 'distributions to investors' to describe such payments. This term will be consistently used throughout the book; however, if you do come across alternative terms elsewhere, it is not an incorrect usage. Funds have a wide degree of latitude in the terminology that they employ in their financial statements.

[3] Subsequent to 2003 the fund introduced a second class of investor – the F Class. This is why a more recent set of financial statements was not considered.

3.2.1: The Statement of Net Assets

Figure 3.1a shows the statement of net assets of the Sprott Canadian Equity Fund.

Figure 3.1a: Statement of Net Assets of the Sprott Canadian Equity Fund

Statements of Net Assets

As at December 31	2003	2002
	$	$
Assets		
Investments, at market value	267,096,468	200,324,284
Cash	3,029,997	2,289,803
Accrued income	199,624	442,105
Due from broker	471,348	447,656
Subscriptions receivable	552,736	691,102
	271,350,173	204,194,950
Liabilities		
Distributions payable	–	11,798,850
Redemptions payable	145,869	276,245
Management fees payable	582,609	403,538
Incentive fees payable	749,576	11,043,358
Due to broker	1,149,992	–
Other accrued liabilities	197,609	853,796
	2,825,655	24,375,787
Net assets at market value representing unitholders' equity	268,524,518	179,819,163
Units outstanding	14,132,567	11,542,456
Unit value	$19.000	$15.579

Source: © Sprott Canadian Equity Fund, 2004. All rights reserved.

Consider some of the items in the statement of net assets (also called the balance sheet). Notice that there are two columns of numbers: one for the current year and one for the previous year. This is done so that investors can see how the fund has progressed from one year to the next.

Starting at the top, the normal practice is to list all the assets of the fund first and then the liabilities (to outsiders) second. For 2003, all of the assets totalled $271,350,173, while all of the liabilities totalled $2,825,655. When the assets are subtracted from the liabilities the result is $268,524,518; this is called 'net assets at market value representing unitholders' equity', which is a longwinded set of words for investors' equity. This amount represents the value of the investor's stake in the fund: it is also called **capital stock, shareholders' equity** and **investors' capital**. The figure $268,524,518 is the amount of money the investors put into the fund plus any net gains the fund has made since (or less any net losses the fund has made).

Assets

Next the assets of the fund will be explained in more detail. In this case, the largest of the figures is the first of the assets: investments at market value ($267,096,468). This represents the total value of all of the investments that the fund now holds. For this fund the investments are Canadian shares; a full list is given in the detail of the financial statements. There are over 120 separate investments. To arrive at this figure, the number of shares held is multiplied by the current price of the shares. The value given represents the current value of the shares (as on 31 December 2003), not the amount that the fund paid for the investments. The original cost of the shares is given in the detail (also called the notes to the financial statements). Going to the detail, it can be ascertained that the shares cost $214,801,274; so the shares have increased substantially in value since purchased. An extract from the last section of the detail of the investments at market value is given in Figure 3.1b (remember that there are over 100 other investments that appear prior to this).

Figure 3.1b: Detail of the Investments at Market Value of the Sprott Canadian Equity Fund – Statement of Net Assets

Quantity	Name of Stock	Cost	Market Value
	Other [1.99%]		
13,000	Bennett Environmental Inc.	285,285	348,140
326,500	Bevo Ágro, Inc.	158,816	195,900
349,931	DiagnoCure Inc.	298,420	958,811
18,742	FTI Consulting Inc.	763,921	566,009
598,538	Global Link Data Solutions Ltd.	150,375	209,488
443,000	Hanfeng Evergreen Inc.	797,444	1,355,580
109,934	KFX Inc.	1,032,320	1,072,575
80,990	Oncolytics Biotech Inc.	668,107	359,594
50,000	Refocus Group Inc.	147,069	32,951
25,000	Refocus Group Inc., Warrants	–	–
590,400	Unisphere Waste Conversion Ltd.	225,000	206,640
		4,526,757	5,305,688
Ounces	**Bullion and Certificates [17.13%]**		
84,528	Gold Bullion	44,119,984	45,423,954
600	Gold Certificates	345,258	322,431
		44,465,242	45,746,385
	Total Investments [100.00%]	214,801,274	267,096,468

As an example, in this case the fund owns 13,000 shares in Bennett Environment Inc. These cost $285,285 and are now worth $348,140. These shares are added to all the other holdings of the fund to give a grand total of $267,096,468.

The next item on the statement of net assets is 'cash'. This is self-explanatory. The fund needs to hold a certain amount of cash ($3,029,997 on 31 December 2003) to pay any investors who would like to withdraw their money and to pay any outstanding liabilities. While the item is called 'cash' it is not held as loose cash; this amount would be held in a bank account (or a number of bank accounts).

Accrued income is an asset of $199,624. To accrue is a technical accounting term that, in this instance, means to accumulate on a periodic basis. Since the item is an asset, the fund is owed that amount of money. This item represents income that the fund has earned but has not yet received; it could, for example, be interest income from cash held on deposit that has been earned but not yet been paid by the bank where the cash is deposited. Accrued income is often called income receivable. Generally, this amount will be received by the fund within the next six months. The opposite of accrued income is accrued expenses – these are expenses that the fund has incurred but not yet paid; this would appear as a liability.

The fund also has an asset termed 'due from broker' ($471,348). When a fund sells investments (e.g. shares in a Canadian company), it often takes a number of days before the money is received. The most likely course of events in this case is that near the year end (31 December) the fund sold some investments for $471,348. The money will be received in a few days (early January of the following year) but at year end the fund is owed the money. This item is often called investments sold receivable or investments sold unsettled.

The last item on the asset side of the statement of net assets is subscriptions receivable ($522,736). When an investor decides to invest in the fund, he or she is issued shares but it often takes a few days for the money to clear the banking/brokerage system before it is received by the fund. Close to year end (31 December) some shareholders invested $522,736; they were issued with shares but the money has not yet been received into the fund's bank account. It will take a few days (sometime in early January) for this to occur, so at year end the fund is owed $522,736 for shares it has issued to new investors. This item is also called subscriptions unsettled or fund shares sold receivable.

Liabilities

The Sprott Canadian Equity Fund has a number of liabilities. The first of these is called distributions payable ($0). This is unusual as the amount owed is zero on 31 December 2003. There is, generally, no need to list liabilities (or assets) that are zero, but, in this instance, in the previous year distributions payable was quite large. Hence the item is included for comparative purposes. When a fund makes a decision to pay a return to its investors it is called a distribution or a dividend. Remember, an investor will give money to a fund to see the investment increase in value (a capital gain) or to get a cash return (generally a dividend/distribution). The fund will announce its intention to pay a dividend but it will take some time before the actual payment is made. Some time before 31 December 2002, the fund decided to pay a distribution to its investors of $11,798,850 but it was not paid until 2003. On 31 December 2002, this amount was owed by the fund to its investors. Moving forward to 31 December 2003, at this time the fund has made no such commitments. Hence there is no liability to investors on 31 December 2003.

Redemptions payable of $145,869 is the next liability. This is the exact opposite of subscriptions receivable. Just before the year end a number of investors ($145,869 worth) applied to take their money out of the fund. Their shares have been cancelled but they have not yet received their money. The procedure takes a few days, so the fund owes this money to its former investors. The amount will be paid in early January 2004. This item is also termed redemptions unsettled or fund shares redeemed payable.

The next two liabilities are very similar: management fees payable ($582,609) and incentive fees payable ($749,576). The largest single expense of a fund is the amount paid to the investment manager. In the case of this fund the investment manager is paid a basic fee of 2.5 per cent of the net assets of the fund and an additional incentive fee if the fund performs extremely well.[4] As at 31 December 2003 the investment managers had performed their duties for the fund but had not yet been paid; they were owed $1,332,185 ($582,609 of basic fees and $749,576 of incentive fees) by the fund. This is standard practice; a fund will not pay the investment managers until they have done the work.

The second last liability is 'due to broker' ($1,149,992). This is the exact opposite to 'due from broker', which was considered earlier as one of the assets of the fund. In this case, the fund has purchased investments (shares in Canadian companies) that it has not yet paid for. This is because the brokerage system takes a few days for the transaction to fully settle. Early in the January 2004 this amount will be paid over to the previous owner of the shares. Consequently, on 31 December 2003 the amount is still owed. This item is also called investments purchased unsettled or investments purchased payable.

The final liability is 'other accrued liabilities' ($197,609). This represents other amounts that the fund owes to those who have provided services to the fund. The administrators, custodians, auditors, legal advisors, and so on would all have done work for the fund and may not have been paid. The fund will only pay once the work is complete, not in advance. At year end all these amounts add to $197,609. These items are also known as accrued expenses or expenses payable.

---

[4] Exact details can be found in the full financial statements. The incentive fee can be generous and investment managers can earn huge payments if their funds outperform the specified market. In 2002 the fund did very well – take a look at the statement of operations in Section 3.2.2 to see just how well the fund performed. The investment manager of the Sprott Canadian Equity Fund is Sprott Asset Management Inc.

Capital

The final section of the statement of net assets is the capital section. This is equal to all of the assets less all of the liabilities (€268,524,518). It represents the value of the investor's interest in the fund. It is also known as shareholders' equity, capital stock or investors' equity. If the fund ceased on 31 December 2003, the investors would receive $268.5 million.

The units outstanding are the number of shares/units that are in existence in the fund. Every time investors wish to put money into the fund they are given shares/units in return. If each investor held just one share/unit, then the fund would have 14,132,576 investors. Fortunately, this is highly unlikely as investors will hold thousands of shares/units each. The more shares/units an investor owns the more the investor is worth.

Each one of those shares/units is worth $19.000 – this is called the **NAV per share** or **unit value**. This is arrived at by dividing the total net assets ($268,524,518) by the units outstanding (14,132,567). If a new investor wanted to buy into this fund, each share/unit would cost $19.000. By the same logic, if an existing investor wanted their money back they would get $19.000 per share/unit. This is an improvement on the same time last year (31 December 2002), when the shares/units were worth just $15.579.

3.2.2: The Statement of Operations

Figure 3.2 shows the statement of operations of the Sprott Canadian Equity Fund.

Figure 3.2:   Statement of Operation of the Sprott Canadian Equity Fund

Statement of Operation

Years ended December 31	2003	2002
	$	$
Investment Income (Loss)		
Income		
Dividends	666,178	189,672
Interest	3,312,677	3,062,099
	3,978,855	3,251,771
Expenses		
Management fees	5,054,166	4,528,882
Incentive fees	1,119,359	11,043,358
Other	391,509	345,294
Goods and services tax	454,697	1,109,494
	7,019,731	17,027,028
Net investment income (loss)	**(3,040,876)**	**(13,775,257)**

(Continued)

Figure 3.2: *(Continued)*

Years ended December 31	2003	2002
	$	$
Realized and Unrealized Gain on Investments		
Realized gain on sale of investments	30,190,007	46,259,667
Realized foreign exchange gain (loss)	(2,711)	(57,243)
Change in unrealized appreciation in the value of investments	29,859,446	3,165,526
Net realized and unrealized gain on investments	**60,046,742**	**49,367,950**
Increase in net assets from operations	**57,005,866**	**35,592,693**

Source:

In this example, the statement of operations is divided into two sections: 'investment income (loss)' and 'realised and unrealised gains on investments'. This is because a fund can generate income from two sources: direct income from its investments (e.g. dividends) and indirect income from its investments (e.g. increase in the value of investments – share price increases). Funds are not required to follow this type of layout but the general format for any fund should be similar. The statement of operations usually reports on a year-long period, up to 31 December 2003 in this case. Comparative figures are also included for the previous year. The Sprott Canadian Equity Fund made a net investment *loss* of $3,040,876 and a net realised and unrealised *gain* on investments of $60,046,742 for the year ended 31 December 2003. This gives a net gain for the year of $57,005,866 (the gain less the loss); the equivalent for a 'normal' company would be 'profit for the year'. The figure €57,046,742 is the profit that the fund has made for 2003.

Income

Funds have only a few sources of direct income; in the example these are dividends and interest. The dividend income represents the dividends that the fund receives from its investments. This fund holds shares in Canadian companies and, from time to time, some of these companies will pay a dividend and the fund will be entitled to its portion. In total, the fund received $666,178 in dividends from companies in its portfolio for 2003. The fund also had money on deposit (in various forms); this money would have earned interest over the year. In total, the fund received $3,312,677 in interest in 2003.

Expenses

The annual expenses of the fund are set out here. These are reasonably self-explanatory. The 'management fee' and 'incentive fee' are the two largest expense items; this is to be expected and full details on their calculation are available in the notes to the financial statements. 'Other fees' includes the cost of all the other services provided to the fund for the year (administration, custody, audit, legal, etc.). Goods and services tax is a Canadian tax (similar to VAT in Ireland and the EU). As the fund enjoys special tax status in Canada, it is unable to reclaim this cost; hence, it is an expense of the fund. This is unique to Canadian funds; Irish funds would not have this line item.

The total expenses of the fund add to $7,019,731. This is subtracted from the income of the fund, $3,987,855, leaving a net investment loss of $3,040,876. The fact that there is a loss is not unusual – many extremely successful funds do not regularly generate enough day-to-day income to meet their expenses. How do you think a fund would meet their expenses in such a situation?[5]

Realised and Unrealised Gain on Investments

This is the second part of the statement of operations and reports on the price performance of the fund's investments over the year. It is comprised of two main items: realised gains (or losses) on investments ($30,190,007) and unrealised gains (or losses) on investments ($29,859,446). The realised gains relate to increases in the value of the equities in the investment portfolio of the fund that have been converted into cash by selling the equities. The unrealised gains represent gains that have been made on equities in the investment portfolio that have not yet been converted into cash because these equities are still held. Not all funds make this distinction, just providing a total gain on investments figure instead. However, under certain circumstances, the distinction can be important as some funds may limit the maximum amount that they can distribute to investors to net realised gains, meaning unrealised gains cannot be distributed.

The fund also made a small loss on foreign exchange ($2,711); the detail on this is not provided by the fund.[6]

The net realised and unrealised gain on investments is $60,046,742. This is the gain made over the year due to the increase in the prices of the equities held by the fund. This is where the expertise of the investment manager (along with some luck) is essential. Many funds generate the bulk of their returns from equity price increases and not from dividends and interest income. The Sprott Canadian Equity Fund is not unusual in this regard.

---

[5] The capital gains on the share portfolio should exceed the net investment loss. However, to meet the expenses the fund might have to sell some shares in its portfolio.

[6] The fund holds a small amount of gold bullion in its portfolio, which is generally quoted in USD. The likelihood is that the foreign exchange loss is due to movements between the CAD and the USD over the period.

3.2.3: Statement of Changes in Net Assets

Figure 3.3 shows the statement of changes in net assets of the Sprott Canadian Equity Fund.

Figure 3.3:   Statement of Changes in Net Assets of the Sprott Canadian Equity Fund

Statement of Changes in Net Assets

Years ended December 31	2003	2002
	$	$
Increase in net assets from operations	57,005,866	35,592,693
Distributions to unitholders		
From net realized capital gains	(16,675,464)	(11,798,850)
Capital unit transactions		
Proceeds from issue of units	91,851,059	167,483,100
Redemption of units	(43,476,106)	(83,475,692)
	48,374,953	84,007,408
Increase in net assets for the year	88,705,355	107,801,251
Net assets, beginning of year	179,819,163	72,017,912
Net assets, end of year	268,524,518	179,819,163

Source: © Sprott Canadian Equity Fund, 2004. All rights reserved.

This is the final report that comprises the financial statements of an investment fund. In this statement, an investor can determine the reasons why the overall value of the fund has increased (or decreased). A fund will increase in total value (net assets) for two potential reasons:

- The investments of the fund have generated returns, either by dividend or interest payments or by price increases less any expenses. The statement of operations provides this information. In the example of the Sprott Canadian Equity Fund, it has already been ascertained that the value of the fund has increased by $57,005,866 for this reason.
- Transactions with investors (subscriptions, redemptions and distributions). The net assets of a fund will increase if more investors put their money into the fund. Conversely, the net assets of a fund will decrease if existing investors withdraw their money from the fund or if all of the investors are given a distribution (dividend payment from the fund).

The statement of changes in net assets will be explained by working from the end of the report to the start. This report explains why the total net assets of the fund have increased from $179,819,163 at the start of the year to $268,524,518 at the end of the year (this is also the figure for total net assets at the end of the statement of net assets on 31 December 2003). This represents an increase in the net assets of $88,705,355.

One of the reasons for the increase in net assets is because new investors put more money into the fund. In total, new investors put $91,851,059 into the fund over the year; in return for their investment, they were issued shares or units in the fund. Hence this is called 'proceeds from the sale of units'. However, some of the existing investors withdrew their money from the fund. This totalled $43,476,106. The fund had to pay these investors this amount and in return they surrendered their shares. Hence this is termed 'redemption of units'. The net effect is that investors put an extra $48,374,953 into the fund.

A second reason for the increase in net assets of $88,705,355 (continuing to work backwards) is because the fund paid investors a distribution of €16,675,464 during the year. Similar to companies (e.g. Vodafone and CRH) that pay a dividend to their shareholders, funds also pay dividends to their investors or shareholders. The larger the distribution, the smaller the fund subsequently becomes. Thus, the fund will have decreased in value by $16,675,464 because of these payments to investors.

The final reason for the increase in net assets is the effect of the performance of the fund's investments (less expenses) over the year. The statement of operations has already highlighted that the fund made a profit (increase in net assets from operations) of €57,005,866. This will cause the value of the investment fund to increase.

So, the €57,005,866 (gain due to the performance of the fund's investments) less $16,675,464 (distributions paid to investors) plus $48,374,953 (net new money invested by investors) explains how the fund has increased in value by $88,705,355.

3.3: Terminology/Jargon and Glossary

Even to this point, a large number of different terms (or jargon) have been explained. These will become more familiar as they will appear over and over again. This is the language of investment fund accounting and it is important that the meaning of each item is understood. Figure 3.4 shows a schematic of where the various terms appear and how they relate to one another.

This list will be added to over time. At this stage, sufficient terms have been explained to allow you to be comfortable with most of the common terms in investment fund accounting.

Figure 3.4: **A Diagram of Accounting Terms and How They Relate to Each Other**

The Statement of Net Assets

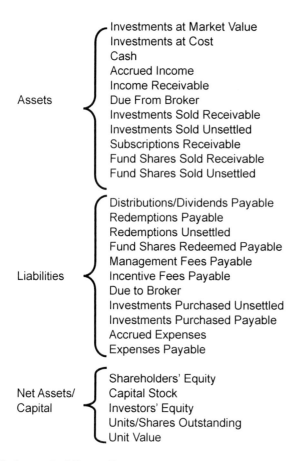

The Statement of Operations

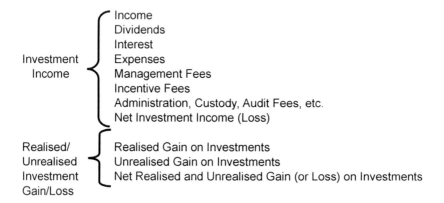

Increase in Net Assets from Operations

(Continued)

Figure 3.4: *(Continued)*

The Statement of Changes in Net Assets

Increase in Net Assets from Operations

Distributions to Unitholders
Dividends to Investors

Capital   { Proceeds from Sales of Units
Transactions { Redemption of Units

3.3.1: A Glossary of Useful Terms

The following is a list of terms/jargon most of which have been already addressed. Notice the large amount of redundancy in terminology as there are many terms to explain the same item.

Account

Any item that a fund would like to track. For example, a fund normally would like to know how much is owed to third parties for investments that it has purchased but not yet paid for, so an investments purchased payable account would be drawn up.

Accrual

The accounting technique of matching the income and expenses of a fund to the period that they relate to, rather than to the period in which the income was received in cash or the expense paid in cash, is a fundamental principle of accounting and applies to the financial reports of all entities. This technique records transactions and events when they are incurred or earned.

Accrued Expenses

Expenses that the fund has incurred but has not yet paid for. The fund has received the service but has yet to pay. This is a liability of the fund. It arises because most expenses are paid in arrears. For example, management expenses are paid quarterly but the service is incurred every day.

Accrued Income

See income receivable.

Asset

An asset is something that is owned by the fund (or business). In more complicated terms, an asset is 'a resource controlled by an entity as a result of past events and from which future economic benefits are expected to flow to an entity'.[7]

Balance Sheet

See statement of net assets.

Balancing an Account

'Balancing' an account is a mechanical procedure that will tell the current position with regard to that account, i.e. how much remains in the account.

Bank

See cash.

Capital Stock

See investors' equity.

Capital Units

See fund shares.

Cash

This represents the money in the fund's bank account; most funds only hold very small amounts in their bank account.

Credit

An accounting convention: the right-hand side of a 'T' account. Assign a credit using the following rule:

- Credit asset and expense accounts with decreases
- Credit liability, capital and income accounts with increases

Debit

An accounting convention: the left-hand side of a 'T' account. Assign a debit using the following rule:

- Debit asset and expense accounts with increases
- Debit liability, capital and income accounts with decreases

---

[7] International Accounting Standards Board (2001).

Distributions to Investors/Unitholders

An investment fund returns cash to its investors from time to time (particularly if the fund is increasing in value). This is done to provide investors with a tangible return on their investment and to manage investor sentiment (i.e. keep investors happy). This is called a dividend or a distribution (in the investment fund business it is more often called a distribution).

Distributions Payable

This is where the 'distribution to investors' has been announced but not yet paid to the investors. Thus, the amount is outstanding or owed by the fund; it is a liability of the fund.

Distributions Reinvested

Some investors elect not to receive their distribution in cash. Instead, they prefer to reinvest the amount that they would have received back into the fund. This represents the total amount of distributions that investors have elected to reinvest in a fund in a period.

Dividend Income

A dividend is a payment to the shareholders of a company from the realised profits of the company. Dividend income is the total amount of dividends that a fund has received in a period from all of its equity investments.

Dividends Receivable/Dividend Income Receivable

This represents dividend income due to the fund that it will receive at some point in the future. It is an asset of the fund.

Due from Broker

See investments sold receivable.

Due to Broker

See investments purchased payable.

Expenses

This is the cost of operating the fund. Expenses typically include investment management fees, administration fees, audit fees, legal fees and so on.

Expenses Payable

See accrued expenses.

Fund Shares

As investors put money into a fund they are issued fund shares in return. The fund shares are valued at the NAV per share (often on a daily basis).

Fund Shares Outstanding

This is the number of fund shares in issue at a particular point in time. The total net assets are divided by this number to give the NAV per share.

Fund Shares Redeemed Payable

This represents money that the fund is due to pay for fund shares redeemed by exiting investors. It tends to take a few days for these transactions to settle, so there can be a delay between the cancelling of shares and the payment of money. This is a liability of the fund.

Fund Shares Redeemed Unsettled

See fund shares redeemed payable.

Fund Shares Sold Receivable

This represents money that the fund is due for fund shares issued to new investors. It tends to take a few days for these transactions to settle, so there can be a delay between issuing the shares and receiving the money. It is an asset of a fund.

Fund Shares Sold Unsettled

See fund shares sold receivable.

Gain/Loss on Investments

This is the amount that the fund has gained (or lost) in a period as a result of the increases (or decreases) in the prices of the shares in its portfolio. This can be split into two:

- The realised gain/loss on investments – this is where the gain (loss) has been converted into cash by selling the shares in the period.
- The unrealised gain/loss on investments – this is where the gain (loss) has not yet been converted into cash as the shares are still in the portfolio.

Incentive Fees

This is an additional fee that is paid to the investment managers if the fund achieves some pre-determined targets. Normally, this should only be paid to the investment managers on foot of exceptional performance.

Income Receivable

Income that the fund has earned but it has not yet received. Dividend income receivable is an example.

Income Statement

See statement of operations.

Increase/Decrease in Net Assets from Operations

This is the total income of a fund less the expenses of running the fund for a period. It is the final figure at the end of the statement of operations and is also called net investment income.

Interest Receivable

This is interest income that the fund has earned on its investments or bank accounts that it has not yet received. It is an asset of the fund.

Investments at Cost

This represents the investments that a fund owns at their original cost to the fund.

Investments at Market Value

This represents the total value of all of the investments that the fund holds. 'Market value of investments' is 'investments at cost' plus 'unrealised appreciation/depreciation'.

Investment Income

This is the income that the fund has generated from all of its investments. It can include the gains (losses) on share prices, dividend income, interest income and so on.

Investments Purchased Payable

This represents the amount that the fund owes to third parties for investments purchased but not yet paid for. There is, generally, a lag of a few days before the previous owner of the shares or investment is paid (the settlement period).

Investments Purchased Unsettled

See investments purchased payable.

Investments Sold Receivable

This represents the amount that the fund is owed by third parties for investments sold but the cash has not yet been received. When a fund sells shares or investments, it will have to wait a few days before it receives the money. This is normal practice; it is called the 'settlement period'. Investments sold receivable is the opposite of investments purchased payable.

Investments Sold Unsettled

See investments sold receivable.

Investors' Equity

This represents the value of the investors' stake in the fund; it is also called capital stock, shareholders' equity and investors' capital. If the fund has performed well then this will increase but if it has performed badly then this will decrease. This is divided by the number of shares in the fund to give a NAV per share (net asset value per share).

Liability

A liability is something that is owed by the fund (or business). In more complicated terms, a liability is 'a present obligation as a result of past events, the settlement of which is expected to result in the outflow of resources'[8] (cash, for example).

Management Fees Payable

This represents the amount of money that the fund owes for management fees that it has incurred but has not yet paid for. It is a subset of accrued expenses and is a liability of the fund.

NAV per Share/Net Asset Value per Share

This is the total net assets of the fund divided by the total number of outstanding investor shares (capital stock). It is the price at which new investors can buy into the fund and existing investors can sell out.

Payable

A payable is an amount of money that is owed by the fund to a third party. It is a liability of the fund, e.g. investments purchased payable.

---

[8] International Accounting Standards Board (2001).

Proceeds from the Sale of Shares

The total amount received by the fund from new investors in a period. This appears in the statement of changes in net assets.

Profit and Loss Account

See statement of operations.

Realised Gain/Loss on Investments

See gain/loss on investments.

Receivable

A receivable is an amount of money that is due to the fund by a third party. It is an asset of the fund, e.g. investments sold receivable.

Redemption/Redeeming Shares

This is the term given to the process where existing shareholders apply to leave a fund and get the current value of their investment back. The shareholders surrender their shares and in return they receive the value of the shares.

Redemptions Payable

See fund shares redeemed payable.

Redemptions Unsettled

See fund shares redeemed payable.

Redemption of Units

The total amount paid by the fund, in a period, to investors who have left the fund. This item appears in the statement of changes in net assets.

Settlement

The process of exchanging securities (equities) for cash once an agreement on price has been reached between the buyer and the seller.

Settlement Period

The time allowed for the settlement to take place. This can be a few days, or longer, depending on the type of security involved. It is the time allowed for the seller to deliver the shares to the buyer and for the buyer to deliver the cash to the seller.

Shareholders' Equity

See investors' equity.

Shares Outstanding

See fund shares outstanding.

Statement of Changes in Net Assets

The statement of changes in net assets is a report that explains how the investors' equity in a fund has increased or decreased from the start of the period to the end of the period. The normal reasons for such changes are new investors coming into the fund, existing investors leaving the fund, distributions to investors and changes in net assets from operations.

Statement of Financial Position

See statement of net assets.

Statement of Net Assets

The statement of net assets of a fund is the list of assets less liabilities. This should equal the investors' equity at a point in time. It is also called a balance sheet or a statement of financial position. In simple terms, it is a list of what the fund owns and owes.

Statement of Operations

The statement of operations is a report that informs shareholders of the returns that the fund's investments have generated and the expenses or cost of running the fund. This is the report that is used to judge the performance of the investment manager. It is also called the income statement or the profit and loss account.

Subscriptions Receivable

See fund shares sold receivable.

'T' Account

A format of laying out an account, making it easier to determine the balance on the account; the left-hand side of the 'T' is the debit side and the right-hand side is the credit side.

Trial Balance

A trial balance is a report that lists the balances on the individual accounts. It is also a useful check on arithmetic as the trial balance should balance (or both sides should be equal).

Unitholders' Equity

See investors' equity.

Units

See fund shares.

Unrealised Appreciation/Depreciation

This represents any subsequent gains or losses on the investments that the fund owns. Investors often like to know if the investments of the fund have gained or lost value since purchase. If the investments have gained in value then the figure is positive; otherwise it is negative. 'Unrealised' means that the gains (or losses) have not yet been converted into cash. This will only happen when the shares are sold. 'Appreciation' is another word for gains and 'Depreciation' is another word for loss. Thus, this account keeps track of the gains (or losses) that the fund has made on its investments, but these gains (or losses) have not yet been converted into cash.

Unrealised Gain/Loss on Investments

See gain/loss on investments. The difference between unrealised gain/loss on investments and unrealised appreciation/depreciation is that the unrealised gain/loss in investments refers to the gain/loss for the current period only, while the unrealised appreciation/depreciation refers to the total gain/loss since the shares were originally purchased (this may have been many years ago).

YTD

Short for year-to-date; for example, management fee YTD, which is the total amount that has been incurred on management fees from the start of the accounting period until the current day (i.e. the year to date).

3.4: TEMPLATE FUND

In Section 3.2, the financial statements of a 'real' fund were considered in detail. In this section a format for a template fund will be introduced. The template fund is the basic example that will be used throughout the remainder of this book. It will be added to as new areas are encountered but the fundamental format should remain the same. It is important to become familiar with this format and how the figures relate to one another. The template fund is very similar to the example of the Sprott Canadian Equity Fund. Table 3.1 shows the three statements of the template fund.

Table 3.1: The Statements of the Template Fund as at 04/04/X8

Statement of Net Assets of the Template Fund as at 04/04/X8

Assets

Investments at Cost	€10,526,700
Unrealised Appreciation/Depreciation	€1,250,300
Investments Sold Receivable	€450,000
Fund Shares Sold Receivable	€120,000
Interest Receivable	€25,520
Cash	€1,400,000
Dividends Receivable	€25,000
Total Assets	*€13,797,520*

Liabilities

Investments Purchased Payable	€255,420
Accrued Expenses	€16,890
Fund Shares Redeemed Payable	€362,460
Distributions Payable	€25,800
Total Liabilities	*€660,570*
Total Net Assets	**€13,136,950**
Capital Stock/Investors' Equity	**€13,136,950**
Outstanding Shares	1,250,300
Net Asset Value (NAV) Per Share	**€10.507**

Statement of Operations for Period from 01/01/X8 to 04/04/X8

Realised Gains/Losses on Investments	€125,550
Unrealised Gain/Losses on Investments	€129,938
Dividend Income	€82,560
Interest Income	€36,180
Total Investment Income/Loss	*€374,228*
Administration Fee Year to Date (YTD)	€16,740
Investment Management Fee YTD	€65,671
Other Fees YTD	€4,700
Auditing Fee YTD	€2,060
Total Fund Expenses	*€89,171*
Increase/Decrease in Net Assets from Operations	**€285,057**

(Continued)

Table 3.1: *(Continued)*

Statement of Changes in Net Assets for Period from 01/01/X8 to 04/04/X8	
Investors' Equity at 01/01/X8	€11,754,700
Distributions to Investors	(€60,500)
Capital Fund Share Transactions	
Proceeds from the Sale of Shares	€1,556,221
Redemption of Units	(€398,528)
Dividend Reinvestment	0
Total	**€1,157,693**
Increase/Decrease in Net Assets from Operations	€285,057
Investors' Equity at End of Period (04/04/X8)	**€13,136,950**

3.4.1: Using the Template with the Spreadsheet Approach

This template will be the starting point for the spreadsheet approach that was explained in Chapter 2. Recall from the previous chapter that the spreadsheet approach was used to explain the recording of transactions in the statement of net assets.

The statement of operations and the statement of changes in net assets are now being introduced. However, the mechanism of recording transactions is the same as has been outlined in Chapter 2. Try to imagine the template as a spreadsheet with each statement (statement of net assets, statement of operations, statement of changes in equity) having an opening column, a column for each transaction and a closing column. Jump forward to Chapter 4, Section 11 (4.11: Bringing it All Together) to see an example of the extended spreadsheet. The operation of the template with the spreadsheet approach will be outlined in the next chapter. In the meantime, to become familiar with the template, try Example 3.1.

Example 3.1

You have been provided with the following balances for the TRIM Growth Fund for the year ended 31/12/X8 (see Table 3.2a).

Table 3.2a: Balances for the TRIM Growth Fund on 31/12/X8

Account Name	Dr €	Cr €
Investments at Cost	12,500,680	
Unrealised Appreciation/Depreciation	85,260	
Investments Purchased Payable		455,600
Investments Sold Receivable	190,000	
Dividends Receivable	1,500	
Distributions Payable		8,500
Fund Shares Sold Receivable	125,600	
Fund Shares Redeemed Payable		26,410
Interest Receivable	3,600	
Cash	800,540	
Expenses Payable		80,500
Gain/Loss on Investments		1,000,780
Dividend Income		55,800
Interest Income		9,506
Administration Fee YTD	15,450	
Investment Management Fee YTD	187,930	
Incentive Fees YTD	55,886	
Custody Fees YTD	19,780	
Audit Fee	4,500	
Investors' Equity at 01/01/X8		9,920,710
Proceeds from Issue of Shares		2,894,160
Redemption of Shares	442,550	
Distributions to Investors	18,690	
Total	*14,451,966*	*14,451,966*

Note: the above format is a trial balance. If in doubt regarding a particular item, here is a little tip: if an item has a debit (dr) balance then it is generally an asset (in the statement of net assets) or an expense (in the statement of operations); if an item has a credit (cr) balance then it is most likely a liability (in the statement of net assets) or an income (in the statement of operations).

Requirement:

1. Prepare the fund financial statements for the year ended 31/12/X8.

Use the template fund in Section 3.4 and fill in the figures. Then calculate the various totals. If the statement of net assets balances, then there is a good chance that your answer is correct, i.e. the total of all the assets less liabilities in the statement of net assets is equal to the investors' equity at the end of the statement of changes in net assets. This should not be a difficult operation; the information in the trial balance is just being presented in a more accessible format for investors.

2. There are 11,450,000 shares in issue – calculate the NAV per share.

Solution 3.1: TRIM Growth Fund

Table 3.2b shows the statement of net assets for the TRIM Growth Fund, while Table 3.2c shows the statement of operations and 3.2d shows the statement of changes in net assets.

Table 3.2b: Statement of Net Assets for the TRIM Growth Fund as at 31/12/X8

Assets	
Investments at Cost	€12,500,680
Unrealised Appreciation/Depreciation	€85,260
Investments Sold Receivable	€190,000
Fund Shares Sold Receivable	€125,600
Interest Receivable	€3,600
Cash	€800,540
Dividends Receivable	€1,500
Total Assets	*€13,707,180*
Liabilities	
Investments Purchased Payable	€455,600
Accrued Expenses	€80,500
Fund Shares Redeemed Payable	€26,410
Distributions Payable	€8,500
Total Liabilities	*€571,010*
Total Net Assets	**€13,136,170**
Capital Stock/Investors' Equity	**€13,136,170**
Outstanding Shares	11,450,000
NAV per Share	**€1.147**

Table 3.2c: Statement of Operations for the TRIM Growth Fund for the Period from 01/01/X8 to 31/12/X8

Gains/Losses on Investments	€1,000,780
Dividend Income	€55,800
Interest Income	€9,506
Total Investment Income/Loss	*€1,066,086*
Administration Fee Year to Date (YTD)	€15,450
Investment Management Fee YTD	€187,930
Incentive Fees YTD	€55,886
Custody Fees YTD	€19,780
Auditing Fee YTD	€4,500
Total Fund Expenses	*€283,546*
Increase/Decrease in Net Assets from Operations	**€782,540**

Table 3.2d: Statement of Changes in Net Assets for the TRIM Growth Fund for the Period from 01/01/X8 to 31/12/X8

Investors' Equity at 01/01/X8	**€9,920,710**
Distributions to Investors	**(€18,690)**
Capital Fund Share Transactions	
Proceeds from the sale of shares	€2,894,160
Redemption of units	(€442,550)
Dividend reinvestment	0
Total	**€2,451,610**
Increase/Decrease in Net Assets from Operations	**€782,540**
Investors' Equity at End of Period (31/12/X8)	**€13,136,170**

3.5: CONCLUSION

There was very little accounting in this chapter. However, there was a lot of information that will be of assistance when the technical accounting is reintroduced, which will begin in the next chapter. Jargon and terminology can often be a barrier to understanding; very often in investment fund accounting the terminology explains very simple concepts. In this chapter much of the terminology was explained. This was done by firstly using a real investment fund, then by setting out many of the terms in detail and finally by outlining a template fund.

The template fund will be the basis for the spreadsheet approach that will be used to explain the recording of transactions in future chapters. This will begin in earnest in the next chapter where the accounting for fund shares (capital stock) will be explained.

3.6: ADDITIONAL QUESTIONS

Question 3.6.1

Table 3.3 shows the balances for the DTM Growth Fund.

Table 3.3: Balances for the DTM Growth Fund

Account Name	Dr €	Cr €
Investments at Cost	58,660,450	
Unrealised Appreciation/Depreciation		4,586,200
Investments Purchased Payable		220,840
Investments Sold Receivable	266,330	
Dividends Receivable	66,280	
Distributions Payable		7,400
Fund Shares Sold Receivable	85,620	
Fund Shares Redeemed Payable		800,120
Interest Receivable	45,690	
Cash	1,000,780	
Expenses Payable		78,590
Gain/Loss on Investments	854,810	
Dividend Income		420,590
Interest Income		100,600
Administration Fee YTD	22,540	
Investment Management Fee YTD	250,450	
Incentive Fees YTD	1,200	
Custody Fees YTD	18,180	
Audit Fee	9,500	
Investors' Equity at 01/01/X8		60,664,740
Proceeds from Issue of Shares		2,894,160
Redemption of Shares	8,450,560	
Distributions to Investors	40,850	
Total	*69,773,240*	*69,773,240*

Requirement:

1. Prepare the fund's financial statements for the year ended 31/12/X8.
(Some of the items on this fund are not as you might expect – is the fund performing very well?)

2. There are 11,450,000 shares in issue – calculate the NAV per share.

Question 3.6.2

Explain the following terms in your own words

- Investments sold receivable
- Fund shares redeemed payable
- Unrealised appreciation/depreciation (on investments)
- Investments at cost
- Dividend income

Question 3.6.3

You work for a fund distributor. A potential client has arrived into your office and has just obtained the financial statements of the fund that he is considering investing in. However, he is a little confused by the information he has received. He is having difficulty understanding:

- The purpose of the statement of changes in net assets
- The difference between the statement of operations and the statement of changes in net assets

Write a short memo to your new client explaining the items that he is having difficulty with.

Chapter 4

Fund Shares/Capital Stock

- Introduction
- The transfer agent
- Transaction fees
- Accounting for transactions in fund shares
- Accounting for subscriptions
- Accounting for redemptions
- Accounting for transfers/switches
- Accounting for distributions
- Distribution reinvestment
- Fund share classes
- Bringing it all together
- Additional questions

LEARNING OUTCOMES

At the end of this chapter you should:

- Be able to explain the role of the transfer agent.
- Be able to describe the types of transaction fees and the accounting implications.
- Be able to record subscriptions into the fund.
- Be able to record redemptions from the fund.
- Be able to understand the implications of transfers/switches.
- Be able to record distributions from the fund.

4.1: INTRODUCTION

This chapter is where the accounting for some typical transactions begins. 'Fund shares' or 'capital stock' refers to transactions in the shares (or units) of the fund.

When investors put money into a fund they are given shares in the fund in return. This process is often called subscription. The opposite occurs when investors withdraw their money: they give back their shares and the shares are cancelled. This process is known as redemption.

The number of shares that new investors obtain and the amount of money that exiting investors receive will be determined by the price of the shares/units in the fund – this is the NAV per share (see Chapter 3). This is where the role of the fund accountant becomes centrally important as the fund accountant is responsible for the calculation of the NAV per share. If this is incorrect, then some investors are likely to be disadvantaged as a result of the miscalculation or negligence of the fund accountant. In these situations the fund accountant (or more correctly the company that employs the fund accountant) is liable for any loss incurred.

The funds accounted for in this book are all variable capital investment funds, which are also known as open-ended investment funds. The implication of this is that when investors wish to buy shares in a fund or exit a fund they deal directly with the fund (often via a distributor or broker). The fund issues and redeems shares as investors buy into or sell out of the fund. Consequently, the number of shares outstanding in the fund is constantly fluctuating. Most mutual funds operate on this basis. The benefit is that there is rarely a liquidity issue if an investor wishes to redeem shares. There is always a price quoted, the NAV per share, at which an investor can choose to redeem his or her investment.

The opposite of a variable capital investment fund is a fixed capital investment fund, also known as a closed-ended investment fund. The implication of this is that the number of shares in issue does not change (on a regular basis). If an investor wishes to buy into the fund, then he or she must locate an investor who wishes to sell out. The two individuals must agree a price between themselves and organise the transfer of shares (they will probably use a broker for this). Transactions in the shares of the fund do not involve the investment fund itself. This is very similar to transactions in the shares of 'normal' companies. Liquidity can be an issue – if an existing investor wishes to sell out of a fund, he or she can only do so if there is an investor who wishes to buy the shares. If there are no interested investors then the price of the shares will fall and fall, which may not be related to the value of the assets of the fund. This type of fund is rarer than the open-ended variety but many property funds commonly use this type of arrangement, for example, Brendan Investments,[1]

---

[1] Brendan Investments was a property fund established by self-styled consumer champion Eddie Hobbs. It failed to generate the expected investment when launched in October 2007, having become embroiled in controversy over excessive fees.

British Land[2] (the largest UK property fund) and Berkshire Hathaway[3] (not a property fund but possibly the most successful fund over the past 30 years). We will not be accounting for these types of funds; in any case, there are very few capital stock transactions in these funds.

Having set the scene, this chapter continues with a consideration of the role of the transfer agent. The controversial issue of sales-related fees is then addressed. This leads to the core section, a discussion on accounting for transactions in fund shares, which is organised under two sub-headings: accounting for subscriptions and accounting for redemptions of fund shares. Transfers and switches between investment funds in the same 'fund family' are also addressed. Then, accounting for distributions and distribution reinvestment is explained. The final section is called 'Bringing It All Together', where all the different elements of accounting for fund shares are reviewed in a comprehensive example.

4.2: THE TRANSFER AGENT

In Section 1.6.4 the role of the transfer agent was considered. In accounting for transactions involving shares and/or investors in the fund, the information flow between the transfer agent and the fund accountant will be of key importance.

The transfer agent responds to all investor enquiries, deals with requests for subscriptions or redemptions and arranges payment, calculates and dispenses all shareholder distributions, provides statements to shareholders and maintains shareholder records. In addition, the transfer agent will deal with situations where investors have lost (or have had stolen) share certificates and will perform any money laundering checks on potential investors where required.

The transfer agent will need to inform the fund accountant of any transactions in the shares of the fund. In return, the fund accountant will need to calculate the NAV per share so that those transactions can be correctly priced. There will also need to be strong lines of communication with the custodian. The custodian takes responsibility for the fund's bank account: any receipts for the sale of shares will need to be monitored along with any payments to be made for shares redeemed. This information will also need to be passed onto the fund accountant.

---

[2] On 6 June 2008 British Land was worth £4.06 billion GBP (British Land, 2009). It owns warehouses, shopping centres, offices and other commercial property. For more details see www.britishland.com. GBP = Great British Pounds.

[3] On 6 June 2008 Berkshire Hathaway was worth $202 billion USD (Berkshire Hataway, 2009). It is run by one of the richest individuals in the world, Warren Buffet. It holds shares in Coca-Cola, American Express and a number of insurance companies (plus over 70 other businesses).

4.3: TRANSACTION FEES

Transaction fees are a controversial topic in the investment funds industry. Very often, these fees are levied when new investors come into a fund and existing investors withdraw.

Accounting for the fees is the important issue from the fund accountant's perspective. These fees can be subdivided into two categories:

- Transaction fees that are not accounted for by the fund accountant because they are taken by the parties involved before the money reaches the fund
- Transaction fees that are accounted for by the fund as they paid by or to the fund

4.3.1: Sales Loads

The most common type of fee on capital fund/share transactions is the 'sales load' fee. This is where an investor is charged a fee when making an investment into a fund (also called a 'front load' fee). There is no limit on the size of the fee but the amount should be set out in the fund's prospectus. A sales load of 5 per cent is not unusual. The sales load is paid directly to the broker or distributor and the remaining amount is invested in the fund. The fund accountant need only record the net amount. These fees are controversial because there is less money being invested in the fund so the investor has already lost money on his or her investment. If an investor with €20,000 wishes to invest in a fund with a 5 per cent front-end sales load, the broker/distributor will take €1,000, leaving €19,000 to invest in the fund. The €1,000 is effectively a commission that is taken by the broker.

In an effort to attract investors, some funds do not charge an up-front (or front-end) sales load and instead charge the sales load when the shareholder withdraws from the fund. This is called a 'back-end sales load' or a 'deferred sales load'. The benefit of this is that the full investment is working for the investor from the beginning. Take the previous example of the investor with €20,000. Now, assume that the fund grows by 20 per cent. In the case of the front-end load fund, the investment is now worth €22,800 (€19,000 + 20 per cent), while the back-end load fund is worth €24,000 (€20,000 + 20 per cent). Generally, when investors are redeeming their shares from a back-end load fund, the load fee is calculated based on the lower of either the percentage fee on the original investment or the percentage fee on the proceeds. In the example, that would amount to 5 per cent of €20,000 (€1,000) or 5 per cent of €24,000 (€1,200). Thus, the investor would pay a fee of €1,000, leaving him with €23,000 (compared with €22,800 for a front-end load fund). Even in this very simple example the investor is €200 better off with a back-end load fund.

A final alternative to sales load fees is the contingent deferred sales charge. This is a variation on the back-end sales load fee. Investors are not charged a fee when they invest in the fund but are charged when they exit the fund. However, the longer the investor leaves their money in the fund, the lower the fee. Thus, the fee is deferred (until exit) and it is contingent (it depends on how long the investor remains in the fund). Often, the fee falls to zero if enough time is allowed to elapse. For example, if an investor leaves a fund within one year the sales fee will be 5 per cent, if an investor leaves after two years the sales fee falls to 4 per cent and so on until the fee falls to 0 per cent after five years. Full details of the sales fees should be disclosed in the fund's prospectus.

4.3.2: Other Investor Transaction Fees

Funds can charge a myriad of other fees. However, these fees must be fully disclosed in the prospectus. Those funds with excessive charges tend not to have very many investors.[4]

The 'purchase fee' is a fee that a fund levies on new investors. While it has the same effect as a front-end sales load (i.e. the investor has less money invested in the fund), it is different to a sales load since, instead of the fee going to the distributor or broker, it goes to the fund. This is because when a new investor enters a fund there is a cost to the fund, i.e. the transfer agent will have to undertake extra work to process the new investor's application and the investment managers will have to decide how to invest the extra money that the fund will now have.

A 'redemption fee' is similar to a purchase fee – it is a fee that the fund will receive to help defray the cost of processing an exiting investor. In addition, the investment managers may also have to carry out extra tasks; they may have to decide which investments to sell so that there will be enough cash in the fund to meet the redemption. Purchase and redemption fees are now less common as the funds industry is extremely competitive. Funds with excessive fee structures find it difficult to recruit investors.

A rarer fee is the exchange fee. This is the fee payable if an investor wishes to move their money from one fund to another in the same stable. For example, Irish Life offers a series of funds under the 'Select' brand – if an investor wishes to switch from one fund to another, this is carried out for free but the fund could have levied an exchange fee. Practically all funds now offer this type of transaction without charge.

---

[4] As an example, the Brendan Investments Property Fund failed to reach its target number of investors. A significant contributory factor was the perceived high fees that were to be charged by the fund.

Sometimes, and particularly for smaller investors, an account fee is levied. This is a fee that will accrue to the fund. It is a charge to discourage investors from holding very small shareholdings. While it costs the same to communicate with a large investor as a small investor, the cost per share invested is a lot more for the small investor. An investor with 1 share or 1,000,000 shares in a fund will each receive one copy of the fund documentation and reports. The cost of producing and sending the report to the investor with one share may even exceed the value of that share.

The final sales based fee that will be considered is the 12b-1 Fee (other expenses of an investment fund will be addressed in more detail in Chapter 7). The 12b-1 Fee is the name given to the costs incurred by a fund to market itself to new investors, to produce the prospectus, to respond to potential investor enquiries, etc. It is a controversial fee. The Financial Industry Regulatory Authority in the US limits this fee to 0.75 per cent of net assets. The reason why the fee is controversial is because it is an annual fee levied on the fund, so existing investors effectively pay the fee. However, existing investors get little benefit from having new investors come into the fund. Hence the reason for the cap on the fee (it is called the 12b-1 Fee because of the US legislation that governs its payment).

Figure 4.1 shows an extract from the prospectus for the Vanguard Emerging Markets Stock Index Fund. This fund has two types of investors: those who buy investor shares and those who buy admiral shares.

Figure 4.1: Shareholder Fees – The Vanguard Emerging Markets Stock Index Fund

Shareholder Fees (Fees paid directly from your investment)	Investor Shares	Admiral Shares
Sales Charge (Load) Imposed on Purchases	None	None
Purchase Fee	None	None
Sales Charge (Load) Imposed on Reinvested Dividends	None	None
Redemption Fee	2%	2%
Account Service Fee (for accounts under $10,000)	$20/year	–

Source: Vanguard International Stock Index Funds Prospectus, February 2009. Available from www.vanguard.com.

The 'sales charge load imposed on purchases' is also called the front-end load. The redemption fee of 2 per cent is waived if the money is left in the fund for over two months (this is given in a footnote to the documentation, not reproduced here). Investor shares are targeted at smaller shareholders (hence the account service fee) while admiral shares are for larger investors (in excess of $100,000 USD).

Figure 4.2 is another example from Irish Life's Select Funds. This is an example of a fund that operates a CDSC (contingent deferred sales charge) structure.

Figure 4.2: CDSC – Irish Life Select Funds

You will pay the following charge on any amount you withdraw from any investment you make in each of the Select investment options.

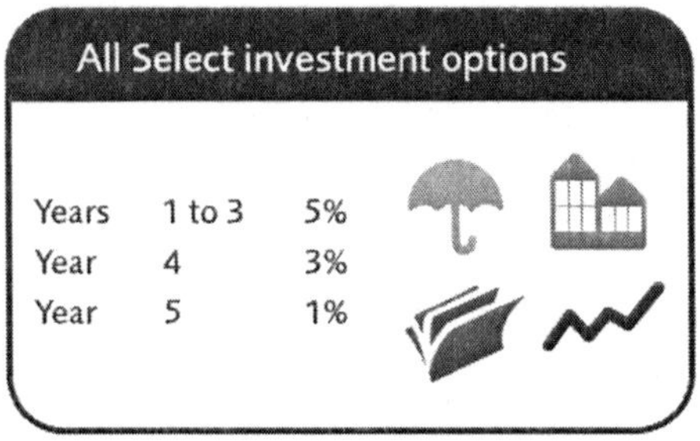

Source: Irish Life (2008), 'Select: Investments to Suit You', April 2008. This is the promotional brochure for the Select family of funds, available from www.irishlife.ie/uploadedFiles/Investments/select(2).pdf.

The longer an investor remains in the fund, the less they will pay in sales charges.

A final word on fees: 'no load' funds (i.e. funds with no sales loads) also exist. Be careful of these funds as there is no such thing as a free lunch – the costs of operating the investment fund (including recruiting investors) must be cleared at some point.[5]

4.4: ACCOUNTING FOR TRANSACTIONS IN FUND SHARES

The most common transactions in fund shares are subscriptions (where investors are putting money into a fund), redemptions (where investors are taking out their money) and transfers (where investors are transferring their money from one fund to another). In accounting for fund shares, it is important to determine the correct price per share as this influences the number of shares that will be involved in the transaction.

The difficulty in the funds industry is that the price of a fund (i.e. its NAV per share) is calculated just once a day. This is different to a share in a 'normal' company, which is continually priced by the stock market. Thus, when an order is received from a new investor, the investor will get the price at the end of that day. Likewise, the same treatment is applied to an investor who is looking to redeem shares. By the time the information flow reaches the fund accountant, it is the following day. Consequently, most fund share transactions will take place at the price from the previous day's NAV per share calculation. This is because the

---

[5] A full discussion on fees can be found on http://thismatter.com/money/Mutual-Funds/Mutual-Fund-Fees-Expenses.htm and www.sec.gov/answers/mffees.htm.

trade date of the transaction is the previous day. Trade date is a technical term – it is the date a transaction occurs. The settlement date (the date when the payment occurs) can be a few days later.

This is an area of the funds industry that is open to abuse. It could be possible for an 'investor' to time their subscriptions and redemptions knowing how the market has been performing during the day but before the NAV per share is determined. By doing this, the 'investor' is guaranteed to make a profit at the expense of the true investors. This is called market timing and, along with late trading,[6] was the source of a major scandal in the funds industry in 2003. In excess of $1 billion USD of fines were paid by a number of different parties, including $675 million by Bank of America.[7] Late trading was (and still is) illegal, while to benefit from market timing is now much more difficult as many funds charge a redemption fee for investors who buy shares in a fund and sell them again within a short period of time.

Notwithstanding the significant difficulties in determining the trade date for fund share transactions, in this book all transactions will take place using the NAV per share from the previous day. It can often take up to three days for the transactions to settle (TD + 3 or Trade Date + 3 days). Thus, if a shareholder comes into a broker on Tuesday to take his or her money out, it will be done at the closing price on Tuesday (Tuesday's NAV per share), recorded by the fund on Wednesday and the shareholder will receive his or her cash from the fund on Trade Date + 3 days, i.e. Friday. For subscriptions it is the same procedure but in reverse.

4.5: ACCOUNTING FOR SUBSCRIPTIONS

A subscription is where a new investor wishes to invest their money in the fund. In return, they will be given shares in the fund.

The accounting tasks are:

- Determine the correct NAV per share (generally this will be the previous day's NAV per share)
- Record the issue of the shares
  - record the money amounts
  - update the number of shares in issue
- Record the receipt of the money (on settlement date, a few days later)

---

[6] Late trading is where fund shares are redeemed after the time that the fund has calculated the NAV per share. This violates US securities laws; the NAV per share of the following day should be used to price the redemption.

[7] See Atkinson (2004) for full details. The companies who paid the fines all settled out of court so were never found guilty of any crime or illegal behaviour.

Example 4.1

An investor applies for shares in a fund; he has €100,000 to invest. The fund has a front-end load of 4 per cent. The first published NAV per share after the application showed a share price of €1.92. The money is received on TD + 3.

Requirements:

- Calculate the amount of money that the fund will receive.
- Calculate the number of shares to be issued.

Solution 4.1

How much will the fund receive?

Full amount invested	€100,000
Less 4 per cent sales load	€4,000
Invested in fund	€96,000

Number of shares to be issued:

Invested in fund	€96,000
Price per share	€1.92
Number of shares issued	50,000 shares

4.5.1: Recording the Issue of Shares

Using the figures from Example 4.1, the fund is owed €96,000 from an investor (the money has not yet been received). Thus, the fund has an asset; the asset is called fund shares sold receivable. It is increasing, so it is a debit.

⇒ Debit fund shares sold receivable by €96,000

On the other side of the transaction, the fund needs to keep track of the total amount of investors' equity outstanding. Thus, the capital base of the fund is increasing. Capital is a liability; it is increasing, resulting in a credit. However, this amount will not be put into capital directly – remember in the statement of changes in net assets there is a category called 'proceeds from the sale of shares'. This is the account (a sub-category of capital) where the fund keeps track of the total subscriptions for the year. So, instead of lumping everything into capital, which would become overcrowded and difficult to analyse, the amount will be put into 'proceeds from the sale of shares', a liability account which is increasing; thus, it is a credit.

⇒ Credit proceeds from fund shares sold by €96,000

The final element of the transaction is to increase the number of shares in the fund.

- Dr fund shares sold receivable   €96,000
- Cr proceeds from fund shares sold   €96,000
- Increase the number of shares in the fund   50,000 shares

Or – for the spreadsheet approach:

- Increase fund shares sold receivable, an asset, by €96,000.
- Increase proceeds from fund shares sold, a liability, by €96,000.
- Increase the number of shares in the fund by 50,000 shares.

4.5.2: Recording the Receipt of the Money

A number of days after the transaction (on the settlement date) the money will be received. In the case of Example 4.1 this is TD + 3, i.e. three days after the trade date.

When the money is received then the cash in the fund increases. Cash is an asset and it is increasing.

⇒ Debit the cash account by €96,000

The other side of the transaction is that the fund is no longer owed any money by this new investor. When the original transaction was recorded, the amount was put into an account called fund shares sold receivable; this represented the fact that the fund was owed money by a new investor. This debt has now been settled by the investor. Thus, fund shares sold receivable, which is an asset, is decreasing.

⇒ Credit fund shares sold receivable by €96,000

To record the receipt of the cash:

- Dr cash   €96,000
- Cr fund shares sold receivable   €96,000

Or – for the spreadsheet approach:

- Increase cash, an asset, by €96,000.
- Decrease fund shares sold receivable, an asset, by €96,000.

That's it: subscriptions into a fund have now been accounted for. It will not be any different in the other examples that will be addressed, just the numbers will change. There is just one potential pitfall – what happens when a fund is starting out and there is no previous day's closing NAV per share? If this is the case then the launch prospectus will detail the initial offering price of a share (generally €1, €10 or €100 per share).

4.5.3: Summary

On trade date, record the issue of shares:

- Dr fund shares sold receivable.
- Cr proceeds from fund shares sold.
- Increase the number of shares in the fund by X shares.

On settlement date, record the receipt of cash:

- Dr cash.
- Cr fund shares sold receivable.

Try Questions 4.12.2 and 4.12.3 at the end of this chapter.

4.6: ACCOUNTING FOR REDEMPTIONS

The opposite of a subscription is a redemption. This is where an investor takes his or her money out of the fund. Generally, when a shareholder applies to redeem shares they are given the price at the end of the day (i.e. the next published NAV per share). However, because of the time it takes for the information flow to reach the fund accountant, redemptions are generally recorded on the following day. A similar situation existed for subscriptions. The settlement date is normally two to three days after the trade date. When recording the redemption of new shares, it is necessary to record the transaction and to update the number of fund shares outstanding.

The accounting tasks are:

- Determine the correct NAV per share (generally, this will be yesterday's NAV per share).
- Record the redemption of the shares:
  - o record the money amounts
  - o update the number of shares in issue
- Record the payment of the money (on settlement date, a few days later).

Example 4.2

An investor applies to redeem shares from a fund. He wishes to redeem 100,000 shares; these shares were originally subscribed for on 15/06/X4 at a price of €8.65.
He makes his application on 24/04/X7.

- The NAV per share quoted at the end of trading on 23/04/X7 was €11.40.
- The NAV per share quoted at the end of trading on 24/04/X7 was €11.49.
- The NAV per share quoted at the end of trading on 25/04/X7 was €11.55.
- The NAV per share quoted at the end of trading on 26/04/X7 was €11.60.
- The NAV per share quoted at the end of trading on 27/04/X7 was €11.66.
- The NAV per share quoted at the end of trading on 28/04/X7 was €11.69.

The fund operates a CDSC, which the broker deducts, depending on when the original investment was made. If an investor withdraws from the fund:

- Within 0 to 3 years of investment, the charge is 5 per cent.
- Between 3 and 4 years after investment, the charge is 3 per cent.
- Over 4 years after investment, the charge is 1 per cent.

Three days later, on 27/04/X7, the money is paid.

Requirements:

- Calculate the amount of money that the fund will pay out.
- Calculate the amount that the investor will receive.

Solution 4.2

The investor will be given the price at the end of 24/04/X7, the closing price on the day the application is made. However, the redemption will not be recorded until 25/04/X7.
The fund will pay out €11.49 × 100,000 or €1,149,000.
The investor will not receive all of this as the fund operates a deferred sales load (CDSC). The original investment was made on 15/06/X4; this is less than three years ago, so a 5 per cent sales load will apply. It is now important to review the prospectus of the fund to determine the exact detail on the calculation of the CDSC. There are two alternative approaches:

- Version 1: the CDSC is based on the redemption proceeds:
  ○ CDSC = €1,149,000 × 5 per cent = €57,450
  ○ the investor receives €1,091,550 (full proceeds less CDSC)

- Version 2: the CDSC is based on the original investment (after all the CDSC is a deferral of the original sales charge):
  - ○ CDSC = €865,000 × 5 per cent = €43,250
  - ○ the investor receives €1,105,750 (full proceeds less CDSC)

Some funds calculate the CDSC using the lower of these two amounts, i.e. €43,250.

4.6.1: Recording the Redemption of Shares

Using the numbers from Example 4.2, the fund owes €1,149,000 to the exiting investor. This fund does not account for the CDSC. The fund will pay the full amount to the broker/distributor and they will calculate and deduct the CDSC. The full proceeds, €1,149,000, are owed, as the money has not yet been paid (the settlement date is not until 27/04/X7). Thus, the fund has a liability; the liability is called fund shares redeemed payable; it is increasing, so it is a credit.
⇒ Credit fund shares redeemed payable by €1,149,000

On the other side of the transaction, the fund needs to keep track of the total amount of investors' equity outstanding. The capital base of the fund is decreasing. Capital is a liability; it is decreasing. Thus it is a debit. However, as noted when dealing with subscriptions for shares, this will not be put into capital directly. In the statement of changes in net assets there is a category called 'redemption of units', the account (a sub-category of capital) where the fund keeps track of the total payments made to exiting investors for the year. So, instead of combining everything into capital, which would become overcrowded and difficult to analyse, it will be put into redemption of units, a liability account, which results in a decrease in capital; thus, it is a debit.
⇒ Debit redemption of units by €1,149,000

The final step in the transaction is to decrease the number of shares in the fund:

- Dr redemption of units   €1,149,500
- Cr fund shares redeemed payable   €1,149,500
- Decrease the number of shares in the fund   100,000 shares

Or – for the spreadsheet approach:

- Increase redemption of units, a capital/liability, by €1,149,000.
- Increase fund shares redeemed payable, a liability, by €1,149,000.
- Decrease the number of shares in the fund by 100,000 shares.

Note: for the spreadsheet approach, while the capital base of the fund is decreasing, the 'redemption of units' is increasing. This category will then be subtracted from the positive proceeds from fund shares sold to give a net figure. Thus, at the end, redemption of units has a negative impact on the capital base of the fund.

4.6.2: Recording the Payment of the Money on Settlement Date

Using the scenario in Example 4.2, a few days later the money is paid to the investor. This date is called the settlement date and in this instance is 27/04/X7 (or TD + 3; three days after the original transaction).

On 27/04/X7 the fund will pay money to the investor. As a result, the cash in the fund will decrease. Cash is an asset and it is decreasing, so it is a credit.

⇒ Credit the cash account by €1,149,000

Once the money is paid, the fund no longer owes any amount to the exiting investor. When the original transaction was recorded, the debt that the fund owed was shown in an account called fund shares redeemed payable – this represented the fact that the fund owed money to an investor. This debt has now been settled. Thus, there is no need for the debt to be shown; fund shares redeemed payable, which is a liability, is decreasing; thus, it is a debit.

⇒ Debit fund shares redeemed payable By €1,149,000

To record the payment of the cash:

- Dr fund shares redeemed payable   €1,149,000
- Cr cash   €1,149,000

Or – for the spreadsheet approach:

- Decrease fund shares redeemed payable, a liability, by €1,149,000.
- Decrease cash, an asset, by €1,149,000.

It will not be any different in the other examples that will be addressed, just the numbers will change.

Note: if on the same day there is an investor who wants to buy into the fund and an investor who wants to withdraw from the fund then these two amounts cannot be netted against one another. This is a basic principle of financial accounting.[8]

---

[8]   International Accounting Standard Board (2008), IAS1, paragraph 32.

4.6.3: Summary

On the trade date, record the redemption of shares:

- Dr redemption of units.
- Cr fund shares redeemed payable.
- Decrease the number of shares in the fund by X shares.

On the settlement date, record the payment of cash:

- Dr fund shares redeemed payable.
- Cr cash.

Try Questions 4.12.4 and 4.12.5 at the end of this chapter.

4.7: Accounting for Transfers/Switches

Many financial institutions offer investors the opportunity to invest in a family of funds. For example, Janus Capital Group[9] offer a range of equity funds (such as the Janus Equity Fund, Janus Orion Fund, Janus Research Fund, Janus Enterprise Fund and Janus Triton Fund). Investors choose which of these funds they would like to invest in. Often investors would like to switch their money from one fund to another; most financial institutions will permit investors (within reason) to switch from one fund to another within the same family for free (no sales loads or other expenses). See Figure 4.3 for an extract from the Janus Equity Investment Funds Prospectus (Janus use the term 'exchange' for transfers or switches).

Investors may wish to switch for a number of reasons; it could be that, having invested in an US equity fund, an investor may believe that the US market is going to suffer from a recession. Therefore, the investor may want to switch their money to a European equity fund, which they believe is going to perform better. Alternatively, an investor may have originally invested in a riskier equity fund and, now that they are getting older, may wish to transfer their investment into a safer bond type fund.

Financial institutions use their range of investment fund offerings as a selling point. Often, retail investors can be nervous about investing in funds; the range of products with differing risk profiles is a source of comfort to investors. They can try a low-risk product first and, as they get familiar with the investment product,

---

[9] Janus Capital Group has over $187 billion USD under management as of March 2008 (source: www.janus.com). The prospectuses for all Janus funds can be found on https://www.janus.com/Janus/Retail/StaticPage?jsp=jsp/Funds/Prospectus/ProspAnnRpts.jsp.

Figure 4.3: Janus Equity Funds Prospectus – Extract on Exchanges

Exchanges

Please note the following when exchanging shares:

- An exchange represents the redemption (or sale) of shares from one Fund and the purchase of shares of another Fund, which may produce a taxable gain or loss in a non-retirement account.

- You may generally exchange shares of a Fund for shares of any fund in the Trust.

- The exchange privilege is not intended as a vehicle for short-term or excessive trading. You may make up to four round trips in a Fund in a 12-month period, although the Funds at all times reserve the right to reject any exchange purchase for any reason without prior notice. Generally, a "round trip" is a redemption out of a Fund (by any means) followed by a purchase back into the same Fund (by any means). Different restrictions may apply if you invest through an intermediary. The Funds will work with financial intermediaries to apply the Funds' exchange limit. However, the Funds may not always have the ability to monitor or enforce the trading activity in such accounts. For more information about the Funds' policy on excessive trading, refer to "Excessive Trading."

Source: Janus Equity Funds Prospectus, February 2009, available from www.janus.com.

they can then try a riskier product (subject to their individual risk preferences and requirements). In addition, by offering a 'no cost' transfer facility, it is a means of locking investors into a fund family. If an investor wishes to transfer their money to another completely different fund operated by a different institution, they could be heavily penalised with charges (potentially a CDSC of up to 5 per cent to withdraw followed by a potential front-end sales load of 5 per cent to reinvest, a total cost of 10 per cent).

The accounting for a transfer is not difficult:

- A switch out of a fund is recorded similar to a redemption.
- A switch into a fund is recorded similar to a subscription.

The same procedure applies with regard to trade dates and settlements, although the settlement may often take place more quickly as it is an easier transaction to arrange.

Example 4.3

You are the fund accountant for the Sharp Fund Family. You are required to account for the following transaction:

On 23/10/X6 an investor in the Sharp Growth Fund with 100,000 shares has applied to transfer her holding to the Sharp Cautious Fund. There is no charge for transferring between funds in the same family. The settlement date is 25/10/X6. Table 4.1 shows the NAV per share.

Table 4.1: Sharp Funds – NAV per Share

Date	Sharp Growth	Sharp Cautious
21/10/X6	€23.10	€45.80
22/10/X6	€22.90	€46.13
23/10/X6	€22.50	€46.17
24/10/X6	€22.36	€46.56
25/10/X6	€22.10	€46.12
26/10/X6	€21.97	€45.94
27/10/X6	€22.23	€45.76

For transactions in fund shares, investors are given the NAV per share at the end of that day.

Solution 4.3

On 24/10/X6 account for the redemption of 100,000 shares in the Sharp Growth Fund; use the NAV per share on 23/10/X6. The amount to be redeemed is €2,250,000 (100,000 × €22.50):

- Dr redemption of units   €2,250,000
- Cr fund shares redeemed payable   €2,250,000
- Decrease the number of shares in the fund   100,000 shares

Or – for the spreadsheet approach:

- Increase redemption of units, a capital/liability, by €2,250,000.
- Increase fund shares redeemed payable, a liability, by €2,250,000.
- Decrease the number of shares in the fund by 100,000 shares.

On 24/10/X6 account for the issue of shares in the Sharp Cautious Fund; use the NAV per share on 23/10/X6. The amount the investor has available is €2,250,000; for that he will get 48,732 shares in the fund. The actual cost is €2,249,956 (funds do not tend to allow the issue of fractions of shares):

- Dr fund shares sold receivable   €2,249,956
- Cr proceeds from fund shares sold   €2,249,956
- Increase the number of shares in the fund   48,732 shares

Or – for the spreadsheet approach:

- Increase fund shares sold receivable, an asset, by €2,249,956.
- Increase proceeds from fund shares sold, a liability, by €2,249,956.
- Increase the number of shares in the fund by 48,732 shares.

On 25/10/X6 the transaction settles and the funds are transferred. The settlement in the Sharp Growth Fund will be recorded as follows:

- Dr fund shares redeemed payable   €2,250,000
- Cr cash   €2,250,000

Or – for the spreadsheet approach:

- Decrease fund shares redeemed payable, a liability, by €2,250,000.
- Decrease cash, an asset, by €2,250,000.

The settlement will also be recorded on 25/10/X6 in the Sharp Cautious Fund:

- Dr cash   €2,249,956
- Cr fund shares sold receivable   €2,249,956

Or – for the spreadsheet approach:

- Increase cash, an asset, by €2,249,956.
- Decrease fund shares sold receivable, an asset, by €2,249,956.

Now try Question 4.12.6.

4.8: ACCOUNTING FOR DISTRIBUTIONS

A distribution is where a fund pays out some of its income to investors. It is very similar to a company paying a dividend; indeed, the terms 'distribution' and 'dividend' are used interchangeably. For investors in funds, any distribution income tends to be low in comparison to the capital gain in the fund's NAV per share (money market funds are an exception).

Often, an investor has a choice to receive their distribution in the form of cash or in the form of shares in the fund. If the investor opts to receive the distribution in the form of shares, then this will be recorded similar to a subscription based on the NAV per share at the time of the distribution; this is called dividend/distribution reinvestment.

Some investors may not react favourably when a fund pays a dividend. This is because it may give rise to a taxable event. For example, an Irish resident investor in an investment fund may be liable to income tax of up to 41 per cent on any dividends received.

When a fund decides to pay a distribution, it is generally the transfer agent that deals with the individual payments. Some funds can have tens of thousands of investors; consequently, the transfer agents need to be given enough time to organise the individual cheques or account transfers. Because of the potentially large amount of administrative work involved, the payment of a distribution follows a predetermined process. There are a number of important dates from the point of view of investment fund accounting:

- The announcement date, which is the date that the fund announces the payment of the distribution.
- The ex-date, which is the date on which all existing investors become entitled to the distribution; any investors who buy into the fund after this date do not receive the distribution. The announcement date and the ex-date can be the same day.[10] This is the important date from a fund accounting perspective. It is on this date that the distribution is first recorded.
- The payment date, which is the date that the fund makes the payment to the individual shareholders.

When a distribution is announced the fund accountant does not record anything in the fund; the announcement details will need to be noted but there is no accounting entry.

On the ex-date, the first of the accounting entries are made. On that date the fund now has a liability to each of its individual investors. The NAV per share of the fund will fall by the amount of the distribution. Why this is the case?

Consider a fund with net assets of €1,000,000 and 100,000 shares in issue. On 22/04/X5 the NAV per share is €10.

On 23/04/X5, the fund declares a distribution of €1 per share with an immediate ex-date and a payment date on 24/04/X5. Assume that nothing else has happened in the fund and the value of its investments has not changed. Table 4.2a shows the NAV per share of the fund at the end of 23/04/X5.

---

[10] Some funds operate a record date, which has a slightly different impact to the ex-date. The record date is the date that the share register is closed for the purposes of receiving the dividend. The record date is always prior to the ex-date. If an investor redeems their shares between the record date and the ex-date then they will not be entitled to a dividend and if they receive a dividend in error they will be required to return it.

Table 4.2a: Calculating the NAV per Share after a Distribution is Declared

Original Net Assets	€1,000,000	
Distribution Owed to Investors	(€100,000)	100,000 shares × €1
Net Assets on 23/04/X5	€900,000	
Number of Shares	100,000	
NAV per Share	€9	

The NAV per share of the fund has fallen from €10 to €9; this is exactly equal to the amount of the distribution, €1. The investors are not worse off because they have an investment in the fund worth €9 and a distribution of €1 on the way. This is equal to their original value of €10 per share.

On the payment date, the payment of the distribution is recorded. This will have no effect on the NAV per share of the fund. This is because cash will leave the fund but an equivalent liability will also disappear.

Continue with the same scenario. Assume nothing else is happening in the fund. 24/04/X5 is the payment date. The fund's cash balance will decrease but the investors will no longer be owed any distribution. Table 4.2b shows the NAV per share at the end of 24/04/X5.

Table 4.2b: Calculating the NAV per Share after a Distribution is Paid

Original Net Assets	€1,000,000	
Less: Cash Paid	(€100,000)	
Revised Net Assets	€900,000	
Distribution Owed to Investors	€0	now paid
Net Assets on 24/04/X5	€900,000	
Number of Shares	100,000	
NAV per Share	€9	

The investors have a share worth €9 and have received the €1 distribution. However, it should be clear that the NAV per share of the fund did not change on the payment date (see Table 4.2c).

Table 4.2c: How the NAV per Share Changes During a Distribution

Date	NAV per Share	Notes
22/04/X5	€10	Before announcement
23/04/X5	€9	(Ex-date) NAV per share falls on ex-date
24/04/X5	€9	(Payment date) No impact on NAV per share

4.8.1: Recording the Distribution – The Ex-Date

On the ex-date, the fund will need to record that it now owes money to its investors. The first step will be to calculate the amount, which will be the number of fund shares outstanding on the ex-date multiplied by the distribution per share. Once the amount is known, it will need to be noted in the records of the fund.

The fund owes money to its investors – this is a liability of the fund, called 'distributions payable'. This account is increasing and is a liability; thus, it is a credit.

$\Rightarrow$ Credit distributions payable with the amount owed

As a fund pays out more to its investors, its capital base is decreasing. Thus, the other side of the transaction relates to capital. Capital is a liability and is decreasing

$\Rightarrow$ Debit a capital account with the amount owed

It is good practice to keep track of the total distributions paid in a period (similar to proceeds from issue of shares/units and payments on redemption of shares/units). So, rather than combining all the transactions in 'capital' it is better practice to group all these items in a separate account called distributions to investors. Distributions to investors is a capital/liability account, as result capital is decreasing; thus, it is a debit.

$\Rightarrow$ Debit distributions to investors with the amount owed

- Dr distributions to investors.
- Cr distributions payable.

Or – for the spreadsheet approach:

- Increase distributions to investors, a capital/liability (statement of changes in net assets).
- Increase distributions payable, a liability (statement of net assets).

Note: for the spreadsheet approach, while the capital base of the fund is decreasing, the distributions to investors is increasing. This category will then be subtracted from the other items in the statement of changes in net assets to give a final figure, investors' equity, at the end of the year.

Example 4.4

On 04/12/X1 WYZ Fund announces a dividend of €0.50 per share. The ex-date is 10/12/X1 and the payment date is 22/12/X1. Table 4.3 shows the NAV per share for each day.

Table 4.3: WYZ Fund – Share Details

Date	Outstanding Fund Shares	NAV per Share
04/12/X1	100,000	€12.30
10/12/X1	110,000	€12.50
22/12/X1	115,000	€12.15

On each of the dates record the appropriate transaction.

Solution 4.4

On 04/12/X1: no transaction recorded.
On 10/12/X1: record distribution.
Total distribution = 110,000 × €0.50 = €55,000

- Dr distributions to investors   €55,000
- Cr distributions payable   €55,000

Or – for the spreadsheet approach:

- Increase distributions to investors, a capital/liability, by €55,000.
- Increase distributions payable, a liability, by €55,000.

On 22/12/X1: record payment of distribution (see next section).

4.8.2: Recording the Payment – The Payment Date

On the payment date, the fund will pay the distribution to the investors. Cash in the fund will decrease. Cash, an asset, is decreasing:
⇒ Credit cash account

The other side of the transaction should not be difficult – a pattern is now emerging as items are paid by the fund. Once the money is paid, the fund no longer owes any amount to the investors. When the original transaction was recorded on the ex-date, the amount that the fund owed was shown in an account called distributions payable; this represented the fact that the fund owed money to its investors. This debt has now been settled. Thus, there is no need for the debt to be shown. Distributions payable, which is liability, is decreasing:
⇒ Debit distributions payable

Solution 4.4 Continued

Using the figures from Example 4.4, on 22/12/X1 the following will be recorded:

- Dr distributions payable   €55,000
- Cr cash   €55,000

Or – for the spreadsheet approach:

- Decrease distributions payable, a liability, by €55,000.
- Decrease cash, an asset, by €55,000.

Now try Question 4.12.7.

4.9: Distribution Reinvestment

When an investor opts for a dividend reinvestment, he or she is given shares in the fund in place of the cash distribution. The key aspect of this is to determine the correct number of shares to issue to the investor in the place of the cash distribution. The fundamental premise is that an investor, at the time of the distribution, should be indifferent between the options.[11]

Example 4.5

A fund with a NAV per share of €10 and 100,000 shares in issue decides to pay a distribution of €1 per share. Assume that the investments in the fund are static and there are no other influences on NAV per share.

The NAV per share of the fund, on the ex-date immediately after recording the distribution, will fall to €9. The investors in the fund now own a share worth €9 and are due a distribution of €1, giving a total value of €10 (as before).

Now consider Investor A with 10,000 shares, who opts for the cash distribution, while Investor B with 5,000 shares opts for the dividend reinvestment.

Investor A is as before – he now has shares in the fund worth €90,000 and a cash distribution of €10,000, a total net worth of €100,000.

---

[11]   This may not be the situation where there are tax implications. Some investors may prefer cash dividends while others prefer to reinvest as their tax liability can be different. This decision will depend on the circumstances of individual investors and the tax laws in different countries.

How many shares should be issued to Investor B? And which NAV per share should be used: €10 or €9 per share? Investor B would have been entitled to a cash distribution of €5,000. This would give 500 shares (at €10) or 555 new shares (at €9). If Investor B was issued with 500 shares then she would own 5,500 shares at €9 each. This would give a total wealth of €49,500 (or, under this option, B would be €500 worse off from before the payment of the distribution). If B was issued with 555 shares then she would own 5,555 shares at €9 each. This gives a net worth of €49,995 (the €5 difference is due to rounding and can be ignored). Thus, if the shares are issued at the price just after the ex–date then both investors are treated equally.

4.9.1: Recording the Distribution Reinvestment

When recording a distribution reinvestment, the approach that will be used is to split the transaction into two:

- Record the distribution as before.
- Record the issue of new shares (as a subscription).

Consider the previous example, assuming that Investor B is the only investor who opts for the reinvestment choice.

The Ex-Date

To make matters a little more transparent, the distribution will be split into two components. The first component will be all those investors who opt for cash. These investors will be recorded as in Section 4.8. This will be done first to get them resolved. Thus, on the ex–date, the fund will have to account for a distribution of €95,000 (95,000 shares by €1 distribution per share). This will be done as normal.

- Dr distributions to investors   €95,000
- Cr distributions payable   €95,000

The second component is to account for the distribution reinvestment. One approach to this is to split the transaction into two: (i) the distribution and (ii) the issue of shares. This transaction can be viewed as the payment of a distribution to Investor B and the immediate purchase of shares in the fund by Investor B.

(i) Record the distribution (same as before: 5,000 shares by €1 distribution per share).

- Dr distributions to investors   €5,000
- Cr distributions payable   €5,000

(ii) Record the issue of new fund shares (i.e. the reinvestment)

- Dr fund shares sold receivable   €5,000
- Cr distributions reinvested   €5,000 (part of the statement of changes of net assets)
- Increase number of shares in the fund by 555.

Part (ii) is a more complex transaction, so why was it accounted for as above? As a result of the reinvestment, the fund will have more capital available to it. Thus, capital, a liability type account, is increasing ⇒ credit to a capital account. As with other capital transactions, it is good practice not to combine all capital items into one account. Instead, they are segregated for better analysis. It would be helpful to keep track of the total amount of distributions reinvested in the fund over a period; hence, an account termed 'distributions reinvested'. This is a capital account and appears in the statement of changes in net assets. The capital base of the fund is increasing as a result of this transaction ⇒ credit distributions reinvested.

The other side of the transaction is less clear and can depend on the circumstances. The shares have not yet been issued (this will occur on the payment date). In essence, the fund is due to receive €5,000 from itself; or, more correctly, it will pay €5,000 to the reinvesting investors and the investors will immediately use that money to pay for the new shares that will be issued. In practice, no money changes hands; just the new shares are issued. However, it is a basic principle of financial accounting that assets and liabilities cannot be netted against one another. So, to record the expected receipt of €5,000 for the new shares, it is necessary to debit the fund shares sold receivable account. The fund is owed money for the issue of shares. This is an asset and is increasing ⇒ debit fund shares sold receivable.

Table 4.4a shows the balances of the fund at the end of the ex-date.

Table 4.4a: The Fund's Balances on the Ex-Date

In the Statement of Net Assets:		
Fund Shares Sold Receivable	€5,000	Asset
Cash	X	Asset
Distributions Payable	(€95,000 + €5,000) = €100,000	Liability
In the Statement of Changes in Net Assets:		
Distributions to Investors	(€95,000 + €5,000) = (€100,000)	Capital – decreasing
Distributions Reinvested	€5,000	Capital – increasing

The Payment Date

Record the payment of the cash distribution as normal:

- Dr distributions payable   €95,000
- Cr cash   €95,000

Record the issue of shares in the place of the dividend:

- Dr distributions payable   €5,000
- Cr fund shares sold receivable   €5,000

On the payment date the investor receives the shares. In essence, the fund pays the €5,000 distribution to the investors and immediately the investors give back the €5,000 to the fund to pay for the shares issued. However, in practice no money enters or leaves the fund; thus, there can be no entry into the cash account. So effectively, the distributions payable is cancelled (as the fund no longer owes €5,000 to the investor) and the fund shares sold receivable is cancelled (as the fund is no longer owed €5,000 from the investor).

Table 4.4b shows the fund's balances at the end of the payment date.

Table 4.4b: The Fund's Balances on the Payment Date

In the Statement of Net Assets:		
Fund Shares Sold Receivable	(€5,000 – €5,000) = €0	Asset
Cash	X – €95,000	Asset
Distributions Payable	(€100,000 – €95,000 – €5,000) = €0	Liability
In the Statement of Changes in Net Assets:		
Distributions to Investors	(€95,000 + €5,000) = (€100,000)	Capital – decreasing
Distributions reinvested	€5,000	Capital – increasing

Now try Example 4.12.7.

4.10: FUND SHARE CLASSES

Many funds offer investors the option of buying different classes of shares. The implication of a different class of share is that shares will have different rights attached to them. For example:

- There can be different classes of shares depending on sales loads:
  - ○ Class A shares have a front-end load and no back-end load
  - ○ Class B shares have a back-end load and no front-end load

- There can be different share classes depending on the amount of money invested in the fund. Investment made in larger amounts can attract lower fees (as they are easier to administer):
  - Class F shares are for investments of over €500,000 and are guaranteed an expense ratio of 1.5 per cent of the NAV per share
  - Class G shares are for investments of under €500,000 and have no guaranteed expense ratio
- Share classes can be based on distribution reinvestment:
  - Class R shares (or growth shares) are where all distributions are automatically reinvested
  - Class S shares (or income shares) are where all distributions are automatically paid in cash

This list can go on and on. One of the innovations in the funds industry in recent times has been to offer investors a range of choices so that they can choose a share class that best reflects their investment preferences.

As time has progressed many of the fund share class designations have become standardised across the industry. The more common share classes are:

- **Class A:** Has a front-end sales load; often, as more is invested in the fund, the sales load percentage tends to diminish. This can have lower expense ratios.
- **Class B:** Has a back-end sales load, often on a CDSC basis, so if an investor leaves their money in the fund for a long period there is no charge. Fund expenses can be higher than for Class A shares.
- **Class C:** Has a lower front-end sales load than Class A and lower back-end sales load than Class B shares – the in-between option.

American Funds operate the Growth Fund of America. This fund has a number of different share classes: Class A, B and C shares are available to retail investors, while Class E and F shares are only available through certain distribution channels. The costs and expenses of the different classes are shown in Figure 4.4 to give a flavour of the types of choices that are available. Imagine that you are an investor in the fund; what is your impression of this essential information?

The accounting for different share classes will be determined by the conditions attached to the shares. Most of the conditions are related to sales loads; these costs are not accounted for by the fund so will have little impact.

Some conditions relate to distribution reinvestment. These will be accounted for using the principles similar to those in Section 4.9. In some funds, new shares are not issued. Instead, the 'distributions reinvested shares' are quoted at a higher price than the 'non-distributions reinvested shares'. The accounting for these types of shares is beyond the scope of an introductory book in investment fund

Figure 4.4:   Share Classes in the Growth Fund of America

Summary of the primary differences among share classes

Class A shares

Initial sales charge	up to 5.75% (reduced for purchases of $25,000 or more and eliminated for purchases of $1 million or more)
Contingent deferred sales charge	none (except that a charge of 1.00% applies to certain redemptions made within one year following purchases of $1 million or more without an initial sales charge)
12b-1 fees	up to .25% annually (for 529-A shares, may not exceed .50% annually)
Dividends	generally higher than other classes due to lower annual expenses, but may be lower than F shares, depending on relative expenses
Purchase maximum	none
Conversion	none

Class B shares

Initial sales charge	none
Contingent deferred sales charge	starts at 5.00%, declining to 0% six years after purchase
12b-1 fees	up to 1.00% annually
Dividends	generally lower than A and F shares due to higher 12b-1 fees and other expenses, but higher than C shares due to lower other expenses
Purchase maximum	see the discussion regarding purchase minimums and maximums in "Purchase and exchange of shares"
Conversion	automatic conversion to A or 529-A shares after eight years, reducing future annual expenses

Class C shares

Initial sales charge	none
Contingent deferred sales charge	1.00% if shares are sold within one year after purchase
12b-1 fees	up to 1.00% annually
Dividends	generally lower than other classes due to higher 12b-1 fees and other expenses
Purchase maximum	see the discussion regarding purchase minimums and maximums in "Purchase and exchange of shares"
Conversion	automatic conversion to F shares after 10 years, reducing future annual expenses (529-C shares will not convert to 529-F shares)

Class 529-E shares

Initial sales charge	none
Contingent deferred sales charge	none
12b-1 fees	currently up to .50% annually (may not exceed .75% annually)
Dividends	generally higher than 529-B and 529-C shares due to lower 12b-1 fees, but lower than 529-A and 529-F shares due to higher 12b-1 fees
Purchase maximum	none
Conversion	none

Class F shares

Initial sales charge	none
Contingent deferred sales charge	none
12b-1 fees	currently up to .25% annually (may not exceed .50% annually)
Dividends	generally higher than B and C shares due to lower 12b-1 fees, and may be higher than A shares, depending on relative expenses
Purchase maximum	none
Conversion	none

Source: American Funds, Growth Fund of America Prospectus 1 Nov 2007, available from http://www.americanfunds.com/funds/prospectuses.htm.

accounting but will involve the splitting of the fund by share class (using a value weighting) to arrive at a NAV per share.

A final common type of share class condition is based on management and administration fees. Different classes of shares are subject to different management fees (generally, the larger the investment the smaller the fee). The accounting for these types of shares is also beyond the scope of this book. It can be a complex area that is alleviated through the use of sophisticated accounting systems but will involve the splitting of the fund by share class (using a value weighting) to arrive at a NAV per share.

4.11: BRINGING IT ALL TOGETHER

This section begins with a short review of the main items from earlier and these will then be combined into a comprehensive example.

4.11.1: Review of Main Points

The most common types of capital/fund share transactions are subscriptions, redemptions and distributions. The accounting entries are reproduced below but, more importantly, try to understand how the debit and credit is assigned to the various accounts. The more familiar this becomes, the easier it will be to apply it to other similar transactions.

Accounting for a Subscription:

On the trade date:

- Dr fund shares sold receivable.
- Cr proceeds from fund shares sold.
- Increase the number of shares in the fund.

Or – for the spreadsheet approach:

- Increase fund shares sold receivable, an asset.
- Increase proceeds from fund shares sold, capital.
- Increase the number of shares in the fund.

On the settlement date:

- Dr cash.
- Cr fund shares sold receivable.

Or – for the spreadsheet approach:

- Increase cash, an asset.
- Decrease fund shares sold receivable, an asset.

Accounting for a Redemption

On the trade date:

- Dr redemption of units.
- Cr fund shares redeemed payable.
- Decrease the number of shares in the fund.

Or – for the spreadsheet approach:

- Increase redemption of units, capital.
- Increase fund shares redeemed payable, a liability.
- Decrease the number of shares in the fund.

On the settlement date:

- Dr fund shares redeemed payable.
- Cr cash.

Or – for the spreadsheet approach:

- Decrease fund shares redeemed payable, a liability.
- Decrease cash, an asset.

Accounting for a Distribution

On the ex-date:

- Dr distributions to investors.
- Cr distributions payable.

Or – for the spreadsheet approach:

- Increase distributions to investors, capital.
- Increase distributions payable, a liability.

On the payment date:

- Dr distributions payable.
- Cr cash.

Or – for the spreadsheet approach:

- Decrease distributions payable, a liability.
- Decrease cash, an asset.

4.11.2: A Comprehensive Question

In this section, the full spreadsheet approach will be used for the first time (see Table 4.5a). It is also an opportunity to practise using Excel (or a similar spreadsheet package). If the computing aspect is too daunting, it is also possible to complete the question on paper.

The spreadsheet should be reasonably intuitive. In the rows are the various accounts split into their appropriate report (statement of net assets, statement of operations and statement of changes in net assets). Have a look at the template fund in the last chapter to see how the various statements interact with one another. The columns are reserved for the recording of each transaction. The opening position of the fund at the start of the day is provided, represented by the figures in the '04/04/XX' column.

Follow the sequence of transactions. Record the transactions that occurred on 05/04/XX and calculate the NAV per share at the end of the day, then do the same for 06/04/XX and 07/04/XX. The detail on the transactions is provided at the end. All of the transactions are capital/fund shares related, making this an excellent vehicle to test the accounting issues addressed to this point.

The Following Transactions Occurred on 05/04/XX

1. Settle all fund shares sold receivable outstanding as of today.
2. An investor has decided to redeem 17,000 shares as of yesterday's NAV per share to settle on TD + 3.
3. An investor has decided to subscribe for 25,000 shares as of yesterday's NAV per share to settle on TD + 2.

The Following Transactions Occurred on 06/04/XX

1. The fund shares redeemed payable outstanding from before 04/04/XX are settled today.

Table 4.5a: Comprehensive Question – Investor Fund – Capital/Fund Shares Transactions

Statement of Net Assets

	04/04/XX	Trans. 1	Trans. 2	Trans. 3	Trans. 4	05/04/XX	Trans. 1	Trans. 2	Trans. 3	06/04/XX	Trans. 1	Trans. 2	Trans. 3	07/04/XX
Assets														
Investments at Cost	€14,720,000													
Unrealised Appreciation/ Depreciation	€3,089,000													
Investments Sold Receivable	€410,000													
Fund Shares Sold Receivable	€40,000													
Interest Receivable	€5,000													
Cash	€1,400,000													
Dividends Receivable	€14,250													
Total Assets	*€19,678,250*													
Liabilities														
Investments Purchased Payable	€52,000													
Accrued Expenses	€18,000													
Fund Shares Redeemed Payable	€80,000													
Distributions Payable	€0													
Total Liabilities	*€150,000*													
Total Net Assets	**€19,528,250**													
Capital Stock/Investors' Equity	**€19,528,250**													
Outstanding Shares	1,000,000													
NAV per Share	**€19.528**													

Table 4.5a: (Continued)

Statement of Operations for the Period from 01/01/XX to YY/04/XX

	04/04/XX	Trans. 1	Trans. 2	Trans. 3	Trans. 4	05/04/XX	Trans. 1	Trans. 2	Trans. 3	06/04/XX	Trans. 1	Trans. 2	Trans. 3	07/04/XX
Gains/Losses on Investments	€300,000													
Dividend Income	€2,000													
Interest Income	€0													
Total Investment Income/Loss	€302,000													
Administration Fee Year to Date (YTD)	€3,000													
Investment Management Fee YTD	€6,000													
Other Fees YTD	€0													
Auditing Fee YTD	€1,000													
Total Fund Expenses	€10,000													
Increase/Decrease in Net Assets from Operations	€292,000													

(Continued)

Table 4.5a: *(Continued)*

Statement of Changes in Net Assets for the Period from 01/01/XX to YY/04/XX

	04/04/XX	Trans. 1	Trans. 2	Trans. 3	Trans. 4	05/04/XX	Trans. 1	Trans. 2	Trans. 3	06/04/XX	Trans. 1	Trans. 2	Trans. 3	07/04/XX
Investors' Equity at 01/01/XX	€19,210,250													
Distributions to Investors	€10,000													
Capital Fund Share Transactions														
Proceeds from the sale of shares	€426,000													
Redemption of units	€390,000													
Dividend reinvestment	€0													
Total	*€36,000*													
Increase/Decrease in Net Assets from Operations	€292,000													
Investors' Equity at End of Period (YY/04/XX)	**€19,528,250**													

2. A shareholder with €100,000 to invest has decided to subscribe at yesterday's NAV per share to settle on TD + 3; front-end fees are 4 per cent.

The Following Transactions Occurred on 07/04/XX

1. At the start of business the fund announces a distribution of €0.40 per share, with an ex-date of 07/04/XX (before the markets open) and a payment date of 10/04/XX. An undisclosed number of investors, holding a total of 100,000 shares, have elected to reinvest the distribution.
2. The subscription from 05/04/XX is settled today.

Requirements:

Using Table 4.5a as provided:

1. Record the transactions for 05/04/XX and calculate the NAV per share for 05/04/XX.
2. Record the transactions for 06/04/XX and calculate the NAV per share for 06/04/XX.
3. Record the transactions for 07/04/XX and calculate the NAV per share for 07/04/XX.

4.11.3: Solution to Comprehensive Question

Each of the transactions will be considered in turn and a final completed solution will be provided at the end of this section (Table 4.5b). The equivalent debit and credit is also presented.

Transactions from 05/04/XX

1. Settle all fund shares sold receivable as of today:
This means that the investors who bought shares in the fund in the days prior to 05/04/XX have now paid cash into the fund.

- Increase cash   €40,000
  - o (dr cash)
- Decrease fund shares sold receivable   €40,000
  - o (cr fund shares sold receivable)

2. An investor wishing to redeem 17,000 shares at yesterday's NAV per share:
Amount to be paid is €19.528 × 17,000 = €331,976

- Increase redemption of units   €331,976
  - o (dr redemption of units)

- Increase fund shares redeemed payable   €331,976
  - ○ (cr fund shares redeemed payable)
- Reduce number of shares in fund by 17,000.

3. An investor subscribes for 25,000 shares at yesterday's NAV per share:
Amount to be received is €19.528 × 25,000 = €488,200

- Increase proceeds from sale of fund shares   €488,200
  - ○ (cr proceeds from sale of fund shares)
- Increase fund shares sold receivable   €488,200
  - ○ (dr fund shares sold receivable)
- Increase number of shares in fund by 25,000.

Now calculate the closing balance for each item. To do this, add across the rows and put the total in the 05/04/XX column. Then calculate the totals for each of the statements and the NAV per share, (see Table 4.5b for solution).

Transactions from 06/04/XX

1. Fund shares redeemed payable from before 04/04/XX was settled:
This means that the investors who exited the fund in the days prior to 04/04/XX have now been paid their cash.

- Decrease cash   €80,000
  - ○ (cr cash)
- Decrease fund shares redeemed payable   €80,000
  - ○ (dr fund shares redeemed payable)

2. A shareholder with €100,000 to invest buys shares in the fund at yesterday's NAV per share; front-end fees of 4 per cent are charged:
The investor has €96,000 to invest in the fund after fees. Yesterday's NAV per share (from 05/04/XX) was €19.528; this will result in 4,916 new shares being issued.

- Increase proceeds from sale of fund shares   €96,000
  - ○ (cr proceeds from sale of fund shares)
- Increase fund shares sold receivable   €96,000
  - ○ (dr fund shares sold receviable)
- Increase number of shares in fund by 4,916.

Now calculate the closing balance for each item. To do this, from and including column 05/04/XX, add across the rows to the right and put the total in the 06/04/XX column. Then calculate the totals for each of the statements and the NAV per share. A solution is provided in Table 4.5b.

Transactions from 07/04/XX

1. Distribution of €0.40 per share; a number of investors, holding a total of 100,000 shares, have opted to reinvest their distribution.

Total distribution will be 1,012,916 shares × €0.40 = €405,166. Of this, €40,000 will be reinvested and €365,166 will be settled by a cash payment.

- Share price at the start of business (time of ex-date): €19.528
- Amount of the distribution: €0.40
- Predicted share price immediately after ex-date: €19.128

Thus, the reinvesting investors will be issued shares at €19.128. They will be issued with €40,000/€19.128 = 2,091 shares.

Cash investors:
- Increase distributions to investors   €365,166
  - (dr distributions to investors)
- Increase distributions payable   €365,166
  - (cr distributions payable)

Reinvesting investors (recording the distribution):
- Increase distributions to investors   €40,000
  - (dr distributions to investors)
- Increase distributions payable   €40,000
  - (cr distributions payable)

Reinvesting investors (recording the issue of shares):
- Increase distributions reinvested   €40,000
  - (cr distributions reinvested)
- Increase fund shares sold receivable   €40,000
  - (dr fund shares sold receivable)
- Increase shares in the fund by 2,091.

2. Subscription on 05/04/XX settles today:

Recall the original transaction on 05/04/XX had a settlement on TD + 2. It is now two days after the original transaction. Assuming that confirmation of the settlement has been received, then the settlement should be recorded. The amount to be received was €488,200 (none of the other transactions were due to settle on 07/04/XX as they had later settlement dates).

- Increase cash   €488,200
  - (dr cash)

- Decrease fund shares sold receivable   €488,200
  - ○ (cr fund shares sold receivable)

Now calculate the closing balance for each item. To do this, add across the rows from and including column 06/04/XX to the right and put the total in the 07/04/XX column. Then calculate the totals for each of the statements and the NAV per share. A solution is provided in Table 4.5b.

The only movement in the NAV per share occurred on 07/04/XX. This fall in the NAV per share of €0.40 is equal to the distribution. In all other respects there was no movement in the NAV per share. The reason for this is that the fund's underlying investments did not change in value. The next chapter will address this issue.

A full solution to the question follows in Table 4.5b. Now try Question 4.12.8 for more practice.

4.12: ADDITIONAL QUESTIONS

Question 4.12.1

You are advising an investor with €60,000 to invest. The client is considering two different funds: one with a front-end sales load of 3 per cent and the other with a back-end load of 5 per cent (at the end the load will be calculated based on the lower of 5 per cent of the original investment or 5 per cent of the final proceeds). The funds will be left in the fund for five years. Advise the investor under the following circumstances:

- Each fund gives an annual return of 5 per cent.
- Each fund gives an annual return of 10 per cent.
- Each fund gives an annual return of 20 per cent.
- The front-end fund gives an annual return of 8 per cent and the back-end fund gives an annual return of 6 per cent.

Hint: use an Excel spreadsheet – this should save a considerable amount of time.

Question 4.12.2

An investor applies for shares in your fund; he has €250,000 to invest. The fund has a front-end load of 3 per cent. The first published NAV per share after the application showed a share price of €2.425. The money is received on TD + 3.

Fund Shares/Capital Stock

Table 4.5b: Solution to Comprehensive Question – Investor Fund – Capital/Fund Shares Transactions

Statement of Net Assets

	04/04/XX	Trans. 1	Trans. 2	Trans. 3	05/04/XX	Trans. 1	Trans. 2	06/04/XX	Trans. 1	Trans. 2	07/04/XX
Assets											
Investments at Cost	€14,720,000				€14,720,000			€14,720,000			€14,720,000
Unrealised Appreciation/ Depreciation	€3,089,000				€3,089,000			€3,089,000			€3,089,000
Investments Sold Receivable	€410,000				€410,000			€410,000			€410,000
Fund Shares Sold Receivable	€40,000	(€40,000)		€488,200	€488,200		€96,000	€584,200	€40,000	(€488,200)	€136,000
Interest Receivable	€5,000				€5,000			€5,000			€5,000
Cash	€1,400,000	€40,000			€1,440,000	(€80,000)		€1,360,000		€488,200	€1,848,200
Dividends Receivable	€14,250				€14,250			€14,250			€14,250
Total Assets	€19,678,250				€20,166,450			€20,182,450			€20,222,450
Liabilities											
Investments Purchased Payable	€52,000				€52,000			€52,000			€52,000
Accrued Expenses	€18,000				€18,000			€18,000			€18,000
Fund Shares Redeemed Payable	€80,000		€331,976		€411,976	(€80,000)		€331,976			€331,976
Distributions Payable	€0				€0	€405,166		€0			€405,166
Total Liabilities	€150,000				€481,976			€401,976			€807,142
Total Net Assets	€19,528,250				€19,684,474			€19,780,474			€19,415,308
Capital Stock/ Investors' Equity	€19,528,250				€19,684,474			€19,780,474			€19,415,308
Outstanding Shares	1,000,000		−17,000	25,000	1,008,000		4,916	1,012,916	2,091		1,015,007
NAV per Share	€19.528				€19.528			€19.528			€19.1283

(Continued)

173

Table 4.5b: *(Continued)*

Statement of Operations for the Period from 01/01/XX to YY/04/XX

	04/04/XX	Trans. 1	Trans. 2	Trans. 3	05/04/XX	Trans. 1	Trans. 2	06/04/XX	Trans. 1	Trans. 2	07/04/XX
Gains/Losses on Investments	€300,000				€300,000			€300,000			€300,000
Dividend Income	€2,000				€2,000			€2,000			€2,000
Interest Income	€0				€0			€0			€0
Total Investment Income/Loss	*€302,000*				*€302,000*			*€302,000*			*€302,000*
Administration Fee Year to Date (YTD)	€3,000				€3,000			€3,000			€3,000
Investment Management Fee YTD	€6,000				€6,000			€6,000			€6,000
Other Fees YTD	€0				€0			€0			€0
Auditing Fee YTD	€1,000				€1,000			€1,000			€1,000
Total Fund Expenses	*€10,000*				*€10,000*			*€10,000*			*€10,000*
Increase/Decrease in Net Assets from Operations	€292,000				€292,000			€292,000			€292,000

Table 4.5b: (Continued)

Statement of Changes in Net Assets for the Period from 01/01/XX to YY/04/XX

	04/04/XX	Trans. 1	Trans. 2	Trans. 3	05/04/XX	Trans. 1	Trans. 2	06/04/XX	Trans. 1	Trans. 2	07/04/XX
Investors' Equity at 01/01/X8	€19,210,250				€19,210,250			€19,210,250			€19,210,250
Distributions to Investors	€10,000				€10,000			€10,000	€405,166		€415,166
Capital Fund Share Transactions											
Proceeds from the sale of shares	€426,000			€488,200	€914,200		€96,000	€1,010,200			€1,010,200
Redemption of units	€390,000		€331,976		€721,976			€721,976			€721,976
Dividend reinvestment	€0				€0			€0	€40,000		€40,000
Total (Note 1)	*€36,000*				*€192,224*			*€288,224*			*€328,224*
Increase/Decrease in Net Assets from Operations	€292,000				€292,000			€292,000			€292,000
Investors' Equity at End of Period (Note 2)	**€19,528,250**				**€19,684,474**			**€19,780,474**			**€19,415,308**

Note 1: To calculate the total of the capital fund share transactions, for example on 07/04/XX, start with proceeds from the sale of shares (€1,010,200), subtract redemption of units (€721,976) and add dividend reinvestment (€40,000). This gives the total of €328,224.

Note 2: To calculate the investors' equity at the end of the period, start with investors' equity at 01/01/X8 (€19,210,250), subtract distributions to investors (€415,166), add total of capital fund share transactions (€328,224) and add increase/decrease in net assets from operations (€292,000). This gives a total of €19,415,308 on 07/04/XX.

Requirements:

- Calculate the amount of money that the fund itself will receive and the number of shares that will be issued.
- Record the issue of the shares.
- Record the receipt of cash.

Question 4.12.3

An investor applies for shares in your fund; he has €50,000 to invest. The fund has a front–end load of 2 per cent. The first published NAV per share after the application showed a share price of €7.14. The money is received on TD + 3.

Requirements:

- Calculate the amount of money that the fund itself will receive and the number of shares that will be issued.
- Record the issue of the shares.
- Record the receipt of cash.

Question 4.12.4

An investor applies to redeem shares from your fund. He wishes to redeem 500,000 shares; these shares were originally subscribed for on 15/06/X1 at a price of €10.90. He makes his application on 26/04/X7.

- The NAV per share quoted at the end of trading on 23/04/X7 was €6.40.
- The NAV per share quoted at the end of trading on 24/04/X7 was €6.49.
- The NAV per share quoted at the end of trading on 25/04/X7 was €6.55.
- The NAV per share quoted at the end of trading on 26/04/X7 was €6.60.
- The NAV per share quoted at the end of trading on 27/04/X7 was €6.66.
- The NAV per share quoted at the end of trading on 28/04/X7 was €6.69.

The fund operates a CDSC, which the broker deducts, depending on when the original investment was made. The CDSC is calculated based on the lower of the original amount invested or the proceeds at redemption. If an investor withdraws from the fund:

- Within 0 to 3 years of investment, the CDSC is 4 per cent.
- Between 3 and 4 years after investment, the CDSC is 3 per cent.
- Over 4 years after investment, the CDSC is 1 per cent.

Three days later, on 29/04/X7, the money is paid.

Requirements:

- Calculate the amount of money that the fund will pay out.
- Calculate the amount that the investor will receive.
- Record the redemption of shares.
- Record the payment of cash.

Question 4.12.5

An investor applies to redeem shares from your fund. She wishes to redeem 25,000 shares; these shares were originally subscribed for on 20/04/X4 at a price of €23.50. She makes her application on 26/04/X7.

- The NAV per share quoted at the end of trading on 23/04/X7 was €46.40.
- The NAV per share quoted at the end of trading on 24/04/X7 was €47.49.
- The NAV per share quoted at the end of trading on 25/04/X7 was €46.55.
- The NAV per share quoted at the end of trading on 26/04/X7 was €49.60.
- The NAV per share quoted at the end of trading on 27/04/X7 was €46.66.
- The NAV per share quoted at the end of trading on 28/04/X7 was €48.69.

The fund operates a CDSC, which the broker deducts, depending on when the original investment was made. The CDSC is calculated based on the lower of the original amount invested or the proceeds at redemption. If an investor withdraws from the fund:

- Within 0 to 3 years of investment, the CDSC is 4 per cent.
- Between 3 and 4 years after investment, the CDSC is 3 per cent.
- Over 4 years after investment, the CDSC is 1 per cent.

Three days later, on 29/04/X7, the money is paid.

Requirements:

- Calculate the amount of money that the fund will pay out.
- Calculate the amount that the investor will receive.
- Record the redemption of shares.
- Record the payment of cash.

Question 4.12.6

You are the fund accountant for the Elecom Fund Family. You are required to account for the following transaction:

On 15/08/X8 an investor in the Elecom Technology Fund with 50,000 shares has applied to transfer his holding to the Elecom Utility Fund. There is no charge for transferring between funds in the same family. The settlement date is 18/08/X8. Table 4.6 shows the NAVs per share for this period.

Table 4.6: The NAVs per Share for Elecom Technology and Elecom Utility

Date	Elecom Technology	Elecom Utility
13/08/X8	€120.56	€34.56
14/08/X8	€121.05	€34.44
15/08/X8	€121.60	€34.23
16/08/X8	€121.96	€34.15
17/08/X8	€122.16	€34.04
18/08/X8	€122.44	€33.97
19/08/X8	€122.49	€33.93

Question 4.12.7

On 13/05/X4 Connect Enterprise Fund announces a dividend of €0.25 per cent share. The ex-date is 22/05/X4 and the payment date is 02/06/X4.

When investors apply for shares in the fund they are asked for their distribution preferences: do they wish to receive a cash distribution or would they prefer to re-invest any distribution back into the fund in the form of new shares? This election is made at the time of investment and once a distribution is announced cannot be revoked. The split of the shares opting for the cash option and the reinvest option is shown in Table 4.7.

Table 4.7: Distribution and Reinvestment Preferences for the Connect Enterprise Fund

Date	NAV per Share	Total Outstanding Fund Shares	Cash Distribution	Reinvest Distribution
13/05/X4	€5.65	1,000,000	900,000	100,000
22/05/X4	€5.68	1,010,000	905,000	105,000
02/06/X4	€5.48	1,150,000	1,043,000	107,000

(The reason why the 'Reinvest Distribution' option is increasing is due to the new investors entering the fund opting for the reinvest option. Between 13/05/X4 and 22/05/X4, 10,000 new shares were issued; 5,000 of these went for the cash option and 5,000 went for the reinvest option).

Record the appropriate transaction on each of the dates.

Table 4.8: Question 4.12.8: Comprehensive Question – Yield Fund

Statement of Net Assets

	04/04/XX	Trans. 1	Trans. 2	Trans. 3	05/04/XX	Trans. 1	Trans. 2	Trans. 3	06/04/XX	Trans. 1	Trans. 2	Trans. 3	07/04/XX
Assets													
Investments at Cost	€22,000,589												
Unrealised Appreciation/ Depreciation	€4,008,970												
Investments Sold Receivable													
Fund Shares Sold Receivable	€86,000												
Interest Receivable													
Cash	€1,400,000												
Dividends Receivable													
Total Assets	*€27,495,559*												
Liabilities													
Investments Purchased Payable													
Accrued Expenses	€18,000												
Fund Shares Redeemed Payable	€125,800												
Distributions Payable	€40,500												
Total Liabilities	*€184,300*												
Total Net Assets	**€27,311,259**												
Capital Stock/Investors' Equity	**€27,311,259**												
Outstanding Shares	1,000,000												
NAV per Share	€27.311												

(Continued)

179

Table 4.8: *(Continued)*

Statement of Operations for Period from 01/01/XX to YY/04/XX

	04/04/XX	Trans. 1	Trans. 2	Trans. 3	05/04/XX	Trans. 1	Trans. 2	Trans. 3	06/04/XX	Trans. 1	Trans. 2	Trans. 3	07/04/XX
Gains/Losses on Investments	€414,186												
Dividend Income	€2,500												
Interest Income													
Total Investment Income/Loss	*€416,686*												
Administration Fee Year to Date (YTD)	€3,000												
Investment Management Fee YTD	€6,000												
Other Fees YTD	€0												
Auditing Fee YTD	€1,000												
Total Fund Expenses	*€10,000*												
Increase/Decrease in Net Assets from Operations	**€406,686**												

Table 4.8: *(Continued)*

Statement of Changes in Net Assets for Period from 01/01/XX to YY/04/XX

	04/04/XX	Trans. 1	Trans. 2	Trans. 3	05/04/XX	Trans. 1	Trans. 2	Trans. 3	06/04/XX	Trans. 1	Trans. 2	Trans. 3	07/04/XX
Investors' Equity at 01/01/XX	€25,807,352												
Distributions to Investors	(€60,500)												
Capital Fund Share Transactions													
Proceeds from the sale of shares	€1,556,221												
Redemption of units	(€398,500)												
Dividend reinvestment	€0												
Total	*€1,157,721*												
Increase/Decrease in Net Assets from Operations	€406,686												
Investors' Equity at End of Period	**€27,311,259**												

Question 4.12.8: Comprehensive Question – Yield Fund

Table 4.8 shows a blank statement of net assets, statement of operations and statement of changes in net assets for the Yield Fund. Read the transactions below and then follow the requirements.

The Following Transactions Occurred on 05/04/XX:

All fund shares sold receivable outstanding are settled today.

A shareholder has decided to redeem 35,000 shares as of yesterday's NAV per share to settle on TD + 2.

A shareholder has decided to subscribe for 104,000 shares as of yesterday's NAV per share to settle on TD + 3.

The Following Transactions Occurred on 06/04/XX:

The fund shares redeemed payable outstanding from before 04/04/XX are settled today.

A shareholder with €250,000 to invest has decided to subscribe at yesterday's NAV per share to settle on TD + 3; front-end fees are 3 per cent.

Distributions payable outstanding from 04/04/XX are paid to investors today.

The Following Transactions Occurred on 07/04/XX:

At the start of business the fund announces a distribution of €1.00 per share with an ex-date of 07/04/XX (before the markets open) and a payment date on 10/04/XX. A number of shareholders, holding a total of 200,000 shares, have opted to reinvest the distribution.

The redemption of 05/04/XX is settled today.

The fund's investments increase in value by €750,000 (try this; we have not yet covered it but have a quick look at the next chapter to see how it might be recorded).

Requirements:

1. Record the transactions for the 05/04/XX and calculate the NAV per share for 05/04/XX.
2. Record the transactions for the 06/04/XX and calculate the NAV per share for 06/04/XX.
3. Record the transactions for the 07/04/XX and calculate the NAV per share for 07/04/XX.

Chapter 5

Accounting for Equities

- Introduction
- Types of equity securities
- Valuing equity securities
- Accounting for the purchase of equities
- Accounting for the daily valuation of equities
- Accounting for the sale of equities
- Summary
- Bringing it all together
- Additional questions

LEARNING OUTCOMES

At the end of this chapter you should:

- Be able to explain the different types of equity securities.
- Be able to describe the issues in valuing equity securities.
- Be able to record purchases of equities by a fund.
- Be able to record changes in the value of equities in a fund.
- Be able to record sales of equities by a fund.

5.1: INTRODUCTION

Investments are the driver of fund value. If the investments increase in value then the shareholders in the fund will be rewarded for the risks they have taken. The most common type of investment that mutual funds make is in equities (also known as shares, common stock, ordinary shares and equity securities). In this chapter the accounting aspects of investing in equities will be addressed.

The discussion will begin with an overview of the types of equity securities. Typically, most funds invest in common stock but there are other types of securities that a fund can purchase. These tend to be accounted for in a similar fashion, so it is appropriate to consider them all together.

Valuing equities is probably the most contentious issue for an equity-based investment fund. Generally, there are few issues. However, when there are difficulties, the impact on the NAV per share can be significant. Some of the more common issues will be discussed as part of Section 5.3.

The next sections address the accounting issues, following a logical sequence: accounting for the purchase of equities will be considered first, then the focus moves to accounting for the valuation of equities and we finish with accounting for the sale of equities.

The chapter concludes with a comprehensive example which will review much of the material that has been addressed, including fund share transactions from the previous chapter. This example will use the spreadsheet format that should now be more familiar.

5.2: TYPES OF EQUITY SECURITIES

5.2.1: Common Stock

When the media or financial press refers to the market what they are normally discussing are the current prices of 'common stock'. Common stock is also known as shares, equities, ordinary shares and equity securities; many writers use these terms interchangeably.

As a fund purchases common stock (for example, 100,000 shares in Intel), it becomes a part owner of that company. This means that the fund is entitled to vote on major issues at the annual general meeting (AGM) of the company. If Intel decides to pay a dividend[1] out of its profits then the fund will get its share of the dividend. In good years this dividend may be quite large, while in poor years it might be small or even zero; the dividend is not guaranteed from year to year. In the case of Intel, the share price on 17 August 2009[2] was $18.45. This means that the cost of the 100,000 shares is $1,845,000. Intel has almost 5.6 billion shares in issue; thus the fund now owns 0.002 per cent of Intel – such a small shareholding will not give the fund much influence over the business.

The fund's liability from its investment in common stock is limited. Should Intel, for example, go bankrupt, owing large sums of money to its banks and creditors,

---

[1] A dividend is a payment that a company makes to its shareholders. The more shares that a shareholder owns the more money that shareholder will receive. Generally, more profitable companies tend to make larger payments. Typically, dividends are paid twice a year (for European companies) or quarterly (for US companies).

[2] Data from www.intel.com as on 17 August 2009.

then the fund will not be liable for any part of the shortfall. The share price of Intel can only fall to zero; it cannot have a negative value.

One of the risks of owning shares is that if the company gets into difficulty, the shareholders will be last in the queue to be repaid. So the assets of the company will be sold off and the resulting money will be used to repay the banks, creditors and any other type of shareholder before the common shareholders receive anything. If this is the scenario then the likelihood is that the common shareholders will receive very little.

In addition, the holders of the common stock have very little certainty. Dividends are at the discretion of the directors. If the company does not perform well then it is likely that any dividend payment will be curtailed. This is in direct contrast to those who provide debt finance to a company: their interest payments are much more certain as the company is legally obliged to pay.

5.2.2: Preferred Stock

Also known as preference shares, preferred stock is a much less used source of finance. The characteristics of preferred stock will depend on the individual issuer (i.e. the individual company). However, often there is a fixed dividend payment that can be paid irrespective of the profits of the company. This fixed payment may appear to be a significant incentive for preference shareholders but if the company does exceptionally well the payment remains the same. While ordinary shareholders can see their dividend cheque grow from year to year, the preference shareholder will remain with their original dividend payment.

Preferred stock can be redeemable or irredeemable. If the stock is redeemable then the company may be required to repay the original value of the shares to the preferred stockholders, whereas, for irredeemable preference stock, the company is under no obligation to repay.

Typically, the holders of preference shares will not get a vote in the major decisions affecting the company. Notice that the difference between preferred stock and a normal loan is very small: the fixed annual dividend is analogous to interest, no vote and the potential requirement to repay the original value is similar to many of the conditions attached to loans. In many cases individual companies are now required to account for preference shares in the same way as they account for a bank loan.[3]

Preference shares are normally riskier than debt or loans. A lender will normally insist on some form of collateral but preference shareholders will not have this type of security. Also, if the company gets into financial difficulty the preference

---

[3] International Accounting Standards Board (2009a), paragraph 18a.

shareholders will be one of the last finance providers to get any payment from the company. The banks and 'normal' debt providers will be paid earlier but the equity shareholders will be paid later.

So why would a fund invest in the preference shares of a company? They do not appear to be very attractive. They are more risky than debt or loan finance and they do not have the same upside as ordinary shares because of the fixed dividend. The answer is that preference shares are somewhere between debt/loan finance and ordinary equity finance. Preference shares are not as risky as ordinary shares but more risky than debt/bank finance. On the potential for gains, preference shares with a fixed dividend have less potential than equity shares. On the positive side, preference shares tend to attract a higher dividend payment than the equivalent interest payment on debt finance. So a fund that is looking for an investment port-folio that will give its investors the opportunity to generate a reasonable return but without taking excessive risks may consider preference shares.

An example of preference stock is an issue by CRH. These are titled the '5% Cumulative Preference Shares'. The 5 per cent relates to the fixed rate of dividend; 5 per cent of the nominal value of the shares is paid as a dividend each year. In this case, the nominal value of CRH 5 per cent cumulative preference shares is €1.27[4] per share. Thus, the annual dividend is just €0.0635 per share (5 per cent of €1.27). Contrast this with the ordinary shares of CRH, which have been experiencing large dividend increases over the past number of years, increasing steadily from €0.1052 per share in 1995 to €0.68 per share in 2007. The 'cumulative' aspect of the shares also conveys the following information to potential investors in these shares: if CRH do not make enough profits in any one year to be able to pay the 5 per cent preference dividend then the dividend will roll forward until next year and beyond until CRH has enough profits to be able to make the payment. In these circumstances, CRH will not be permitted to pay the ordinary shareholders a dividend at any point until the preference shareholders have been paid all of their outstanding dividends (see Figure 5.1).

Figure 5.1:   CRH 5% Cumulative Preference Shares Details

(ii) 5% Cumulative Preference Shares
The holders of the 5% Cumulative Preference Shares are entitled to a fixed cumulative preferential dividend at a rate of 5% per annum and priority in a winding-up to repayment of capi-tal, but have no further right to participate in profits or assets and are not entitled to be present or vote at general meetings unless their dividend is in arrears. Dividends on the 5% Cumulative Preference Shares are payable half-yearly on 15th April and 15th October in each year.

Source: CRH Annual Report for year ended 31 December 2008, p. 108, available from www.crh.ie.

---

[4]   €1.27 is the equivalent of an old Irish Punt, 1 IEP.

Volkswagen is an example of another company that uses preference shares in its financing. Take a look at www.volkswagenag.com to see the particulars of the preference shares; navigate to the annual financial report where a short summary can normally be found. The dividend payment attached to Volkswagen's preference shares is unusual; can you determine the exact nature of the dividend payment?[5] An investor should be aware of these arrangements before investing in the preference shares of Volkswagen. This is a reason for investing through a fund, as the investment managers will be aware of this small but essential information, which an individual private investor may not know. Compare the share price of Volkswagen ordinary shares to Volkswagen preference shares. Use one of the many charting tools available online to track historic movements; there are numerous free charting facilities, try http://moneycentral.msn.com/investor/charts/chartdl.aspx as an example.[6]

5.2.3: American Depository Receipts (ADRs)

American Depository Receipts (ADRs) can be thought of as common stock. There is essentially no difference. ADRs are an innovation of the American financial system. They are a repackaging of the common stock of foreign companies to be sold mainly (but not exclusively) to American investors. The ADRs are then traded on the US markets, usually in dollars.

ADRs are issued by American financial institutions representing shares in foreign companies. They were originally a means of reducing tax and duty when buying shares in companies that were located in jurisdictions with unfavourable taxes. An American bank would purchase shares in a French company (as an example). The shares would be held in custody overseas, often in the country where the company was domiciled. Then if the American bank had a client who was looking to buy shares in the French company they would issue the client with an ADR; each ADR could represent one share in the French company and would be backed up by the shares in the French company that the bank held. There would be no change in ownership of the French company shares but the ADR could be traded by the client without a resultant French tax liability.

Elan, the Irish pharmaceutical research company, has both ordinary shares (listed on the Irish Stock Exchange) and Elan ADRs (quoted on the New York Stock Exchange (NYSE)). One ADR represents one Elan Ordinary Share. On 20 June 2008, Elan ordinary shares were trading at €20.79 while Elan ADRs were trading

---

[5] The holders of Volkswagen AG preference shares are entitled to a dividend of €0.06 over and above any dividend paid to the ordinary shareholders.

[6] In October 2008 there was a large spike in Volkswagen shares connected to a protracted takeover battle.

at \$32.95. On 20 June 2008 the EUR–USD exchange rate was 1.5605 (€1 = \$1.5605). Is it possible to explain most of the difference between the prices?[7]

A GDR is a Global Depository Receipt: similar in structure to an ADR but giving companies exposure to non-US global financial markets. GDRs tend to trade in London or Luxembourg and are denominated in Sterling or Euro.

The benefit of ADRs, from an individual company's perspective, is that they offer a new means of raising equity capital. They broaden the company's shareholder base and this often results in an increase in liquidity. There is also a further spin-off benefit in that more research analysts should follow the company, raising the company's visibility and leading to greater levels of liquidity. Finally, for some foreign companies there are limits on foreign ownership, which can restrict the growth of the company as its access to capital is constrained. ADRs can be structured to avoid some of these limitations.

The benefits of ADRs for investors is that they are easy to purchase and have a lower holding cost (custody charges are often zero), there are fewer language issues as the company is obliged to issue information in the language of the ADRs' home currency and there can also be tax benefits.[8]

A good source of information on ADRs can be found on www.adr.com; this is a JPMorgan site which promotes the ADR and GDR market.

5.2.4: Warrants

Warrants are a type of share option that are issued directly by a company. A warrant (and share option) gives the holder an option, but not an obligation, to purchase shares in a company at a fixed price (the strike price), some time in the future (the exercise date).

British Energy is an example of a company that has used warrants (see Figure 5.2). As part of a restructuring of the business in January 2005, it offered shareholders warrants in the company.[9] The shareholders have the option of

---

[7] Sources for price information: www.yahoofinance.com (US prices), www.goodbody.ie. (Dublin prices). The remaining difference can be explained by timing effects between the various quotes. If this was not the situation then an astute investor could make a risk-free profit by playing one market against the other. This is often referred to as arbitrage.

[8] For example, if an investor purchases shares in an Irish company then they must pay Irish stamp duty of 1 per cent. If an ADR in the same Irish company is purchased then, under certain circumstances, there may be no exposure to Irish stamp duty.

[9] The warrants were offered to shareholders as part of a larger package, which also included ordinary shares. For full details see www.british-energy.com or the annual report of British Energy for the year ended 31 March 2005.

purchasing shares in British Energy at 98p (the strike price) at any time up to five years after the date of the restructuring (the final exercise date). Once the ordinary share price of British Energy exceeds 98p then it will be in the warrant holder's interest to pay 98p and get one share in British Energy. These warrants are tradable: the warrant holder can sell the warrant to someone else. The value of the warrant depends on a number of factors, including the price of the associated share.

Figure 5.2: British Energy Warrants

Warrants
On Restructuring, 29,298,286 Warrants of £0.98 were allotted. The Warrants are freely exercisable at the option of the Warrant holder. The subscription rights may be exercised at any time in respect of certificated Warrants on lodging of a duly completed subscription notice and remittance of the subscription price or, in respect of Warrants held in uncertificated form, if CREST Co. Limited receives a properly authenticated dematerialised instruction and payment through CREST in accordance with its rules. In the year ended 31 March 2008 6,955,809 (2007: 6,399,439) of these Warrants were exercised leaving 6,764,057 (2007:13,719,866) unexercised. The Warrants entitle the holder to subscribe to acquire an equivalent number of ordinary shares at a subscription price of £0.98 per share within five years of Restructuring.

Source: British Energy Group Annual Report, 31 March 2008, p. 89, available from www.british-energy.com.

On 24 June 2008, shares in British Energy were trading at 700.5p[10] while, at the same time and date, British Energy warrants were trading at 602.5p. The difference between the two prices is 98p – the amount that a warrant holder will have to pay to buy the ordinary shares in British Energy. A potential investor has two options: they could buy shares in British Energy for 700.5p or they could buy a warrant for 602.5p and then exercise the warrant by paying 98p, resulting in the investor holding one ordinary share in British Energy. Whichever option the investor takes, the end result is the same: they own one ordinary share at a total cost of 700.5p. If this were not the case there would be an opportunity for investors to make windfall gains for taking no risk (arbitrage). If the warrant price fell to 590p this would result in a rush of traders buying the warrant instead of the ordinary share; this increase in demand would cause the price of the warrant to rise until it reaches 602.5p.

The British Energy warrants are currently exercisable and are 'in the money' (the current share price of 700.5p is well in excess of the strike price of the warrant at 98p). Consequently, the difference in the two prices is equal to the strike price of the warrant. This will not always be the case. In these situations warrants can still have a value. Warrants with exercise dates many years in the future can have a value even if the current ordinary share price is not higher than the strike price. This is because there is ample time for the ordinary share price to increase and exceed the exercise price.

---

[10]   All British Energy share prices are from www.londonstockexchange.com.

There can be a variety of different types of warrants so it is important to read the conditions of the warrant before purchasing.

Warrants are not very common. Companies often issue them to act as a sweetener for investors. In the case of British Energy, the company was going through a difficult restructuring. As part of the plan, finance providers in the old British Energy were given shares in the new British Energy along with warrants; the warrants were offered to encourage investors to accept the plan. The warrants give investors a chance to make large gains if the company does exceptionally well. Warrants are sometimes issued in situations where companies are trying to raise bond finance; again the objective is to encourage potential bondholders to participate in the bond issue.

5.2.5: Other Types of Equity Securities

Other types of equity securities include rights issues and convertible bonds. Rights issues display characteristics that are very similar to those of warrants but they tend to have shorter lives. In the case of British Energy the warrant had a five-year life; a rights issue may only have a life of two months. The value of a right will be determined to some extent by the price of the associated ordinary share. This will be addressed in more detail in Chapter 6 (Accounting for Corporate Actions).

Investors who purchase convertible bonds give finance to a company in return for an annual interest payment and the return of the principal amount at the end of the term (similar to a loan). However, at the end of the life of the bond (or at other specified intervals), the bondholder has the option to 'convert' the bond into a predetermined number of shares in the company. If this option is taken, the bondholder will not get the principal back at the end of the life but will receive shares instead. Whether or not the bondholder takes this option will depend on the number of shares that will be offered and the current share price. Convertible bonds are popular with investors who do not want the risk of owning shares outright in a company but would like some of the potential returns. The price of a convertible bond is determined by a number of factors, including the price of the associated ordinary share. The accounting for convertible bonds is outside the scope of this book.

5.3: VALUING EQUITY SECURITIES

The NAV per share of an investment fund is published at regular intervals, such as daily, weekly or monthly. The exact specification of this will be stated in the fund's prospectus, even down to the time of day when the NAV per share should be calculated, for example, at the close of business of the Irish Stock Exchange (or the New York Stock Exchange or any other exchange). Every time that the NAV per share is calculated, this will result in the valuation of the investment portfolio of the fund.

To value an investment portfolio that is made up of equities, the fund accountant will have to determine the current market price for the shares multiplied by the number of shares held. This is normally a straightforward procedure as most equities can be valued using the official published information from the appropriate stock markets.

One issue that can arise is which share price should be used. Table 5.1 shows a series of quotes for BP (British Petroleum) on 24 June 2008 at 10:16am.

Table 5.1:   Quotes for BP on 24 June 2008 at 10:16 a.m. (15 Minute Delay)

BP (LSE: BP.L)			
Last Trade:	**577.50 p**	Day's Range:	571.50 – 581.75
Trade Time:	10:01AM	52wk Range:	495.00 – 657.25
Change:	**↑2.75 (0.48%)**	Volume:	7,897,081
Prev Close:	574.75	Avg Vol (3m):	53,069,800
Open:	575.00	Market Cap:	£108.63 B
Bid:	577.25	P/E:	10.65 x
Ask:	577.75	EPS (Growth):	54.20p (–8.37%)
1y Target Est:	693.30p	Dividend:	6.83p (9-Jun-08)

Source: Yahoofinance.

There are a number of prices that can be used:

- Last trade: the price at which the last trade was executed (577.5p for BP).
- Previous close: the price at which the shares closed on the previous day (574.50p on 23 June 2008 for BP).
- Open: the price at which the shares opened on the current day (575p on 24 June 2008 for BP). There can be differences between the previous close and the opening price due to overnight trading and the effect of overnight events.
- Bid price: the price that investors are willing to buy at (currently 577.25p for BP).
- Asked/offer price: the price that investors are willing to sell at (currently 577.75p for BP).
- Mean price: average of the bid and offer price.
- Official closing price: the official closing price as issued by the relevant exchange. Most stock exchanges provide this information using a defined procedure. The procedures of the Irish Stock Exchange can be found on www.ise.ie/index.asp?locID=335&docID=278.

The fund's prospectus should give the pricing policy; funds tend to use the official closing price (unless there are overriding reasons not to). Figure 5.3 shows the policy of BlackRock Global Funds for valuing its portfolios.

Figure 5.3: Extract from BlackRock Global Funds Prospectus – Portfolio Valuation Procedures

13. The value of all securities and other assets forming any particular Fund's portfolio is determined by last known prices upon close of the exchange on which those securities or assets are traded or admitted for trading. For securities traded on markets closing after the time of the valuation, last known prices as of this time or such other time may be used. If net transactions in Shares of the Fund on any Dealing Day exceed the threshold referred to in paragraph 16(c) below, then additional procedures apply. The value of any securities or assets traded on any other regulated market is determined in the same way. Where such securities or other assets are quoted or dealt in on or by more than one stock exchange or regulated market the Directors may in their discretion select one of such stock exchanges or regulated markets for such purposes.
14. If a security is not traded on or admitted to any official stock exchange or any regulated market, or in the case of securities so traded or admitted the last known price is not considered to reflect their true value, the Directors will value the securities concerned with prudence and in good faith on the basis of their expected disposal or acquisition price. Cash, bills payable on demand and other debts and prepaid expenses are valued at their nominal amount, unless it appears unlikely that such nominal amount is obtainable.

Source: BlackRock Global Funds Prospectus, June 2008, p. 35, available from www.blackrock.com.

5.3.1: Valuation Issues – Selling Costs

When an equity is valued in the portfolio of an investment fund, no allowance is made for the costs of selling that equity. This has the effect of slightly overvaluing the portfolio of the fund. If the cost of selling an equity position is 1 per cent of the value of the equity then this could represent an overvaluation of 1 per cent on the NAV per share of the investment fund.

However, it is highly unlikely that all of the holdings of an investment fund will be sold at the same time, resulting in large selling costs. Consequently, the overvaluation is unlikely to have a material impact on investors (or potential investors) in the fund.

Some investment funds do give themselves the latitude to reduce the NAV per share of the fund in situations where there are large redemptions from the fund. Many redemptions over a short period will result in the fund selling a large portion of its portfolio, thereby resulting in high selling costs. See Figure 5.4 for an example from BlackRock Global Funds Prospectus.

This part of the prospectus is written using legal terminology but the result is that the directors of the fund have the option to adjust the NAV per share by up to 1.25 per cent in situations where there are a large number of redemptions.

Figure 5.4:   Extract from BlackRock Global Funds Prospectus – Portfolio Valuation Procedures (Multiple Transactions)

16(c)   If on any Dealing Day the aggregate transactions in Shares of all Classes of a Fund result in a net increase or decrease of Shares which exceeds a threshold set by the Directors from time to time for that Fund (relating to the cost of market dealing for that Fund), the Net Asset Value of the relevant Fund will be adjusted by an amount (not exceeding 1.25%, or 3% in the case of the High Yield Funds, of that Net Asset Value) which reflects both the estimated fiscal charges and dealing costs that may be incurred by the Fund and the estimated bid/offer spread of the assets in which the Fund invests. The adjustment will be an addition when the net movement results in an increase of all Shares of the Fund and a deduction when it results in a decrease. As certain stock markets and jurisdictions may have different charging structures on the buy and sell sides, the resulting adjustment may be different for net inflows than for net outflows. Where a Fund invests substantially in government bonds or money market securities, the Directors may decide that it is not appropriate to make such an adjustment.

Source: BlackRock Global Funds Prospectus, June 2008, p. 35, available from www.blackrock.com.

5.3.2: Valuation Issues – Thin Trading

Thin trading is where there are very few transactions in the shares of a particular company. This results in share prices that can be out of date as the last transaction in that particular share may have taken place some time ago (even weeks ago). Shares that are thinly traded can be subject to large price fluctuations as there are very few buyers and sellers. In addition, information on these shares can be hard to find as thinly traded companies tend to be small and attract only sporadic interest from analysts.

There is no interval between trades that defines thin trading. However, consider the following example from the Irish Stock Market. Merrion Pharmaceuticals is a company listed on the Irish Enterprise Exchange. For the month of February 2008 there were no transactions in Merrion Pharmaceuticals shares; the share price at the start of the month was 410c and at the end of the month it was quoted at 410c (as there was no other transaction during the month) (see Figure 5.5).[11]

The chart shown in Figure 5.5 is typical of a share that is thinly traded. The share price moves in big discrete jumps and the volume chart at the bottom shows little activity. Once a share has been identified as thinly traded, the issue then moves to how to value these shares.

The approach may depend on the number of shares held – if the fund only holds a small number of shares then it may be possible to sell them on the market. Even for a company as thinly traded as Merrion Pharmaceuticals it was possible to sell blocks of 15,000 shares in May, although there was an impact on the price. Thus, for small shareholdings relative to the size of the company it may still be appropriate to use the official closing price as quoted by the relevant exchange.

---

[11]   ISE Monthly Report for February 2008, p. 20.

Figure 5.5: Share Price Chart for Merrion Pharmaceuticals (Jan–Jun 2008)

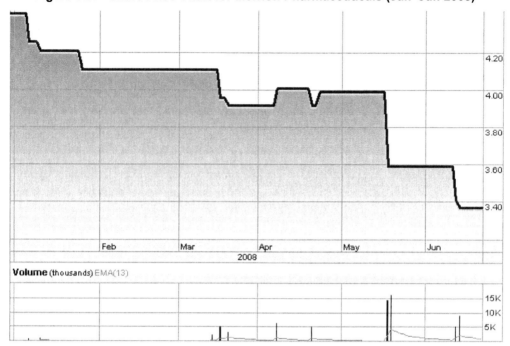

Source: www.businessweek.com.

As an alternative, there may be periodic valuations available from pricing services, brokers or analysts. Another option is to use a valuation model by applying industry-wide benchmarks to the company under consideration.[12] The value of thinly traded equities should be reviewed on a regular basis to ensure that their value has not shifted dramatically from their assigned value.

There is also a sector of the funds industry that invests in companies that are not traded on any exchange. This is a strategy followed by venture capital funds: these funds invest in high-potential small companies in the hope that they will eventually float on the stock market and provide the fund with significant returns. Valuing these types of investments is particularly hazardous as there is no equivalent share price to even act as a guide.[13] 3i is a large venture capital company that has a portfolio of investments under management totalling over £6 billion[14] GBP. As only

---

[12] Industry benchmarks that can be used include PE ratios and market-to-book ratios. For further information on the use of these techniques please consult the valuation chapters of any introductory book on corporate finance.

[13] The television programme *Dragon's Den* is an extreme example of this. The valuations and the percentage of the companies on offer tend to be very fluid as small start-up companies are difficult to value.

[14] 3i Annual Report for year ended 31 March 2008, p. 81.

15 per cent of the 3i portfolio is quoted on a stock market, the company must use a variety of methods to value its portfolio. These include cost, earnings-based (using versions of the PE ratio), asset-based and potential disposal valuations. Full details of the valuation process can be found in the 3i Annual Report (www.3igroup.com). This is a highly specialised aspect of investment fund accounting and, consequently, is outside the scope of this book.

5.4: ACCOUNTING FOR THE PURCHASE OF EQUITIES

This is where the accounting for equities really begins. The first issue that needs to be considered is how to account for the purchase of equities. Similar to fund share transactions, the purchase of equities will be accounted for separately to the settlement (payment) of the transaction. This is because equity transactions generally take three days to settle. If a purchase takes place today, on the trade day (TD), the fund will only get delivery on the settlement date, which is normally three days later – TD + 3 (trade date plus three days). The fund accountant will record the purchase of the equities immediately (this could be on TD + 1 because it may take a day for the information to reach the fund accountant). Then on TD + 3 the fund accountant will record the settlement; on that day the fund gets delivery of the shares and makes the payment to the previous owner.

This time delay can give rise to some differences between the fund accountant's records and the custodian's records. The custodian will not record the shares until they have been delivered but the fund accountant recognises the shares on the date they are purchased (the trade date). Regular reconciliations will need to be performed between the fund accountant's records and the custodian's records to ensure that any differences can be explained by these types of circumstances. Differences that are unexplained or differences that do not resolve themselves after a few days should be thoroughly investigated – these could be symptomatic of failed trades or errors.

5.4.1: Recording the Purchase of Equities

When a fund purchases equity investments for its portfolio, the fund accountant must:

- Determine the total cost of the equities purchased.
- Record the purchase.
- Record the settlement (normally, TD + 3).

The first step is to determine the cost of the shares that have just been purchased. Generally, the cost of purchase includes the cost of the shares plus any fees, commissions and taxes associated with the purchase of the shares.

Example 5.1: Purchase of Equities

On 15/02/X7 a fund purchased 10,000 shares in McInerney Holdings Plc. The trade price was €1.90 per share. Stamp duty of 1 per cent is due on the transaction and the broker commission was €250.

In this instance the amount to be recorded is 10,000 × €1.90 = €19,000 + 1% Duty + €250. That gives a total of €19,000 + €190 + €250 = €19,440.

Next, this amount needs to be recorded. The fund now owes €19,440 to the previous owner of the shares (to be more specific, €19,000 is owed to the previous owner, €190 to the government and €250 to the broker, but the broker will collect the full amount and then distribute the proceeds appropriately). As the amount is owed, this means that it is a liability of the fund. A separate account will be created for this liability as it is a common type of transaction, and will be entitled 'investments purchased payable'. This account represents the amounts owed to third parties for investments that were purchased for the fund's portfolio. As stated, investments purchased payable is a liability. It is increasing; thus, it is a credit.

⇒ Credit investments purchased payable.

On the other side of the transaction, the fund now owns equities. These are part of the investments that the fund has made. The assets of the fund are increasing. When a fund purchases investments it is a good idea to track this kind of information, so these amounts will be put into an account called investments at cost. This account will allow investors to easily determine how much the fund has paid for all of its current investments. The account is an asset (as the fund owns the equities) and it is increasing (the fund now has more shares than before this transaction); thus, it is a debit.

⇒ Debit investments at cost.

- Dr investments at cost   €19,440
- Cr investments purchased payable   €19,440

Or – for the spreadsheet approach:

- Increase investments at cost, an asset, by €19,440.
- Increase investments purchased payable, a liability, by €19,440.

5.4.2: Recording the Subsequent Payment

If the transaction proceeds as normal, three days later (TD + 3) the fund will receive delivery of the equities and payment will be made.

In Example 5.1 the fund will pay €19,440 to the broker of the previous owner of the shares, as a result the cash in the fund will decrease. Cash is an asset and it is decreasing; thus, it is a credit.

⇒ Credit the cash account.

On the other side of the transaction, once the money is paid the fund no longer owes any amount to the previous owner. When the original transaction was recorded the debt that the fund owed was shown in an account called investments purchased payable – this represented the fact that the fund owed money to the previous owner of the shares. This debt has now been settled. Thus, there is no need for the debt to be shown. Investments purchased payable, which is a liability, is decreasing; thus, it is a debit.

⇒ Debit investments purchased payable.

- Dr investments purchased payable   €19,440
- Cr cash   €19,440

Or – for the spreadsheet approach:

- Decrease investments purchased payable, a liability, by €19,440.
- Decrease cash, an asset, by €19,440.

5.4.3: Accounting for Purchase of Equities – Summary of Accounting Entries

Determine the total cost of the shares purchased (including any fees, commissions and taxes).

On the trade date record the purchase of the equities:

- Dr investments at cost.
- Cr investments purchased payable.

On the settlement date record the payment:

- Dr investments purchased payable.
- Cr cash.

Now try Question 5.9.6 at the end of this chapter.

5.5: ACCOUNTING FOR THE DAILY VALUATION/DAILY PRICE MOVEMENTS

Unlike many other organisations, investment funds value their assets (i.e. their portfolio of equities and other investments) at market value on a regular basis, often daily. As the value of the shares held by the fund change, the generally accepted approach is not to adjust the investments at cost account. Instead, all the share price movements are accumulated and recorded in a separate account called unrealised appreciation/depreciation on investments. This conveys much more information to investors on the performance of the fund as it is easy to determine if the investments in the fund have increased in value (the unrealised appreciation/depreciation account is positive) or if the investments have lost value since purchased (the unrealised appreciation/depreciation account is negative).

5.5.1: Daily Valuation – Calculating the Appreciation or Depreciation on a Fund's Portfolio

Arriving at the figure for the daily valuation will be the most challenging task so far. It is a relatively obvious calculation if the fund has just one or two shares in its portfolio. If a fund has just 10,000 shares in Ryanair in its portfolio and the share price increases from €3.90 to €3.95 then arriving at the increase in the value of the portfolio is not onerous. In this example, the share price has increased by €0.05 and the fund holds 10,000 shares, giving a total increase of €500.

The calculations that are used need to be robust for situations where the fund has hundreds of equities in its portfolio, purchases equities over the day and sells equities over the day. However, try to remember the following two points and it may help to explain the logic of the process:

- The objective is to arrive at the increase/decrease in the value of the portfolio for the day (or period), not the total increase/decrease.
- The total of the investments at cost account (at the end of the day) plus the unrealised appreciation/depreciation account (at the end of the day) should equal the market value of the fund's portfolio (at the end of the day).

Step 1: Calculate the Market Value of the Portfolio

The first step in arriving at the increase/decrease in the value of the portfolio is to calculate the total market value of the portfolio at the end of the period in question. This is an easy task: just multiply the share price by the number of shares in the portfolio and add the resulting totals. Remember from Section 5.3 that most funds tend to use the 'official closing price' when valuing shares.

Example 5.2a: Calculating the Market Value of a Portfolio

Consider a fund with the portfolio shown in Table 5.2a.

Table 5.2a: Irish Blue-Chip Fund Portfolio

Share	Quantity	Closing Price 05/05/X6
AIB	10,000	€20.50
Bank of Ireland	5,000	€14.56
Ryanair	8,000	€7.45
Waterford Wedgwood	60,000	€0.05
Grafton Group	2,000	€10.61
Irish Continental Group	5,000	€25.00
C & C	11,000	€7.10

Calculate the market value of the portfolio as on 05/05/X6.

Solution 5.2a: Calculating the Market Value of a Portfolio

All you need to do is multiply the quantity of shares by the price to give the market value for each shareholding. The individual market values are then added to arrive at an overall total (see Table 5.2b).

Table 5.2b: Irish Blue-Chip Fund Market Value

Share	Quantity	Closing Price 05/05/X6	Market Value 05/05/X6
AIB	10,000	€20.50	€205,000
Bank of Ireland	5,000	€14.56	€72,800
Ryanair	8,000	€7.45	€59,600
Waterford Wedgwood	60,000	€0.05	€3,000
Grafton Group	2,000	€10.61	€21,220
Irish Continental Group	5,000	€25.00	€125,000
C & C	11,000	€7.10	€78,100
Total			€564,720

Step 2: Calculate the Total Unrealised Appreciation/Depreciation

The next step is to compare the market value of the portfolio with the cost of the portfolio at the end of the day/period. The difference will give the total unrealised appreciation/depreciation – the final number that we are hoping to arrive at. There are two approaches to this:

1. Get the cost of each holding in the portfolio and add them up or
2. Go to the investments at cost account and get the closing balance of this account (opening investments at costs + purchases of new holdings – disposals of holdings).

Returning to the previous example:

Example 5.2b: Calculating the Total Unrealised Appreciation/Depreciation

Table 5.2c shows the total cost of the Irish Blue–Chip Fund's holdings.

Table 5.2c: Irish Blue-Chip Fund Original Cost

Share	Quantity	Closing Price 05/05/X6	Cost	Commission
AIB	10,000	€20.50	€19.70	€400
Bank of Ireland	5,000	€14.56	€14.44	€300
Ryanair	8,000	€7.45	€7.50	€100
Waterford Wedgwood	60,000	€0.05	€0.05	€100
Grafton Group	2,000	€10.61	€10.65	€400
Irish Continental Group	5,000	€25.00	€24.50	€100
C & C	11,000	€7.10	€7.00	€100

Calculate the total cost of the portfolio and the total unrealised appreciation/ depreciation on the portfolio on 05/05/X6. The shares, the quantity held and the closing price on 05/05/X6 are the same as in the previous example.

Remember that the cost of a holding includes the commissions, non–refundable taxes (if any) and other fees.

Solution 5.2b: Calculating the Total Unrealised Appreciation/Depreciation

To calculate the total cost of each holding the quantity is multiplied by the cost and the commission is then added. The total cost of each holding is then added to arrive at an overall total (€554,500 – see Table 5.2d).

Table 5.2d: Irish Blue-Chip Fund Total Cost

Share	Quantity	Cost	Cost × Quantity	Commission	Total Cost
AIB	10,000	€19.70	€197,000	€400	€197,400
Bank of Ireland	5,000	€14.44	€72,200	€300	€72,500

(Continued)

Table 5.2d: *(Continued)*

Share	Quantity	Cost	Cost × Quantity	Commission	Total Cost
Ryanair	8,000	€7.50	€60,000	€100	€60,100
Waterford Wedgwood	60,000	€0.05	€3,000	€100	€3,100
Grafton Group	2,000	€10.65	€21,300	€400	€21,700
Irish Continental Group	5,000	€24.50	€122,500	€100	€122,600
C & C	11,000	€7.00	€77,000	€100	€77,100
Total					€554,500

Finally, Table 5.2e shows the calculation of the total unrealised appreciation/ depreciation.

Table 5.2e: Calculating the Total Unrealised Appreciation/Depreciation of the Irish Blue-Chip Fund

Total Market Value of Portfolio on 05/05/X6	€564,720	(Table 5.2b)
Total Cost of Portfolio on 05/05/X6	€554,500	(Table 5.2d)
Total Unrealised Appreciation/Depreciation	€10,220	(Market Value less Cost)

What does the unrealised appreciation/depreciation of €10,220 represent? Since the holdings in the portfolio were purchased they have gained (appreciated) €10,220 in value. This is good news for the investors in the fund. If this was a negative figure − the cost of the portfolio exceeded the market value − then there would have been an unrealised depreciation in the value of the portfolio; the portfolio would have lost value. In both cases, the gains or losses are unrealised as the fund still holds these shares and has not yet sold them; when the shares are sold then any gains or losses become realised.

A quick review of the holdings in the portfolio shows that some have gained substantially whereas others have lost value since purchase.[15] At this stage it is only the net figure that is important. Remember, this is a small portfolio; if it was made up of 200 holdings then the calculations would be more complex.

---

[15] AIB, Bank of Ireland, Irish Continental Group and C & C have increased in value. Ryanair and Grafton have decreased in value While Waterford Wedgwood's value has not changed.

Step 3: Calculating the Daily Unrealised Appreciation/Depreciation

At this point, the total unrealised appreciation on the portfolio is known (€10,220 in the example). However, this gain (or loss) has been made over many days, even months. The shares in AIB could have been bought on 01/01/X5; hence, any increase in value has been generated since then. In order to arrive at the NAV per share of a fund for a particular day, the unrealised appreciation/depreciation for just that day needs to be calculated (05/05/X6 in the example).

To calculate the daily unrealised appreciation/depreciation, a starting point is yesterday's unrealised appreciation. If yesterday's total unrealised appreciation/depreciation is known and today's total unrealised appreciation/depreciation is also known, then the difference should be the unrealised appreciation/depreciation for the current day.

There is just one complication which will be left until later (Section 5.6) but a line will be added here for completeness. The unrealised appreciation/depreciation from yesterday needs to be adjusted for any unusual movements during the day – these nearly exclusively relate to the sale of holdings in the portfolio.[16]

Table 5.3a shows how to calculate the daily unrealised appreciation/depreciation.

Table 5.3a: How to Calculate the Daily Unrealised Appreciation/Depreciation

Total Unrealised Appreciation/Depreciation – Today		€X (Note 1)
Total Unrealised Appreciation/Depreciation – Yesterday	€A (Note 2)	
Add (or Subtract) any Increases (or Decreases) in Unrealised Appreciation/Depreciation during the Day (Note 3)	€B	(€A – €B) = €Y
Daily Change in Unrealised Appreciation/Depreciation	(€X – €Y)	€Z

Note 1: This is the amount already calculated (see Example 5.2b, Table 5.2e).
Note 2: This will be known from yesterday's NAV per share calculation.
Note 3: This will be zero for the moment. Any item included here is usually due to sales of equities.

Example 5.2c: Calculating the Daily Unrealised Appreciation/Depreciation

On 04/05/X6 the following balances are noted for the Irish Blue-Chip Fund:

- Investments at cost account   €554,500   (dr balance)
- Unrealised appreciation/depreciation account   €7,800   (dr balance)

---

[16] When the sale of equities is addressed (in Section 5.6), this point will be returned to in much more detail.

This information can be found in the previous day's NAV per share calculation. If the fund is new then both will be zero.

Calculate the unrealised appreciation/depreciation for 05/05/X6. The shares, the quantity held and the closing price on 05/05/X6 are the same as in the previous example.[17]

Solution 5.2c: Calculating the Daily Unrealised Appreciation/Depreciation

Table 5.3b shows the calculation for the daily unrealised appreciation/depreciation for the Irish Blue–Chip Fund on 05/05/X6.

Table 5.3b: Calculating the Daily Unrealised Appreciation/Depreciation for the Irish Blue-Chip Fund

Total Unrealised Appreciation/Depreciation – 05/05/X6 (Today)		€10,220
Total Unrealised Appreciation/Depreciation – 04/05/X6 (Yesterday)	€7,800	
Add (or Subtract) any Increases (or Decreases) in Unrealised Appreciation/Depreciation during the Day (Sales of Equities)	€0	€7,800
Daily Change in Unrealised Appreciation/Depreciation		€2,420

Yesterday, 04/05/X6, the portfolio had gained €7,800 since it was originally purchased (figure provided in the information to this example). By today, 05/05/X6, this had increased to a total gain since the portfolio was originally purchased of €10,220 (as calculated in the solution in Example 5.2b). Thus, over the day of 05/05/X6, the portfolio gained €2,420. It is this amount that should be recorded.

Summary of Solution to Example 5.2a, Example 5.2b and Example 5.2c

This may appear quite tedious but once a few examples have been attempted, it is amazing how quickly the concepts behind this calculation can be mastered. Use the template in Table 5.4 as a guide (the figures are taken from the previous examples).

---

[17] In the previous example, 5.2b, the total unrealised appreciation/depreciation since the equities were originally purchased was calculated at €10,220. The current discussion centres around how much of that €10,220 gain was generated today.

Table 5.4: A Template for Calculating the Daily Unrealised Appreciation/Depreciation

Market Value of the Portfolio (today) – Step 1		€564,720	Example 5.2a
Less: Cost of the Portfolio (today) – Step 2		€554,500	Example 5.2b
Total Unrealised Appreciation/Depreciation – Step 2		€10,220	Example 5.2b
Unrealised Appreciation/Depreciation from Yesterday – Step 3	€7,800		Example 5.2c
+/– Movements in Unrealised Appreciation/Depreciation – Step 3	€0	€7,800	Example 5.2c
Unrealised Appreciation/Depreciation for Today – Step 3		€2,420	Example 5.2c

5.5.2: Daily Valuation – The Accounting Entry

The difficult aspect of the daily valuation is now complete; all that remains is to consider the accounting entry. The accounting entry for the daily valuation will always be the same but will depend on whether the value of the fund's portfolio is increasing or decreasing. The logic of the transaction for an unrealised appreciation will be outlined; the only difference in the case of an unrealised depreciation is that the entries are reversed.

As stated earlier, any change in the value of the fund's portfolio will be kept in a separate account: unrealised appreciation/depreciation on investments (often shortened to 'unreal app/depr'). This makes it easier for investors to appraise the performance of the fund from the perspective of the current portfolio. Table 5.5 shows the relationship between the different portfolio asset accounts.

Table 5.5: Relationship between Portfolio Asset Accounts

Investments at Cost A/c	Keeps track of the cost of all the holdings in the portfolio
Unrealised Appreciation/Depreciation A/c	Keeps track of the movement in the value of the holdings in the portfolio
Inv at Cost A/c + Unreal App/Depr A/c	Adding both accounts together gives the current market value of the portfolio

As the value of the fund's portfolio increases then the assets of the fund are increasing. Thus, debit the unrealised appreciation/depreciation account in the statement of net assets (recall the rule: debit asset and expense accounts with increases).

The other side of the transaction is to an account in the statement of operations. If the value of the portfolio is increasing then the fund is generating 'profits' (often called 'gains') for its investors. It is also worthwhile to keep track of the total profits/gains that the fund has made over a period for its investors – we will call this account 'gains/losses on investments'. This is an income/gain type account. As the value of the portfolio increases, the income of the fund also increases ⇒ credit gains/losses on investments in the statement of operations (recall the rule: credit liability and income accounts with increases).

Using the figures from Example 5.2:

- Dr unrealised appreciation/depreciation   €2,420
- Cr gains/losses on investments   €2,420

Or – for the spreadsheet approach:

- Increase unrealised appreciation/depreciation, an asset, by €2,420 (in the statement of net assets).
- Increase gains/losses on investments, a gain/income, by €2,240 (in the statement of operations).

If the portfolio had lost value over the period then the entries would just be reversed:

- Dr gains/losses on investments   €X
- Cr unrealised appreciation/depreciation   €X

Or – for the spreadsheet approach:

- Decrease gains/losses on investments, a gain/income, by €X.
- Increase unrealised appreciation/depreciation, an asset, by €X.

Example 5.3: Calculating the Daily Movement in the Value of a Fund's Portfolio

Consider a fund with a portfolio as shown in Table 5.6a.

Table 5.6a: Irish Blue-Chip Fund – Closing Prices

Share	Quantity	Cost	Commission	Closing Price 05/05/X6	Closing Price 06/05/X6	Closing Price 07/05/X6	Closing Price 08/05/X6
AIB	10,000	€19.70	€400	€20.50	€20.64	€20.80	€21.20
Bank of Ireland	5,000	€14.44	€300	€14.56	€14.50	€14.74	€14.96
Ryanair	8,000	€7.50	€100	€7.45	€7.40	€7.25	€7.10

(Continued)

Table 5.6a: *(Continued)*

Share	Quantity	Cost	Commission	Closing Price 05/05/X6	Closing Price 06/05/X6	Closing Price 07/05/X6	Closing Price 08/05/X6
Waterford Wedgwood	60,000	€0.05	€100	€0.05	€0.05	€0.04	€0.04
Grafton Group	2,000	€10.65	€400	€10.61	€10.69	€10.75	€10.72
Irish Continental Group	5,000	€24.50	€100	€25.00	€25.20	€25.45	€25.60
C & C	11,000	€7.00	€100	€7.10	€7.15	€7.20	€5.50

This is the same fund from Example 5.2. The earlier calculations have yielded the following results at the end of 05/05/X6:

- Investments at cost account   €554,500   (dr balance)
- Unrealised appreciation/   €10,220   (dr balance)
  depreciation account

Requirements:

For each day (06/05/X6, 07/05/X6, 08/05/X6):

1. Calculate the market value of the portfolio.
2. Calculate the total cost of the portfolio (the investments at cost account).
3. Calculate the movement in unrealised appreciation/depreciation.
4. Record the entries to give effect to the movement in the value of the portfolio.

Show the entries and calculate the daily balance on the following accounts:

- Investments at cost account
- Unrealised appreciation/depreciation account

Note: during the period in question the fund did not purchase or sell any investments.

Solution 5.3: Calculating the Daily Movement in the Value of a Fund's Portfolio

Taking each day in turn, begin with 06/05/X6.

1. Market value of the portfolio – see Table 5.6b.

Table 5.6b: Market Value of the Irish Blue-Chip Fund on 06/05/X6

Share	Quantity	Closing Price 06/05/X6	Market Value
AIB	10,000	€20.64	€206,400
Bank of Ireland	5,000	€14.50	€72,500
Ryanair	8,000	€7.40	€59,200
Waterford Wedgwood	60,000	€0.05	€3,000
Grafton Group	2,000	€10.69	€21,380
Irish Continental Group	5,000	€25.20	€126,000
C & C	11,000	€7.15	€78,650
Total			*€567,130*

2. Total cost of the portfolio on 06/05/X6:
As there were no additions or disposals since 05/05/X6, the cost of the portfolio remains at €554,500.

3. Movement in unrealised appreciation/depreciation for 06/05/X6 – first calculate the total unrealised appreciation/depreciation and then compare this with the total from yesterday (05/05/X6) – see Table 5.6c.

Table 5.6c: Daily Unrealised Appreciation/Depreciation for the Irish Blue-Chip Fund for 06/05/X6

Market Value of the Portfolio (today, 06/05/X6) – Step 1		€567,130
Less: Cost of the Portfolio (today, 06/05/X6) – Step 2		€554,500
Total Unrealised Appreciation/Depreciation – Step 2		€12,630
Unrealised Appreciation/Depreciation from Yesterday – Step 3	€10,220	
+/– Movements in Unrealised Appreciation/Depreciation – Step 3	€0	€10,220
Unrealised Appreciation/Depreciation for Today		€2,410

The portfolio has now gained €12,630; this compares with total gains of €10,220 from 05/05/X6. From this it can be deduced that the portfolio has gained €2,410 during the day.

4. The accounting entry:
The portfolio is increasing in value:

- Dr unrealised appreciation/depreciation   €2,410
- Cr gains/losses on investments   €2,410

Or – for the spreadsheet approach:

- Increase unrealised appreciation/depreciation, an asset, by €2,410.
- Increase gains/losses on investments, a gain/income, by €2,410.

Now moving to 07/05/X6:

1. Market value of the portfolio – see Table 5.6d.

Table 5.6d: Market Value of the Irish Blue-Chip Fund on 07/05/X6

Share	Quantity	Closing Price 07/05/X6	Market Value
AIB	10,000	€20.80	€208,000
Bank of Ireland	5,000	€14.74	€73,700
Ryanair	8,000	€7.25	€58,000
Waterford Wedgwood	60,000	€0.04	€2,400
Grafton Group	2,000	€10.75	€21,500
Irish Continental Group	5,000	€25.45	€127,250
C & C	11,000	€7.20	€79,200
Total			*€570,050*

2. Total cost of the portfolio on 07/05/X6:
As there were no additions or disposals since 06/05/X6, the cost of the portfolio remains at €554,500.

3. Movement in unrealised appreciation/depreciation for 07/05/X6 – first calculate the total unrealised appreciation/depreciation and then compare this with the total from yesterday (06/05/X6) – see Table 5.6e.

Table 5.6e: Daily Unrealised Appreciation/Depreciation for the Irish Blue-Chip Fund for 07/05/X6

Market Value of the Portfolio (today, 07/05/X6) – Step 1		€570,050
Less: Cost of the Portfolio (today, 07/05/X6) – Step 2		€554,500
Total Unrealised Appreciation/Depreciation – Step 2		€15,550
Unrealised Appreciation/Depreciation from Yesterday – Step 3	€12,630	
+/– Movements in Unrealised Appreciation/Depreciation – Step 3	€0	€12,630
Unrealised Appreciation/Depreciation for Today		€2,920

The portfolio has now gained €15,550; this compares with total gains of €12,630 from 06/05/X6. From this it can be deduced that the portfolio has gained €2,920 during the day.

4. The accounting entry:
The portfolio is increasing in value:

- Dr unrealised appreciation/depreciation   €2,920
- Cr gains/losses on investments   €2,920

Or – for the spreadsheet approach:

- Increase unrealised appreciation/depreciation, an asset, by €2,920.
- Increase gains/losses on investments, a gain/income, by €2,920.

Now moving to 08/05/X6:

1. Market value of the portfolio – see Table 5.6f.

Table 5.6f: Market Value of the Irish Blue-Chip Fund on 08/05/X6

Share	Quantity	Closing Price 08/05/X6	Market Value
AIB	10,000	€21.20	€212,000
Bank of Ireland	5,000	€14.96	€74,800
Ryanair	8,000	€7.10	€56,800
Waterford Wedgwood	60,000	€0.04	€2,400
Grafton Group	2,000	€10.72	€21,440
Irish Continental Group	5,000	€25.60	€128,000
C & C	11,000	€5.50	€60,500
Total			€555,940

2. Total cost of the portfolio on 08/05/X6:
As there were no additions or disposals since 07/05/X6, the cost of the portfolio remains at €554,500.

3. Movement in unrealised appreciation/depreciation for 08/05/X6 – first calculate the total unrealised appreciation/depreciation and then compare this with the total from yesterday (07/05/X6) – see Table 5.6g.

Table 5.6g: Daily Unrealised Appreciation/Depreciation for the Irish Blue-Chip Fund for 08/05/X6

Market Value of the Portfolio (today, 08/05/X6) – Step 1		€555,940
Less: Cost of the Portfolio (today, 08/05/X6) – Step 2		€554,500
Total Unrealised Appreciation/Depreciation – Step 2		€1,440
Unrealised Appreciation/Depreciation from Yesterday – Step 3	€15,550	
+/– Movements in Unrealised Appreciation/Depreciation – Step 3	€0	€15,550
Unrealised Appreciation/Depreciation for Today		−€14,110

Over 08/05/X6 the portfolio lost value. Although the market value of the portfolio is greater than the cost of the portfolio, this differential has fallen dramatically. The portfolio has now gained just €1,440 – this compares with total gains of €15,550 from 07/05/X6. From this it can be deduced that the portfolio has lost €14,110 during the day.

4. The accounting entry:

- Dr gains/losses on investments   €14,110
- Cr unrealised appreciation/depreciation   €14,110

Or – for the spreadsheet approach:

- Decrease gains/losses on investments, a gain/income, by €14,110.
- Increase unrealised appreciation/depreciation, an asset, by €14,110.

Recording the Entries and Calculating the Daily Balance

Figure 5.6 shows the entries to the 'T' accounts for these transactions.

A final check: the total of the investments at cost account and the unrealised appreciation/deprecation account should equal the market value of the portfolio for that day (see Table 5.7).

5.5.3: Daily Valuation – Control Issues

In the previous examples, the calculations were performed manually. In most practice-based situations, these calculations are carried out by the fund accounting system: the prices are downloaded automatically from a pricing service (such as Bloomberg or Reuters) and the unrealised gain/loss is then computed.

It would be a mistake to accept the output of the system without question. The most common source of error in the calculation of daily NAVs per share is often connected with the daily valuation of the fund's investment portfolio. As a result, a number of checks should be performed – these can vary from fund to fund but the

Figure 5.6: Entering the Irish Blue-Chip Fund's Transactions in the 'T' Accounts

dr   Investments at Cost A/c   cr

Date	Description	€	Date	Description	€
06/05	Opening Bal	554,500			
06/05	Additions	0	06/05	Disposals	0
			06/05	Balance	554,500
		554,500			554,500
06/05	Closing Bal	554,500			
07/05	Additions	0	07/05	Disposals	0
			07/05	Balance	554,500
		554,500			554,500
07/05	Closing Bal	554,500			
08/05	Additions	0	08/05	Disposals	0
			08/05	Balance	554,500
		554,500			554,500
08/05	Closing Bal	554,500			

dr   Unrealised Appreciation/Depreciation A/c   cr

Date	Description	€	Date	Description	€
06/05	Opening Bal	10,220			
06/05	Gain on Inv	2,410			
			06/05	Balance	12,630
		12,630			12,630
06/05	Closing Bal	12,630			
07/05	Gain on Inv	2,920			
			07/05	Balance	15,550
		15,550			15,550
07/05	Closing Bal	15,550			
			08/05	Loss on Inv	14,110
			08/05	Balance	1,440
		15,550			15,550
08/05	Closing Bal	1,440			

objective is to ensure you are confident in the reliability of the information produced by the system.

Any errors should be investigated in detail – reassurance will need to be obtained on whether the error is a once-off event in relation to a single pricing issue or if there is a more endemic problem with the specification of the system or how the

Table 5.7: Reconciliation of Portfolio Asset Accounts to Market Value

	05/05/X6	06/05/X6	07/05/X6	08/05/X6
Investments at Cost A/c	€554,500	€554,500	€554,500	€554,500
Unrealised Appreciation/Depreciation A/c	€10,220	€12,630	€15,550	€1,440
Total	*€564,720*	*€567,130*	*€570,050*	*€555,940*
Market Value of Portfolio	€564,720	€567,130	€570,050	€555,940
Difference	*€0*	*€0*	*€0*	*€0*

basic information is obtained. The checks that are performed will only point to the likelihood of an error. A subsequent investigation will confirm whether a mistake has been made and the source of the mistake.

The types of checks that are undertaken include:

- Checking the movement in the share price of each individual holding in the portfolio: if the share price fluctuates by a preset percentage (this will be set by the fund administrator) then this should trigger an investigation.
- Checking the overall movement in the portfolio: if the movement deviates from a relevant benchmark by a preset percentage then this should trigger an investigation.
- Reconciling the holdings in the portfolio to those of the custodian. Remember that the custodian holds the shares on behalf of the fund. Their list should equal that of the fund accountant, except for the timing differences surrounding additions, disposals and corporate actions. Any unexplained differences (or persistent differences) should be investigated.
- Undertaking periodic reviews to ensure that the correct securities are being valued. Some companies are quoted on different markets and have different types of shares; all types of shares have a unique identifier called the CUSIP (generally for US shares) or SEDOL (for UK and RoI shares). These will help in this regard.[18]

This is not an exhaustive list of checks. Other checks are performed depending on the nature of the fund, the type of accounting system in operation and the potential for misstatement. In the previous example, a check was performed to provide assurance on the accuracy of the calculations. The total of the investments at cost account was added to the unrealised appreciation/deprecation account to

---

[18] CUSIP is short for Committee on Uniform Security Identification Procedures; SEDOL stands for Stock Exchange Daily Official List.

check if it equalled the market value of the portfolio. This type of check will only identify some arithmetic errors and has only limited power. It will not identify any pricing errors. It is, however, beneficial to carry out the check due to the emphasis on manual processing and calculations.

The most common sources of error are pricing issues, stock splits,[19] dividends and the impact of news stories and rumours. These will all potentially impact on the price of a share; it is equally important to investigate situations where a share price has increased unexpectedly as decreased unexpectedly.

Example 5.4: Investigation of Portfolio Movements

Consider Example 5.3. The fund operates a 5 per cent threshold, any movement of +/−5% or more on an individual share should be investigated. The fund is benchmarked against the ISEQ index and the investigation threshold is +/−1%. Thus, if the portfolio movement exceeds the index movement by more than 1 per cent then this should be investigated. Values for the index are provided below:

05/05/X6	4,400
06/05/X6	4,428
07/05/X6	4,437
08/05/X6	4,377

Requirement:

Perform any checks considered to be appropriate to determine if there are any items that require further investigation.

Solution 5.4: Investigation of Portfolio Movements

Consider the individual share price movements – the increase or decrease in share prices as a percentage of the previous day's prices. See Table 5.8 for the share price movements of the Irish Blue-Chip Fund.

Table 5.8: Individual Share Price Movements in the Irish Blue-Chip Fund

Share	06/05/X6 % Change	07/05/X6 % Change	08/05/X6 % Change
AIB	1%	1%	2%
Bank of Ireland	0%	2%	1%
Ryanair	−1%	−2%	−2%
			(Continued)

---

[19] Stock splits will be explained in Section 6.6.

Table 5.8: *(Continued)*

Share	06/05/X6 % Change	07/05/X6 % Change	08/05/X6 % Change
Waterford Wedgwood	0%	−20%	0%
Grafton Group	1%	1%	0%
Irish Continental Group	1%	1%	1%
C & C	1%	1%	−24%

Two movements require further investigation: Waterford Wedgwood on 07/05/X6 and C & C on 08/05/X6:

- The decrease in Waterford Wedgwood share price can probably be accepted as legitimate because while the percentage fall is large it only represents a 1c movement.
- The decrease in C & C would require further investigation – check if C & C paid an unusually large dividend, had a share/stock split, announced some bad news or had another event that could explain this large fall in their share price.

Consider the overall movement in the portfolio relative to the index benchmark (see Table 5.9).

Table 5.9: **Overall Movements in the Irish Blue-Chip Fund Portfolio**

Date	Opening Market Value of Portfolio	Closing Market Value of Portfolio	% Change in Market Value of Portfolio	Opening ISEQ	Closing ISEQ	Percentage Change in ISEQ	Percentage Difference Relative to ISEQ
06/05/X6	€564,720	€567,130	0.4%	4400	4428	0.6%	−0.2%
07/05/X6	€567,130	€570,050	0.5%	4428	4437	0.2%	0.3%
08/05/X6	€570,050	€555,940	−2.5%	4437	4377	−1.4%	−1.1%

As can be seen from the above analysis, the movements on 08/05/X6 require further investigation. On that day, the portfolio fell in value by 2.5 per cent but the ISEQ index only fell by 1.4 per cent. The excess poor performance of the fund is most likely down to the adverse movement in C & C. C & C comprise approximately 11 per cent of portfolio but do not make up 11 per cent of the ISEQ. The likelihood is that C & C accounts for a much smaller percentage of the ISEQ.[20]

---

[20] The exact weighting of any individual company in the ISEQ index can be found on www.ise.ie. The weights change over time. On 31 July 2009, C & C represented 1.80% of the ISEQ.

Thus, the Irish Blue-Chip Fund is overweight on C & C shares relative to the index; hence, a fall in C & C shares will have a disproportionate impact on the fund as compared to the index. So, if the C & C movement can be explained (from the previous analysis) then this should also help to explain this difference.

(For ease of analysis, the portfolio of the fund in the example does not fully reflect the ISEQ – in order to mirror the ISEQ, over 30 holdings in the portfolio would be required. This would be difficult to manage in the context of a manual example. The fact that the portfolio is not fully diversified will explain a lot of the differences between the portfolio performance and the index performance.)

5.5.4: Accounting for Daily Valuation – Summary

There are two aspects to the valuation of the portfolio of an investment fund.

1. Calculating the unrealised appreciation/depreciation (see Table 5.10).

Table 5.10:   Approach for Calculating the Daily Gain/Loss (Unrealised Appreciation/Depreciation)

Market Value of the Portfolio (today) – Step 1		€564,720
Less: Cost of the Portfolio (today) – Step 2		€554,500
Total Unrealised Appreciation/Depreciation – Step 2		€10,220
Unrealised Appreciation/Depreciation from Yesterday – Step 3	€7,800	
+/– Movements in Unrealised Appreciation/Depreciation – Step 3	€0	€7,800
Unrealised Appreciation/Depreciation for Today – Step 3		€2,420

2. Recording the unrealised appreciation/depreciation:
If the value of the portfolio is increasing:

- Dr unrealised appreciation/depreciation   €X
- Cr gains/losses on investments   €X

If the value of the portfolio is decreasing:

- Dr gains/losses on investments   €X
- Cr unrealised appreciation/depreciation   €X

The accounts involved are the same; the entries are reversed for a fall in value. Now try Question 5.9.7.

5.6: ACCOUNTING FOR THE SALE OF EQUITIES

Recall the purchase of equities. This transaction generally takes three days to settle. A similar situation persists when selling shares. This will impact on the accounting for the sale of equities. The fund accountant will record the sale of the equities immediately (this could be on TD + 1 because it may take a day for the information to reach the fund accountant). Then, on TD + 3 the fund accountant will record the settlement – on that day the fund gets the money it is due and makes the delivery of the equities to the new owner.

This time delay can give rise to some differences between the fund accountant's records and the custodian's records. The custodian may not record the disposed shares until they have been delivered (the settlement date) but the fund accountant removes the shares from the portfolio on the date they are sold (the trade date). Regular reconciliations will need to be performed between the fund accountant's records and the custodian's records to ensure that any differences can be explained by these types of differences. Differences that are unexplained or differences that do not resolve themselves after a few days should be thoroughly investigated – these could be symptomatic of failed trades or errors.

5.6.1: Recording the Sale of Equities – Calculating the Figures

There are a number of issues that arise on the sale of equities:

- Calculate the proceeds.
- Identify the equities sold.
- Determine the original cost of the equities sold.
- Determine the realised gain/loss on the equities sold.

Calculate the Proceeds

This is relatively straightforward – it is the number of shares sold multiplied by the share price less any fees, commissions and taxes.

Example 5.5a: Disposal of Equities

On 04/10/X4, B.I.G. Fund sold 10,000 shares in Elan for €22.50 each; the commission charged in the transaction is €2,500. The settlement date is 07/10/X4.
    Calculate the proceeds of the sale.

Solution 5.5a: Disposal of Equities

Amount that will be received by the fund will be $10,000 \times €22.50 − €2,500 = €222,500$.

Identify the Equities Sold

Often a fund will have a number of holdings of shares in a company that were purchased on different periods at different prices. It will be necessary to identify which shares are being sold. A number of approaches can be used:

- FIFO = First In First Out – the oldest shares of the particular company in the portfolio are sold first.
- LIFO = Last In First Out – the newest shares of the particular company in the portfolio are sold first.
- Weighted average = shares being sold represent an average of all those shares of that company in the portfolio.
- Less common methods
  - highest cost – the fund disposes of the shares of the particular company in the portfolio with the highest cost.
  - lowest cost – the fund disposes of the shares of the particular company in the portfolio with the lowest cost.
  - specific identification – check which shares are actually sold and use their original cost.

Of the different methods, the most common is the FIFO method – practically all funds use this approach. The method used may be outlined in the fund documentation (the prospectus or the trust deed/articles).

Example 5.5b: Disposal of Equities

Using the same basic information:
On 04/10/X4, B.I.G. Fund sold 10,000 shares in Elan for €22.50 each; the commission charged in the transaction is €2,500. The settlement date is 07/10/X4.

The fund has a number of holdings in Elan, details of which are provided in Table 5.11a.

Table 5.11a: Shares in Elan held by B.I.G. Fund

Company	Trade Date	Quantity	Cost	Commission
Elan	01/02/X1	4,000	€10.50	€1,000
Elan	01/02/X2	3,000	€11.75	€1,200
Elan	01/02/X3	5,000	€12.50	€1,500
Elan	01/02/X4	6,000	€14.90	€1,800

Requirement:

Identify the shares that were sold, the fund uses the FIFO method of identification.

Solution 5.5b: Disposal of Equities

The oldest shares are sold first, so the batch purchased on 01/02/X1 is disposed of first. This batch is comprised of 4,000 shares; 6,000 shares to be sold still remain. Then the second oldest batch (originally purchased on 01/02/X2) is sold – this batch is made up of 3,000 shares; 3,000 shares to be sold still remain. The third oldest batch is then considered. This batch (originally purchased on 01/02/X3) comprises 5,000 shares, of which 3,000 shares are being disposed; the remaining 2,000 shares are unsold. See Table 5.11b.

Table 5.11b: Shares in Elan sold by B.I.G. Fund

Company	Trade Date	Quantity	Sold	Remaining
Elan	01/02/X1	4,000	4,000	0
Elan	01/02/X2	3,000	3,000	0
Elan	01/02/X3	5,000	3,000	2,000
Elan	01/02/X4	6,000	0	6,000
Total		18,000	10,000	8,000

Determine the Original Cost of the Equities Sold

Once the actual shares sold are identified then the cost of those shares will need to be calculated. Remember that the cost includes the commissions and fees paid on purchase. The calculation gets difficult where only part of a batch was sold (the 01/02/X3 batch in the previous example). An apportionment will need to be made in these circumstances. This apportionment will be based on the shares sold relative to the total number of shares in the batch.

Example 5.5c: Disposal of Equities

Using the same basic information:

On 04/10/X4, B.I.G. Fund sold 10,000 shares in Elan for €22.50 each; the commission charged in the transaction is €2,500. The settlement date is 07/10/X4.

The fund has a number of holdings in Elan, details of which are given in Table 5.11a.

Requirement:

Identify the shares that were sold and calculate the cost of the shares sold; the fund uses the FIFO method of identification.

Solution 5.5c: Disposal of Equities

The 'total cost' is the (quantity × cost) + commissions.

The entire first batch (01/02/X1) was sold – hence the full cost is included under column 'cost sold'; similarly for the second batch (01/02/X2). However, from the previous example (Example 5.5b), only 3,000 shares of the 5,000 from the third batch shares were sold. Thus, the total cost now needs to be apportioned – the total cost of the batch is €64,000. 3,000 shares of 5,000 shares were sold; hence €64,000 × 3,000/5,000 gives €38,400; the balance of the cost is remaining. None of the final batch (01/02/X4) was sold. See Table 5.11c.

Table 5.11c: Cost of Shares in Elan sold by B.I.G. Fund

Company	Trade Date	Quantity	Cost	Commission	Total Cost	Cost Sold	Cost Remaining
Elan	01/02/X1	4,000	€10.50	€1,000	€43,000	€43,000	€0
Elan	01/02/X2	3,000	€11.75	€1,200	€36,450	€36,450	€0
Elan	01/02/X3	5,000	€12.50	€1,500	€64,000	€38,400	€25,600
Elan	01/02/X4	6,000	€14.90	€1,800	€91,200	€0	€91,200
Total		18,000			€234,650	€117,850	€116,800

The total cost of the shares sold is €117,850 (or the total of the 'cost sold' column).

Determine the Gain/Loss on the Equities Sold

This is the last step in the process. The proceeds are known and the cost is known. Hence the gain (or loss) is just the difference between the two.

Example 5.5d: Disposal of Equities

Using the information given already and the results to date for Example 5.5, calculate the gain/loss on disposal.

Solution 5.5d: Disposal of Equities

Table 5.11d shows the gain or loss on the disposal.

Table 5.11d: The Gain or Loss on the Disposal of Elan Shares

Proceeds (Example 5.5a)	€222,500
Cost of Shares Sold (Example 5.5c)	€117,850
Gain/Loss on Disposal	€104,650

5.6.2: Recording the Sale of Equities – The Accounting Entries – Trade Date

Now that the figures have been calculated the next stage will be to record these in the accounting system.

Firstly, the fund is due to receive money (€222,500 in the example) in three days' time. It makes good sense to track this amount in an account called 'investments sold receivable'. This account represents money that the fund is owed on investments that it has sold but has not yet settled. It is an asset as the fund is owed money and it is increasing; thus, it is a debit.

⇒ Debit investments sold receivable with the proceeds.

On the other side of the transaction, shares which originally cost €117,850 are leaving the portfolio. Thus, one of the assets in the portfolio is decreasing (soon to be converted into cash). The investments at cost account is where the cost of the shares was originally recorded when purchased. Hence it makes sense that this should be the account to be used when shares leave the portfolio. As this account only records cost then only the cost of the shares sold will be removed from here. Investments at cost, an asset, is decreasing; thus, it is a credit.

⇒ Credit investments at cost with the original cost of the shares sold.

However, this only makes up part of the transaction (the debits do not equal the credits). The difference is the gain/loss on the disposal. The unrealised gains which were previously recognised in the unrealised appreciation/depreciation account are also leaving the portfolio – they are being converted into cash (in three days' time). In the case of a gain, unrealised appreciation/depreciation, an asset, is decreasing; thus, it is a credit.

⇒ Credit unrealised appreciation/depreciation with the gain on the sale (€104,650 in the example).

Notice that, even though a gain is made on the disposal, all of the above transactions are to accounts that appear in the statement of net assets (the balance sheet). None of the transactions involve the statement of operations (the income statement). This is because the gain has already been recognised over the previous days', months and years as the price of the shares increased over time.

Some funds do draw a distinction between gains that are realised and unrealised – this does not have any impact on the NAV per share so, for the purposes of this book, it will not be specifically addressed. In any case, a quick reallocation of gains can be made for reporting purposes if needs be. This is not an onerous calculation and with a little experience it is not difficult to reason it out.

When selling equities where gains are being realised:

- Dr investments sold receivable   €222,500
- Cr investments at cost   €117,850
- Cr unrealised appreciation/depreciation   €104,650

Or – for the spreadsheet approach:

- Increase investments sold receivable, an asset, by €222,500.
- Decrease investments at cost, an asset, by €117,850.
- Decrease unrealised appreciation/depreciation, an asset, by €104,650.

The only difference when the shares are sold at a loss is that the entry into the unrealised appreciation/depreciation account is reversed. Let's assume that shares which originally cost €25,000 are subsequently sold for €21,500, realising a loss of €3,500 (this loss would have been recognised in the NAV per share of the preceding days, weeks and months).

When selling equities where losses are being realised:

- Dr investments sold receivable   €21,500
- Cr investments at cost   €25,000
- Dr unrealised appreciation/depreciation   €3,500

Or – for the spreadsheet approach:

- Increase investments sold receivable, an asset, by €21,500.
- Decrease investments at cost, an asset, by €25,000.
- Increase unrealised appreciation/depreciation, an asset, by €3,500.

This may appear counterintuitive – why should the unrealised appreciation/depreciation account increase when shares are sold at a loss? Remember that the unrealised appreciation/depreciation account represents the gains and losses from all of the holdings in the funds portfolio. The holdings with unrealised losses cause this account to be less than it would otherwise be. So when these loss-making holdings are sold, it has the effect of removing some of the 'deadweights' in the account, causing the account to rise. Losses which were previously reducing the unrealised appreciation/depreciation account are now no longer in the portfolio. Hence, the account increases.

This little quirk can give rise to some unusual behaviour by investment managers around the financial reporting dates of a fund. To give the portfolio an appearance of stronger performance, some investment managers sell off loss-making holdings. This will not impact on the NAV per share (except for the trading costs involved but these are relatively small), but it can show the investment manager in a better light. If an investor was to scan the portfolio of the fund all the shares would be showing gains and none would be showing losses. This would give the impression that the investment managers are excelling in their role. This practice is called window dressing. Try a search on any search engine for the term 'investment fund window dressing'; the extent of the results will indicate how widespread the practice is believed to be.

5.6.3: Recording the Sale of Equities – The Accounting Entries – Settlement

A number of days after the transaction (the trade date) the money will be received. In the case of Example 5.5, this is TD + 3, i.e. three days after the trade date.

When the money is received then the cash in the fund goes up. Cash is an asset and it is increasing; thus, it is a debit.

⇒ Debit the cash account.

The other side of the transaction is the fund is no longer owed any money by the new owner of the shares. When the original transaction was recorded the amount was put into an account called investments sold receivable – this represented the fact that the fund was owed money by the new owner (in effect, the cash will be paid through a broker). This debt has now been settled by the new owner. Thus, investments sold receivable, which is an asset, is decreasing, making a credit.

⇒ Credit investments sold receivable.

Using the figures from Example 5.5, record the receipt of the cash:

- Dr cash   €222,500
- Cr investments sold receivable   €222,500

Or – for the spreadsheet approach:

- Increase cash, an asset, by €222,500.
- Decrease investments sold receivable, an asset, €222,500.

Accounting for the sale of equities is a complex transaction. Try to understand the logic behind it; it will not be any different in the other examples that will be addressed, just the numbers will change.

Now try Questions 5.9.8 and 5.9.9.

5.6.4: Interaction of Purchases and Disposals with the Daily Movement Calculation

As the fund purchases and sells investments, this will impact on the calculation of the daily movement on the unrealised appreciation/depreciation account. Consider the following example:

Example 5.6: The Food Fundamentals Fund

On 01/06/X6 the fund had holdings as shown in Table 5.12a.

Table 5.12a: Holdings of the Food Fundamentals Fund

Company	Trade Date	Quantity	Cost	Commission	Total Cost	31/05/X6 Share Price	31/05/X6 Market Value
Glanbia	03/07/X4	15,000	€4.70	€1,200	€71,700	€5.20	€78,000
Greencore	04/07/X4	30,000	€3.50	€2,400	€107,400	€3.80	€114,000
Fyffes	06/05/X5	36,000	€1.10	€1,800	€41,400	€1.30	€46,800
Danone	04/12/X5	5,000	€35.00	€5,000	€180,000	€38.10	€190,500
Parmalat	02/09/X5	19,000	€2.50	€850	€48,350	€1.90	€36,100
Total					*€448,850*		*€465,400*

Recalculate the 'total cost' column and the 'market value' column to check that it is correct (this is not a trick; it is just good practice).

The difference between the market value and the total cost columns gives the total unrealised appreciation/depreciation on 31/05/X6: €465,400 less €448,850 gives €16,550. The following balances exist in the statement of net assets:

- Investments at cost account   €448,650   (dr balance)
- Unrealised appreciation/depreciation account   €16,550   (dr balance)

During 01/06/X6 the following transactions occurred:

- 5,000 shares in Glanbia were sold for €5.25 each, commission of €500, settlement date on 04/06/X6.
- 7,000 shares in Kerry Group were purchased for €18.10 each, commission of €1,400, settlement on 04/06/X6.

Table 5.12b shows the following official closing prices at the end of 01/06/X6.

Table 5.12b: Closing Prices for the Food Fundamentals Fund's Holdings on 01/06/X6

Company	01/06/X6 Share Price
Glanbia	€5.30
Greencore	€3.90
Fyffes	€1.25
Danone	€38.40
Parmalat	€1.95
Kerry	€18.20

Requirements:

- Record the sale of shares in Glanbia.
- Record the purchase of shares in Kerry Group.
- Record the movement in the unrealised appreciation/depreciation account for the day.
- Show the investments at cost account and the unrealised appreciation/depreciation account.

Solution 5.6: The Food Fundamentals Fund

Recording the sale of shares in Glanbia:

1. Sales proceeds = $(5,000 \times €5.25) - €500 = €25,750$
2. Identify the shares sold: just one batch in the portfolio but not all of that batch was sold; 5,000 shares out of the batch of 15,000 were sold.
3. Determine the cost of shares sold = $€71,700 \times 5,000/15,000 = €23,900$
4. Calculate the gain on the sale = €25,750 (sales proceeds) − €23,900 (cost) = €1,850

- Dr investments sold receivable   €25,750
- Cr investments at cost   €23,900
- Cr unrealised appreciation/depreciation   €1,850

Or – for the spreadsheet approach:

- Increase investments sold receivable, an asset, by €25,750.
- Decrease investments at cost, an asset, by €23,900.
- Decrease unrealised appreciation/depreciation, an asset, by €1,850.

Recording the purchase of shares in Kerry:

Calculate the cost of the shares = $(7,000 \times €18.10) + €1,400 = €128,100$

- Dr investments at cost   €128,100
- Cr investments purchased payable   €128,100

Or – for the spreadsheet approach:

- Increase investments at cost, an asset, by €128,100.
- Increase investments purchased payable, a liability, by €128,100.

Note: commission increases the cost of purchasing shares; hence, they are added to the cost. Commission reduces the proceeds from the sale of shares; hence, it is subtracted from the proceeds.

Recording the movement in the unrealised appreciation/depreciation account:

1. Calculate the market value of the portfolio at the end of 01/06/X6 (see Table 5.12c).

Table 5.12c: Market Value of the Food Fundamentals Fund's Portfolio on 01/06/X6

Company	01/06/X6 Share Price	01/06/X6 Quantity	01/06/X6 Market Value
Glanbia	€5.30	10,000	€53,000
Greencore	€3.90	30,000	€117,000
Fyffes	€1.25	36,000	€45,000
Danone	€38.40	5,000	€192,000
Parmalat	€1.95	19,000	€37,050
Kerry	€18.20	7,000	€127,400
Total			€571,450

Note that the new shares purchased in Kerry have been added to the portfolio, while the shares sold in Glanbia have been removed (leaving just 10,000 Glanbia shares in the portfolio).

2. Calculate the cost of the portfolio as at the end of 01/06/X6. This can be done by calculating the cost of each holding in the portfolio or by taking yesterday's cost and adjusting for the cost of purchases and sales during the current day. The latter approach is often much faster and will be used in the solution to this example (see Table 5.12d).

Table 5.12d: Cost of the Food Fundamentals Fund's Portfolio at end of 01/06/X6

Total Cost at End of 31/05/X6	€448,850
+ Cost of Shares Purchased during 01/06/X6 (Kerry)	€128,100
– Cost of Shares Sold during 01/06/X6 (Glanbia)	(€23,900)
Total Cost at End of 01/06/X6	€553,050

3. Fill in the daily valuation table (see Table 5.12e).

Table 5.12e: Daily Valuation Table for the Food Fundamentals Fund

Market Value of the Portfolio (today, 01/06/X6) – Step 1, Table 5.12c		€571,450
Less: Cost of the Portfolio (today, 01/06/X6) – Step 2, Table 5.12d		€553,050
Total Unrealised Appreciation/Depreciation – Step 2		€18,400
Unrealised Appreciation/Depreciation from Yesterday (31/05/X6)	€16,550	
– Gain Realised on Sale of Glanbia Shares	(€1,850)	€14,700
Unrealised Appreciation/Depreciation for Today		€3,700

The portfolio is increasing in value:

- Dr unrealised appreciation/depreciation   €3,700
- Cr gains/losses on investments   €3,700

Or – for the spreadsheet approach:

- Increase unrealised appreciation/depreciation, an asset, by €3,700
- Increase gains/losses on investments, a gain/income, by €3,700

This is where a change has occurred from the previous examples. In total, on 01/06/X6 the portfolio has gained €18,400. However, this is not the same portfolio as existed on 31/05/X6. In order to calculate the gain it is important to compare like with like. On 31/05/X6 the portfolio had gained €16,550; some of these gains relate to shares that have now been sold. The shares sold had gains of €1,850. This €1,850 is included in the €16,550 of gains from the previous day. Thus, in equivalent terms, the same portfolio as existed on the two days had gains of €14,700 at the end of 31/05/X6. This is the total unrealised gains from 31/05/X6 but doesn't include the gains on the Glanbia shares that have been sold.

Table 5.12f: Gain/Loss on Each Holding on 01/06/X6

Company	31/05/X6 Share Price	01/06/X6 Share Price	Difference	Quantity	Gain/Loss
Glanbia	€5.20	€5.30	€0.10	10,000	€1,000
Greencore	€3.80	€3.90	€0.10	30,000	€3,000
Fyffes	€1.30	€1.25	−€0.05	36,000	−€1,800
Danone	€38.10	€38.40	€0.30	5,000	€1,500
Parmalat	€1.90	€1.95	€0.05	19,000	€950
Kerry	€18.10	€18.20	€0.10	7,000	€700
Total Gain/Loss					*€5,350*
Add: Gain on Glanbia[1]					€250
Less: Commission on Sale of Glanbia[2]					(€500)
Less: Commission on Purchase of Kerry[3]					(€1,400)
Net Gain for the Day					*€3,700*

Notes: 1. Before the sale of the shares in Glanbia, those shares had increased from €5.20 (yesterday's share price) to €5.25 (transaction share price) – a gain of €0.05 × 5,000 shares, which gives €250.
2. This is the cost of the commission on the sale of Glanbia; this will reduce any gains made for the day.
3. Again the commission on the Kerry shares will reduce the gains for the day – the fund will not show a profit on the Kerry shares until the price rises above the cost plus commission.

Hence, yesterday the portfolio had gains of €14,700. The same portfolio has gained €18,400 by the end of today (06/01/X6). This gives a gain for the day of €3,700. This may appear long-winded; however, when there are 100 holdings in the portfolio, it reduces the calculations considerably. An alternative approach is to consider the gain on each holding as adjusted for some of the transactions that have occurred over the day – see Table 5.12f.

Try to imagine a portfolio of 100 holdings, with regular purchases and sales; this would be more long-winded than the approach already outlined.

The individual 'T' accounts are shown in Figure 5.7.

Figure 5.7:   The 'T' Accounts for the Food Fundamentals Fund

dr			Investments at Cost A/c			cr
Date	Description	€	Date	Description	€
1/6	Opening Bal	448,850	1/6	Disposals	23,900
1/6	Additions	128,100			
			1/6	Balance	553,050
		576,950			576,950
1/6	Closing Bal	553,050			

dr			Unrealised Appreciation/Depreciation A/c			cr
Date	Description	€	Date	Description	€
1/6	Opening Bal	16,550	1/6	Disposals	1,850
1/6	Gain on Inv	3,700			
			1/6	Balance	18,400
		20,250			20,250
1/6	Closing Bal	18,400			

Notice that the balance on the two accounts equals the market value of the portfolio (see Table 5.13).

Table 5.13:   Balancing the Accounts of the Food Fundamentals Fund

Investments at Cost	€553,050
Unrealised Appreciation/Depreciation	€18,400
Market Value of Portfolio as Calculated Earlier	€571,450

The key issue to note with this example is the impact that the purchase and sale have in the calculation of the daily valuation of the portfolio. As holdings are purchased and sold, remember to:

- Update the holdings in the portfolio so that the market value of the portfolio can be calculated.
- Update the investments at cost account so that the cost of the portfolio can be determined, which will allow the closing unrealised appreciation/ depreciation to be calculated.
- Adjust the opening unrealised appreciation/depreciation account so that the daily movement in the unrealised appreciation/depreciation account can be calculated.

Now try Question 5.9.10.

5.7: SUMMARY

From an accounting perspective, there are three aspects to accounting for equities: the purchase of equities, the sale of equities and the daily valuation of equities.

Recording the Purchase of Equities

- Calculate the cost (cost + commission).
- Record transaction and settlement as two separate transactions.

On the trade date record the purchase of the equities:

- Dr investments at cost   €X
- Cr investments purchased payable   €X

On the settlement date record the payment:

- Dr investments purchased payable   €X
- Cr cash   €X

Recording the Sale of Equities

- Calculate the proceeds (cost − commission).
- Identify the shares sold.
- Calculate the cost of the shares sold.
- Calculate the gain/loss on the shares sold.
- Record the transaction and the settlement as two separate transactions.

On trade date – selling equities where gains are being realised (X (proceeds) = Y (cost) + Z (gain)):

- Dr investments sold receivable   €X
- Cr investments at cost   €Y
- Cr unrealised appreciation/depreciation   €Z

On trade date – when selling equities where losses are being realised (X (proceeds) = Y (cost) − Z (loss)):

- Dr investments sold receivable   €X
- Cr investments at cost   €Y
- Dr unrealised appreciation/depreciation   €Z

On settlement date record the receipt:

- Dr cash   €X
- Cr investments sold receivable   €X

Recording the Daily Valuation

Calculate the amount of the movement in the unrealised appreciation/depreciation account using the approach given in Table 5.14.

Table 5.14: Approach for Calculating the Daily Gain/Loss (Unrealised Appreciation/Depreciation)

Market Value of the Portfolio (today) – Step 1		€A
Less: Cost of the Portfolio (today) – Step 2		−€B
Total Unrealised Appreciation/Depreciation – Step 2		€C
Less: Unrealised Appreciation/Depreciation from Yesterday – Step 3	€D	
+/− Movements in Unrealised Appreciation/Depreciation – Step 3	€E	−€F
Unrealised Appreciation/Depreciation for Today – Step 3		€G

For Table 5.14, 'D' can be found in the previous day's NAV per share calculation; 'E' is the gain (or loss) on the shares sold.

Recording the unrealised appreciation/depreciation:

- If the value of the portfolio is increasing:
  - Dr unrealised appreciation/depreciation   €G
  - Cr gains/losses on investments   €G
- If the value of the portfolio is decreasing:
  - Dr gains/losses on investments   €G
  - Cr unrealised appreciation/depreciation   €G

In the next section there is a comprehensive question that addresses virtually all of the topics covered up to this point. The question is in a spreadsheet format – please refer back to Chapter 4 for some guidance in completing the spreadsheet-type questions. The approach to this question should be the same.

5.8: BRINGING IT ALL TOGETHER

5.8.1: Comprehensive Question – Euro Equity Fund

Shown in Table 5.15a is the statement of net assets, statement of operations and statement of changes in net assets for the Euro Equity Fund. Table 5.15b shows the investment portfolio for the fund on 04/04/XX.
  The following transactions occurred on 05/04/XX:

1. Settle investments sold receivable and fund shares sold receivable as of today.
2. Purchased 20,000 shares in CRH for €8.20 and commission of €1,000 – to be settled on TD + 3.

Current share prices on 05/04/XX:

- CRH   €8.20
- Irish Life and Permanent   €10.45
- Kingspan   €7.20
- Smurfit   €5.80
- AIB   €23.00

The following transactions occurred on 06/04/XX:

1. Sold 186,000 shares in Irish Life and Permanent for €10.45 and commission of €3,000 – to be settled on TD + 3.
2. A new shareholder buys 20,000 shares in the fund at yesterday's NAV per share – to be settled on TD + 3.
3. Settle distributions payable as of today.

Current share prices on 06/04/XX:

- CRH   €8.30
- Irish Life and Permanent   €10.50
- Kingspan   €7.50
- Smurfit   €6.00
- AIB   €23.30

Table 5.15a: Comprehensive Question – Euro Equity Fund

Statement of Net Assets

	04/04/XX	Trans. 1	Trans. 2	Daily Valuation 05/04/XX	Trans. 1	Trans. 2	Trans. 3	Daily Valuation 06/04/XX	Trans. 1	Trans. 2	Trans. 3	Daily Valuation 07/04/XX
Assets												
Investments at Cost	€23,850,500											
Unrealised Appreciation/ Depreciation	€1,012,750											
Investments Sold Receivable	€265,000											
Fund Shares Sold Receivable	€25,000											
Interest Receivable	€0											
Cash	€1,400,000											
Dividends Receivable	€0											
Total Assets	*€26,553,250*											
Liabilities												
Investments Purchased Payable	€0											
Accrued Expenses	€18,000											
Fund Shares Redeemed Payable	€0											
Distributions Payable	€15,000											
Total Liabilities	*€33,000*											
Total Net Assets	**€26,520,250**											
Capital Stock	**€26,520,250**											
Outstanding Shares	1,000,000											
NAV per Share	**€26.52**											

(Continued)

Table 5.15a: *(Continued)*

Statement of Operations for the Period from 01/01/XX to YY/04/XX

	04/04/XX	Trans. 1	Trans. 2	Daily Valuation 05/04/XX	Trans. 1	Trans. 2	Trans. 3	Daily Valuation 06/04/XX	Trans. 1	Trans. 2	Trans. 3	Daily Valuation 07/04/XX
Gains/Losses on Investments	€414,186											
Dividend Income	€2,500											
Interest Income	€0											
Total Investment Income/Loss	*€416,686*											
Administration Fee YTD	€3,000											
Investment Management Fee YTD	€2,000											
Other Fees YTD	€5,000											
Auditing Fee YTD	€0											
Total Fund Expenses	*€10,000*											
Increase/Decrease in Net Assets from Operations	**€406,686**											

Table 5.15a: (Continued)

Statement of Changes in Net Assets for the Period from 01/01/XX to YY/04/XX

	04/04/XX	Trans. 1	Trans. 2	Daily Valuation 05/04/XX	Trans. 1	Trans. 2	Trans. 3	Daily Valuation 06/04/XX	Trans. 1	Trans. 2	Trans. 3	Daily Valuation 07/04/XX
Investors' Equity at 01/01/XX	€25,016,343											
Distributions to Investors	€60,500											
Capital Fund Share Transactions												
Proceeds from sale of shares	€1,556,221											
Redemption of units	€398,500											
Dividend reinvestment	€0											
Total	*€1,157,721*											
Increase/Decrease in Net Assets from Operations	€406,686											
Investors' Equity at End	**€26,520,250**											

Table 5.15b: Holdings of the Euro Equity Fund

Security	Date Purchased	Cost Price	Quantity	Commission	Total Cost	04/04/XX Market Price	04/04/XX Market Value
CRH	01/01/X1	€10.00	250,000	€1,500	€2,501,500	€8.00	€2,000,000
CRH	01/01/X2	€10.50	300,000	€1,500	€3,151,500	€8.00	€2,400,000
CRH	01/01/X3	€11.00	500,000	€2,000	€5,502,000	€8.00	€4,000,000
Irish Life and Permanent	01/01/X1	€8.00	150,000	€2,500	€1,202,500	€10.50	€1,575,000
Irish Life and Permanent	01/01/X2	€7.50	180,000	€2,500	€1,352,500	€10.50	€1,890,000
Irish Life and Permanent	01/01/X3	€7.25	190,000	€1,500	€1,379,000	€10.50	€1,995,000
Kingspan	01/01/X1	€6.00	80,000	€2,000	€482,000	€7.25	€580,000
Kingspan	01/01/X2	€5.30	125,000	€2,500	€665,000	€7.25	€906,250
Smurfit	01/01/X3	€4.50	505,000	€3,000	€2,275,500	€5.90	€2,979,500
Smurfit	01/01/X4	€5.20	125,000	€1,000	€651,000	€5.90	€737,500
AIB	01/01/X3	€18.50	100,000	€1,600	€1,851,600	€23.20	€2,320,000
AIB	01/01/X4	€18.90	150,000	€1,400	€2,836,400	€23.20	€3,480,000
Total					€23,850,500		€24,863,250

The following transactions occurred on 07/04/XX:

1. An existing shareholder wishes to redeem 12,000 shares at yesterday's NAV per share – to be settled on TD + 3.
2. Sold 144,000 shares in Irish Life and Permanent for €10.68 and commission of €2,500 – to be settled on TD + 3.
3. Fund declares a distribution to shareholders of €0.50 per share payable on TD + 5. Ex-date is today. Redeeming shareholder is not entitled to the distribution.

Current share prices on 07/04/XX:

- CRH   €8.45
- Irish Life and Permanent   €10.65
- Kingspan   €7.25
- Smurfit   €6.05
- AIB   €23.50

Requirements:

Using the template provided (Table 5.15a):

1. Record the transactions for 05/04/XX. Calculate and record the daily movement in the unrealised appreciation/depreciation account and calculate the NAV per share for 05/04/XX.

2. Record the transactions for the 06/04/XX. Calculate and record the daily movement in the unrealised appreciation/depreciation account and calculate the NAV per share for 06/04/XX.
3. Record the transactions for the 07/04/XX. Calculate and record the daily movement in the unrealised appreciation/depreciation account and calculate the NAV per share for 07/04/XX.

5.8.2: Solution to Comprehensive Question

Each of the transactions will be considered in turn and a final completed solution will be provided at the end of this section.

Transactions from 05/04/XX

1. Settle investments sold receivable and fund shares sold receivable as of today.

This means that the fund will receive any outstanding amounts (in cash) that it is due in respect of investments that were sold and fund shares that it issued over the past few days. On 04/04/XX the balance on the investments sold receivable account was €265,000 and the balance on the fund shares sold receivable account was €25,000 – these amounts were received.

- Increase cash (€265,000 + €25,000) by €290,000 (dr cash).
- Decrease investments sold receivable by €265,000 (cr investments sold receivable).
- Decrease fund shares sold receivable by €25,000 (cr fund shares sold receivable).

2. Purchase 20,000 shares in CRH for €8.20 and a commission of €1,000 – settle on TD + 3.

The fund has purchased but not paid for shares in CRH. The total cost of the shares is (20,000 × €8.20) + €1,000 = €165,000.

- Increase investments at cost by €165,000 (dr investments at cost).
- Increase investments purchased payable by €165,000 (cr investments purchased payable).

3. Value the investment portfolio – use Table 5.15c.

- Increase unrealised appreciation/depreciation by €59,750 (dr unrealised appreciation/depreciation).
- Increase gains/losses on investments by €59,750 (cr gains/losses on investment).

Table 5.15c: Market Value of Portfolio on 05/04/XX

Shares	Price	Quantity	05/04/XX Market Value
CRH (Note 1)	€8.20	1,070,000	€8,774,000
Irish Life and Permanent	€10.45	520,000	€5,434,000
Kingspan	€7.20	205,000	€1,476,000
Smurfit	€5.80	630,000	€3,654,000
AIB	€23.00	250,000	€5,750,000
Market Value of Portfolio (today)			€25,088,000
Cost of Portfolio (today) (Note 2)			€24,015,500
Total Unrealised Appreciation/Depreciation			€1,072,500
Unrealised Appreciation/Depreciation from yesterday, 04/04/XX (Note 3)		€1,012,750	
Movements on day		€0	€1,012,750
Gain for Day (record in 'Value' column)			**€59,750**

Note 1: CRH Shares: Original quantity of 1,050,000 shares plus 20,000 shares purchased today gives a total quantity of 1,070,000

Note 2: Cost of Portfolio:

Opening Investments at Cost	€23,850,500
CRH shares purchased	€165,000
Investments at Cost at end of day	€24,015,500

Note 3: Unrealised appreciation/depreciation from yesterday: This can be found on the Statement of Net Assets from 04/04/XX, see Table 5.15a.

Now calculate the closing balance for each item. Add across the rows and put the total in the 05/04/XX column. Then calculate the totals for each of the statements and the NAV per share. See completed solution in Table 5.15f – column 05/04/XX.

Transactions from 06/04/XX

1. Sell 186,000 shares in Irish Life and Permanent for €10.45 and a commission of €3,000 to settle on TD + 3.
   a) Calculate the proceeds: (186,000 × €10.45) – €3,000 = €1,940,700.
   b) Identify the shares sold: the entire first batch (150,000 shares) is sold and 36,000 of the second batch (180,000 shares) are sold.
   c) Calculate the cost of the shares sold:
      €1,202,500 + €1,352,500 × 36,000/180,000 = €1,473,000
      (Batch 1)   (Batch 2)
   d) Calculate the gain on the sale: €1,940,700 – €1,473,000 = €467,700.

   • Increase investments sold receivable by €1,940,700 (dr investments sold receivable).

- Reduce investments at cost by €1,473,000 (cr investments at cost).
- Reduce unrealised appreciation/depreciation by €467,700 (cr unrealised appreciation/depreciation).

2. A new shareholder buys 20,000 shares in the fund at yesterday's NAV per share.

This is a transaction that was addressed in Chapter 4. The NAV per share at the end of the previous day (05/04/XX) has been calculated as €26.580 (see solution in Table 5.15f below). Amount to be received is €26.580 × 20,000 = €531,600.

- Increase proceeds from sale of fund shares by €531,600 (cr proceeds from sale of fund shares).
- Increase fund shares sold receivable by €531,600 (dr fund shares sold receivable).
- Increase number of shares in fund by 20,000.

3. Settle distributions payable as of today.

This means that investors who were previously promised a distribution from the fund will receive their cash today. The balance on the distributions payable account is €15,000 – this was paid today.

- Decrease cash by €15,000 (cr cash).
- Decrease distributions payable by €15,000 (dr distributions payable).

4. Value the investment portfolio – use Table 5.15d.

- Increase unrealised appreciation/depreciation by €383,200 (dr unrealised appreciation/depreciation).
- Increase gains/losses on investments by €383,200 (cr gains/losses on investment).

Now calculate the closing balance for each item. Add across the rows from the 05/04/XX column to the right (Trans. 1, Trans. 2, Trans. 3 and Value) and put the total in the 06/04/XX column. Then calculate the totals for each of the statements and the NAV per share.

Transactions from 07/04/XX

1. An existing shareholder wishes to redeem 12,000 shares at yesterday's NAV per share.

This is a transaction from Chapter 4. The NAV per share at the end of the previous day (06/04/XX) has been calculated as €26.956 (see solution in Table 5.15f below). Amount to be paid is €26.956 × 12,000 = €323,472.

Table 5.15d: Market Value of Portfolio on 06/04/XX

Shares	Price	Quantity	06/04/XX Market Value
CRH	€8.30	1,070,000	€8,881,000
Irish Life and Permanent (Note 1)	€10.50	334,000	€3,507,000
Kingspan	€7.50	205,000	€1,537,500
Smurfit	€6.00	630,000	€3,780,000
AIB	€23.30	250,000	€5,825,000
Market Value of Portfolio (today)			€23,530,500
Cost of Portfolio (today) (Note 2)			€22,542,500
Total Unrealised Appreciation/Depreciation			€988,000
Unreal Appreciation/Depreciation from Yesterday, 05/04/XX		€1,072,500	
Less: Gain Sold (Irish Life and Permanent)		€467,700	€604,800
Gain for Day (record in 'Value' column)			**€383,200**

Note 1: Irish Life and Permanent shares: Original quantity of 520,000 shares less 186,000 shares sold today gives a total quantity of 334,000

Note 2: Cost of Portfolio:

Opening Investments at Cost from Yesterday, 05/04/XX	€24,015,500
Less: Irish Life and Permanent Shares Sold	€1,473,000
Investments at Cost at end of day	€22,542,500

- Increase redemption of units by €323,472 (dr redemption of units).
- Increase fund shares redeemed payable by €323,472 (cr fund shares redeemed payable).
- Reduce number of shares in fund by 12,000.

2. Sell 144,000 shares in Irish Life and Permanent for €10.68 and commission of €2,500.

    a) Calculate the proceeds: (144,000 × €10.68) – €2,500 = €1,535,420.

    b) Identify the shares sold: all the remainder of the second batch is sold.

    c) Calculate the cost of the shares sold: €1,352,500 × 144,000/180,000 = €1,082,000.

    d) Calculate the gain on the sale: €1,535,420 – €1,082,000 = €453,420.

- Increase investments sold receivable by €1,535,420 (dr investments sold receivable).
- Reduce investments at cost by €1,082,000 (cr investments at cost).
- Reduce unrealised appreciation/depreciation by €453,420 (cr unrealised appreciation/depreciation).

3. Fund declares a distribution of €0.50 per share; ex–date is today.

Calculate the amount of the distribution (the redeeming investor does not get distribution). On 06/04/XX there were 1,020,000 fund shares in existence; during the day, 12,000 fund shares were redeemed. Thus there are 1,008,000 fund shares still outstanding:

Number of shares outstanding	1,008,000
Distribution rate	€0.50
Total distribution	€504,000

- Increase distributions to investors by €504,000 (dr distributions to investors).
- Increase distributions payable by €504,000 (cr distributions payable).

4. Value the investment portfolio – see Table 5.15e.

Table 5.15e: Market Value of Portfolio on 07/04/XX

Shares	Price	Quantity	07/04/XX Market Value
CRH	€8.45	1,070,000	€9,041,500
Irish Life and Permanent (Note 1)	€10.65	190,000	€2,023,500
Kingspan	€7.25	205,000	€1,486,250
Smurfit	€6.05	630,000	€3,811,500
AIB	€23.50	250,000	€5,875,000
Market Value of Portfolio (today)			€22,237,750
Cost of Portfolio (today) (Note 2)			€21,460,500
Total Unrealised Appreciation/Depreciation			€777,250
Unrealised Appreciation/Depreciation from Yesterday, 06/04/XX		€988,000	
Less: Gain Sold (Irish Life and Permanent sale 2)		€453,420	€534,580
Gain for Day (record in 'Value' column)			**€242,670**

Note 1: Irish Life and Permanent shares: Original quantity of 334,000 shares less 144,000 shares sold today gives a total quantity of 190,000

Note 2: Cost of Portfolio:

Opening Investments at Cost from Yesterday	€22,542,500
Less: Irish Life and Permanent Shares Sold – sale 2	€1,082,000
Investments at Cost at end of day	€21,460,500

- Increase unrealised appreciation/depreciation by €242,670 (dr unrealised appreciation/depreciation).
- Increase gains/losses on investments by €242,670 (cr gains/losses on investments).

Now calculate the closing balance for each item. Add across the rows from the 06/04/XX column to the right (Trans. 1, Trans. 2, Trans. 3 and Value) and put the total in the 07/04/XX column. Then calculate the totals for each of the statements and the NAV per share.

A full solution to the question follows in Table 5.15f. Try the questions that follow in Section 5.9 for more practice.

5.9: ADDITIONAL QUESTIONS

Question 5.9.1

Find a company with preference shares as part of its financing structure. Determine the characteristics of the preference shares (the annual report should provide this information). Then compare the price of the preference shares with the price of the ordinary shares for the same company. What do you notice?

Question 5.9.2

Go to www.adr.com. Find a company that has an ADR issue in addition to its own shares. What are the characteristics of the company? What are the characteristics of the ADR issue?

Question 5.9.3

Find a company that has recently issued warrants. What are the characteristics of the warrant (strike price, exercise date, etc)? This information may be found in the company's annual report. Compare the price of the ordinary shares with the price of the warrants for the same company. What do you notice?

Question 5.9.4

Your fund has a holding of 5,000 shares in ASD Corp. ASD is untraded and you are wondering how to value the company. The company operates in the medical devices industry. Similar companies in that industry trade on 14 times earnings (their PE ratio is 14 times).[21] The earnings of ASD are €15 million. ASD has a total of 30 million shares in issue. What value would you place on the fund's holding of ASD shares?

---

[21]   The PE ratio is a measure of the value of a company to its earnings. If a company is in an industry that 'trades' on a PE ratio of 14 then, on average, if the company has earnings of €20 million then it's value is €280 million. 'Earnings' is another word for profit. This is just a crude measure as there are many other unique factors that impact on the value of a company. However, it is often a good starting point in determining corporate value.

Table 5.15f: Solution to Comprehensive Question – Euro Equity Fund

Statement of Net Assets

	04/04/XX	Trans. 1	Trans. 2	Daily Value	05/04/XX	Trans. 1	Trans. 2	Trans. 3	Daily Value	06/04/XX	Trans. 1	Trans. 2	Trans. 3	Daily Value	07/04/XX
Assets															
Investments at Cost	€23,850,500		€165,000		€24,015,500	–€1,473,000				€22,542,500		–€1,082,000			€21,460,500
Unrealised Appreciation/ Depreciation	€1,012,750			€59,750	€1,072,500	–€467,700			€383,200	€988,000		–€453,420		€242,670	€777,250
Investments Sold Receivable	€265,000	–€265,000			€0	€1,940,700				€1,940,700		€1,535,420			€3,476,120
Fund Shares Sold Receivable	€25,000	–€25,000			€0		€531,600			€531,600					€531,600
Interest Receivable	€0				€0					€0					€0
Cash	€1,400,000		€290,000		€1,690,000			–€15,000		€1,675,000					€1,675,000
Dividends Receivable	€0				€0					€0					€0
Total Assets	*€26,553,250*				*€26,778,000*					*€27,677,800*					*€27,920,470*
Liabilities															
Investments Purchased Payable	€0		€165,000		€165,000					€165,000					€165,000
Accrued Expenses	€18,000				€18,000					€18,000					€18,000
Fund Shares Redeemed Payable	€0				€0					€0	€323,472				€323,472
Distributions Payable	€15,000				€15,000			–€15,000		€0			€504,000		€504,000
Total Liabilities	*€33,000*				*€198,000*					*€183,000*					*€1,010,472*

(Continued)

Table 5.15f: (Continued)

	04/04/XX	Trans. 1	Trans. 2	Daily Value 05/04/XX	Trans. 1	Trans. 2	Trans. 3	Daily Value 06/04/XX	Trans. 1	Trans. 2	Trans. 3	Daily Value 07/04/XX
Total Net Assets	€26,520,250			€26,580,000				€27,494,800				€26,694,350
Capital Stock	€26,520,250			€26,580,000				€27,494,800				€26,909,998
Outstanding Shares	1,000,000			1,000,000	20,000			1,020,000	−12,000			1,008,000
NAV per Share	€26.520			€26.580				€26.956				€26.696

Statement of Operations for the Period from 01/01/XX to YY/04/XX

	04/04/XX	Trans. 1	Trans. 2	Daily Value 05/04/XX	Trans. 1	Trans. 2	Trans. 3	Daily Value 06/04/XX	Trans. 1	Trans. 2	Trans. 3	Daily Value 07/04/XX
Gains/Losses on Investments	€414,186		€59,750	€473,936	€383,200			€857,136	€242,670			€1,099,806
Dividend Income	€2,500			€2,500				€2,500				€2,500
Interest Income	€0			€0				€0				€0
Total Investment Income/Loss	*€416,686*			*€476,436*				*€859,636*				*€1,102,306*
Administration Fee YTD	€3,000			€3,000				€3,000				€3,000
Investment Management Fee YTD	€2,000			€2,000				€2,000				€2,000
Other Fees YTD	€5,000			€5,000				€5,000				€5,000
Auditing Fee YTD	€0			€0				€0				€0
Total Fund Expenses	*€10,000*			*€10,000*				*€10,000*				*€10,000*
Increase/ Decrease in Net Assets from Operations	€406,686			€466,436				€849,636				€1,092,306

Table 5.15f: *(Continued)*

Statement of Changes in Net Assets for the Period from 01/01/XX to YY/04/XX

	04/04/XX	Trans. 1	Trans. 2	Daily Value 05/04/XX	Trans. 1	Trans. 2	Trans. 3	Daily Value 06/04/XX	Trans. 1	Trans. 2	Trans. 3	Daily Value 07/04/XX
Investors' Equity at 01/01/XX	€25,016,343			€25,016,343				€25,016,343				€25,016,343
Distributions to Investors	€60,500			€60,500				€60,500			€504,000	€564,500
Capital Fund Share Transactions												
Proceeds from sale of shares	€1,556,221			€1,556,221		€531,600		€2,087,821				€2,087,821
Redemption of units	€398,500			€398,500				€398,500	€323,472			€721,972
Dividend reinvestment	€0			€0				€0				€0
Total	*€1,157,721*			*€1,157,721*				*€1,689,321*				*€1,365,849*
Increase/Decrease in Net Assets from Operations	€406,686			€466,436				€849,636				€1,092,306
Investors' Equity at End	**€26,520,250**			**€26,580,000**				**€27,494,800**				**€26,909,998**

Question 5.9.5

Your fund has a portfolio as shown in Table 5.16.

Table 5.16: Holdings of ACD Fund

Company	Number of Shares	Currency	Price	Total Value (local)	Total Value (EUR)
Microsoft	20,000	USD			
IBM	10,000	USD			
Intel	15,000	USD			
Bank of Ireland	100,000	EUR			
CRH	75,000	EUR			
Vodafone	400,000	GBP			
Accor	30,000	EUR			
RWE	150,000	EUR			
Fortis	25,000	EUR			
ABB	100,000	SEK			

Key:
USD = US Dollars
GBP = British Pound (Sterling)
EUR = Euro
SEK = Swedish Kroner

Complete the table and calculate the total value of the complete portfolio in Euros.

Pricing details and currency rates can be found on numerous sites but you need to be sure that you are getting the correct price and currency rate (i.e. not a tourist rate).

Question 5.9.6

You are the accountant to a fund that has just made some purchases. On 23/05/X7 you received two trade tickets,[22] a summary of which are set out below:

- Ticket No. 1: purchase of 100,000 equity securities in EDF at a price of €14.50 each. There is no stamp duty, just broker's commission of €1,500. Settlement date is 26/05/X7.

---

[22] In bygone days when a transaction in equities took place, a trade ticket was generated. This was a piece of paper that set out the details of the sale (price, quantity, company, etc.). This now takes place electronically; however, the term still remains. It describes the terms of a transaction in equities and is the source information that the fund accountant uses to record a share transaction.

- Ticket No. 2: purchase of 140,000 equity securities in Carrefour at a price of €40.65 each. There is a non-refundable French government duty of 0.5 per cent and broker's commission of €1,250. Settlement date is 27/05/X7.

Requirement:

- Calculate the amount of each purchase.
- Record the purchase.
- Record the settlement.
- Specify the balance on the investments at cost account and the investments purchased payable account for each day from 23/05/X7 to 27/05/X7 inclusive.

Question 5.9.7

Table 5.17 shows the holdings of the Euro Stock Stable Fund.

Table 5.17: Holdings of the Euro Stock Stable Fund

Share	Quantity	Cost	Commission	Closing Price 08/08/X7	Closing Price 09/08/X7	Closing Price 10/08/X7	Closing Price 11/08/X7
Fortis	22,000	€9.00	€2,200	€10.20	€10.30	€10.15	€10.54
Renault	5,000	€45.75	€2,600	€52.91	€53.10	€53.05	€53.60
Vinci	6,000	€35.80	€2,300	€39.88	€39.75	€39.50	€39.25
ENEL	30,000	€7.50	€2,000	€6.90	€6.60	€8.50	€6.70
RWE	3,000	€80.22	€2,400	€78.40	€78.90	€77.10	€77.80
Total	4,500	€45.10	€3,000	€52.90	€54.00	€52.95	€53.30
Volkswagen	1,500	€145.60	€3,200	€177.50	€180.50	€179.50	€177.20

At the end of 07/08/X7 you note the following balances:

- Investments at cost account   €1,546,260   (dr balance)
- Unrealised appreciation/   €125,800   (dr balance)
  depreciation account

The fund operates a 5 per cent threshold; any movement of +/−5% or more on an individual share should be investigated. The fund is benchmarked against the

EuroStoxx index where the investigation threshold is +/−1%; values for the index are provided below:

07/08/X6	3,356
08/08/X6	3,363
09/08/X6	3,375
10/08/X6	3,329
11/08/X6	3,355

Note: during the periods in question the fund did not purchase or sell any investments.

Requirements:

1. Check (reconcile) the opening balance on the investments at cost account.
2. For each day (08/08/X7, 09/08/X7, 10/08/X7 and 11/08/X7) you are required to do the following:
   a) Calculate the market value of the portfolio.
   b) Calculate the total cost of the portfolio (the investments at cost account).
   c) Calculate the movement in unrealised appreciation/depreciation.
   d) Record the entries to give effect to the movement in the value of the portfolio.
3. Show the entries and calculate the daily balance on the following accounts:
   o investments at cost account
   o unrealised appreciation/depreciation account
4. Perform any checks that you consider to be appropriate to determine if there are any items that require further investigation.

Question 5.9.8

Table 5.18 shows a fund's holdings in GST Plc.

Table 5.18:   A Fund's Holdings in GST Plc

Company	Date Purchased	Quantity	Cost	Commission
GST	01/02/X3	10,000	€2.00	€1,000
GST	01/02/X4	20,000	€3.00	€2,400
GST	01/02/X5	50,000	€4.00	€3,000

On 01/01/X7 the fund sells 15,000 shares at €5.00 each with commission of €1,800. The transaction will settle on 04/04/X7. The fund uses the FIFO method of share identification.

Requirements:

- Calculate the sales proceeds.
- Determine the cost of the shares that have been sold (use FIFO).
- Calculate the gain/loss on the sale.
- Record the sale.
- Record the settlement.

Question 5.9.9

You are the fund accountant to Fin-index Growth Fund. You have been asked to record the following transactions as they relate to AIB, one of the holdings of the fund:

- On 15/01/X2 100,000 shares in AIB were purchased for the price shown in Table 5.19; commission charged was €3,000. This amount was paid on 18/01/X2.
- On 23/01/X2 50,000 shares in AIB were sold for the price shown in Table 5.19; the commission charged was €3,500. This amount was received on 26/01/X2.

Table 5.19:   Fin-index Growth Fund's Holdings in AIB

AIB	Price
15/01/X2	€12.11
16/01/X2	€12.27
17/01/X2	€12.58
18/01/X2	€12.75
19/01/X2	Saturday
20/01/X2	Sunday
21/01/X2	€12.65
22/01/X2	€12.82
23/01/X2	€13.02

Requirements:

1. In respect of the purchase of the AIB shares:
   - calculate the amount of the purchase (on 15/01/X2)
   - record the purchase (on 15/01/X2)
   - record the settlement (on 18/01/X2)
2. For each day (15/01, 16/01, 17/01, 18/01, 21/01, 22/02, 23/01) you are required to do the following:
   - calculate the market value of the portfolio
   - calculate the total cost of the portfolio (the investments at cost account)

  o calculate the movement in unrealised appreciation/depreciation

  o record the entries to give effect to the movement in the value of the portfolio

3. In respect of the sale of the AIB shares

  o calculate the sales proceeds

  o determine the cost of the shares that have been sold (use FIFO)

  o calculate the gain/loss on the sale

  o record the sale

  o record the settlement

4. Show the entries and calculate the daily balance for each day (15/01, 16/01, 17/01, 18/01, 21/01, 22/02, 23/01) on the following accounts:

  o investments at cost account

  o unrealised appreciation/depreciation account

  o investments purchased payable account

  o investments sold receivable account

  Hint – using Excel may save some time and make the calculations easier.

Question 5.9.10

You are the fund accountant for the Euro Airline Fund. Table 5.20a shows the fund's holding on 18/07/X9.

Table 5.20a: Holdings of Euro Airline Fund on 18/07/X9

Company	Purchase Date	Quantity	Cost	Commission	Total Cost	17/07/X9 Share Price	17/07/X9 Market Value
Ryanair	02/05/X3	10,000	€4.70	€1,000	€48,000	€4.95	€49,500
Ryanair	19/12/X5	12,000	€4.40	€2,400	€55,200	€4.95	€59,400
Aer Lingus	31/10/X4	30,000	€3.50	€2,400	€107,400	€3.55	€106,500
EADS	10/08/X4	6,000	€40.50	€1,800	€244,800	€42.00	€252,000
SAS	09/12/X7	14,000	€3.50	€2,100	€51,100	€4.40	€61,600
Air Berlin	02/09/X5	19,000	€2.50	€850	€48,350	€2.75	€52,250
Total					€554,850		€581,250

You should be able to calculate the 'Total Cost' column and the 'Market Value' column. The answer is provided but it is always good practice to check if they are correct.

From the information above, the following balances exist in the statement of net assets:

- Investments at cost account   €554,850   (dr balance)
- Unrealised appreciation/   €26,400   (dr balance)
  depreciation account

During 18/07/X9 the following transactions occurred:

- 14,000 shares in Ryanair were sold for €5.00 each, commission of €2,800, settlement date on 21/07/X9.
- 20,000 shares in Air France/KLM were purchased for €3.10 each, commission of €1,500, settlement on 21/07/X9.

Table 5.20b shows the official closing prices at the end of 18/07/X9.

Table 5.20b: Official Closing Prices of Euro Airline Fund's Holdings on 18/07/X9

Company	18/07/X9 Share Price
Ryanair	€5.05
Aer Lingus	€3.65
EADS	€43.15
SAS	€4.20
Air Berlin	€2.90
Air France/KLM	€3.15

Requirements:

- Record the sale of the shares in Ryanair.
- Record the purchase of the shares in Air France/KLM.
- Record the movement in the unrealised appreciation/depreciation account for the day.
- Show the investments at cost account and the unrealised appreciation/depreciation account.

Question 5.9.11: Start-Up Fund (Comprehensive Question)

Table 5.21 provides another comprehensive question.

This is a new fund which has just commenced with the shareholders investing €2,000,000, for which they received 2,000,000 shares in the fund.

Table 5.21: Question 5.9.11: Start-Up Fund (Comprehensive Question)

Statement of Net Assets

	04/04/XX	Trans. 1	Trans. 2	Daily Valuation 05/04/XX	Trans. 1	Trans. 2	Daily Valuation 06/04/XX	Trans. 1	Trans. 2	Daily Valuation 07/04/XX
Assets										
Investments at Cost	€0									
Unrealised Appreciation/ Depreciation	€0									
Investments Sold Receivable	€0									
Fund Shares Sold Receivable	€0									
Interest Receivable	€0									
Cash	€2,000,000									
Dividends Receivable	€0									
Total Assets	*€2,000,000*									
Liabilities										
Investments Purchased Payable	€0									
Accrued Expenses	€0									
Fund Shares Redeemed Payable	€0									
Distributions Payable	€0									
Total Liabilities	*€0*									
Total Net Assets	**€2,000,000**									
Capital Stock/Investors' Equity	**€2,000,000**									
Outstanding Shares	2,000,000									
NAV per Share	**€1.000**									

(Continued)

Table 5.21: *(Continued)*

Statement of Operations for the Period from 01/01/XX to YY/04/XX

	04/04/XX	Trans. 1	Trans. 2	Daily Valuation 05/04/XX	Trans. 1	Trans. 2	Daily Valuation 06/04/XX	Trans. 1	Trans. 2	Daily Valuation 07/04/XX
Gains/Losses on Investments	€0									
Dividend Income	€0									
Interest Income	€0									
Total Investment Income/ Loss	€0									
Administration Fee Year to Date	€0									
Investment Management Fee YTD	€0									
Other Fees YTD	€0									
Auditing Fee YTD	€0									
Total Fund Expenses	€0									
Increase/Decrease in Net Assets from Operations	**€0**									

(Continued)

Table 5.21: (Continued)

Statement of Changes in Net Assets for the Period from 01/01/XX to YY/04/XX

	04/04/XX	Trans. 1	Trans. 2	Daily Valuation 05/04/XX	Trans. 1	Trans. 2	Daily Valuation 06/04/XX	Trans. 1	Trans. 2	Daily Valuation 07/04/XX
Investors' Equity at 01/01/XX	€0									
Distributions to Investors	€0									
Capital Fund Share Transactions										
Proceeds from the sale of shares	€2,000,000									
Redemption of units	€0									
Dividend reinvestment	€0									
Total	*€2,000,000*									
Increase/Decrease in Net Assets from Operations	€0									
Investors' Equity at End	**€2,000,000**									

The following transactions occurred on 05/04/XX:

1. The fund purchased 30,000 shares in Ryanair for €8.00 and commission of €2,000 to settle on TD + 3.
2. The fund purchased 40,000 shares in Total Produce for €2.35 and commission of €2,500 to settle on TD + 3.

The closing price of the shares on 05/04/XX:

- Ryanair   €8.20
- Total Produce   €2.55

The following transactions occurred on 06/04/XX:

1. The fund purchased 60,000 shares in AIB for €22.00 and commission of €2,000 to settle on TD + 3.
2. The fund purchased 50,000 shares in Blackrock Land for €2.95 and commission of €2,500 to settle on TD + 3.

The closing price of the shares on 06/04/XX:

- Ryanair   € 8.30
- Total Produce   € 2.80
- AIB   € 23.50
- Blackrock Land   € 3.20

The following transactions occurred on 07/04/XX:

1. The fund sold 15,000 shares in Ryanair for €8.40 and commission of €500 to settle on TD + 3.

The closing price of the shares on 07/04/XX:

- Ryanair   € 8.40
- Total Produce   € 2.85
- AIB   €23.45
- Blackrock Land   €3.10

Requirements:

1. Record the transactions for 05/04/XX. Calculate and record the daily movement in the unrealised appreciation/depreciation account and calculate the NAV per share for 05/04/XX.

2. Record the transactions for 06/04/XX. Calculate and record the daily movement in the unrealised appreciation/depreciation account and calculate the NAV per share for 06/04/XX.

3. Record the transactions for 07/04/XX. Calculate and record the daily movement in the unrealised appreciation/depreciation account and calculate the NAV per share for 07/04/XX.

Chapter 6

Accounting for Corporate Actions

- Introduction
- Corporate actions explained
- Dividends
- Stock dividends
- Return of capital and share buy backs
- Bonus issues/stock splits
- Rights issues
- Mergers and acquisitions
- Bringing it all together
- Additional questions

LEARNING OUTCOMES

At the end of this chapter you should:

- Be able to describe corporate actions and explain their impact on a fund.
- Be able to explain the different types of corporate actions.
- Be able to describe the issues in accounting for corporate actions.

6.1: INTRODUCTION

In Chapter 5, issues surrounding the purchase, sale and valuation of equities were discussed. However, there are other transactions that occur as a result of holding equities. Many of these transactions impact on the portfolio and assets of the fund. This current chapter will address these 'other' transactions, which will be loosely collected together under the title of 'corporate actions'. These include transactions such as dividend payments, share buy backs, stock dividends and bonus issues.

This chapter will begin with a more detailed discussion on corporate actions. Each of the different types of corporate action will then be discussed in turn. This will involve an explanation of the individual categories of corporate action and the impact they can have on an investment fund. The accounting for the particular corporate action will then be outlined. This chapter will only consider corporate actions that affect equity holders; debt-related corporate actions will not be addressed.

A comprehensive example will conclude the chapter. This will review much of the material that has been addressed so far, including fund share transactions and equity transactions from previous chapters. This example will use the spreadsheet format that should now be more familiar.

6.2: CORPORATE ACTIONS EXPLAINED

Keeping proper and effective control over an equity portfolio is more than just recording purchases, sales and valuations. Efficient portfolio management also involves proper and timely recording of corporate actions.

According to Simmons and Dalgleish,[1] a corporate action is an event in the life of an equity, instigated by the company, which affects a position in that equity. Normally, it involves the distribution of benefits to the equity holders (e.g. a dividend) or a change in the structure of the equity (e.g. a bonus issue or capital reconstruction). Since many corporate actions can have a significant impact on the company's structure and financing, it is not unusual for all the shareholders involved to have a vote to approve the action.

The most common types of corporate actions are:

- Dividends – where the company decides to make a payment to the equity holders from the realised profits of the business. This can take the form of a cash payment or a stock/share payment (where the company gives the equity holder more shares in the business instead of a cash payment, often referred to as a stock dividend).
- Share buy backs – this is where the company offers to repurchase its own shares from its existing shareholders. In some cases, the shareholders are given a choice as to whether or not they would like to participate in the share buy back. In other situations, all shareholders are obliged to participate. This can also be called a capital repayment or a return of capital.
- Bonus issues – from time to time, companies give their shareholders 'free' shares. This will alter the structure of the company's capital and affect the share price.
- Rights issues – a company has a number of mechanisms to raise finance. One such mechanism is a rights issue. This is where the existing equity holders

---

[1]   Simmons and Dalgleish (2006), *Corporate Actions: A Guide to Securities Event Management.* The terminology of the definition has been slightly altered to suit the language used in this book.

have the option to invest more money in the company at a price lower than the market price. It is considered to be a corporate action; general share issues, which are at full price, are not considered to be corporate actions (they are treated as a purchase of equities).

- Equity restructuring – this is where a company radically alters its shareholder structure. They tend to be relatively rare events in the life of a company and can be broken into two subcategories: equity restructuring actions and mergers and acquisitions:

  o Equity restructuring – companies in financial difficulty can sometimes undergo an equity restructuring. There is no set formula for this and the end result can take many different forms. Often it will involve the debt holders (e.g. the banks) or the government (for strategically important businesses) taking an equity stake in the company at the expense of the original equity shareholders. This is likely to have an impact on the original equity shareholders, which will need to be reflected in the portfolio of a fund. After the 2008 credit crisis some of the nationalisations in the banking sector would have been achieved by an equity restructuring.[2] These events will not be addressed in this book as they are relatively rare and tend to be unique to the circumstances of the companies concerned.

  o Mergers and acquisitions – some mergers and acquisitions can be considered to be corporate actions. For example, if Company X is taking over Company Y, the shareholders in Company Y could be offered shares in Company X in exchange for their shares. This potentially changes the capital structure of both companies – if a fund held shares in Company Y, this event would certainly need to be recorded even though no cash changed hands.

The remainder of this chapter will address the more significant of these corporate actions in detail and consider any fund accounting implications.

6.3: DIVIDENDS

Dividends are the most common type of corporate action. A dividend is a payment to the shareholders of a company from the realised profits of the company. Dividends are generally paid on a per share basis, for example, €0.04 per share.

---

[2] In the UK, Northern Rock was nationalised by the government. Effectively, the existing shareholders had their shares taken by the government. Had an investment fund held shares in Northern Rock, the shares would have had to be removed from the portfolio as they are now worthless and there is little chance of compensation. The nationalisation of Anglo Irish Bank in Ireland was similar.

Thus, if the fund held 10,000 shares in this company it would receive €400. Dividends are proposed by the board of directors and voted on by the shareholders; it is very rare that shareholders would vote against a dividend.

European companies tend to pay a dividend twice a year, whereas, in the US, companies regularly make quarterly dividend payments. Dividends are seen by the market as a fundamental signal of the health of a company. If a company fails to declare a dividend as expected, it can have a significant negative impact on its share price. Companies that pay regular and increasing dividends are generally prized by the market; this is because they are predictable companies.

The dividend history of a company can be a key driver of investment choice for some investment funds. A company that can afford to pay a regular dividend is often a very safe business with a proven profitability record. In addition, the fund can use the dividend as income and in turn pay a distribution to its investors. The drawback of investing in a company with a strong commitment to paying dividends is that there is less cash for reinvestment, so the potential for large increases in share prices may be limited.

Microsoft is an example of a company that, for many years, never paid a dividend; it needed all of its cash to reinvest and grow the business. As a result, the share price of the company grew dramatically from when it first floated on the stock market in 1986. By 2003, Microsoft was a hugely profitable business but was running out of investment opportunities (it was so profitable that it had generated over $40 billion USD of cash). The company opted to begin to pay a dividend. Since then, it has grown its dividend from $0.08 USD per quarter in 2004/2005, $0.09 USD per quarter in 2005/2006, $0.10 USD per quarter in 2006/2007 and $0.11 USD per quarter in 2007/2008 – it is easy to see the pattern. It is not difficult to predict the future dividends for Microsoft.[3] Financial meltdown notwithstanding, Microsoft is now a stable dividend payer and has moved into a different phase in its financial evolution. This type of stability is attractive to some investors; however, there is a compromise since Microsoft's share price is unlikely to increase at the same rate in the next fifteen years as over the past fifteen years.

Dividends are also an important element of the investing strategy of an investment fund. Some funds deliberately target companies with high and regular dividend payments. This is because the fund can in turn use the dividends it receives to fund its distributions to its investors. An investment fund that follows this objective is often categorised as an 'income fund'; this is because it can generally provide its investors with a regular cash income, but large increases in the NAV

---

[3] Have a look at www.microsoft.com; go to the 'Investor Relations' page under 'About Microsoft' to find out the dividend payouts for 2008/2009 and forward.

per share are compromised as a result. The opposite type of fund is a 'growth fund'. This type of fund invests in companies that are still in a growth phase. These companies do not pay a dividend; they reinvest their profits in the business with the intention of increasing share price. These types of companies are a lot riskier than the more stable dividend payers. However, the potential for large share price gains are much greater. Hence, the funds that invest in these types of companies tend to pay only a small distribution to their investors, with the objective of increasing the NAV per share as the share prices of its underlying investments increase.

The Growth Fund of America and the Income Fund of America[4] illustrate the differences between the two types of funds (see Figure 6.1).

Notice the differing objectives of the two funds. Also, as can be seen, the growth fund has performed much better from a capital appreciation perspective but the income fund has paid out much more in distributions over the twenty-year period (the darker section of the performance graphs). While both funds pay relatively similar amounts in total distributions, the amount paid by the income fund represents 6.8 per cent of NAV per share, whereas the growth fund pays a more modest 3.8 per cent of NAV per share in distributions. Finally, consider the portfolios of the two funds (just the top five were included as the individual portfolios consist of over 100 holdings). The growth fund is invested in technology and exploration companies – organisations that typically do not pay large dividends – whereas the income fund is invested in utility and financial services companies, which would tend to be more stable dividend payers (credit crunches not withstanding).

Figure 6.2 highlights the differences between a growth and income fund. It should be possible to see how the dividends from the companies are passed on to investors as distributions from the fund.

What is the difference between a dividend and a distribution? Effectively, nothing; they are both payments out of the profits of a company, or a fund, to its shareholders. This book uses 'distribution' when referring to payments made by investment funds to its investors and uses 'dividend' when referring to payments made by companies to its shareholders. This is done for clarity purposes only and the terms are used interchangeably.

---

[4] All data in Figure 6.1 are from the prospectuses and annual reports of the relevant funds, available from www.americanfunds.com. The investment objectives are stated in the prospectuses of the funds. The results graphs and holdings data are available in the annual reports of the funds.

**Figure 6.1:   Growth Funds versus Income Funds – An Illustration
from American Funds**

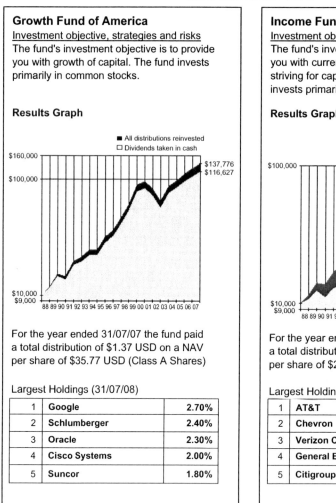

Growth Fund of America

Investment objective, strategies and risks
The fund's investment objective is to provide you with growth of capital. The fund invests primarily in common stocks.

Results Graph

■ All distributions reinvested
□ Dividends taken in cash

$160,000
$137,776
$116,627
$100,000

$10,000
$9,000
88 89 90 91 92 93 94 95 96 97 98 99 00 01 02 03 04 05 06 07

For the year ended 31/07/07 the fund paid a total distribution of $1.37 USD on a NAV per share of $35.77 USD (Class A Shares)

Largest Holdings (31/07/08)

1	Google	2.70%
2	Schlumberger	2.40%
3	Oracle	2.30%
4	Cisco Systems	2.00%
5	Suncor	1.80%

Income Fund of America

Investment objectives, strategies and risks
The fund's investment objectives are to provide you with current income while secondarily striving for capital growth. Normally, the fund invests primarily in income-producing securities.

Results Graph

■ All distributions reinvested
□ Dividends taken in cash

$100,000
$85,398

$29,171

$10,000
$9,000
88 89 90 91 92 93 94 95 96 97 98 99 00 01 02 03 04 05 06 07

For the year ended 31/07/07 the fund paid a total distribution of $1.39 USD on a NAV per share of $20.54 (Class A Shares)

Largest Holdings (31/07/08)

1	AT&T	3.10%
2	Chevron	2.70%
3	Verizon Communications	1.90%
4	General Electric	1.60%
5	Citigroup	1.30%

Source: www.americanfunds.com.

6.3.1: Dividends – The Dates

When a company announces a dividend it can take some time before the shareholders receive their cash. This is because many large companies have thousands of shareholders, resulting in an inevitable administrative delay. In order to facilitate this, the payment of dividends follows a predetermined process. Similar to when an investment fund pays a distribution (see Chapter 4), there are a number of important dates. These dates have an impact on when the dividend will be accounted for by the fund.

Figure 6.2: Growth Fund versus Income Fund – Generic Illustration

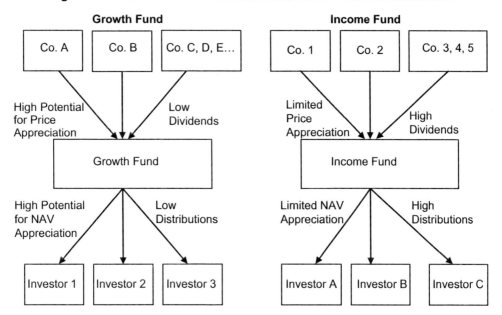

- Declaration (announcement) date: the date when the directors of the company announce that a dividend will be paid to all shareholders on the share register on the record date. This will happen sometime in the future.
- Ex-dividend date: on this date the owner of the shares is entitled to receive the dividend. If after this date the shares are traded, the previous owner of the shares keeps the dividend even though they may not own the shares on the payment date. For this reason, on the ex-dividend date the share price of company normally falls by the amount of the dividend (normal share price movements notwithstanding). This date will be some time after the declaration date. There is no specified time gap but the period is usually a number of weeks.
- Record date: the date on which a shareholder must be on the share register to receive a declared dividend. When a fund purchases shares it takes up to three days before the fund is entered on the company's share register as the owner of the shares. If a fund purchases shares prior to the ex-dividend date, but is not on the share register on the record date, then, depending on the arrangements, the dividend will be paid to the previous owner, who will pass it on to the fund. Generally, the record date is two days after the ex-dividend date.
- Payment date: the date on which the dividend is paid. This will take place some time after the ex-dividend date, often up to six weeks later.

From the fund accounting perspective, the ex-dividend date is the important date – if the fund owns the shares on this date, then it is entitled to the dividend. Hence, this is the date that the dividend should be recorded by the fund as income. It is also on this date that the value of the shares will fall by the amount of the dividend. See the following illustration for an explanation of why this is the case.

Consider a shareholder who holds shares in Company XYZ; the shares are quoted at €10 each. Assume that there is no change in the underlying business of XYZ so, for the purposes of this illustration, the share price remains constant at €10. Then, on 04/05/X5, the directors announce a €2 per share dividend with an ex-date on 17/05/X5 and a payment date on 22/05/X5.

- Prior to the announcement, each shareholder has an interest in the company valued at €10.
- On the announcement date, 04/05/X5, the company still has the same assets and liabilities as the day before, so the share price will remain at €10 per share.
- In effect each shareholder now has an interest in the assets less liabilities of the company of €8 and a 'guaranteed' dividend of €2 cash. Remember, the company has done nothing different except announce a dividend and committed itself to making a €2 per share payment. The €2 per share payment will be funded from the assets of the company. These assets were originally worth €10 per share, so now, after the dividend, there is just €8 per share remaining. If the total interest in the company was greater than €10 per share then the company would have created value out of nothing; it would be a money-making machine, which is illogical.
- If a shareholder sells the shares before the ex-date, they would not sell the shares for less than €10 each (this is because the new shareholder would get the €2 dividend plus the €8 of company value).
- If the shareholder sells the shares after the ex-date then the new shareholder should not pay more than €8 per share. The new shareholder will not get the dividend and will be left with just €8 per share of company value. At this stage the original shareholder would have a €2 per share dividend, which they will still receive, and €8 per share for the sale of the shares – giving a total of €10 per share.
- The only difference is that before the ex-date the shares were trading for €10 each (€8 of value + €2 of dividend) but after the ex-date the shares trade for €8 each (€0 dividend + €8 of value).
- On the payment date, 22/05/X5, whoever was entitled to the dividend as on the ex-date will receive their cash, leaving the company valued at €8 per share.

6.3.2: Accounting for Dividends – Calculating the Dividend

The accounting implications of dividends can be broken into the following:

- Calculate the amount of dividend to be received.
- Record the dividend (on the ex-date).[5]
- Record the payment of the dividend (on the payment date).

The first step is to determine the amount of dividend that the fund is entitled to receive. This is generally straightforward: dividends are quoted in an amount per share. In the case of Microsoft above, the company paid a dividend of $0.11 USD per share in Quarter 1, 2007. The more shares a fund owns, the greater the total dividend. The fund accountant will need to refer to the detailed portfolio (or contact the custodian) to determine the extent of the holding and multiply this by the dividend per share.

Example 6.1: Dividend Income

You are the fund accountant for a fund that holds European equities. The fund owns 50,000 shares in Allied Irish Banks (AIB). You received a dividend notification from AIB (see Figure 6.3).

Figure 6.3: Dividend Notification from AIB

Ex-Div Date	Issuer Name	Security Name	Curr Code	Net Div €(c)	Tax	Tax Credit	Gross Div €(c)	Record Dt/ Coupon No.	Payment Date
27-FEB-08	ALLIED IRISH BANKS PLC	Ordinary Shares	EUR		W		51.2000	29-FEB-08	23-APR-08

Requirements:

1. Calculate the amount of dividend that the fund will receive.
2. When the dividend is recorded, set out the accounting entries.
3. When the dividend is received, set out the accounting entries.

---

[5] Notice the terminology has changed slightly – the 'ex-dividend date' has been shortened to the 'ex-date'. This 'ex-date' concept will repeat itself again when bonus issues and rights issues are considered. It has a similar meaning in these contexts; hence it tends to be shortened to 'ex-date'.

Solution 6.1 – Part 1: Dividend Income

The amount to be received will be $50,000 \times €0.512 = €25,600$. The solutions to the other requirements follow in the subsequent sections.

6.3.3: Accounting for Dividends – The Ex-Dividend Date

On the ex-date, the fund becomes entitled to the dividend but it has not yet received any cash. Thus, the fund is owed €25,600 by AIB. Consequently, the fund has an asset, which will be called dividends receivable; it is increasing ⇒ debit dividends receivable (debit asset accounts with increases).

On the other side of the transaction, the fund needs to keep track of the total dividends that it has received in a period. The fund probably has holdings in many companies that pay dividends at different times. The dividend that the fund receives is income for the fund. The account that will be used to monitor the dividend income for a period will be called dividend income. This is an income-type account in the statement of operations; the account is increasing as the fund generates dividend income ⇒ credit dividend income (credit income accounts with increases).

Using the figures from Example 6.1 (this is the solution to Requirement 2), on the ex-date, 27/02/08, record the following:

- Dr dividends receivable by €25,600.
- Cr dividend income by €25,600.

Or – for the spreadsheet approach:

- Increase dividends receivable, an asset, by €25,600.
- Increase dividend income, an income item (in the statement of operations) by €25,600.

6.3.4: Accounting for Dividends – The Payment Date

On the payment date, the fund will receive the amount owed from the company. In the case of AIB from Example 6.1, this will occur on 23/04/08, two months after the ex-date. This gives AIB plenty of time to determine who their shareholders were on the ex-date and to organise all the dividend cheques for their thousands of shareholders.

The fund now has more money in its bank account. Thus cash, an asset, is increasing ⇒ debit cash.

The other side of the transaction is to the dividends receivable account. The company no longer owes any dividend to the fund; thus the dividends receivable asset is no longer required. Hence, dividends receivable, an asset, is decreasing ⇒ credit dividends receivable.

Using the figures from Example 6.1 (this is the solution to Requirement 3), on the payment date, 23/04/08, record the following:

- Dr cash by €25,600.
- Cr dividends receivable by €25,600.

Or – for the spreadsheet approach:

- Increase cash, an asset, by €25,600.
- Decrease dividends receivable, an asset, by €25,600.

6.3.5: Accounting for Dividends – Summary

The most common type of corporate action has now been accounted for. It is important to understand the nature of the dividend payments and to be able to account for the transactions underlying dividends.

1. Calculating the dividend: number of shares owned × dividend rate per share
2. On the ex-dividend date record the following:
   o dr dividends receivable
   o cr dividend income
3. On the payment date record the following:
   o dr cash
   o cr dividends receivable

Now try Question 6.10.1.

6.3.6: Dividend Withholding Tax

Dividend withholding tax (DWT) is a tax that exists in many countries. The rates and conditions vary considerably but they tend to follow a similar basis.

As a general rule in taxation, when individuals or companies receive income then they are liable to income tax on that income. So, when an Irish (or UK, or French) company, for example, pays a dividend, the recipients of that dividend should pay Irish (or UK, or French) income tax on that dividend. However, non-resident individuals, companies or investment funds may not be liable to Irish (or UK, or French) income tax. So, to prevent a leakage of tax revenue and to ensure that all shareholders are treated equally, the revenue authorities in many countries require that tax should be deducted at source by the company paying the dividend.

Thus, the non-resident entity receives the dividend less any tax automatically deducted by the company. This regulation whereby the tax on dividends is deducted at source by the dividend paying company is called dividend withholding tax (DWT).[6]

Example 6.2a: Dividend Withholding Tax

Company XYZ is located in Walterland. The government of Walterland has put a tax of 30 per cent on all payments of dividends. An Irish fund holds 100,000 shares in Company XYZ. Recently the company declared a dividend of €0.50 per share.

Calculate the dividend that the fund will receive.

Solution 6.2a: Dividend Withholding Tax

In these circumstances the fund will receive €35,000, with the government of Walterland getting €15,000. This deduction will be made by Company XYZ and paid directly to the revenue authorities of Walterland.

If these regulations did not exist then it would be more beneficial for non-residents to invest in Irish (or UK, or French) companies than Irish residents. The non-residents would receive a dividend tax-free, whereas the resident investors would have to pay tax on their dividend income. This would cause an imbalance in the capital markets, which could create increased difficulties for Irish companies to raise finance. Irish companies would find it more competitive to attract finance from abroad, while Irish investors would find it more advantageous to invest abroad. This is counterintuitive as companies often find it easier to raise finance closer to their base of operations. The DWT is one means of levelling the playing field as a result of the distortions caused by other taxation regulations.

There is a negative effect of DWT. The tax discourages companies from sending profits outside of the host country, instead keeping the cash in the country where it was generated. This was originally the justification for DWT. Politically it is easy to justify to the electorate the argument that 'profits generated in Ireland/UK/Japan should stay in the country'. However, many countries noticed that if they relaxed these provisions, they found it easier to attract inward investment. Multinational companies are more likely to invest in countries where they can easily extract their profits.

---

[6] Resident shareholders may also pay DWT but are usually given a credit in their income tax return for such deductions. The regulations on DWT will differ from country to country.

Thus, DWT is a balancing act between ensuring a level playing field for all investors, generating tax revenue for a country and attracting inward investment.

Many countries have reduced their DWT rates or have offered exemptions to certain types of investors. Investment funds are often exempt from DWT. If this is not the case there may be a further provision whereby an investment fund can reclaim any DWT deducted. The difficulty with these provisions is that it is necessary to be aware of the tax situation in a number of different countries – for example, an Irish domicile investment fund with US investors and investments in European companies will require expert tax advice regarding all these specific circumstances.

For a fund that receives foreign dividend income, the following possibilities exist:

1. No DWT exists. Therefore there are no accounting implications. Record the dividend as outlined earlier.
2. DWT exists but the fund is exempt from DWT. In these circumstances, the fund may have to show the revenue authorities of the foreign country that it is eligible for the exemption. This is likely to involve some paperwork but, generally, once the paperwork is in place then, unless there is a change in circumstances, the exemption holds for future foreign dividends. If the fund is exempt then the company paying the dividend is permitted to pay it without deducting any tax. Consequently, there are no accounting implications. Record the dividend as outlined earlier.
3. DWT exists and is charged but the fund can subsequently reclaim the tax paid. This is quite a common arrangement. It can involve some form filling and a lengthy wait for the repayment. If the fund is in receipt of many of these dividends then there will need to be a system in place to ensure that the fund fully reclaims any tax it is due; this can be a costly process. There are accounting implications; these are outlined in the next section.
4. DWT exists, is charged and the fund cannot reclaim the tax paid. This also has accounting implications, which are outlined in the next section.

6.3.7: Dividend Withholding Tax – Accounting Implications

Firstly, consider a fund that can reclaim any DWT that it has been charged (scenario 3 above).

Example 6.2b – DWT Revisited

Company XYZ is located in Walterland. The government of Walterland has put a tax of 30 per cent on all payments of dividends. The fund holds 100,000 shares in

Company XYZ. On 13/05/X6 the fund announces a dividend. The ex-date is 28/05/X6 and the payment date is 28/07/X6. The dividend is €0.50 per share.

The tax system in Walterland allows foreign funds to reclaim any DWT deducted by companies located in Walterland. The fund is only able to reclaim the DWT once it is paid and it takes up to four months for any tax to be returned to the fund. On 30/07/X6 the fund submitted the claim for tax repayment and on 22/11/X6 the fund received the DWT that had been paid.

Set out the accounting entries to record the events described.

Solution 6.2b – DWT Revisited

In these circumstances, on 28/07/X6 the fund will receive €35,000 with the government of Walterland getting €15,000. These amounts will be paid by Company XYZ. Then, on 22/11/X6, the fund receives €15,000 from the government of Walterland – its DWT refund.

There are a number of methods of accounting for this; the simplest assumes that the claim for DWT will be made by the fund and the government will repay the tax as expected. Then on the ex-date (28/05/X6) record the dividend and split the receivable in two – one from the company and the other from the government of Walterland:

- Dr dividends receivable €35,000.
- Dr DWT receivable €15,000.
- Cr dividend income €50,000.

On the payment date (28/07/X6) record the portion of the dividend received from the company:

- Dr cash €35,000.
- Cr dividends receivable €35,000.

On the date the government repays the DWT (22/11/X6) record the receipt of this amount:

- Dr cash €15,000.
- Cr DWT receivable €15,000.

Now consider a situation where it is not possible to reclaim the DWT.

Example 6.2c – DWT Revisited Again

Company XYZ is located in Walterland. The government of Walterland has put a tax of 30 per cent on all payments of dividends. The fund holds 100,000 shares in Company XYZ. On 13/05/X6, the fund announces a dividend. The ex-date is 28/05/X6 and the payment date is 28/07/X6. The dividend is €0.50 per share. The taxation system in Walterland does not permit foreign funds to reclaim DWT paid.

Set out the accounting entries to record the events described.

Solution 6.2c – DWT Revisited Again

In these circumstances, on 28/07/X6 the fund will receive €35,000, with the government of Walterland getting €15,000. This deduction will be made by Company XYZ. The fund will not be permitted to get this €15,000 back.

There are two methods of accounting for this. The first is just to account for the net amount of €35,000. The second is to account for the gross amount of the dividend (€50,000) and show a tax expense of €15,000. It is the second method that is more widely used as it can give investors an indication of the tax the fund is leaking as a result of investing in companies in Walterland and similar countries (it could be that there is a requirement on the investment managers to invest a certain percentage of the fund in Walterland – the fund's prospectus will indicate this).

Then on the ex-date (28/05/X6) record the dividend – record the full dividend as income and show the DWT as a tax expense:

- Dr dividends receivable €35,000.
- Dr taxation expense €15,000.
- Cr dividend income €50,000.

On the payment date (28/07/X6) record the payment of the dividend:

- Dr cash €35,000.
- Cr dividends receivable €35,000.

There are no further transactions required.

It is not necessary to be an expert in the taxation regulations of every country on the planet. It is likely that any investment fund only invests in the equities (or bonds) of companies located in a limited number of countries. It is also likely that these countries are developed economies and that someone else has come across this situation before. Consequently, in many fund accounting organisations, there is probably a list of countries and their DWT regimes. If not, seek expert tax advice to determine the exact arrangement between the country in which the fund is domiciled and the country in which the dividend-paying company is domiciled.[7] A final note of caution – tax regulations can change over time, so it is important to have access to a reliable source of information on any new variations.

Try Question 6.10.2.

6.4: STOCK DIVIDENDS

A stock dividend is where the fund takes a dividend in the form of shares or equities in the company instead of cash. There are two types of stock dividends:

1. Where all shareholders in the company have no choice but to receive the dividend in the form of shares. This is the same as a bonus or scrip issue (see Section 6.6). It is also called a scrip dividend.
2. Where shareholders are given the choice to receive their dividend as shares or cash. This is the most common type of stock dividend and will be considered in the remainder of this section.

6.4.1: Cash versus Stock Dividend – Which Is Best?

Most large companies routinely give their shareholders this option. They even offer a dividend reinvestment programme (DRIP or DRP) to encourage shareholders to take the stock dividend option (a stock dividend is also known as dividend reinvestment). The reinvestment option is often very attractive to smaller investors. There are a number of benefits:

- Shareholders get to purchase the shares without any transaction and brokerage costs.
- Shareholders are often given the opportunity to purchase more shares beyond their dividend entitlement (subject to a limit) at the same time, without any transaction costs.
- Many companies offer the shares at a discount. Those shareholders who take the reinvestment option obtain the shares at a price lower than the market.

---

[7] Domicile, resident and ordinarily resident are complex constructs in taxation. The terms are defined differently for individuals and companies. Indeed, the area has been the subject of much case law as tax practitioners have sought clarifications on numerous occasions. For the purposes of this book, the detail on these issues will not be considered. You can assume that an 'Irish' fund is registered and domiciled in Ireland, and subject to the regulations of the Irish financial regulator.

For example, Macquarie Group regularly gives their shareholders a 2.5 per cent discount when taking the reinvestment option (this can actually rise to 5 per cent in some circumstances).[8]

Generally, when making this decision, there is no impact on the total wealth of the shareholder. The individual shareholder's need for cash is what often guides the decision. Since many funds use dividends to generate cash to pay the expenses of the fund and to support its own distributions, then most funds tend to take the cash option. Most small investors do not have an immediate need for cash (otherwise they would not be buying shares), so they often take the reinvestment option. Example 6.3 will illustrate the dynamic involved.

Example 6.3: Dividend Reinvestment – The Decision

Consider a company that is worth €100,000 and has 100,000 shares in issue. Each share is worth €1.00 (€100,000/100,000 shares).

Next, the company announces a €0.40 dividend per share and all shareholders are given the option of using their dividend to buy shares at €0.60. In this example, assume that nothing else is happening in this company (imagine, for instance, that the company has just one asset – a bank account with €100,000). The price at which the shareholders can buy shares in the company should be the price just after the ex-dividend date (€1.00 less the dividend of €0.40 = €0.60).

Let's assume that a number of shareholders holding a total of 30 per cent of the shares will take the option to reinvest:

- They would have been entitled to a dividend of €12,000 (30,000 shares × €0.40).
- The shareholders will be issued with 20,000 shares (€12,000 dividend/€0.60).
- There will now be 120,000 shares in issue (100,000 original shares + 20,000 new shares).
- All the other shareholders will receive €28,000 cash (70,000 shares × €0.40 dividend), leaving the company worth €72,000 (€100,000 less €28,000).
- The value of each share will be €0.60 (€72,000/120,000 shares).

Consider a cash shareholder who held 120 shares:

- He or she has received a dividend of €48 (120 shares × €0.40).
- He or she still owns 120 shares worth €0.60 each = €72.

---

8   See www.macquarie.com.au/au/about_macquarie/acrobat/drp_summary_Aug07.pdf for the rules on the Macquarie Group DRP.

- This gives a total wealth of €120 (the same as before the dividend, 120 shares at €1 each – remember the company has done nothing other than declare a dividend).

Consider a reinvesting shareholder who held 120 shares:

- He or she gets no dividend.
- The dividend of €48 is reinvested to give 80 new shares (€48/€0.60 = 80 shares).
- He or she now owns 200 shares (120 original shares + 80 new shares) worth €0.60 each = €120.
- This also gives a total wealth of €120.

Notice that both shareholders are equally well off. The cash shareholders have their wealth in both cash and shares, whereas the reinvesting shareholders have their wealth in shares only.

The important issue when making the decision on dividend reinvestment is the determination of the share price at which the reinvestment takes place. Example 6.3 is an abstraction from reality because it was assumed that nothing else was happening in the company.

There are a number of approaches used. Macquarie, for example, uses the average share price for the four days around the record date, Shell buys the shares on the open market as soon as is practicable after the payment date and Honeywell uses the average of the high and low share price on the dividend payment date.[9]

Bank of Ireland uses a different approach, announcing the rate at which they will allow reinvesting shareholders to buy shares in advance of the ex–dividend date – this has the effect of freezing the number of shares that a shareholder can obtain before the payment date. In 2008 Bank of Ireland announced a dividend of €0.394 per share with an ex–dividend date of 28/05/08 and a payment date of 23/07/08. Shareholders were given the option of using their dividend to purchase Bank of Ireland shares at €8.10, which was very close to the closing price on the ex–dividend date (the closing price of Bank of Ireland shares on 28/05/08 was €8.07). Thus, the dividend reinvestment option appeared fair to all shareholders. However, between the ex–dividend date and the payment date, the share price of Bank of Ireland fell dramatically – by 26/06/08 the share price had fallen to €5.97. Although they were not obliged to, the directors decided to cancel the dividend reinvestment option and gave all those shareholders the original cash dividend

---

[9] See www.shell.com and www.honeywell.com for information on their dividend reinvestment plans (located on the investor relations pages).

instead. They could now use their cash dividend to purchase much more shares in Bank of Ireland if they wished (or spend the dividend on other items). This let the reinvesting shareholders off the hook, i.e. they didn't have to reinvest in a company whose share price was in freefall.[10]

When making the decision to reinvest, a shareholder may not know in advance at what price the shares will be issued. However, the price will tend to reflect either the share price just after the ex-date or after the payment date. As seen in the case of Bank of Ireland, if the shareholders are going to suffer greatly as a result of their decision, then the option may be revoked and cash given instead. This can reduce some of the risk of this option, but the Bank of Ireland example will only occur in the most extreme circumstances.

6.4.2: Accounting for a Dividend Reinvestment

This can be a complex set of transactions, but if it is broken into its components it is easier to process:

1. The fund receives a dividend (record as if a normal dividend).
2. The fund effectively uses the dividend to buy equities (record as if a normal purchase of equities).
3. The fund receives the equities (offset the receivable with the payable).

Transaction 1

On the ex-dividend date record the dividends receivable as before. It doesn't matter if the dividend is the form of cash or shares. The fund is entitled to the dividend in either form on the ex-date (a separate account can be opened, a 'stock dividends receivable' account, if warranted). Recall from earlier the entry to record the dividend:

- Dr dividends receivable.
- Cr dividend income.

---

[10] See www.boi.ie for more details – the events described are set out in various announcements made by the company. Go to the investor relations page and then to stock exchange releases. In March 2009, the share price of Bank of Ireland reached an all-time low of just €0.12 – much lower than the dividend paid! One of the reasons for the decision to cancel the stock dividend is that the reinvesting shareholders would not have been able to sell their shares as the share price fell – they were not due to receive the shares until July 2008.

Or – for the spreadsheet approach:

- Increase dividends receivable, an asset.
- Increase dividend income, an income account.

Funds can treat this as income but, depending on the fund's rules, this income may not form part of a distribution to investors; the fund's distribution policy for this item should be stated. If no policy is stated then it is assumed that this type of income is distributable.

Transaction 2

On the date that the company announces the price at which the reinvestment will occur, the fund will need to record the shares that it will now receive. Remember that the fund is effectively purchasing shares with the proceeds of the dividend. As a consequence, this transaction will be recorded similarly to an equity purchase. It will still take some time before the share certificates are finally issued in the fund's name. The fund now effectively has shares in its investment portfolio which cost the same amount as the dividend income foregone. Thus, the investments at cost account, an asset, is increasing ⇒ debit investments at cost account.

The other side of the transaction is that the fund owes money for the shares until the shares are received by the fund. This debt is offset by the receivable for the dividends (an asset) for the same amount with the same company. Accounting regulations (IAS 1[11]) do not permit offsetting assets with liabilities. Thus, it is good practice to show them separately. The fund is using the money it would have received in dividends to pay for the equities, but while it is owed the dividend, the fund owes for the equities. This amount can be put into the investments purchased payable account, a liability account, which is increasing ⇒ credit investments purchased payable. A separate account can be used but it is not absolutely necessary; this account could be called 'dividend reinvestment purchased payable'.

- Dr investments at cost.
- Cr investments purchased payable.

Or – for the spreadsheet approach:

- Increase investments at cost, an asset.
- Increase investments purchased payable, a liability.

---

[11] International Accounting Standards Board (2009b), paragraph 32 (applies to all entities, including 'normal' companies and investment funds).

At this stage, the shares are added to the portfolio and become part of the daily valuation. Any increases/decreases in the value of the shares now have an effect on the NAV per share calculation.

Transaction 3

After some time the shares will be received; this can take a number of weeks, particularly if the company is issuing new shares (some companies just use the dividends foregone to buy shares on the open market, in which case the shares are often acquired faster).

When the shares are received, then the company no longer owes the dividend to the fund and the fund no longer owes that dividend back to the company to buy shares. Thus, there is no need for the amount to be in the dividends receivable account, this account is an asset and it is decreasing ⇒ credit dividends receivable. Likewise, there is no need for the amount to be in the investments purchased payable account, this account is a liability and it is decreasing ⇒ debit investments purchased payable account.

- Dr investments purchased payable.
- Cr dividends receivable account.

Or – for the spreadsheet approach:

- Decrease investments purchased payable, a liability.
- Decrease dividends receivable account, an asset.

Example 6.4: Dividend Reinvestment

You are the fund accountant for a fund that holds 15,000 shares in Brace Plc. The shares were purchased for €2.50 each along with commission of €1,000. On 31/03/X5 the share price of Brace Plc was €5.50.

Requirement:

1. Calculate the balance on the investments at cost account and the unrealised appreciation/depreciation account on 31/03/X5.

On 01/04/X5 Brace Plc announce a dividend of €1.50 per share. The ex-dividend date is 03/04/X5 and the payment date is 05/04/X5. On 01/04/X5 Brace Plc also gave shareholders the option to accept the dividend in the form of shares in Brace Plc. The price at which the shares are to be issued will be the closing price on the ex-dividend date. The fund opted to take its full dividend entitlement in the form of shares in Brace Plc. The shares were received by the fund on 07/04/X5 (for this example the dates are very close together. This simplification permits the highlighting of all of the accounting implications without tedious repetition – in reality, this process takes place over many weeks).

The daily share prices of Brace Plc are provided in Table 6.1.

Table 6.1: Daily Share Prices in Brace Plc

Date	01/04/X5	02/04/X5	03/04/X5	04/04/X5	05/04/X5	06/04/X5	07/04/X5	08/04/X5
Price	€5.60	€5.90	€4.50	€4.30	€4.40	€4.50	€4.55	€4.58

Requirements:

2. Set out the entry to record the various stages of the dividend reinvestment.
3. For each day from 01/04/X5 to 07/05/X5 inclusive, show the balance on the following accounts:

- Investments at cost account
- Unrealised appreciation/depreciation account
- Dividends receivable account
- Investments purchased payable account/dividend reinvestment purchased payable account

Solution 6.4: Dividend Reinvestment

Requirement 1:

Investments at Cost Account = 15,000 shares × €2.50 + €1,000 commission = €38,500

Market value of shares on 31/03/X5 = 15,000 shares × €5.50 = €82,500
Less Investments at Cost $\qquad$ = €38,500
Unrealised Appreciation/(Depreciation) $\qquad$ = €44,000

Requirement 2:

Dividend Income = 15,000 × €1.50 = €22,500
Number of shares in Brace Plc that the company will receive = 5,000 (€22,500/€4.50)

Accounting Entries:

To record the dividend income on 03/04/X5 (ex-dividend date):

- Dr dividends receivable, an asset, by €22,500.
- Cr dividend income, an income account, by €22,500.

Or – for the spreadsheet approach:

- Increase dividends receivable, an asset, by €22,500.
- Increase dividend income, an income account, by €22,500.

To record the dividend reinvestment on 03/04/X5 (date the price for reinvestment is given):

- Dr investments at cost, an asset, by €22,500.
- Cr investments purchased payable, a liability, €22,500.

Or – for the spreadsheet approach:

- Increase investments at cost, an asset, by €22,500.
- Increase investments purchased payable, a liability, by €22,500.

Add 5,000 Brace Plc Shares to Portfolio.

To record receipt of equities in Brace Plc (on 07/04/X5):

- Dr investments purchased payable, a liability, by €22,500.
- Cr dividends receivable account, an asset, by €22,500.

Or – for the spreadsheet approach:

- Decrease investments purchased payable, a liability, by €22,500.
- Decrease dividends receivable account, an asset, by €22,500.

Requirement 3:

In this solution the daily valuation calculation is provided for on 01/04/X5 and 03/04/X5. The other dates are not shown – the approach for these dates is the same so recalculating it should not be difficult. The only other transactions that need to be recorded are the dividend and dividend reinvestment on 03/04/X5 (the ex-date) and the payment of the dividend and receipt of shares on 07/04/X5 (the payment date). See Table 6.2.

Table 6.2: Solution to Example 6.4, Requirement 3

	Investments at Cost A/c	Unrealised Appreciation/ Depreciation A/c	Dividends Receivable A/c	Investments Purchased Payable A/c	Remarks
01/04/X5 Opening Balance	€38,500	€44,000	€0	€0	See Requirement 1
Transaction on 01/04/X5					No accounting on announcement date
Valuation 01/04/X5		€1,500			Note 1
01/04/X5 Closing Balance	€38,500	€45,500	€0	€0	Closing Balance from 01/04/X5
02/04/X5 Opening Balance	€38,500	€45,500	€0	€0	
Transaction on 02/04/X5					No transaction Same approach as 01/04/X5
Valuation on 02/04/X5		€4,500			
02/04/X5 Closing Balance	€38,500	€50,000	€0	€0	
03/04/X5 Opening Balance	€38,500	€50,000	€0	€0	Closing Balance from 02/04/X5
Transaction on 03/04/X5			€22,500		Recording the dividend
Transaction on 03/04/X5	€22,500			€22,500	Recording the reinvestment
Valuation on 03/04/X5		-€21,000			Note 2
03/04/X5 Closing Balance	€61,000	€29,000	€22,500	€22,500	

04/04/X5 Opening Balance	€61,000	€29,000	€22,500	Closing Balance from 03/04/X5
Transaction on 04/04/X5				No transaction Same method as previously
Valuation on 04/04/X5		−€4,000		
04/04/X5 Closing Balance	€61,000	€25,000	€22,500	
05/04/X5 Opening Balance	€61,000	€25,000	€22,500	Closing Balance from 04/04/X5
Transaction on 05/04/X5				No transaction Same method as previously
Valuation on 05/04/X5		€2,000		
05/04/X5 Closing Balance	€61,000	€27,000	€22,500	
06/04/X5 Opening Balance	€61,000	€27,000	€22,500	Closing Balance from 05/04/X5
Transaction on 06/04/X5				No transaction Same method as previously
Valuation on 06/04/X5		€2,000		
06/04/X5 Closing Balance	€61,000	€29,000	€22,500	
07/04/X5 Opening Balance	€61,000	€29,000	€22,500	Closing Balance from 06/04/X5
Transaction on 07/04/X5			−€22,500	Payment and receipt of shares Same method as previously
Valuation on 07/04/X5		€1,000		
07/04/X5 Closing Balance	€61,000	€30,000	€0	

(Continued)

Table 6.2: *(Continued)*

Note 1: Valuation on 01/04/X5

This approach uses the method described in Chapter 5. It is longwinded as it is more suited to situations where there are numerous holdings in the portfolio. The approach is taken to ensure consistency with previous examples.

Step 1: Calculate Market Value

	Shares	Market Price	Value	Notes
Brace Plc	15,000	€5.60	€84,000	

Step 2: Calculate Total Cost of Portfolio

Yesterday's Investments at Cost A/c	€38,500
Additions/Disposals	€0
Today's Total Cost	€38,500

Step 3: Calculate Unrealised Appreciation/Depreciation

Market Value of Portfolio		€84,000
Total Cost of Portfolio		€38,500
Total Unrealised Appreciation/Depreciation		€45,500
Yesterday's Unrealised Appreciation/Depreciation	€44,000	
Gain/Loss on Shares Sold	€0	€44,000
Unrealised Appreciation/Depreciation for the Day		€1,500

Note 2: Valuation on 03/04/X5

There are now 5,000 additional shares in the portfolio. This will need to be reflected in the daily valuation. The approach uses the method described in Chapter 5. It is longwinded as it is more suited to situations where there are numerous holdings in the portfolio. The approach is taken to ensure consistency with previous examples.

Step 1: Calculate Market Value

	Shares	Market Price	Value	Notes
Brace Plc	20,000	€4.50	€90,000	

Step 2: Calculate Total Cost of Portfolio

Yesterday's Investments at Cost A/c	€38,500	
Additions/Disposals	€22,500	Dividend reinvested
Today's Total Cost	€61,000	

Step 3: Calculate Unrealised Appreciation/Depreciation

Market Value of Portfolio		€90,000
Total Cost of Portfolio		€61,000
Total Unrealised Appreciation/Depreciation		€29,000
Yesterday's Unrealised Appreciation/Depreciation	€50,000	
Gain/Loss on Shares Sold	€0	€50,000
Unrealised Appreciation/Depreciation for the Day		−€21,000

The loss in value of €21,000 is offset by the dividend income of €22,500, which is recorded on this day.

Now try Question 6.10.3.

6.5: Share Buy Backs/Return of Capital

'Share buy backs' and 'return of capital' are very similar corporate actions. They both involve a transfer of money from the company to its shareholders. However, they operate under different mechanisms. They are also relatively infrequent events – dividend payments can be made quarterly but share buy backs and return of capital tend to occur when a company has an amount of excess cash. The excess cash could be as a result of a once-off transaction (e.g. selling off part of the business) or built up over time (e.g. as a result of profitable activities over a period of time). Companies that engage in share buy backs and return of capital transactions are, more than likely, past their growth phase and do not need the money for investment. So, rather than waste their excess cash on spurious investments, they decide to return it to shareholders in large once-off payments.

6.5.1: Share Buy Backs

A share buy back is where a company repurchases its own shares from existing shareholders. There are a number of different types of share buy back programmes:

- Equal access programme – this is where all shareholders participate in proportion to their existing shareholding. For example, Company X has 10 million shares outstanding; your fund holds 10,000 of these shares. The company announces that it will repurchase 1 million of its existing shares on an equal access basis. This represents 10 per cent of its outstanding capital. Thus, the fund will be obliged to submit 1,000 of their shares for repurchase. Note: the fund has no choice but to participate in the share buy back.
- Optional buy back programme – this is where shareholders have the option to participate in the buy back. The company will repurchase shares from those shareholders who wish to sell their shares back to the company. An overall limit is set, in advance, by the company. If the limit is exceeded, then there will be an agreed procedure to decide which shareholders get to sell their shares to the company (this could be on a pro-rata basis or on a first-come, first-served basis).
- Open market repurchase – this is where the company participates in the market like any other investor buying shares whenever it gets an opportunity. This is the most common type of share repurchase. It is effectively a type of optional buy back programme as only those shareholders who wish to sell their shares get to participate. There is substantial regulation surrounding open market repurchases. For example, the company cannot establish a

programme in situations where it has price–sensitive information. Also, the company shouldn't use its substantial purchasing power to distort the market. Often the company will limit itself to 105 per cent of the most recently quoted price when buying shares.

- Fixed price offer – this is where the company sets the price at which it is willing to repurchase shares along with the number of shares it wishes to buy. Shareholders are then given the option to participate in the programme. These are not very common.

Consider the example in Figure 6.4 where Diageo announces a share repurchase programme.

Figure 6.4:   Diageo Press Release Announcing Buy Back Programme

---

Diageo puts in place programme to enable the buy back of shares in forthcoming closed period

12 December 2007

Diageo plc announces that it has put in place an irrevocable, non-discretionary programme to allow the company to buy back shares during the closed period which precedes the interim results announcement on 14 February 2008. The buy-back programme during the closed period will be managed by an independent third party, which will make its trading decisions in relation to the company's securities independently of, and uninfluenced by, the company.

Share buy backs will be effected during the period between 2 January 2008 and 14 February 2008 within pre-set parameters. The buy backs will be in accordance with Diageo's general authority to repurchase shares and in accordance with Chapter 12 of the Listing Rules. Consequently the maximum price per Share shall be no more than the higher of (i) an amount equal to 105% of the average of the middle market quotations for a Share (as derived from the London Stock Exchange Daily Official List) for the 5 days when the London Stock Exchange is open for dealing immediately preceding the day on which the Share is contracted to be purchased and (ii) the higher of the price of the last independent trade and the highest current independent bid on the London Stock Exchange official list at the time the purchase is carried out. The shares repurchased will be cancelled on a daily basis.

In announcing this Diageo confirms that currently it has no inside information. Diageo will announce interim results for the six months ending 31 December 2007 on 14 February 2008.

Source: www.diageo.com/newsmedia/pages/resource.aspx?id=399.

A number of items should be noted regarding the share buy back programme (these are not necessarily unique to Diageo):

- This is an open market programme – Diageo will be buying shares on the market just like any other investor.
- The buying decisions will be made by a third party, independent of Diageo. This is to ensure that Diageo does not use any information that may come into its possession to the detriment of its shareholders.
- The time frame for the repurchase programme is preset as 2 January 2008 to 14 February 2008 – this is the closed period. The closed period is normally

two months prior to an earnings announcement, during which time directors and officers of the company are not permitted to purchase shares in the company.

- The maximum price that Diageo (through the third party) will pay for the shares is limited so that the company does not influence the share price.
- Diageo also confirms that it is not in possession of any inside information (not released to the public) that may influence the share price.

Share buy backs have become increasingly popular in recent years. This is because companies can use them to distribute cash to their shareholders without being committed to an annual dividend-style payment. Also, it gives investors the choice – they can sell their shares and take their money or they can stay invested in the company. A further benefit is that it allows companies to change their capital structure relatively quickly (a share buy back will increase any debt in the company relative to equity).[12] In 2004, the top 500 US companies returned more money to shareholders via share repurchases than dividends ($197 billion on share buy backs versus $181 billion on dividends),[13] and the gap has widened since.

6.5.2: Accounting for Share Buy Backs

Accounting for a share buy back is exactly the same as the sale of equities – effectively, the fund is selling part of its portfolio back to the original company. In the case of open market buy backs, the transaction will settle within a few days. For non–open-market share buy backs, it can take some more time for the transaction to settle but the accounting will be the same.

Recall from Chapter 5 the procedure for recording the sale of equities. This will be applied in exactly the same manner when dealing with share buy backs:

- Calculate the proceeds (for share buy backs there may be no commission charged).
- Identify the shares sold (the most common approach is to sell the oldest shares first – FIFO).
- Calculate the cost of the shares sold (remember to include the commission on the original purchase of the shares).
- Calculate the gain/loss on the shares sold.
- Record the transaction and the settlement as two separate transactions.

---

[12] It may appear counterintuitive that a company will want to increase its debt levels. However, in recent times (2000–2008), debt finance has been relatively cheap and freely available.

[13] Dobozs (2005) – citing Standard and Poor's research data.

On the trade date, share buy backs where gains are being realised $(X = Y + Z)$:

- Dr investments sold receivable   €X
- Cr investments at cost   €Y
- Cr unrealised appreciation/depreciation €Z

On the trade date, share buy backs where losses are being realised $(X = Y - Z)$:

- Dr investments sold receivable   €X
- Cr investments at cost   €Y
- Dr unrealised appreciation/depreciation €Z

On the settlement date record the receipt:

- Dr cash   €X
- Cr investments sold receivable   €X

Example 6.5: Share Buy Backs

You are the fund accountant for UK Equities Fund (all amounts are in GBP so there are no foreign exchange issues). Recall the Diageo example above. Table 6.3 shows the holdings the fund has in Diageo.

Table 6.3: Holdings in Diageo of UK Equities Fund

Company	Trade Date	Quantity	Cost	Commission
Diageo	01/02/X1	4,000	£5.50	£1,000
Diageo	01/02/X2	3,000	£6.75	£1,200
Diageo	01/02/X3	5,000	£7.50	£1,500
Diageo	01/02/X4	6,000	£9.90	£1,800

On 12 December 2007 Diageo announces a share buy back programme. On 10 January 2008 the fund agrees to participate in the programme by selling back 6,000 shares to Diageo at a selling price of £12.25 and zero commission; the transaction will settle on 15 January 2008.

Requirement:

Record the above transaction on the relevant dates.

Solution 6.5: Share Buy Backs

A. On 12 December 2007: recording the share buy back in Diageo – no transaction occurs on 12 December as this is just the announcement date.

B. On 10 January 2008: the company offers its shares to Diageo and the shares are accepted by Diageo; this is the trade date.

1. Sales Proceeds = $6,000 \times £12.25 - £0 = £73,500$.
2. Identify the shares repurchased – all of the first batch of 4,000 shares and 2,000 of the second batch are sold.
3. Determine the cost of shares repurchased:
   Batch 1 = $4,000 \times £5.50 + £1,000 = £23,000$
   Batch 2 = $(3,000 \times £6.75 + £1,200) \times 2,000/3,000 = £14,300$
   Batch 1 + Batch 2 = $£37,300$
4. Calculate the gain on the share buy back: $£73,500 - £37,300 = £36,200$.

- Dr investments sold receivable by £73,500.
- Cr investments at cost by £37,300.
- Cr unrealised appreciation/depreciation by £36,200.

Or – for the spreadsheet approach:

- Increase investments sold receivable, an asset, by £73,500.
- Decrease investments at cost, an asset, by £37,300.
- Decrease unrealised appreciation/depreciation, an asset, by £36,200.

C. On 15 January 2008 the fund receives its cash and gives 6,000 shares back to Diageo:

- Dr cash by £73,400.
- Cr investments sold receivableby £73,400.

Or – for the spreadsheet approach:

- Increase cash, an asset, by £73,400.
- Decrease investments sold receivable, an asset, £73,400.

6.5.3: Return of Capital/Special Dividend

A return of capital is sometimes called a special dividend. It is very similar to a share buy back – the fund will receive a significant amount of cash from the company it had invested in. However, after the transaction the fund will still have the same number of shares as before, whereas with a share buy back the fund will end up with fewer shares.

The dividend history of Microsoft is shown in Figure 6.5. In 2004, the company paid a special dividend of $3 per share when the normal dividend was running at $0.10 per share. The reason for such a special dividend (or return of capital) was because there was a change in tax law in the US making it more advantageous to pay dividends and Microsoft had a large pool of excess cash available.

Figure 6.5: Extract from Microsoft's Dividend History

Quarterly Dividend

Dividend Period	Amount	Announcement Date	Ex-Dividend Date	Record Date	Payable Date
FY2006 Q1	$0.08	September 22, 2005	November 15, 2005	November 17, 2005	December 8, 2005
FY2005 Q4	$0.08	June 15, 2005	August 15, 2005	August 17, 2005	September 08, 2005
FY2005 Q3	$0.08	March 23, 2005	May 16, 2005	May 18, 2005	June 09, 2005
FY2005 Q2	$0.08	December 08, 2004	February 15, 2005	February 17, 2005	March 10, 2005
FY2005 Q1	$0.08	September 15, 2004	November 15, 2004	November 17, 2004	December 02, 2004
Special	$3.00	July 20, 2004	November 15, 2004	November 17, 2004	December 02, 2004
FY2004 Q4	$0.08	July 20, 2004	August 23, 2004	August 25, 2004	September 14, 2004

Source: selected extract from www.microsoft.com/msft/FAQ/dividend.mspx.

On the ex-dividend date of a special dividend (or return of capital), a significant drop in share price is expected (by up to $3 per share). This should occur on 15 November 2004. On 14 November 2004 Microsoft was trading at $29.97 per share; this fell to €27.39 by the end of 15 November 2004 – a fall of nearly $3.00 (the fall is not exactly $3.00 because of trading activity in the share over the day).[14]

---

[14] Source for price data is www.yahoofinance.com. The code for Microsoft is MSFT. Put this code (MSFT) into the 'Get Quotes' box. This will give the current details on Microsoft's share price. Use the 'Interactive Chart' option to get the historic data on Microsoft. This information is available for free – try to use the 'Interactive Chart' tool for yourself to see the movements in share price for Microsoft in November 2004.

From a fund accounting perspective, the issue is how to account for this. There are two alternatives (the final result will be the same):

- Treat the payment as any other dividend (i.e. treat it as income).
- Treat the payment as a return of capital (i.e. treat it as capital).

The distinction being made will not have any impact on the NAV per share but it may have an impact on the distributions made by the fund to its investors. If the first option is taken and the fund has a policy of distributing all of its income to its investors, then a large distribution may have to be made to the fund's investors. If the second option is taken then there will be no reason for a large payment.

Either option is acceptable. From a purely theoretical perspective, there is a distinction between a return of capital and a dividend. A dividend is not a return of capital as dividends should be distributions of profits; more correctly, a dividend is a return *on* capital. For example, suppose today a shareholder invests €100,000 in a new start-up company. The following day, the company announces a return of capital of €30,000 to its investors. It gives €30,000 back and the remaining investment is worth €70,000. A shareholder would not view this €30,000 as a 30 per cent return on investment. Alternatively, consider a shareholder who invests €100,000 in a company and one year later the company has made a profit of €10,000. This increases the value of the investment to €110,000. Next, the company announces a dividend of €10,000. The investor receives €10,000 cash, while the remaining investment is worth €100,000. An investor would probably view this as a 10 per cent return on the original investment. This highlights the difference between a return of capital and a dividend: dividends are seen as being recurring payments from the profits of a business (although not guaranteed), whereas returns of capital and share buy backs are one-off events.

6.5.4: Accounting for Return of Capital/Special Dividends

As noted earlier, there are two basic approaches: treat the payment as income (i.e. a dividend) or treat it as capital. Figure 6.6 illustrates the possible treatments.

A: Treat the Payment as Income/Dividend

The procedure is exactly the same as for any other dividend (this may be accompanied by a loss on the daily valuation on the ex-date, but one should cancel the other). Recall, from earlier, the entries for dividend income:

On the ex-dividend date record the following:

- Dr dividends receivable.
- Cr dividend income.

Figure 6.6: Return of Capital – Accounting Treatments

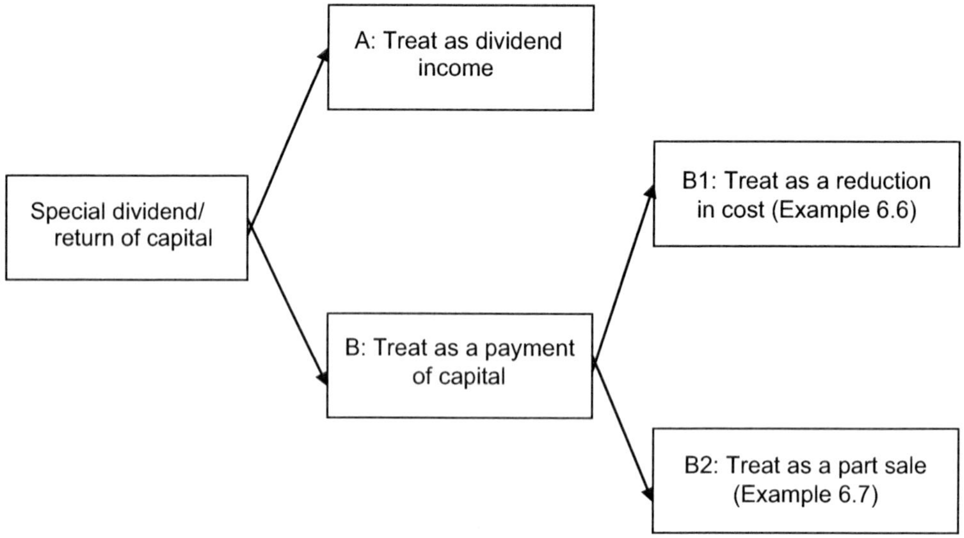

On the payment date record the following:

- Dr cash.
- Cr dividends receivable.

This is a common approach. For an example see the Bridges Investment Fund.[15] This fund had a significant holding in Microsoft shares in 2004. As a consequence of the Microsoft special dividend, the fund generated a large income from operations. As the fund was required to pay any surplus income from operations as distributions, the fund paid an unexpectedly large distribution in 2004.

B: Treat the Payment as Capital

There are two potential methods of accounting as capital.

- B1: treat as a reduction in cost.
- B2: treat as a part sale (i.e. part realising any gains).

When a company returns capital to its shareholders then this can be viewed as a reduction in the base cost of the investment (option B1). Consider the following chain of events in Example 6.6.

---

[15] Bridges Investment Fund Annual Report for the year ending 31 December 2004. See page 3 of the Shareholders' Letter.

Example 6.6: Return of Capital – Reduction in Cost (B1)

Day 1: fund invests €1,000,000 in Company Y; market value of the investment is €1,000,000.

Day 2: company Y announces and pays a return of capital and the fund receives €100,000. The market value of Company Y is now €902,000.

Day 3: the market value of Company Y is €910,000.

Solution 6.6: Return of Capital – Reduction in Cost (B1)

Day 1

Day 1 transaction would be accounted for by (as normal):

- Dr investments at cost by €1,000,000.
- Cr investments purchased payable by €1,000,000.

The valuation of the portfolio at the end of the day reveals that the investment has neither appreciated nor depreciated in value.

- Dr unrealised appreciation/depreciation by €0.
- Cr gains/losses on investments by €0.

Day 2

Next, the fund needs to decide how to report the return of capital on Day 2. Has the investment lost €98,000 (the €1,000,000 invested less the current value of €902,000) or has the investment gained €2,000 (the €1,000,000 invested less €100,000 return of capital, giving €900,000, which can be compared against the current value of €902,000)? The latter is probably more reflective of the underlying events.

Thus, to give this effect, reduce investments at cost by €100,000; investments at cost, an asset, is decreasing ⇒ credit investments at cost. At the same time, the fund is due to receive €100,000 from Company Y (this will settle in a number of days depending on the exact arrangements in place). A separate account can be set up for these amounts – return of capital receivable. This account is an asset and is increasing ⇒ debit return of capital receivable.

- Dr return of capital receivable by €100,000.
- Cr investments at cost by €100,000.

Next the daily movement in the value of the investment needs to be calculated and recorded. This is a simple calculation (€2,000 increase in value), but the standard approach will be used, as often a fund can have hundreds of investments in its portfolio and these items can easily be lost in a sea of numbers. So recall from Chapter 5 the approach that was used; it will be exactly the same again here (see Table 6.4).

Table 6.4: Day 2 – Unrealised Appreciation/Depreciation

	Price	Quantity	Market Value
Company Y	?	?	€902,000
Market Value of Portfolio (today, day 2)			€902,000
Cost of Portfolio (today, day 2) (Note 1)			€900,000
Total Unrealised Appreciation/Depreciation			€2,000
Unrealised Appreciation/Depreciation from Yesterday		€0	
Less Gain Sold		€0	€0
Gain for Day			**€2,000**

Note 1: Cost of Portfolio:

Opening Investments at Cost from Yesterday	€1,000,000
Less Return of Capital	€100,000
Investments at Cost at End of Day	€900,000

Thus, the gain for the day is €2,000. This is recorded as follows (from Chapter 5):

- Dr unrealised appreciation/depreciation by €2,000 (in statement of net assets).
- Cr gains/losses on investments by €2,000 (in statement of operations).

Day 3

This is a 'normal' day – just the daily movement needs to be recorded. Again, this is not a difficult calculation, an increase of €8,000, using the standard format; Table 6.5 shows the calculation.

This is recorded as follows (from Chapter 5):

- Dr unrealised appreciation/depreciation by €8,000.
- Cr gains/losses on investments by €8,000.

Recall, from Figure 6.6 on return of capital accounting treatments, that there is an alternative method of accounting for a return of capital. In Example 6.6 it was assumed that the return of capital was to be treated as a reduction in cost. However, it can also be treated as a part sale. The part sale treatment (B2) will be described in Example 6.7.

Table 6.5:   Day 3 – Unrealised Appreciation/Depreciation

	Price	Quantity	Market Value
Company Y	?	?	€910,000
Market Value of Portfolio (today, day 3)			€910,000
Cost of Portfolio (today, day 3) (Note 1)			€900,000
Total Unrealised Appreciation/Depreciation			€10,000
Unrealised Appreciation/Depreciation from Yesterday		€2,000	
Less Gain Sold		€0	€2,000
Gain for the Day			**€8,000**

Note 1: Cost of Portfolio:

Opening Investments at Cost from Yesterday	€900,000
Less Movements on Day	€0
Investments at Cost at End of Day	€900,000

Example 6.7: Return of Capital – Part Sale (B2)

On 01/01/X1: fund invests €1,000,000 in Company Y.

On 14/05/X6: this investment has increased in value over the years to be now worth €3,000,000.

On 15/05/X6: company Y announces and pays a return of capital and the fund receives €1,200,000. The market value of Company Y is now €1,802,000.

On 16/05/X6: the market value of Company Y is €1,810,000.

Solution 6.7: Return of Capital – Part Sale (B2)

14/05/X6

The following balances exist in the funds records

- Dr investments at cost by €1,000,000.
- Dr unrealised appreciation/depreciation by €2,000,000.

15/05/X6

What is the most appropriate way of reporting on the return of capital? The transaction is not a dividend, so it may not be appropriate to treat it as dividend income (treatment option A). Also, if the full €1,200,000 of the return of capital was treated as a reduction in cost, then the cost would become negative, which is not logical (treatment option B1).

The return of capital of €1,200,000 is partly a return of the original investment and partly a return of the gains made since (this is similar to a sale of equities). This split can be done based on the proportion of cost to market value on the day before the return of capital.

On the day before the return of capital, cost made up 33 per cent of the market value (€1 million of the €3 million market value) and unrealised appreciation/deprecation made up 67 per cent of the market value (€2 million of the €3 million market value). Thus, 33 per cent of the return of capital of €1,200,000 is a reduction in cost, i.e. €400,000, and 67 per cent of €1,200,000 is a reduction in the unrealised appreciation, i.e. €800,000. To record this, the transaction is:

- Dr return of capital receivable by €1,200,000.
- Cr investments at cost by €400,000.
- Cr unrealised appreciation/depreciation by €800,000.

Next, the daily movement in the value of the investment needs to be calculated and recorded. As before, this is a simple calculation (€2,000 increase in value) but the standard approach will be used. Recall from Chapter 5 the approach that was used; it will be exactly the same again here, as shown in Table 6.6.

Table 6.6:   15/05/X6 – Unrealised Appreciation/Depreciation

	Price	Quantity	Market Value
Company Y	?	?	€1,802,000
Market Value of Portfolio (today, 15/05/X6)			€1,802,000
Cost of Portfolio (today, 15/05/X6) (Note 1)			€600,000
Total Unrealised Appreciation/Depreciation			€1,202,000
Unrealised Appreciation/Depreciation from Yesterday		€2,000,000	
Less Gain Realised		€800,000	€1,200,000
Gain for the Day			**€2,000**
Note 1: Cost of Portfolio:			
Opening Investments at Cost from Yesterday	€1,000,000		
Less Return of Capital at Cost	€400,000		
Investments at Cost at End of Day	€600,000		

Thus, the gain for the day is €2,000. This is recorded as follows (from Chapter 5):

- Dr unrealised appreciation/depreciation by €2,000.
- Cr gains/losses on investments by €2,000.

16/05/X6

This is a 'normal' day – just the daily movement needs to be recorded. Again, this is not a difficult calculation – an increase of €8,000. Using the standard format it can be calculated as shown in Table 6.7.

Table 6.7: 16/05/X6 – Unrealised Appreciation/Depreciation

	Price	Quantity	Market Value
Company Y	?	?	€1,810,000
Market Value of Portfolio (today, 16/05/X6)			€1,810,000
Cost of Portfolio (today, 16/05/X6) (Note 1)			€600,000
Total Unrealised Appreciation/Depreciation			€1,210,000
Unrealised Appreciation/Depreciation from Yesterday		€1,202,000	
Less Gain Sold		€0	€1,202,000
Gain for the Day			**€8,000**
Note 1: Cost of Portfolio:			
Opening Investments at Cost from Yesterday	€600,000		
Less Movements on Day	€0		
Investments at Cost at End of Day	€600,000		

This is recorded as follows (from Chapter 5):

- Dr unrealised appreciation/depreciation by €8,000.
- Cr gains/losses on investments by €8,000.

6.5.5: Accounting for Return of Capital/Special Dividends – Which Method?

There were three methods outlined above for accounting for a return of capital or a special dividend. The method to be used is a matter of choice.

- A: treat as a dividend.
- B1: treat as a reduction in cost.
- B2: treat as a part sale (i.e. part-realising any gains).

The method of accounting will not impact on the NAV per share but may impact on the distributable profits of the fund.

If the amount is small relative to the value of the investment then option A is acceptable. Where the amounts become more significant relative to the value of the investment then option B2 is probably more appropriate.

6.5.6: Return of Capital and Share Buy Back – Summary

Example 6.8: Share Buy Back and Return of Capital

You are the fund accountant for the Timkara Fund. On 17/07/X8 the fund had holdings as shown in Table 6.8 (assume all holdings are in EUR).

Table 6.8: Portfolio of the Timkara Fund on 17/07/X8

Company	Trade Date	Quantity	Cost	Commission	Total Cost	17/07/X8 Share Price	17/07/X8 Market Value
Microsoft	02/05/X3	10,000	€14.70	€1,000	€148,000	€29.97	€299,700
Microsoft	19/12/X5	12,000	€18.40	€2,400	€223,200	€29.97	€359,640
SAP	31/10/X4	30,000	€29.00	€2,400	€872,400	€35.00	€1,050,000
Datalink	10/08/X4	6,000	€25.00	€1,800	€151,800	€41.00	€246,000
Intel	09/12/X7	14,000	€22.00	€2,100	€310,100	€24.00	€336,000
Sql IT	02/09/X5	19,000	€18.50	€850	€352,350	€32.11	€610,090
Total					€2,057,850		€2,901,430

You should be able to calculate the 'total cost' and 'market value' columns. From the information above the following balances exist in the statement of net assets:

- Investments at cost account   €2,057,850   (dr balance)
- Unrealised appreciation/depreciation account   €843,580   (dr balance)

During 18/07/X8 the following events occurred:

- Sql IT had previously announced a share buy back programme. On 18/07/X8 the fund agrees to sell 5,000 shares back to Sql IT at a price of €32.30 per share, no commission and a settlement date of 27/07/X8.
- Microsoft had previously announced a special dividend of €3 per share; the ex-date is 18/07/X8. The special dividend is to be recorded as income (Option A) with a settlement on 21/08/X8.
- SAP had previously announced a return of capital of €18 per share, the ex-date is 18/07/X8. The return of capital is to be recorded as a reduction in cost (Option B1) with a settlement on 01/08/X8.
- Datalink had previously announced a return of capital of €24.60 per share; the ex-date is 18/07/X8. The return of capital is to be recorded as a partial reduction in cost and a partial reduction in unrealised appreciation/depreciation (Option B2) with a settlement on 01/08/X8.

Table 6.9 shows the official closing prices at the end of 18/07/X8.

Table 6.9: Selected Official Closing Prices on 18/07/X8

Company	18/07/X8 Share Price
Microsoft	€27.05
SAP	€18.75
Datalink	€17.00
Intel	€25.00
Sql IT	€32.40

Requirements:

- Record the share buy back in Sql IT.
- Record the special dividend and return of capital in Microsoft, SAP and Datalink.
- Record the movement in the unrealised appreciation/depreciation account for the day.
- Show the investments at cost account and the unrealised appreciation/depreciation account.

Solution 6.8: Share Buy Back and Return of Capital

Record the Share Buy Back in Sql IT

1. Sales proceeds: $5,000 \times €32.30 - €0$ (commission) $= €161,500$
2. Identify the shares repurchased: 5,000 of the only batch purchased (19,000) were surrendered.
3. Determine the cost of shares repurchased:
   Batch $1 = (19,000 \times €18.50 + €850) \times 5,000/19,000 = €92,724$
4. Calculate the gain on the share buy back: $€161,500 - €92,724 = €68,776$

- Dr investments sold receivable by €161,500.
- Cr investments at cost by €92,724.
- Cr unrealised appreciation/depreciation by €68,776.

Or – for the spreadsheet approach:

- Increase investments sold receivable, an asset, by €161,500.
- Decrease investments at cost, an asset, by €92,724.
- Decrease unrealised appreciation/depreciation, an asset, by €68,776.

Record the Microsoft Special Dividend (to be recorded as dividend income)

1. Calculate the amount of income: $(10,000 + 12,000) \times €3 = €66,000$

- Dr dividends receivable by €66,000.
- Cr dividend income by €66,000.

Or – for the spreadsheet approach:

- Increase dividends receivable, an asset, by €66,000.
- Increase dividend income, an income, by €66,000.

Record the SAP Return of Capital (to be recorded as a reduction in cost)

1. Calculate the amount to be received: $30,000 \times €18 = €540,000$

- Dr return of capital receivable by €540,000.
- Cr investments at cost by €540,000.

Or – for the spreadsheet approach:

- Increase return of capital receivable, an asset, by €540,000.
- Reduce investments at cost, an asset, by €540,000.

Record the Datalink Return of Capital (to be recorded as a partial reduction in cost and unrealised gains/losses)

1. Calculate the amount to be received: $6,000 \times €24.60 = €147,600$
2. Calculate the percentage of cost to market value and percentage unrealised appreciation/depreciation to market value:

- Total cost of Datalink investment = €151,800 ($6,000 \times €25.00 + €1,800$).
- Market value of Datalink on 17/07/X8 = €246,000 ($6,000 \times €41.00$).
- Percentage cost to market value = €151,800/€246,000 $\times 100\% = 62\%$.
- Percentage gains to market value = 38% ($100\% - 62\%$).

3. Calculate the amount of the proceeds that represents 'Cost' returned to the fund: €147,600 $\times 62\% = €91,512$
4. Calculate the amount of the proceeds the represents 'Gains' returned to the fund: €147,600 $\times 38\% = €56,088$

- Dr return of capital receivable by €147,600.
- Cr investments at cost by €91,512.
- Cr unrealised appreciation/depreciation by €56,088.

Or – for the spreadsheet approach:

- Increase return of capital receivable, an asset, by €147,600.
- Reduce investments at cost, an asset, by €91,512.
- Reduce unrealised appreciation/depreciation, an asset, by €56,088.

Calculate the Daily Unrealised Appreciation/Depreciation

Table 6.10 shows the calculation of the unrealised appreciation/depreciation of the Timkara Fund for 18/07/X8.

Table 6.10: Unrealised Appreciation/Depreciation of the Timkara Fund for 18/07/X8

	Price	Quantity	Market Value
Microsoft	€27.05	22,000	€595,100
SAP	€18.75	30,000	€562,500
Datalink	€17.00	6,000	€102,000
Intel	€25.00	14,000	€350,000
Sql IT (less 5,000 shares)	€32.40	14,000	€453,600
Market Value of Portfolio (today, 18/07/X8)			€2,063,200
Cost of Portfolio (today, 18/07/X8) (Note 1)			€1,333,614
Total Unrealised Appreciation/Depreciation			€729,586
Unrealised Appreciation/Depreciation from Yesterday		€843,580	
Less Gain Sold with SQL Shares		€68,776	
Less Gain Returned with Datalink		€56,088	€718,716
Gain for the Day			**€10,870**
Note 1: Cost of Portfolio:			
Opening Investments at Cost from Yesterday			€2,057,850
Less Cost of SQL Shares			€92,724
Less SAP Return of Capital			€540,000
Less Datalink Return of Capital			€91,512
Investments at Cost at End of Day			€1,333,614

This is recorded as follows (from Chapter 5):

- Dr unrealised appreciation/depreciation by €10,870.
- Cr gains/losses on investments by €10,870.

Or – for the spreadsheet approach:

- Increase unrealised appreciation/depreciation, an asset, by €10,870.
- Increase gains/losses on investments, an income item, by €10,870.

Now try Question 6.10.4.

6.6: Bonus Issues/Scrip Issues/Stock Splits

A bonus issue, scrip issue and stock split are different terms used to describe the same event. It is where a company gives its shareholders new shares at no cost. Stock splits only take place on rare occasions, depending on the rate of growth in the company's share price, among other factors.

Consider the following scenario. Growco's share price has increased substantially over the past number of years. The company has 10,000,000 shares in issue, each with a share price of €120 – giving a total value of €1,200 million. The directors are concerned that the share price is so high that it is discouraging some smaller investors from buying shares in the company. So the directors decide to make a bonus issue of 2 for 1 – all existing investors in the company will be given two shares for every one share that they originally owned.

This will effectively double the number of shares in issue from 10 million to 20 million. Nothing has happened to the company itself – it still has the same assets and liabilities, products and profitability. Thus the value of the company will remain at €1,200 million. A bonus issue is not a money-making machine; otherwise companies would be engaging in bonus issues every other day. The share price will fall from €120 to €60, or €1,200 million divided by 20 million shares.

While the share price of Growco has fallen by €60, the shareholders are no better or worse off than before. Say a fund originally held 4,000 shares in Growco. These would have originally been worth 4,000 × €120 = €480,000. After the bonus issue, the shares are now worth €60 but the fund has twice as many shares, 8,000 shares, giving a total value of 8,000 × €60 = €480,000.

6.6.1: The Bonus Rate

In the example above the bonus rate was 2 for 1. This can vary depending on the circumstances; the rate of bonus can be whatever the directors decide upon. For example, it could be a 3 for 1 stock split or a 3 for 2 split. See Table 6.11 for the impact the differing rates can have on the outstanding shares of a company.

Table 6.11:   Impact of Different Bonus Rates on Share Prices

Bonus Rate	Number of Shares pre Bonus	Share Price pre Bonus	Market Value pre Bonus	Number of Shares post Bonus	Market Value post Bonus	Share Price post Bonus
2 for 1	10 million	€120	€1,200 million	20 million	€1,200 million	€60
3 for 1	10 million	€120	€1,200 million	30 million	€1,200 million	€40
3 for 2	10 million	€120	€1,200 million	15 million	€1,200 million	€80
5 for 4	10 million	€120	€1,200 million	12.5 million	€1,200 million	€96

As can be seen from Table 6.11, the rate of the bonus will impact on the subsequent share price after the issue. No matter what the bonus rate is, the impact on the value of the company and the total value of an investor's holding will remain unchanged.

Consider the example in Table 6.12 from Bank of Ireland. On 19 July 1999 Bank of Ireland had a 2 for 1 bonus issue. After the bonus issue the share price of Bank of Ireland decreased by nearly 50 per cent, representing the increased number of shares in issue. Theoretically, we would expect the share price to be €9.05 (half of €18.10), but the share price increased by €0.20 to €9.25 based on movements over the day.

Table 6.12: Bank of Ireland Bonus Issue

Date	Share Price	Market Value
15 July 1999	€17.65	€9,158
16 July 1999	€18.10	€9,392
19 July 1999	€9.25	€9,636
20 July 1999	€8.95	€9,324

Source: www.ise.ie[16]

Microsoft is an example of a fast-growth company that has had numerous bonus issues since it was first quoted on the stock market in 1986. Figure 6.7 shows the stock split history of Microsoft. If an investor had purchased one share in 1986, he or she would now hold 288 shares in Microsoft today. At a share price of $29.63 (on 18 March 2010), this gives a total value of $8,533; had Microsoft not engaged in any bonus issues each share would be worth $8,533.[17] Such a high price per share may discourage many smaller investors who may have much smaller sums of money to invest.

Figure 6.7: Stock Split History of Microsoft

Payable Date	Type of Split	Closing Price Before	Closing Price After
September 18, 1987	2 for 1	$114.50 (Sep 18)	$53.50 (Sept 21)
April 12, 1990	2 for 1	$120.75 (Apr 12)	$60.75 (Apr 16)
June 26, 1991	3 for 2	$100.75 (Jun 26)	$68.00 (Jun 27)
June 12, 1992	3 for 2	$112.50 (Jun 12)	$75.75 (Jun 15)
May 20, 1994	2 for 1	$97.75 (May 20)	$50.63 (May 23)
December 6, 1996	2 for 1	$152.875 (Dec 6)	$81.75 (Dec 9)
February 20, 1998	2 for 1	$155.13 (Feb 20)	$81.63 (Feb 23)
March 26, 1999	2 for 1	$178.13 (Mar 26)	$92.38 (Mar 29)
February 14, 2003	2 for 1	$48.30 (Feb 14)	$24.96 (Feb 18)

Source: www.microsoft.com/msft/FAQ/stocksplit.mspx.

Based on the information provided in Figure 6.7 for Microsoft, try to recalculate the 288 shares that a fund would now hold in Microsoft had it purchased one share in the company in 1986. Take care to note that each stock split is compounded on all of the previous stock splits. Thus, after the first stock split on 18 September 1987, the fund would hold two Microsoft shares (on an original notional share-holding of one share). After the second stock split on 12 April 1990, the fund

---

[16] Most commercial pricing sources (for example, DataStream) adjust historic prices to remove the effect of stock splits. The official prices of the Irish Stock Exchange do not perform this adjustment – the prices are given as originally quoted. To find historic prices on the Irish Stock Exchange go to www.ise.ie, select the company in question, follow the link to 'equity price history' and enter the appropriate dates.

[17] All Microsoft information is taken from www.microsoft.com/msft/.

would hold four Microsoft shares. Continue with this logic to show that, after the last stock split on 14 February 2003, the fund would hold 288 shares (based on an original notional shareholding of one share before 18 September 1987).

The decision to have a bonus issue rests with the directors of the company. Some companies have decided not to split their shares (these types of companies are rare). However, there is a famous example of such a company: Berkshire Hathaway. Berkshire Hathaway is one of the largest companies in the world. One of the richest men in the world, Warren Buffet, owns a significant portion of it. Since 1965, the company has never had a share split. As a result its shares are worth $123,412 each (as on 18 March, 2010). Owning a share in Berkshire Hathaway gives the investor membership of a very exclusive club! However, the high share price does mean smaller investors may be unable to invest in Berkshire Hathaway.[18]

6.6.2: Accounting for Bonus Issues

Accounting for bonus issues is straightforward – there is no accounting; no debit or credit is required. Instead, it is important to update the number of shares in the fund's portfolio. On the ex-date of the bonus issue the share price of the company concerned will decrease. A failure to increase the number of shares in the portfolio will result in a misstatement of the value of the portfolio.

Example 6.9: Bonus Issues

Table 6.13 shows the portfolio of Fund Z.

From the information in Table 6.13 the following balances exist in the statement of net assets:

- Investments at cost account   €1,431,000   (dr balance)
- Unrealised appreciation/depreciation account   €361,500   (dr balance)

On 18/07/X8 the following events take place:

- It is the ex-date for a bonus issue in EDF (who had announced this bonus issue on a previous date). The rate of the bonus issue is 3 for 1.
- It is the ex-date for a bonus issue in E.On (who had previously announced this bonus issue on an earlier date). The rate of the bonus issue is 5 for 2.

---

[18] Berkshire Hathaway does have B shares that are targeted at smaller investors. These shares have 1/1,500th of the rights of the main shares (in terms of dividends and liquidation rights) and only 1/10,000th of the voting rights of a full share. These shares were trading at $82.28 as on 18 March 2010. All Berkshire Hathaway information is taken from www.berkshirehathaway.com. Stock price information is available on http://finance.yahoo.com/q?s=BRK-A&d=t.

Table 6.13:   Portfolio of Fund Z

Company	Trade Date	Quantity	Cost	Commission	Total Cost	17/07/X8 Share Price	17/07/X8 Market Value
EDF	02/05/X3	5,000	€22.00	€2,000	€112,000	€35.00	€175,000
EDF	19/12/X5	7,000	€28.00	€2,800	€198,800	€35.00	€245,000
E.On	31/10/X4	22,000	€4.50	€2,200	€101,200	€7.50	€165,000
France Telecom	10/08/X4	7,000	€14.00	€2,100	€100,100	€18.00	€126,000
Telefonica	09/12/X7	15,000	€22.00	€3,000	€333,000	€24.00	€360,000
Vinci	02/09/X5	12,000	€18.50	€2,400	€224,400	€30.00	€360,000
Total					*€1,069,500*		*€1,431,000*

Table 6.14 shows the official closing prices on 18/07/X8.

Table 6.14:   Closing Prices for Fund Z's Portfolio on 18/07/X8

Company	18/07/X8 Share Price
EDF	€11.70
E.On	€3.10
France Telecom	€18.25
Telefonica	€24.10
Vinci	€30.00

Requirements:

- Record the bonus issue in EDF.
- Record the bonus issue in E.On.
- Record the movement in the unrealised appreciation/depreciation account for the day.

Solution 6.9: Bonus Issues

1: Record the Bonus Issue in EDF

No accounting entries are required.
   Today is the ex-date $\Rightarrow$ adjust the number of shares in the portfolio.

- Total number of EDF shares in portfolio: $5,000 + 7,000 = 12,000$
- Bonus rate: 3 for 1
- Number of shares after the bonus issue: $12,000 \times 3/1 = 36,000$

2: Record the Bonus Issue in E.On

No accounting entries are required.
   Today is the ex-date $\Rightarrow$ adjust the number of shares in the portfolio.

- Total number of E.On shares in portfolio: 22,000
- Bonus rate: 5 for 2
- Number of shares after the bonus issue: $22,000 \times 5/2 = 55,000$

3: Record the Daily Valuation

Table 6.15 shows the calculation of the daily valuation for Fund Z's holdings.

Table 6.15: Daily Valuation for Fund Z's Portfolio

	Price	Quantity	Market Value
EDF	€11.70	36,000	€421,200
E.On	€3.10	55,000	€170,500
France Telecom	€18.25	7,000	€127,750
Telefonica	€24.10	15,000	€361,500
Vinci	€30.00	12,000	€360,000
Market Value of Portfolio (today, 18/07/X8)			€1,440,950
Cost of Portfolio (today, 18/07/X8) (see Table 6.13)			€1,069,500
Total Unrealised Appreciation/Depreciation			€371,450
Unrealised Appreciation/Depreciation from Yesterday		€361,500	
Less Gains Sold		€0	€361,500
Gain for the Day			**€9,950**

This is recorded as follows (from Chapter 5):

- Dr unrealised appreciation/depreciation by €9,950.
- Cr gains/losses on investments by €9,950.

Or – for the spreadsheet approach:

- Increase unrealised appreciation/depreciation, an asset, by €9,950.
- Increase gains/losses on investments, an income item, by €9,950.

What would have happened had the number of shares not been adjusted? See Table 6.16.

Table 6.16: Daily Valuation for Fund Z's Portfolio without Adjustment of Shares

	Price	Quantity	Market Value
EDF	€11.70	12,000	€140,400
E.On	€3.10	22,000	€68,200
France Telecom	€18.25	7,000	€127,750
Telefonica	€24.10	15,000	€361,500
Vinci	€30.00	12,000	€360,000
Market Value of Portfolio (today, 18/07/X8)			€1,057,850
Cost of Portfolio (today, 18/07/X8)			€1,069,500
Total Unrealised Appreciation/Depreciation			−€11,650
Unrealised Appreciation/Depreciation from Yesterday		€361,500	
Less Gains Sold		€0	€361,500
Loss for the Day			**−€373,150**

As can be seen, a failure to record a bonus issue correctly can have a significant impact on the valuation of the fund. A properly recorded gain of €9,950 becomes an incorrectly recorded loss of €373,150. This is simply because, in the second instance, there was a failure to show the increase in the number of shares held by the fund.

Thus, to summarise accounting for bonus issues:

- There are no accounting entries.
- Adjust the number of shares in the portfolio by the bonus rate (the increase in the number of shares will be offset by the fall in the shares price).

Now try Question 6.10.5.

6.7: RIGHTS ISSUES

A rights issue is where a company attempts to raise additional cash from its existing shareholders. Companies may wish to do this from time to time, often to fund expansion or to recoup losses. For example, after the mortgage losses incurred by banks during the credit crunch of 2008–2009, many banks had to raise extra capital to stabilise their balance sheets. A rights issue was one of the mechanisms used to raise this additional capital.

A rights issue is remarkable for two reasons:

1. Existing shareholders are given first option to purchase new shares in proportion to their existing shareholdings.
2. The new shares are often given at a discount to the current market price.

Considering item #1 above, if a company were to issue new shares outside of the rights issue mechanism then the existing shareholders would suffer a dilution of their holding. This means that if they owned 10 per cent of the company before the share issue then afterwards they would own a lower percentage of the company; albeit a lower percentage of a larger company. Under a rights issue, if a shareholder owned 10 per cent of a company before a rights issue and took up all of their rights, then after the rights issue they would be guaranteed to own at least 10 per cent of the company. As a result, rights issues are normally couched in terms similar to bonus issues. For example, under a 1 for 5 rights issue all existing shareholders are given the option to buy one new share in Company X for every five existing shares that they hold. Thus, if the company had 1,000,000 shares and a fund held 25,000 shares (or 2.5 per cent of the company), then after the rights issue there would be a maximum of 1,200,000 shares in issue, and if the fund took up all its rights it would then own 30,000 shares – the same 2.5 per cent of a larger company.

A further attribute of rights issues is that the shares are often given at a discount to the market price (item two above). Existing shareholders are given the option to buy the shares for less than what they are currently quoted as on the market. This discounted price is known as the exercise price. This acts as an incentive to encourage shareholders to participate in the rights issue. For example, Company X announces a 1 for 5 rights issue at a price of €5 per share when the current market price is €7.50 per share.

An example of a rights issue is provided by CRH. It announced a 1 for 4 rights issue at an exercise price of €10.50 when the share price was trading at over €20. Prior to the rights issue there were 414,489,240 CRH shares in issue. Every shareholder is given the option to purchase one new share in CRH for every four shares they already own; thus, over 103 million new shares will be issued (414,489,240 × 1/4). The announcement of the rights issue is shown in Figure 6.8.

Figure 6.8:   CRH Rights Issue, Official Stock Exchange Announcement

1 FOR 4 RIGHTS ISSUE OF UP TO 103,622,311 NEW ORDINARY SHARES AT EURO 10.50 PER NEW ORDINARY SHARE

CRH today announces that it is raising approximately euro 1.1 billion, net of expenses, by the issue of up to 103,622,311 Rights Shares at a price of euro 10.50 per share. The issue is being made by way of a rights issue to qualifying shareholders (other than certain overseas shareholders) on the basis of one Rights Share for every four existing ordinary shares held at the close of business on 2 March 2001.

The Board believes that an equity input by way of a rights issue at this point in time is desirable, to back the extensive resources committed to development and to ensure that the Group is not constrained in its plans to take full advantage of acquisition opportunities as they arise in its various geographic, product and sectoral markets. The Rights Issue announced today will contribute to the further expansion of the Group.

Application has been made to the UK Listing Authority, the London Stock Exchange plc (the "LSE") and The Irish Stock Exchange Limited for up to 103,622,311 Rights Shares to be admitted to the Official List of the UK Listing Authority and for admission to trading on the LSE's market for listed securities and on the Irish Stock Exchange, respectively. It is expected that admission of the Rights Shares, nil paid, will become effective on 7 March 2001.

This announcement does not constitute an offer of securities for sale in the United States. The information contained herein is not for publication or distribution to persons in the United States. The securities have not been and will not be registered under the U.S. Securities Act of 1933 (the "Securities Act") and may not be offered or sold in the United States unless they are registered with the U.S. Securities and Exchange Commission or pursuant to an exemption from the registration requirements of the Securities Act.

Source: www.crh.ie/crhcorp/media/press/2001/2001-03-05/, 5 March 2001.

6.7.1: The Controversy with Rights Issues

Rights issues do come with a financial health warning. While shareholders are given an opportunity to purchase shares at a seemingly lower price, in reality shareholders are not any better off. Even worse, if a shareholder decides not to exercise their rights, they will end up poorer than before. This is because the share price of a company will usually fall on the ex-rights date. Thus, from a share-holder's perspective a rights issue is often seen as bad news since they will not be any better off and could easily end up being worse off. Also, while an individual shareholder may wish to participate in a rights issue, they may be experiencing cash flow problems, making it difficult for them to raise the required cash. So, for reasons outside their control, the timing of the announcement of the rights issue may result in some shareholders being unable to take up their rights and thus end up worse off. The example below will illustrate this problem.

Example 6.10: Rights Issues

Consider the example from earlier. Company X announces a 1 for 5 rights issue, at a price of €5 per share when the current market price is €7.50 per share. Prior to the rights issue the company had 1,000,000 shares in issue. Fund Z holds 40,000 shares in the fund.

Requirements:

- Assuming all shareholders participate in the rights issue, determine the share price of Company X just after the rights issue (this is called the theoretical ex-rights price). For this requirement assume that there is no other reason for the share price of the company to change.
- Evaluate the wealth of Fund Z, both before and after the rights issue, on the basis that the fund takes up its rights.
- Evaluate the wealth of Fund Z, both before and after the rights issue, on the basis that the fund does not take up its rights.

Solution 6.10: Right Issue

The Share Price of Company X after the Rights Issue (Theoretical Ex-Rights Price)

Share price before rights issue	€7.50
Number of shares in issue	1,000,000
Value of company before rights issue	€7,500,000
Total funds raised by rights issue:	
Number of shares issued	200,000 (1,000,000 × 1/5)
Issue price	€5
Funds raised	€1,000,000

A rights issue is not a money-making machine: the company still has the same sales, profits, products, etc. as it had before the rights issue. It does, however, have €1 million more in its bank account. Thus, the total value of the company after the rights issue is:

Value of company before rights issue	€7,500,000
Plus funds raised	€1,000,000
Value of company after rights issue	€8,500,000

Total number of shares in issue after the rights issue:

Shares in issue before rights issue	1,000,000
New shares issued	200,000
Shares in issue after rights issue	1,200,000

The value of a share after the rights issue is the total value (€8.5 million) divided by the number of shares in issue (1.2 million), giving a value per share of €7.083.

Thus, while shareholders were able to buy shares at a cheaper rate (€5) than the market price (€7.50) at the time, the value of their original holding has decreased (to €7.083 per share).

Wealth of Fund Z if it Participates in the Rights Issue

Wealth of Fund Z before the rights issue:

Number of shares held	40,000
Market price per share	€7.50
Total value	€300,000

If Fund Z wishes to participate in the rights issue it will be able to purchase 8,000 shares (40,000 × 1/5) at a low price of €5.00.

Cost of new shares (8,000 × €5.00)	€40,000

At this point the fund has €340,000 invested in the company: the original €300,000 and the extra €40,000.

The value of Fund Z's holding is:

Number of shares in company	48,000 (40,000 + 8,000)
Value of each share after rights issue	€7.083 (from first requirement)
Total value of holding	€340,000[19]

---

[19] The calculations for this example have eliminated the effects of rounding. The actual ex-rights price is €7.08333333. If the unrounded price was used then the actual value is €340,000. Using €7.083, the total value is €339,984. Any difference is not significant.

Thus, the fund is no better off after investing in the rights issue. Before the rights issue its holding was worth €300,000. It then invested an extra €40,000, giving a total investment of €340,000. This is exactly what the shareholding is worth after the rights issue (€340,000). So the incentive of offering shareholders the opportunity to buy shares at a lower price is only a ruse; there is no net benefit to investors.

The downside is when shareholders decide not to invest in a rights issue – this is the next requirement.

Wealth of Fund Z if it Does Not Participate in the Rights Issue

Wealth of Fund Z before the rights issue:

Number of shares held	40,000
Market price per share	€7.50
Total value	€300,000

As the fund decides not to participate in the rights issue, it will not make any payment to purchase any shares. At this point the fund has €300,000 invested in the company: the original €300,000 and nothing extra.

The value of Fund Z's holding is:

Number of shares in company	40,000 (40,000 + 0)
Value of each share after rights issue	€7.083 (from first requirement)
Total value of holding	€283,333[20]

Notice that the value of the share will still fall to €7.083 as all the other shareholders are assumed to participate in the rights issue.[21] In this case, the value of the fund's investment has fallen by nearly €17,000. By deciding not to participate, the fund has lost money.

The above example highlights why rights issues are unpopular with shareholders. Even though they get the option to buy shares cheaper than the market price, they are, at best, no better off and could be worse off. In addition, the rights issue may come at a time when the shareholder may not have the spare cash for investment, so they may be forced into not participating. In the example above, if the fund did

---

[20]   The calculations here have also eliminated the effects of rounding. The actual ex-rights price is €7.08333333. If the unrounded price was used then the total value would be €283,333. Using €7.083, the total value would be €283,320.

[21]   The share price may not fall all the way down to €7.083 as one shareholder with 40,000 shares (Fund Z) has not participated. But this shareholder owns just 4 per cent of the company, so any difference will be very small (the actual share price after the rights issue, assuming all other shareholders exercise their rights, will be €7.097 – a 1.4 cent difference, which is not significant).

not have €40,000 available then it would not be in a position to invest in the rights issue and could easily lose almost €17,000. In order to get the €40,000, the fund may have to sell some other investments, which it may not wish to do.

Now try Question 6.10.6.

6.7.2: Selling/Trading 'Rights'

In the previous section, a key difficulty with rights issues was outlined: shareholders may not wish to exercise their rights but also do not want to lose any value. There is a solution. It may be possible to trade or sell the rights. Rights that are tradeable are called renounceable rights or nil paid rights. In essence, this means that rights are transferable – if an investor does not wish to exercise them, he or she can sell them to someone else who is prepared to participate in the rights issue. Generally, there is no restriction on who an investor can sell their rights to; it is not a condition to sell to existing shareholders. Returning to the example from CRH (Figure 6.8), notice that these rights are tradeable.

This gives rise to a number of issues:

1. How are rights traded?
2. Why would someone wish to buy rights?
3. How much should the rights trade for?

1. Trading rights is similar to trading shares. There is one difference: the window for trading is quite short. Rights can generally only be traded between the ex-rights date and the application closing date; this could be just a matter of days. Rights can be quoted on the market just like the underlying shares.

2. A third party may be prepared to buy rights as they get the option to purchase shares at a cheaper price than on the open market. In Example 6.10 the rights issue gives the holder an option to buy the shares for €5 when they are worth €7.50. Thus, they clearly have a value – think of them in terms of a money-off coupon when doing the food shopping.

Consider a €1 money-off coupon for cornflakes but the holder of the coupon does not like cornflakes. The expiry date on the coupon is approaching. The holder has two choices: let the coupon lapse and throw it in the bin or sell the coupon to someone else who is buying cornflakes (the holder could also give the coupon away but such charity is rare on the stock market). An individual who is purchasing cornflakes should be prepared to pay up to €1 for the coupon. The final price reached will be a matter for negotiation. It should be between €0 and €1 to give both sides something from the deal. It is unlikely that there will be much negotiation over a cornflakes coupon, but if there was €10,000 or €100,000 at stake then the parties will not be as reticent.

3. The maximum that the rights should trade for is the post–rights issue price less the rights price. Using the details from Example 6.10, the pre–rights issue share price was €7.50, the post–rights issue share price was expected to be €7.08 and the rights price was €5.00.

Whoever buys the rights will have to pay €5.00 to buy the shares. Once this has been paid, the shares will trade for €7.08 (the post–rights issue price). Thus, the most the purchaser should be prepared to pay for a right to buy one share is €7.08 less €5.00, or €2.08. This represents the maximum price that the purchaser would pay; the actual price will be less than this.

In the examples that have been used, it has been assumed that there were no other influences on the price of the underlying shares in the companies concerned. However, this does not happen in reality. Normally, the price of the share fluctuates on a daily basis; therefore, the price of the rights will fluctuate daily also. Indeed, the price fluctuation (in percentage terms) will tend to be much higher for the rights than for the underlying shares. Trading in rights is effectively trading in a derivative product; this is because the value of a right is derived from the value of the underlying share.

6.7.3: Rights Issues – The Dates

As with dividends, stock splits and so on, there are a number of dates used when engaging in a rights issue transaction. These have a similar implication as before:

- Announcement date – there is no accounting implication. However, if a fund purchases shares in a company that has announced a rights issue, care is required because the fund may end up having to contribute more cash to the company. This is especially true if the fund buys the shares between the rights announcement date and the ex-rights date.
- Ex-rights date – if the shares are owned before the ex-rights date then the owner is entitled to participate in the rights issue. If, however, the shares are purchased after the ex-rights date then the purchaser is not permitted to participate in the rights issue (the previous owner gets this entitlement). On the ex-rights date the share price of the underlying share will fall. The ex-rights date is an important milestone for accounting purposes as it is on this date that the rights will have to be valued (if tradeable).
- Application closing date/payment date – this is the last day on which the holders of the rights have to make up their mind (to either exercise their rights or allow them to lapse). Generally payment should accompany the application on this date. The new shares will be issued sometime after this date (it could take a few weeks). This date also has accounting implications.

6.7.4: Accounting for Rights Issues

There are a number of accounting implications with rights issues. The ex-rights date and the application closing date are two key dates that will impact on when to account for rights issues. Also, the particular course of action taken by the fund will determine how the rights issue will be accounted for.

The first accounting transaction will occur on the ex-rights date. On that day, the rights acquire a value while the underlying share will fall in value (one should offset the other). The accounting for this is not difficult:

- Calculate the number of rights that the fund is entitled to (this will depend on the number of shares held and the rights issue rate).
- Include the rights in the portfolio.
- Value the portfolio as normal at the end of the day (including the shares and the rights in the company concerned).
- There is no individual debit or credit as the effect should be subsumed within the daily valuation calculation.

Once the ex-date has passed there are three potential outcomes to a rights issue:

1. The rights are exercised.
2. The rights are sold.
3. The rights are allowed to lapse (this outcome will result in a loss to the fund and is the least favourable outcome).

The accounting for each outcome is explained in Table 6.17.

Example 6.11 below considers each of the above outcomes. This will be used to explain the accounting for rights issues.

Example 6.11 – Accounting for Rights Issues

The Value Fund has the following holdings, as shown in Table 6.18a.

On 01/06/X3 Kerry Group announces a rights issue of 1 for 5 at €10 per share, CRH announces a rights issue of 2 for 5 at €14 per share and Ryanair announces a rights issue of 1 for 2 at €5 per share.

All of the rights issues have a record date of 03/06/X3, an ex-rights date of 06/06/X3 and a payment/application closing date of 10/06/X3 (this is quite a short time period; normally it is much longer). Table 6.18b shows the share prices for the shares over this period.

Table 6.17: Accounting for Rights Issues

Include value of rights from ex-rights date (all options)
Include the correct number of rights in the portfolio and value as part of the daily valuation process

Rights Exercised	Rights Sold	Rights Allowed to Lapse
On the date the rights are exercised: • Record the payment and increase the cost of shares in the portfolio (assumes payment is made on the same day) • Increase the number of shares in the portfolio • Remove the rights from the portfolio	On the date the rights are sold: • Record the sale of the rights – assume the rights have zero cost • Remove the rights from the portfolio	On the date the decision is taken to allow the rights to lapse or on the application closing date: • Remove the rights from the portfolio
Accounting entries: • Dr investments at cost • Cr cash (or investments purchased payable, if not paid for on same day)	Accounting entries: • Dr investments sold receivable • Cr unrealised appreciation/ depreciation See Note 1	Accounting entries: • None – there will be a fall in unrealised appreciation/ depreciation but this will be automatically calculated when the portfolio is valued
Spreadsheet entries: • Increase investments at cost • Decrease cash	Spreadsheet entries: • Increase investments sold receivable • Decrease unrealised appreciation/depreciation	Spreadsheet entries: • None

Note 1:
When the rights are being sold this is treated the same as the sale of any other investment. However, there is one unusual aspect – as the rights did not cost the fund anything then there is no need to check which batch was sold and no need to ascribe a cost to the rights sold. Thus, all of the proceeds are gains that are being sold. More correctly, the accounting entries should be:
• Dr investments sold receivable   Proceeds
• Cr investments at cost   Zero
• Cr unrealised appreciation/depreciation   Proceeds
   There is an alternative approach which attempts to ascribe some of the original cost of the shares to the rights issue sold. This can be a convoluted calculation (particularly where there are multiple batches) and is beyond the scope of this book.

On 08/06/X3 the following occurs:

1. The Value Fund takes up its rights in Kerry (i.e. the fund pays €11,000 for 1,100 shares).
2. The fund sells its rights in CRH (i.e. the fund will receive 3,000 × €8.15 (€24,450) on TD + 3).
3. The fund allows its rights in Ryanair to lapse (it neither buys more shares nor sells the rights).

Table 6.18a: Holdings of the Value Fund

Shares	Date of Purchase	Number of Shares	Cost Price
Kerry Group	01/01/X1	1,000	€12.30
Kerry Group	01/05/X1	2,000	€14.30
Kerry Group	01/03/X2	2,500	€19.50
CRH	01/03/X1	1,500	€15.30
CRH	01/06/X1	2,500	€17.30
CRH	01/09/X2	3,500	€21.50
Ryanair	01/04/X1	2,500	€5.60
Ryanair	01/05/X1	1,500	€7.30
Ryanair	01/10/X2	3,000	€7.50

Table 6.18b: Share Prices

Date	Kerry Shares	Kerry Rights	CRH Shares	CRH Rights	Ryanair Shares	Ryanair Rights
01/06/X3	€21.00		€25.20		€10.00	
02/06/X3	€21.50		€25.40		€10.10	
03/06/X3	€21.55		€25.40		€10.20	
04/06/X3	€21.60		€25.50		€10.20	
05/06/X3	€21.50		€25.60		€10.30	
06/06/X3	€19.65	€9.00	€22.30	€8.00	€8.53	€3.50
07/06/X3	€19.75	€9.10	€22.40	€8.10	€8.56	€3.52
08/06/X3	€19.80	€9.12	€22.45	€8.15	€8.58	€3.53
09/06/X3	€19.90	€9.40	€22.55	€8.10	€8.60	€3.54
10/06/X3	€20.00		€22.60		€8.75	
11/06/X3	€20.10		€22.70		€8.70	

Requirement:

Account for the above transactions on a daily basis, from 05/06/X3 to 10/06/X3 inclusive.

Solution 6.11 – Accounting for Rights Issues

This is a long solution but take one day at a time.

The announcement date (01/06/X3) has no impact on accounting for the fund. At this stage it would be advisable to note the details of the announcement.

The Closing Position on 04/06/X3

The starting point is to determine the total cost of the shares and the unrealised appreciation/depreciation on 04/06/X3. The closing position on 04/06/X3 will give the opening position on 05/06/X3 (see Table 6.19a).

Table 6.19a: Closing Position of the Value Fund on 04/06/X3

	Cost of Shares		
Shares	**Number of Shares**	**Cost**	**Total Cost**
Kerry	1,000	€12.30	€12,300
Kerry	2,000	€14.30	€28,600
Kerry	2,500	€19.50	€48,750
CRH	1,500	€15.30	€22,950
CRH	2,500	€17.30	€43,250
CRH	3,500	€21.50	€75,250
Ryanair	2,500	€5.60	€14,000
Ryanair	1,500	€7.30	€10,950
Ryanair	3,000	€7.50	€22,500
Total			*€278,550*

	Market Value of Shares		
Shares	**Number of Shares**	**Price**	**Market Value**
Kerry	5,500	€21.60	€118,800
CRH	7,500	€25.50	€191,250
Ryanair	7,000	€10.20	€71,400
Total			*€381,450*

Unrealised Appreciation/Depreciation	
Market Value	€381,450
Cost	€278,550
Unrealised Appreciation	*€102,900*

Thus on 04/06/X3 the following balances existed:

- Dr investments at cost   €278,500
- Dr unrealised appreciation/depreciation   €102,900

Record the Events on 05/06/X3

Nothing occurred on 05/06/X3 (the rights issue only needs to be recorded on 06/06/X3, from the ex-rights date). Thus, all that happens on 05/06/X3 is to record the daily movement on the portfolio (see Table 6.19b).

To record this transaction:

- Dr unrealised appreciation/depreciation by €900.
- Cr gains/losses on investments by €900 (in the statement of operations).

Table 6.19b: Daily Movement of the Value Fund's Portfolio on 05/06/X3

Shares	Price	Quantity	Market Value
Kerry	€21.50	5,500	€118,250
CRH	€25.60	7,500	€192,000
Ryanair	€10.30	7,000	€72,100
Market Value of Portfolio (today, 05/06/X3)			€382,350
Cost of Portfolio (today, 05/06/X3)			€278,550
Total Unrealised Appreciation/Depreciation			€103,800
Unrealised Appreciation/Depreciation from Yesterday		€102,900	
Less Gains Sold		€0	€102,900
Gain for the Day			**€900**

An extract from the statement of net assets is shown in Table 6.19c.

Table 6.19c: Extract from the Statement of Net Assets of the Value Fund on 05/06/X3

Assets	04/06/X3	Valuation	05/06/X3
Investments at Cost	€278,550		€278,550
Unrealised Appreciation/Depreciation	€102,900	€900	€103,800

Record the Events on 06/06/X3

It is on this date that the shares went ex-rights. Thus, on this date we need to include the value of the rights in the portfolio. The increase in the value of the rights should be offset by a fall in the price of the individual shares (daily share price movements notwithstanding).

As the rights did not cost anything then no adjustment is required to the investments at cost account. Thus, all that has to be done is to calculate the daily movement in the value of the portfolio, including the new rights. (Try to determine if the value of the rights is reasonable – what would the rights have been expected to trade at?)

- The fund held 5,500 shares in Kerry. The rights issue was 1 for 5; thus the fund has acquired the right to purchase 1,100 shares in Kerry.
- The fund held 7,500 shares in CRH. The rights issue was 2 for 5; thus the fund has acquired the right to purchase 3,000 shares in CRH.
- The fund held 7,000 shares in Ryanair. The rights issue was 1 for 2; thus the fund has acquired the right to purchase 3,500 shares in Ryanair.

Table 6.19d shows the daily movement of the Value Fund's Portfolio on 06/06/X3.

Table 6.19d: Daily Movement of the Value Fund's Portfolio on 06/06/X3

Shares	Price	Quantity	Market Value
Kerry	€19.65	5,500	€108,075
Kerry Rights	€9.00	1,100	€9,900
CRH	€22.30	7,500	€167,250
CRH Rights	€8.00	3,000	€24,000
Ryanair	€8.53	7,000	€59,710
Ryanair Rights	€3.50	3,500	€12,250
Market Value of Portfolio (today, 06/06/X3)			€381,185
Cost of Portfolio (today, 06/06/X3)			€278,550
Total Unrealised Appreciation/Depreciation			€102,635
Unrealised Appreciation/Depreciation from Yesterday		€103,800	
Less Gains Sold		€0	€103,800
Loss for the Day			**−€1,165**

To record this transaction:

- Cr unrealised appreciation/depreciation by €1,165.
- Dr gains/losses on investments by €1,165 (in the statement of operations).

An extract from the statement of net assets is shown in Table 6.19e.

Table 6.19e: Extract from the Statement of Net Assets of the Value Fund on 06/06/X3

Assets	05/06/X3	Valuation	06/06/X3
Investments at Cost	€278,550		€278,550
Unrealised Appreciation/Depreciation	€103,800	(€1,165)	€102,635

Record the events on 07/06/X3

On this date nothing new occurred. We just need to record the daily movement on the portfolio, including the rights again (see Table 6.19f).

To record this transaction:

- Dr unrealised appreciation/depreciation by €1,990.
- Cr gains/losses on investments by €1,990 (in the statement of operations).

An extract from the statement of net assets is shown in Table 6.19g.

Table 6.19f: Daily Movement of the Value Fund's Portfolio on 07/06/X3

Shares	Price	Quantity	Market Value
Kerry	€19.75	5,500	€108,625
Kerry Rights	€9.10	1,100	€10,010
CRH	€22.40	7,500	€168,000
CRH Rights	€8.10	3,000	€24,300
Ryanair	€8.56	7,000	€59,920
Ryanair Rights	€3.52	3,500	€12,320
Market Value of Portfolio (today, 07/06/X3)			€383,175
Cost of Portfolio (today, 07/06/X3)			€278,550
Total Unrealised Appreciation/Depreciation			€104,625
Unrealised Appreciation/Depreciation from Yesterday		€102,635	
Less Gains Sold		€0	€102,635
Loss for the Day			**€1,990**

Table 6.19g: Extract from the Statement of Net Assets of the Value Fund on 07/06/X3

Assets	06/06/X3	Valuation	07/06/X3
Investments at Cost	€278,550		€278,550
Unrealised Appreciation/Depreciation	€102,635	€1,990	€104,625

Record the Events on 08/06/X3

This is the date on which most of the relevant transactions occur.

1. Exercise of the Kerry rights:

- The fund has the opportunity to purchase 1,100 shares in Kerry for €10. This will cost €11,000 in total.
- Increase the number of Kerry shares in the portfolio by 1,100.
- Remove the Kerry rights from the portfolio.
- Record the transaction:
  - dr investments at cost by €11,000
  - cr cash by €11,000

This assumes that the cash was paid immediately. The actual shares will be received in a number of weeks.

2. Sale of CRH rights:

- Calculate the proceeds of the rights sold. The rights to purchase 3,000 shares in CRH were sold at €8.15 per right. This gives proceeds of €24,450.

- The cost of the rights were zero (this solution assumes that no attempt is made to apportion the cost of the rights over the original holdings).
- Thus the gains sold were €24,450.
- Remove the CRH rights from the portfolio.
- Record the transaction:
  - dr investments sold receivable by €24,450 (due on TD + 3)
  - cr investments at cost by €0
  - cr unrealised appreciation/depreciation by €24,450

3. Lapse of Ryanair rights:

- The decision to allow the rights to lapse was taken today; thus, while the fund still owns the rights until the application closing date, they should be removed from the portfolio immediately.
- Remove the Ryanair rights from the portfolio.
- No other action is required – the calculation of the daily movement on the portfolio should show a significant loss as a consequence.

4. Calculate the daily movement on the portfolio (see Table 6.19h).

Table 6.19h: Daily Movement of the Value Fund's Portfolio on 08/06/X3

Shares	Price	Quantity	Market Value
Kerry	€19.80	6,600	€130,680
Kerry Rights	€9.12	–	€0
CRH	€22.45	7,500	€168,375
CRH Rights	€8.15	–	€0
Ryanair	€8.58	7,000	€60,060
Ryanair Rights	€3.53	–	€0
Market Value of Portfolio (today, 08/06/X3)			€359,115
Cost of Portfolio (today, 08/06/X3) (see Note 1)			€289,550
Total Unrealised Appreciation/Depreciation			€69,565
Unrealised Appreciation/Depreciation from Yesterday		€104,625	
Less Gains Sold (CRH Rights)		€24,450	€80,175
Loss for the Day			**–€10,610**

Note 1: Cost of Portfolio:

Cost from Yesterday (07/06/X3)	€278,550
Add Cost of Kerry Shares	€11,000
Less Cost of CRH Rights Sold and Ryanair Rights Lapsed	€0
Cost of Portfolio	€289,550

To record this transaction:

- Cr unrealised appreciation/depreciation by €10,610.
- Dr gains/losses on investments by €10,610 (in the statement of operations).

The large loss is due to the lapse of the Ryanair rights; these were worth €12,320 yesterday. The balance is made up of the daily movement in the other shares. An extract from the statement of net assets is shown in Table 6.19i.

Table 6.19i: Extract from the Statement of Net Assets of the Value Fund on 08/06/X3

Assets	07/06/X3	Kerry Purchase	CRH Rights Sale	Ryanair Lapse	Daily Value	08/06/X3
Investments at Cost	€278,550	€11,000	(€0)			€289,550
Unrealised Appreciation/ Depreciation	€104,625		(€24,450)		(€10,610)	€69,565
Cash	€XXX	(€11,000)				
Investments Sold Receivable	€YYY		€24,450			

Record the Events on 09/06/X3

On this date nothing new occurred. We just need to record the daily movement on the portfolio (see Table 6.19j); as all of the rights were either exercised, sold or lapsed on 08/06/X3, these are no longer in the portfolio.

Table 6.19j: Daily Movement of the Value Fund's Portfolio on 09/06/X3

Shares	Price	Quantity	Market Value
Kerry	€19.90	6,600	€131,340
Kerry Rights	€9.40	–	€0
CRH	€22.55	7,500	€169,125
CRH Rights	€8.10	–	€0
Ryanair	€8.60	7,000	€60,200
Ryanair Rights	€3.54	–	€0
Market Value of Portfolio (today, 09/06/X3)			€360,665
Cost of Portfolio (today, 09/06/X3)			€289,550
Total Unrealised Appreciation/Depreciation			€71,115
Unrealised Appreciation/Depreciation from Yesterday		€69,565	
Less Gains Sold		€0	€69,565
Gain for the Day			€1,550

319

To record this transaction:

- Dr unrealised appreciation/depreciation by €1,550.
- Cr gains/losses on investments by €1,550 (in the statement of operations).

An extract from the statement of net assets is shown in Table 6.19k.

Table 6.19k: Extract from the Statement of Net Assets of the Value Fund on 09/06/X3

Assets	08/06/X3	Valuation	09/06/X3
Investments at Cost	€289,550		€289,550
Unrealised Appreciation/Depreciation	€69,565	€1,550	€71,115

Record the Events on 10/06/X3

There were no new transactions on this day. Only the daily valuation needs to be calculated. Using the same procedure as for the previous days should result in an unrealised gain for the day of €2,085.

To record this transaction:

- Dr unrealised appreciation/depreciation by €2,085.
- Cr gains/losses on investments by €2,085 (in the statement of operations).

An extract from the statement of net assets is shown in Table 6.19l.

Table 6.19l: Extract from the Statement of Net Assets of the Value Fund on 10/06/X3

Assets	09/06/X3	Valuation	10/06/X3
Investments at Cost	€289,550		€289,550
Unrealised Appreciation/Depreciation	€71,115	€2,085	€73,200

Table 6.19m shows an extract for all of the days concerned. This outlines how the investments at cost account and the unrealised appreciation/depreciation account moves from day to day. Notice that on 06/06/X3, the day all of the shares went ex-rights, there was no large fluctuation in the daily valuation. This is because the increase in value caused by the new rights is offset by a decrease in value in the underlying shares. In addition, the only day that the fund suffered a large loss was the day that the Ryanair rights were allowed to lapse. Failure to either sell or take up rights will almost certainly cause a fund to lose value and should be the last option under such circumstances.

Table 6.19m: Statement of Net Assets of the Value Fund (Extract)

Assets	04/06/X3	Daily Value	05/06/X3	Daily Value	06/06/X3	Daily Value	07/06/X3	Kerry Rights Purchase	CRH Rights Sale	Daily Value	08/06/X3	Daily Value	09/06/X3	Daily Value	10/06/X3
Investments at Cost	€278,550		€278,550		€278,550		€278,550	€11,000			€289,550		€289,550		€289,550
Unrealised Appreciation/ Depreciation	€102,900	€900	€103,800	−€1,165	€102,635	€1,990	€104,625		−€24,450	−€10,610	€69,565	€1,550	€71,115	€2,085	€73,200

Now try Question 6.10.7.

In Section 6.9 there is a comprehensive question that combines all of the items learned to date. This example includes corporate actions, equity transactions and fund share transactions. The question is quite detailed and will pose a significant challenge. However, an ability to master this example will underpin the learning achieved thus far.

6.8: MERGERS AND ACQUISITIONS

An acquisition is where one company purchases the shares of another company.[22] Nominally, once 50 per cent plus one share is purchased then the purchasing company has control over the other; however, often the purchasing company buys all (100 per cent) of the shares. Mergers, takeovers and buyouts are similar terms that broadly describe the same practice.

There are significant regulations on mergers and acquisitions. These regulations set out how both parties should conduct themselves in an acquisition situation but are not hugely relevant from a fund accounting perspective.

The accounting for an acquisition can take a number of different forms; this will be dependent on the vehicle used for the acquisition. Unfortunately, there are a wide variety of methods used to give effect to an acquisition; this book will only consider the more common approaches.

When a company (the acquirer) buys the shares of another (the acquiree), this will usually result in a fund accounting implication. As a general rule, if an investment fund holds shares of the acquirer there are limited (or no) accounting implications[23] but if an investment fund is a shareholder of the acquiree then it is almost certain that an accounting transaction will need to be recorded. The exact nature of this will depend on how the transaction was structured.

There are three broad methods of structuring an acquisition:

- An all-cash deal – where the acquirer pays cash to the shareholders of the acquiree for their shares in the acquiree

---

[22] An acquisition can also be effected by purchasing the individual assets and associated liabilities of a company. This is less common and has fewer, if any, implications from an investment fund accounting perspective.

[23] Remember that this is just a general rule – the area of mergers and acquisitions is quite complex and this section will only consider the more common approaches.

- An all-share deal – where the acquirer gives its own shares to the shareholders of the acquiree for their shares in the acquiree
- A cash and share deal – a combination of the two previous structures

Example 6.12 – Acquisition Structures

The following examples describe the three methods outlined previously.

An All-Cash Deal

In November 2008, after protracted negotiations, InBev paid $52 billion for all the shares of Anheuser Busch. This represented an all-cash payment of $70 per share of Anheuser Busch. As a result of this transaction, if an investment fund held shares in Anheuser Busch, it would receive $70 per share and have no further interest in either company. InBev is a Belgian/Brazilian brewing company owning a large number of beer brands including Stella Artois and Becks, while Anheuser Busch's main beer brand is Budweiser.

An All-Share Deal

In December 2000, Glaxo Wellcome and SmithKline Beecham merged in an all-share deal where the original shareholders in Glaxo Wellcome were given one share in the new company for each old share they held and the original shareholders in SmithKline Beecham were given 0.455 shares in the new company for each old share they held. The new company was called GlaxoSmithKline (GSK). Thus, if an investment fund held 10,000 shares in Glaxo Wellcome and 10,000 shares in SmithKline Beecham, it would now own 14,550 shares in GlaxcoSmithKline (10,000 shares as a result of its shareholding in Glaxo Wellcome and 4,550 shares as a result of its shareholding in SmithKline Beecham). Both Glaxo Wellcome and SmithKline Beecham were global pharmaceutical companies.

A Combination Deal

In March 2004, Morrisons acquired Safeway for close to £3 billion. As part of the deal the shareholders in Safeway were given one Morrisons share plus £0.60 cash for each of their Safeway shares. Thus, a fund that held 10,000 shares in Safeway would now own 10,000 shares in Morrisons and £6,000 cash. Both Morrisons and Safeway were food retailers in the UK.

6.8.1: Accounting for Mergers and Acquisitions

The accounting for these transactions will be dependent on the format of the acquisition.

For all-cash transactions (see the InBev acquisition of Anheuser Busch):

- If the investment fund holds shares in the acquiree (Anheuser Busch in the example), this is accounted for as a sale of equities. The price per share is the value of the cash deal per share; this is $70 per share in the InBev takeover of Anheuser Busch. See Section 5.6, 'Accounting for the Sale of Equities', which outlines how a sale of equities should be accounted for.
- If the investment fund holds shares in the acquirer (InBev in the example), then there is no accounting implication.

There are two methods of accounting for all-share transactions (see the Glaxo Wellcome and SmithKline Beecham merger):

- Method 1: Treat as a disposal of shares and an immediate acquisition:
  - Using the figures in Example 6.12, say an investment fund held 10,000 shares in Glaxo Wellcome. Then, these shares are disposed of at their market value on the ex-date and the proceeds are used to acquire 10,000 shares in GSK (the merged company). This is accounted for as a sale of equities and then as a purchase of equities.
  - Say an investment fund held 10,000 shares in SmithKline Beecham. Then these shares are disposed of at their market value on the ex-date and the proceeds are used to acquire 4,550 shares in GSK (the merged company). This is accounted for as a sale of equities and then as a purchase of equities.
  - The rates of conversion and the appropriate dates will be supplied by the companies to their investors. Sometimes these transactions can be very high-profile events, be wary of using information in the media as these deals can be often misreported.
- Method 2: Do not treat as a disposal; just transfer the original cost to the new shareholding:
  - Using the figures in Example 6.12, say an investment fund held 10,000 shares in Glaxo Wellcome. After the transaction, the fund will own 10,000 shares in GSK (the merged company). Just transfer the cost of the original

Glaxo Wellcome shares to the new GSK shares and then remove the Glaxo Wellcome shares from the portfolio to be replaced with the 10,000 GSK shares. Under this option, there is no real accounting.

o Say an investment fund held 10,000 shares in SmithKline Beecham. After the transaction, the fund will own 4,550 shares in GSK (the new merged company). Transfer the cost of the original SmithKline Beecham shares to the new GSK shares and then remove the SmithKline Beecham shares from the portfolio to be replaced with the 4,550 GSK shares. Under this option, there is no real accounting.

For a combination transaction (see the Morrisons and Safeway example):

- If the investment fund holds shares in the acquiree (Safeway in the example), this is accounted for as a sale of equities. The price per share is the value of the total deal per share. The non-cash element of the deal is then used to buy the new shares in the acquirer (Morrisions in the example). Say an investment fund held 10,000 shares in Safeway and on the ex-date of the transaction Morrisons were quoted at £2.50. The value of the transaction is one share in Morrisons plus £0.60 cash. This gives disposal proceeds of 10,000 × £2.50 plus 10,000 × £0.60, £31,000 in total. Thus, account for the sale of 10,000 Safeway shares at £31,000. Then £25,000 of the proceeds is used to buy 10,000 shares in Morrisons – account for this as a purchase of equities.
- If the investment fund holds shares in the acquirer (Morrisons in the example) then there is no accounting implication.
- There is an alternative method of accounting for this transaction. It involves treating the transaction as a part disposal (the amount that relates to the cash element of the deal) and as a part transfer of cost (the amount that relates to the share element of the deal). This is a convoluted calculation which does not add to the functionality of the resulting information. As a consequence, it will not be addressed in this section.

6.9: BRINGING IT ALL TOGETHER – CORPORATE ACTIONS

6.9.1: Comprehensive Question – Euro Equity Fund

Tables 6.20a and 6.20b give the statements and holdings of the Euro Equity Fund.

Table 6.20a: Comprehensive Question – Euro Equity Fund

Statement of Net Assets

	04/04/X8	Trans. 1	Trans. 2	Trans. 3	Trans. 4	Trans. 5	Trans. 6	Trans. 7	Trans. 8	Value 05/04/X8
Assets										
Investments at Cost	€23,850,500									
Unrealised Appreciation/Depreciation	€1,012,750									
Investments Sold Receivable	€265,000									
Fund Shares Sold Receivable	€25,000									
Return of Capital Receivable	€0									
Cash	€880,000									
Dividends Receivable	€520,000									
Total Assets	*€26,553,250*									
Liabilities										
Investments Purchased Payable	€0									
Accrued Expenses	€18,000									
Fund Shares Redeemed Payable	€0									
Distributions Payable	€15,000									
Total Liabilities	*€33,000*									
Total Net Assets	**€26,520,250**									
Capital Stock	**€26,520,250**									
Outstanding Shares	1,000,000									
NAV per Share	€26.52									

(Continued)

Table 6.20a: *(Continued)*

Statement of Operations for the Period from 01/01/X8 to 05/04/X8

	04/04/X8	Trans. 1	Trans. 2	Trans. 3	Trans. 4	Trans. 5	Trans. 6	Trans. 7	Trans. 8	Value 05/04/X8
Gains/Losses on Investments	€14,186									
Dividend Income	€602,500									
Interest Income	€0									
Total Investment Income/Loss	*€616,686*									
Administration Fee YTD	€3,000									
Investment Management Fee YTD	€202,000									
Other Fees YTD	€5,000									
Auditing Fee YTD	€0									
Dividend Withholding Tax	€0									
Total Fund Expenses	*€210,000*									
Increase/Decrease in Net Assets from Operations	**€405,686**									

(Continued)

Table 6.20a: (Continued)

Statement of Changes in Net Assets from the Period from 01/01/X8 to 05/04/X8

	04/04/X8	Trans. 1	Trans. 2	Trans. 3	Trans. 4	Trans. 5	Trans. 6	Trans. 7	Trans. 8	Value 05/04/X8
Investors' Equity at 01/01/X8	€25,016,343									
Distributions to Investors	€60,500									
Capital Fund Share Transactions										
Issue of shares	€1,556,221									
Redemption of units	€398,500									
Dividend reinvestment	€0									
Total	*€1,157,721*									
Increase/Decrease in Net Assets from Operations	€406,686									
Investors' Equity at End	**€26,520,250**									

Table 6.20b: Holdings of the Euro Equity Fund

Security	Date Purchased	Cost Price	Quantity	Commission	Total Cost	04/04/X8 Market Price	04/04/X8 Market Value
CRH	01/01/X1	€10.00	250,000	€1,500	€2,501,500	€8.00	€2,000,000
CRH	01/01/X2	€10.50	300,000	€1,500	€3,151,500	€8.00	€2,400,000
CRH	01/01/X3	€11.00	500,000	€2,000	€5,502,000	€8.00	€4,000,000
Irish Life and Permanent	01/01/X1	€8.00	150,000	€2,500	€1,202,500	€10.50	€1,575,000
Irish Life and Permanent	01/01/X2	€7.50	180,000	€2,500	€1,352,500	€10.50	€1,890,000
Irish Life and Permanent	01/01/X3	€7.25	190,000	€1,500	€1,379,000	€10.50	€1,995,000
Kingspan	01/01/X1	€6.00	80,000	€2,000	€482,000	€7.25	€580,000
Kingspan	01/01/X2	€5.30	125,000	€2,500	€665,000	€7.25	€906,250
Smurfit	01/01/X3	€4.50	505,000	€3,000	€2,275,500	€5.90	€2,979,500
Smurfit	01/01/X4	€5.20	125,000	€1,000	€651,000	€5.90	€737,500
AIB	01/01/X3	€18.50	100,000	€1,600	€1,851,600	€23.20	€2,320,000
AIB	01/01/X4	€18.90	150,000	€1,400	€2,836,400	€23.20	€3,480,000
Total					€23,850,500		€24,863,250

The following transactions occur on 05/04/X8:

1. On 02/04/X8 CRH announced a stock split of 2 for 1. The ex-date for the split is 05/04/X8.
2. On 30/03/X8 Irish Life and Permanent announced a share buy back. The company offered to purchase any investors' shares at the closing market price on 05/04/X8; the fund did not take the offer.
3. On 05/04/X8 the fund purchases 20,000 shares in Bank of Ireland for €8.60 each and commission of €1,000. Settlement date is TD + 3.
4. On 27/03/X8 Smurfit announced a €1 per share dividend. The ex-dividend date is 05/04/X8 with a payment date on 12/04/X8. When paying the dividend Smurfit will deduct 30 per cent dividend withholding tax. This DWT cannot be reclaimed by the fund.
5. On 05/04/X8 120,000 shares in AIB are sold for €23.10 and commission of €3,000 to settle on TD + 3.
6. On 22/03/X8 Kingspan announced a return of capital of €3.00 per share. The ex-date for the return of capital is 05/04/X8 and the payment date is 30/04/X8. The fund has decided to treat the return of capital as a reduction in cost (Option B1 in Chapter 6).
7. There are dividends receivable of €520,000 on the statement of net assets. This represents a dividend payment of €1.00 from Irish Life and Permanent. The ex-date for the dividend was 22/03/X8 and the payment date is 05/04/X8. At the time of paying the dividend, Irish Life and Permanent gave its shareholders a choice of receiving the dividend in cash or in shares. The price at which the shares are to be issued will be the closing price on the payment date (today's closing price of €10.75). The fund opted to take its full dividend entitlement in the form of shares in Irish Life and Permanent. The shares were received today.
8. A shareholder wishes to purchase 8,000 shares in the fund at yesterday's NAV per share – to settle on TD + 3.

Table 6.20c shows the closing prices of the Euro Equity Fund's holdings on 05/04/X8.

Requirements:

Using the template provided and showing any workings clearly:

1. Record transactions 1–8 for 05/04/X8.
2. Calculate and record the daily movement in the unrealised appreciation/depreciation account for 05/04/X8.
3. Calculate the NAV per share for 05/04/X8.

Table 6.20c: Closing Prices on 05/04/X8

Share	Closing Price
CRH	€4.10
Irish Life and Permanent	€10.75
Kingspan	€4.45
Smurfit	€4.85
AIB	€23.05
Bank of Ireland	€8.70

6.9.2: Solution to Comprehensive Question – Workings

Each of the transactions will be considered in turn and a final completed solution will be provided at the end of this section.

Transaction 1

No accounting entry is required. Increase the number of outstanding shares in CRH from 1,050,000 to 2,100,000.

Transaction 2

No accounting entry is required – fund did not take up offer of share buy back.

Transaction 3

Calculate total cost of purchase:
$$20,000 \text{ shares} \times €8.60 + €1,000 = €173,000$$

- Dr investments at cost by €173,000.
- Cr investments purchased payable by €173,000.

Or – for the spreadsheet method:

- Increase investments at cost by €173,000.
- Increase investments purchased payable by €173,000.

Remember to adjust the portfolio for the extra 20,000 Bank of Ireland shares.

Transaction 4

Calculate the amount of the dividend and the DWT:
Gross dividend: $630,000 \times €1 = €630,000$
DWT: $€630,000 \times 30\% = €189,000$
Net dividend: $€630,000 - €189,000 = €441,000$

- Dr dividends receivable by €441,000.
- Cr dividend income by €630,000.
- Dr dividend withholding tax by €189,000.

Or – for the spreadsheet method:

- Increase dividends receivable, an asset, by €441,000.
- Increase dividend income, an income, by €630,000.
- Increase dividend withholding tax, an expense, by €189,000.

Transaction 5

1. Calculate the sales proceeds:
   120,000 shares × €23.10 – €3,000 = €2,769,000

2. Identify the shares sold:

- All of the first batch of 100,000 shares
- 20,000 of the second batch of 150,000 shares

3. Calculate the cost of the shares sold:
   Batch 1: €18.50 × 100,000 + €1,600 = €1,851,600
   Batch 2: (€18.90 × 150,000 + €1,400) × 20,000/150,000 = €378,187
   Total cost: €1,851,600 + €378,187 = €2,229,787

4. Calculate the gain realised:
   Sales proceeds less cost: €2,769,000 – €2,229,787 = €539,213

- Dr investments sold receivable by €2,769,000.
- Cr investments at cost by €2,229,787.
- Cr unrealised appreciation/depreciation by €539,213.

Or – for the spreadsheet method:

- Increase investments sold receivable, an asset, by €2,769,000.
- Decrease investments at cost, an asset, by €2,229,787.
- Decrease unrealised appreciation/depreciation, an asset, by €539,213.

Transaction 6

Calculate the amount of the return of capital:
   205,000 shares × €3 = €615,000

- Dr return of capital receivable by €615,000.
- Cr investments at cost by €615,000.

Or – for the spreadsheet approach:

- Increase return of capital receivable, an asset, by €615,000.
- Reduce investments at cost, an asset, by €615,000.

Transaction 7

Today is the effective date that the shares are received:

- Total number of shares to be received: €520,000/€10.75 = 48,372 shares.
- Increase the number of shares in the portfolio.
- Account for the transaction:
  o dr investments at cost by €520,000
  o cr dividends receivable by €520,000

Or – for the spreadsheet method:

- Increase investments at cost, an asset, by €520,000.
- Decrease dividends receivable, an asset, by €520,000.

Transaction 8

Calculate the amount to be received: 8,000 shares × €26.52 = €212,160

- Dr fund shares sold receivable by €212,160.
- Cr proceeds from the issue of shares by €212,160.
- Increase the number of outstanding fund shares by 8,000.

Or – for the spreadsheet approach:

- Increase fund shares sold receivable, an asset, by €212,160.
- Increase issue of shares, a capital item, by €212,160.
- Increase the number of outstanding fund shares by 8,000.

Daily Valuation

See Table 6.20d for the daily valuation of the fund on 05/04/X8.

Table 6.20d: Daily Valuation of Euro Equity Fund on 05/04/X8

Share	Price	Quantity	Market Value
CRH	€4.10	2,100,000	€8,610,000
Irish Life and Permanent	€10.75	568,372	€6,109,999
Kingspan	€4.45	205,000	€912,250
Smurfit	€4.85	630,000	€3,055,500
AIB	€23.05	130,000	€2,996,500
Bank of Ireland	€8.70	20,000	€174,000
Market Value of Portfolio (today, 05/04/X8)			€21,858,249
Cost of Portfolio (today, 05/04/X8) (Note 1)			€21,698,713
Total Unrealised Appreciation/Depreciation			€159,536
Unrealised Appreciation/Depreciation from Yesterday		€1,012,750	
Less Gains Sold (AIB Sale)		−€539,213	€473,537
Gain/(Loss) for Day			**−€314,001**

Note 1: Cost of Portfolio:	
Total Cost from Yesterday (04/04/X8)	€23,850,500
Add Bank of Ireland Purchase	€173,000
Less AIB Sale, Original Cost	−€2,229,787
Less Kingspan Return of Capital	−€615,000
Add Irish Life and Permanent Stock Dividend	€520,000
Total Cost of Portfolio Today (05/04/X8)	€21,698,713

To record this transaction:

- Dr gains/losses on investments by €314,001 (in the statement of operations).
- Cr unrealised appreciation/depreciation by €314,001.

Or – for the spreadsheet approach:

- Decrease gains/losses on investments, an income, by €314,001.
- Decrease unrealised appreciation/depreciation, an asset, by €314,001.

Note that in this instance there was a loss on the portfolio for the day ⇒ the transaction is reversed from the 'normal' situation (i.e. a gain).

The third requirement is to calculate the NAV per share on 05/04/X8. This is a matter of completing the final column in the spreadsheet. Follow the approach used in previous chapters; a full solution is provided in the next section (Section 6.9.3).

6.9.3: Solution to Comprehensive Question – Euro Equity Fund

Table 6.20e provides the spreadsheet solution to the comprehensive question.
  Now try Question 6.10.8.

6.10: ADDITIONAL QUESTIONS

Question 6.10.1: Dividend Payments

You are the fund accountant for the Irish Equity Investment Fund. Figure 6.9 shows the listing of all the equity dividends approved by companies on the Irish Stock Exchange for April 2008.
  Your fund has holdings in many of these companies:

- Smurfit Kappa   150,000 shares
- IAWS   50,000 shares
- Total Produce   75,000 shares
- Fyffes   250,000 shares
- Kerry Group   115,000 shares

Requirements:

For each of the holdings that the fund has:

1. Calculate the amount of dividend that the fund will receive.
2. When the dividend is recorded, set out the accounting entries.
3. When the dividend is received, set out the accounting entries.

  Show the following accounts for the month of April:

- Dividends receivable account (note some of the companies may have paid their dividend during April)
- Dividend income account

Question 6.10.2

You are the accountant for an Irish resident fund that holds 75,000 shares in Picod Ltd, a company that is resident in Realand. On 11/01/X1 the directors of Picod announce a dividend of €0.40 per share. The ex-date is 31/01/X1 and the payment date is 29/03/X1.

  You are required to show clearly the accounting entries, the amounts and the dates those entries should be recorded under each of the following circumstances (see page 342):

Table 6.20e: Solution to Comprehensive Question – Euro Equity Fund

Statement of Net Assets

	04/04/X8	Trans. 1	Trans. 2	Trans. 3	Trans. 4	Trans. 5	Trans. 6	Trans. 7	Trans. 8	Value	05/04/X8
Assets											
Investments at Cost	€23,850,500			€173,000		-€2,229,787	-€615,000	€520,000			€21,698,713
Unrealised Appreciation/ Depreciation	€1,012,750					-€539,213				-€314,001	€159,536
Investments Sold Receivable	€265,000					€2,769,000					€3,034,000
Fund Shares Sold Receivable	€25,000								€212,160		€237,160
Return of Capital Receivable	€0						€615,000				€615,000
Cash	€880,000										€880,000
Dividends Receivable	€520,000				€441,000			-€520,000			€441,000
Total Assets	*€26,553,250*										*€27,065,409*
Liabilities											
Investments Purchased Payable	€0			€173,000							€173,000
Accrued Expenses	€18,000										€18,000
Fund Shares Redeemed Payable	€0										€0
Distributions Payable	€15,000										€15,000
Total Liabilities	€33,000										€206,000
Total Net Assets	**€26,520,250**										**€26,859,409**
Capital Stock	**€26,520,250**										**€26,859,409**
Outstanding Shares	1,000,000								8,000		1,008,000
NAV per Share	**€26.52**										**€26.646**

(Continued)

Table 6.20e: *(Continued)*

Statement of Operations for the Period from 01/01/X8 to 05/04/X8

	04/04/X8	Trans. 1	Trans. 2	Trans. 3	Trans. 4	Trans. 5	Trans. 6	Trans. 7	Trans. 8	Value	05/04/X8
Gains/Losses on Investments	€14,186									-€314,001	-€299,815
Dividend Income	€602,500				€630,000						€1,232,500
Interest Income	€0										€0
Total Investment Income/Loss	*€616,686*										*€932,685*
Administration Fee YTD	€3,000										€3,000
Investment Management Fee YTD	€202,000										€202,000
Other Fees YTD	€5,000										€5,000
Auditing Fee YTD	€0										€0
Dividend Withholding Tax	€0				€189,000						€189,000
Total Fund Expenses	*€210,000*										*€399,000*
Increase/Decrease in Net Assets from Operations	**€406,686**										**€533,685**

(Continued)

Table 6.20e: *(Continued)*

Statement of Changes in Net Assets for the Period from 01/01/X8 to 05/04/X8

	04/04/X8	Trans. 1	Trans. 2	Trans. 3	Trans. 4	Trans. 5	Trans. 6	Trans. 7	Trans. 8	Value 05/04/X8
Investors' Equity at 01/01/X8	€25,016,343									€25,016,343
Distributions to Investors	€60,500									€60,500
Capital Fund Share Transactions										
Issue of shares	€1,556,221								€212,160	€1,768,381
Redemption of units	€398,500									€398,500
Dividend reinvestment	€0									€0
Total	*€1,157,721*									*€1,369,881*
Increase/Decrease in Net Assets from Operations	€406,686									€533,685
Investors' Equity at End	**€26,520,250**									**€26,859,409**

Figure 6.9: Irish Stock Exchange – Dividend Listing for April 2008

Ex-Div Date	Issuer Name	Security Name	Curr Code	Net Div €(c)	Tax	Tax Credit	Gross Div €(c)	Record Dt/ Coupon No.	Payment Date
02-APR-08	SMURFIT KAPPA GROUP PLC	Ordinary Shares	EUR		W		16.0500	04-APR-08	16-MAY-08
09-APR-08	IAWS GROUP PLC	Ordinary Shares	EUR		W		8.6400	11-APR-08	21-APR-08
23-APR-08	TOTAL PRODUCE PLC – IEX	Ordinary Shares	EUR		W		1.1500	25-APR-08	29-MAY-08
23-APR-08	GLANBIA PLC	Ordinary Shares	EUR		W		3.5800	25-APR-08	20-MAY-08
23-APR-08	TESCO PLC	Ordinary Shares	GBP	7.7000	10/90			25-APR-08	04-JUL-08
23-APR-08	IRISH LIFE AND PERMANENT PLC	Ordinary Shares	EUR		W		52.5000	25-APR-08	28-MAY-08
16-APR-08	TULLOW OIL PLC	Ordinary Shares	GBP	4.0000	10/90			18-APR-08	21-MAY-08
02-APR-08	ABBEY PLC – IEX	Ordinary Shares	EUR	12.0000	10/90			04-APR-08	30-APR-08
02-APR-08	FYFFES PLC – IEX	Ordinary Shares	EUR		W		1.0000	04-APR-08	01-MAY-08
16-APR-08	KERRY GROUP PLC	Ordinary Shares	EUR		W		13.9000	18-APR-08	23-MAY-08
16-APR-08	INDEPENDENT NEWS & MEDIA PLC	Ordinary Shares	EUR		W		9.1300	18-APR-08	13-JUN-08

Source: http://www.ise.ie/uploadedfiles/Monthly_Reports/Monthly_Reports_2008/Apr08.pdf – Irish Stock Exchange, monthly statistical publication, April 2008.

1. Realand does not have a dividend withholding tax; the full amount of the dividend will be paid to the fund.
2. Realand does have a DWT of 20 per cent on all dividends but there is an agreement between the revenue authorities of Realand and Ireland to exempt investment funds located in either country from the other's DWT. This is subject to a number of conditions, but you can assume that your fund qualifies for the exemption and is exempt from the DWT. Picod have been informed of the fund's exempt status and is thus permitted to pay the full dividend direct to the fund.
3. Realand does have a DWT of 20 per cent on all dividends. There is a double taxation agreement between Realand and Ireland. Under the agreement, companies are require to deduct DWT on dividends paid to all non-residents but some non-residents (including investment funds) are permitted to reclaim the DWT paid from the revenue authorities of the tax collecting country. This can only be initiated once the dividend has been paid. On 04/04/X1 the fund submitted a claim to the authorities in Realand for a refund of the DWT paid by Picod. On 14/09/X1 the refund was paid.
4. Realand does have a DWT of 20 per cent on all dividends. There is no double taxation agreement between the governments of Realand and Ireland. The DWT cannot be reclaimed.

Question 6.10.3

Your fund holds 10,000 shares in Tram Biotech. The shares were purchased for €2.50 each, along with commission of €1,000. On 31/03/X5 the share price of Tram Biotech was €4.50.

Requirement:

*   Calculate the balance on the investments at cost account and the unrealised appreciation/depreciation account on 31/03/X5.

On 01/04/X5 Tram Biotech announce a dividend of €1.00 per share. The ex-date is 03/04/X5 and the payment date is 05/04/X5. On 01/04/X5 Tram Biotech also gave shareholders the option to accept the dividend in the form of shares in Tram Biotech. The price at which the shares are to be issued will be the closing price on the payment date. The fund opted to take its full dividend entitlement in the form of shares in Tram Biotech. The shares were received by the fund on 07/04/X5. Table 6.21 shows the daily share prices in Tram Biotech.

Table 6.21:   Daily Share Prices in Tram Biotech

Date	01/04/X5	02/04/X5	03/04/X5	04/04/X5	05/04/X5	06/04/X5	07/04/X5	08/04/X5
Price	€4.60	€4.70	€3.75	€3.80	€3.77	€3.82	€3.85	€3.82

Requirements:

- Set out the entry to record the various stages of the stock dividend reinvestment.
- For each day from 01/04/X5 to 08/04/X5 inclusive, show the balance on the following accounts:
  - investments at cost account
  - unrealised appreciation/depreciation account
  - dividends receivable account
  - investments purchased payable account/dividend reinvestment purchased payable account

Question 6.10.4

You are the fund accountant for the Infra–util Fund. Table 6.22a shows the fund's holdings on 17/07/X8 (assume all holdings are in EUR).

Table 6.22a: Holdings of the Infra-util Fund on 17/07/X8

Company	Trade Date	Quantity	Cost	Commission	Total Cost	17/07/X8 Share Price	17/07/X8 Market Value
EDF	02/05/X3	5,000	€22.00	€2,000	€112,000	€35.00	€175,000
EDF	19/12/X5	7,000	€28.00	€2,800	€198,800	€35.00	€245,000
E.On France	31/10/X4	22,000	€4.50	€2,200	€101,200	€7.50	€165,000
Telecom	10/08/X4	7,000	€14.00	€2,100	€100,100	€18.00	€126,000
Telefonica	09/12/X7	15,000	€22.00	€3,000	€333,000	€24.00	€360,000
Vinci	02/09/X5	12,000	€18.50	€2,400	€224,400	€30.00	€360,000
Total					*€1,069,500*		*€1,431,000*

You should be able to calculate the 'Total Cost' column and the 'Market Value' column.

From the information in Table 6.22a, the following balances exist in the statement of net assets:

- Investments at cost account   €1,431,000   (dr balance)
- Unrealised appreciation/depreciation account   €361,500   (dr balance)

341

During 18/07/X8 the following events occurred:

- EDF had previously announced a share buy back programme. On 18/07/X8 the fund agreed to sell 8,000 shares back to EDF at a price of €35.50 per share, no commission and a settlement date of 27/07/X8.
- E.On had previously announced a special dividend of €2.50 per share; the ex-date was 18/07/X8. The special dividend is to be recorded as income, settlement on 21/08/X8.
- France Telecom had previously announced a return of capital of €7 per share; the ex-date was 18/07/X8. The return of capital is to be recorded as a reduction in cost; settlement on 01/08/X8.
- Telefonica had previously announced a return of capital of €15 per share; the ex-date was 18/07/X8. The return of capital is to be recorded as a partial reduction in cost and a partial reduction in unrealised appreciation/depreciation (Option B2); settlement on 01/08/X8.
- The fund sold 4,000 shares in Vinci for €30.50 less commission of €2,000, to settle on TD + 3.

Table 6.22b shows the official closing prices at the end of 18/07/X8.

Table 6.22b: Closing Prices for Infra-util Fund's Holdings on 18/07/X8

Company	18/07/X8 Share Price
EDF	€35.75
E.On	€5.10
France Telecom	€11.50
Telefonica	€9.25
Vinci	€30.25

Requirements:

- Record the share buy back in EDF.
- Record the special dividend and return of capital in E.On, France Telecom and Telefonica.
- Record the sale of Vinci shares.
- Record the movement in the unrealised appreciation/depreciation account for the day.

Question 6.10.5

You are the fund accountant for the Kilsheelan Investment Fund. Table 6.23a shows the fund's portfolio.

Table 6.23a: Holdings Portfolio of the Kilsheelan Investment Fund

Company	Trade Date	Quantity	Cost	Commission	Total Cost	17/07/X8 Share Price	17/07/X8 Market Value
Enel	02/05/X3	6,000	€14.50	€2,400	€89,400	€27.00	€162,000
Enel	19/12/X5	8,000	€18.50	€3,200	€151,200	€27.00	€216,000
Renault	31/10/X4	15,000	€22.00	€3,000	€333,000	€32.25	€483,750
Thales	10/08/X4	6,000	€14.00	€1,800	€85,800	€18.00	€108,000
Carrefour	09/12/X7	10,000	€26.45	€5,000	€269,500	€38.00	€380,000
Fortis	02/09/X5	13,000	€32.00	€2,600	€418,600	€35.00	€455,000
Total					€1,347,500		€1,804,750

From the information in Table 6.23a the following balances exist in the statement of net assets:

- Investments at cost account   €1,347,500   (dr balance)
- Unrealised appreciation/depreciation account   €457,250   (dr balance)

On 18/07/X8 the following events took place:

- This is the ex-date for a bonus issue in Renault (which had previously announced a bonus issue). The rate of the bonus issue is 3 for 2.
- This is the ex-date for a bonus issue in Enel (which had previously announced a bonus issue). The rate of the bonus issue is 5 for 2.

Table 6.23b shows the official closing prices at the end of 18/07/X8.

Requirements:

- Record the bonus issue in Renault.
- Record the bonus issue in Enel.
- Record the movement in the unrealised appreciation/depreciation account for the day.

Question 6.10.6

Waterford Wedgwood is an example of a company that has had a number of rights issues over the past number of years. A list of the rights issues is presented below:

Table 6.23b: Closing Prices of the Kilsheelan Investment Fund's Holdings on 18/07/X8

Company	18/07/X8 Share Price
Enel	€11.00
Renault	€21.75
Thales	€18.25
Carrefour	€37.70
Fortis	€35.25

- On 01/01/03 Waterford Wedgwood had 776 million shares in issue.
- A 3 for 11 rights issue at €0.18 per share was declared in November 2003, raising €38.5 million. In November 2003, before the rights issue, Waterford Wedgwood was trading at €0.26 per share.
- A 5 for 3 rights issue at €0.06 per share was declared in October 2004, raising €99.7 million.
- A 7 for 11 rights issue at €0.06 per share was declared in June 2005, raising €101.5 million.
- A 3 for 13 rights issue at €0.06 per share was declared in June 2006, raising €60 million.

On 01/01/03, before the first rights issue, your fund held 40,000 shares in the fund.

Requirements:

- Assuming all shareholders participate in the rights issue, determine the share price of the company just after the **first** rights issue (this is called the theoretical ex-rights price). For this requirement, assume that there is no other reason for the share price of the company to change.
- Evaluate the wealth of the fund, both before and after the **first** rights issue, on the basis that the fund takes up its rights.
- Evaluate the wealth of the fund, both before and after the **first** rights issue, on the basis that the fund does not take up its rights.
- Assuming that your fund participated fully in each of the rights issues:
  - how many shares in Waterford Wedgwood would the fund hold by the end of June 2006?
  - how much money would the fund have invested in Waterford Wedgwood as a result of the four rights issues?

Question 6.10.7

Your fund is an equity fund. Consequently the fund has a number of investments in equities. Details of two of its investments are shown in Table 6.24a.

Table 6.24a: Details of Two of the Investments of the Equity Fund

Equity	Date of Purchase	Number of Shares	Cost Price per Share
ASD	03/03/01	3,000	€3.00
ASD	04/04/02	2,000	€5.00
Econo Co	05/05/05	8,000	€4.00
Econo Co	06/06/06	9,000	€6.00

On 24/04/07 ASD Corporation announces a rights issue. The company will issue two new shares for every five held, at a price of €5 per share. The ex-rights date is 01/05/07, on which date the rights will commence trading, and the payment date is 05/05/07, which is also the date that the rights will cease trading.

On 28/04/07 Econo Co announces a rights issue. The company will issue one new share for every four held, at a price of €4 per share. The ex-rights date is 02/05/07, on which date the rights will commence trading, and the payment date is 06/05/07, which is also the date that the rights will cease trading.

On 04/05/07 the fund sold its rights in ASD for €7.90 per right to buy one share and this was settled immediately.

On 04/05/07 the fund exercised its rights in Econo Co and this was settled immediately.

Table 6.24b shows the prices for the holdings.

Table 6.24b: Prices for the Holdings of the Equity Fund from 30/04/07 to 07/05/07

Date	30/04/07	01/05/07	02/05/07	03/05/07	04/05/07	05/05/07	06/05/07	07/05/07
ASD Share Price	€15.50	€12.60	€12.80	€13.00	€13.30	€13.60	€13.80	€13.90
ASD Rights Price		€7.40	€7.60	€7.70	€8.00			
Econo Co Share Price	€10.40	€10.50	€9.20	€9.00	€9.10	€9.15	€9.30	€9.50
Econo Co Rights Price			€5.10	€4.85	€4.90	€5.00		

Requirements:

For each day from 30/04/07 to 06/05/07 inclusive, set out the balance at the end of the day in the following accounts:

- The investments at cost account
- The unrealised appreciation/depreciation on investment account

345

Question 6.10.8

Table 6.25a and Table 6.25b show the financial statements and holdings of the Pan-European Investment Fund.

The following transactions occurred on 05/04/X8:

1. InBev announces a rights issue of 1 for 1 at €10 per share; the record date and the ex-date are 05/04/X8. The payment date is 07/04/X8.
2. Renault announces a rights issue of 1 for 4 at €50 per share; the record date and the ex-date are 05/04/X8. The payment date is 07/04/X8.
3. Generali announces a rights issue of 4 for 3 at €45 per share; the record date and the ex-date are 05/04/X8. The payment date is 07/04/X8.
4. A new shareholder buys 20,000 shares in the fund at yesterday's NAV per share, to settle on TD + 3.

Share prices on 05/04/X8:
- InBev   €13.60
- Renault   €84.00
- BASF   €61.00
- Nokia   €71.00
- Generali   €53.00
- InBev Rights   €3.50 per right to buy one share
- Renault Rights   €32.00 per right to buy one share
- Generali Rights   €6.50 per right to buy one share

The following transactions occurred on 06/04/X8:

1. The fund purchased 10,000 shares for €27.80 in Philips; commission of €3,000 to settle on TD + 3.
2. The fund sold rights in InBev for €3.60, with no commission and settled immediately.
3. Nokia announces a share split of 1 for 1 with a record and ex-date today.

Share prices on 06/04/X8:
- InBev   €13.70
- Renault   €84.50
- BASF   €62.00
- Nokia   €36.00
- Generali   €54.00
- InBev Rights   €3.55 per right to buy one share
- Renault Rights   €33.00 per right to buy one share
- Generali Rights   €7.75 per right to buy one share
- Philips   €28.00

Table 6.25a: Comprehensive Question 6.10.8

Statement of Net Assets

	04/04/X8	Trans. 1	Trans. 2	Value 05/04/X8	Trans. 1	Trans. 2	Trans. 3	Value 06/04/X8	Trans. 1	Trans. 2	Trans. 3	Value 07/04/X8
Assets												
Investments at Cost	€3,602,850											
Unrealised Appreciation/ Depreciation	€62,900											
Investments Sold Receivable	€450,000											
Fund Shares Sold Receivable	€120,000											
Interest Receivable	€0											
Cash	€1,400,000											
Dividends Receivable	€25,000											
Total Assets	*€5,660,750*											
Liabilities												
Investments Purchased Payable	€0											
Accrued Expenses	€15,000											
Fund Shares Redeemed Payable	€0											
Distributions Payable	€0											
Total Liabilities	*€15,000*											
Total Net Assets	**€5,645,750**											
Capital Stock	**€5,645,750**											
Outstanding Shares	1,000,000											
NAV per Share	**€5.646**											

Table 6.25a: *(Continued)*

Statement of Operations for the Period from 01/01/X8 to 07/04/X8

	04/04/X8	Trans. 1	Trans. 2	Value 05/04/X8	Trans. 1	Trans. 2	Trans. 3	Value 06/04/X8	Trans. 1	Trans. 2	Trans. 3	Value 07/04/X8
Gains/Losses on Investments	€414,186											
Dividend Income	€2,500											
Interest Income	€0											
Total Investment Income/Loss	*€416,686*											
Administration Fee YTD	€16,740											
Investment Management Fee YTD	€65,671											
Other Fees YTD	€4,700											
Auditing Fee YTD	€2,060											
Total Fund Expenses	*€89,171*											
Increase/Decrease in Net Assets from Operations	**€327,515**											

(Continued)

Table 6.25a: (Continued)

Statement of Changes in Net Assets for Period from 01/01/X8 to 07/04/X8

	04/04/X8	Trans. 1	Trans. 2	Value 05/04/X8	Trans. 1	Trans. 2	Trans. 3	Value 06/04/X8	Trans. 1	Trans. 2	Trans. 3	Value 07/04/X8
Investors' Equity at 01/01/X8	€4,221,014											
Distributions to Investors	(€60,500)											
Capital Fund Share Transactions												
Proceeds from the sale of shares	€1,556,221											
Redemption of units	(€398,500)											
Dividend reinvestment	€0											
Total	*€1,157,721*											
Increase/Decrease in Net Assets from Operations	€327,515											
Investors' Equity at End of Period	**€5,645,750**											

Table 6.25b: Holdings of the Fund

Security	Date Purchased	Cost Price	Quantity	Commission	Total Cost	04/04/X8 Market Price	Market Value
InBev	01/01/X1	€15.30	12,000	€2,500	€186,100	€17.00	€204,000
InBev	01/01/X2	€15.90	15,000	€3,000	€241,500	€17.00	€255,000
InBev	01/01/X3	€16.50	10,000	€3,500	€168,500	€17.00	€170,000
Renault	01/01/X1	€80.50	5,000	€2,500	€405,000	€90.00	€450,000
Renault	01/01/X2	€84.50	6,000	€3,750	€510,750	€90.00	€540,000
Renault	01/01/X3	€88.50	2,000	€4,250	€181,250	€90.00	€180,000
BASF	01/01/X1	€56.25	4,000	€4,500	€229,500	€60.50	€242,000
BASF	01/01/X2	€58.30	5,000	€5,500	€297,000	€60.50	€302,500
Nokia	01/01/X3	€74.25	6,000	€3,000	€448,500	€70.50	€423,000
Nokia	01/01/X4	€78.25	6,000	€1,000	€470,500	€70.50	€423,000
Generali	01/01/X3	€61.00	5,000	€1,600	€306,600	€63.50	€317,500
Generali	01/01/X4	€62.50	2,500	€1,400	€157,650	€63.50	€158,750
Total					€3,602,850		€3,665,750

The following transactions occurred on 07/04/X8:

1. The fund allowed its rights in Renault to lapse.
2. The fund exercised its rights in Generali, to be settled immediately.
3. BASF goes ex-dividend today, the dividend is €1.00 per share with a payment date on 01/05/X8.

Share prices on 07/04/X8:
- InBev   €14.00
- Renault   €85.00
- BASF   €61.00
- Nokia   €36.50
- Generali   €54.50
- Philips   €28.00

Requirements:

Part A – (25 Marks)
Record the transactions from 05/04/X8 and calculate the daily NAV per share (using the templates provided; complete the statement of net assets, the statement of operations and the statement of changes in net assets).

Part B – (35 Marks)

Record the transactions from 06/04/X8 and calculate the daily NAV per share (using the templates provided, complete the statement of net assets, the statement of operations and the statement of changes in net assets)

Part C – (30 Marks)

Record the transactions from 07/04/X8 and calculate the daily NAV per share (using the templates provided, complete the statement of net assets, the statement of operations and the statement of changes in net assets)

Chapter 7

Accounting for Fund Expenses

- Introduction
- Review of how a fund works
- Types of fund expenses
- Investor reaction to fund expenses
- Accounting for fund expense accruals
- Accounting for the payment of fund expenses
- Accounting for unexpected expenses, under-/over-accruals, caps and waivers
- Summary
- Bringing it all together
- Additional questions

LEARNING OUTCOMES

At the end of this chapter you should:

- Be able to explain the different types of fund expenses.
- Be able to evaluate investor reaction to fund expenses.
- Be able to record fund expenses on a daily basis.
- Be able to cope with unexpected expenses and under-/over-accruals.
- Be able to incorporate fund expenses with your knowledge so far in a comprehensive fund scenario.

7.1: INTRODUCTION

This chapter looks at the sometimes controversial issue of fund expenses. It begins with a review of how a fund works (Section 7.2) as this has a big impact on the expense environment of a fund. Then the different types of fund expenses will be considered (Section 7.3). As can be imagined, investors in a fund do not appreciate high fees; this is the issue that is explored in Section 7.4.

Sections 7.5 and 7.6 consider the accounting implications of expenses, in particular the problem of allocating expenses into the daily/weekly/monthly NAV per share calculation. The payment of expenses does not present significant accounting difficulties. However, in Section 7.7, some of the more thorny accounting problems are addressed: under-/over-accrual of expenses, and accounting for expense caps and waivers.

Section 7.8 is a summary of the main accounting implications, while Section 7.9 is a comprehensive example of fund expenses. This example incorporates much of the learning from previous chapters.

7.2: REVIEW OF HOW A FUND WORKS

Recall Section 1.6, where it was highlighted that a fund does not have any employees. Instead, the fund contracts out all the services it requires to third parties. For example, a fund will not hire an employee to act as its investment advisor; it will pay a company that specialises in investment advice. Similarly, a fund will not hire an accountant; it will pay a company that specialises in investment fund accounting. This pattern is repeated for every service that is required to run an investment fund; every function is contracted to third parties.

This does give an investment fund a remarkable degree of flexibility. If the investment advisors are not performing then it is not difficult to remove them and take investment advice from another company of investment advisors. However, often it is not that simple. Many funds are set up by financial institutions. The investment management arm of the financial institution is given the investment advice contract. The fund accounting subsidiary of the financial institution is awarded the fund accounting contract. The custody division gets the custody job and so on. This is not underhand – the companies that have been awarded the various contracts are clearly outlined in the prospectus of the fund.

7.3: TYPES OF FUND EXPENSES

The different types of major expenses should be outlined in the prospectus, along with (where possible) an indication of the level of expenses. Generally there will be a contract between the service provider and the fund; this should be consistent with the expenses detail given in the prospectus.

The normal types of expenses that a fund will have to pay are:

- Advisory fees, also called investment fees or management fees
- Custodian fees
- Fund administration/accounting fees
- Legal fees

- Audit fees
- Cost of providing reports to shareholders
- Foreign withholding tax on dividends (see Section 6.3.6 for a lengthy discussion on withholding tax on dividends)
- Directors/trustee fees
- Registration fees

Note there are some fees that the fund does not pay, these are paid directly by the investor (for example, when an investor buys into a fund there is a sales load or sales charge – see Section 4.3 for a discussion on sales charges).[1]

An example from the prospectus of a fund is given in Figure 7.1. It is taken from Brendan Investments Pan European Property Plc, a type of property investment fund.

Figure 7.1: Extract from Prospectus of Brendan Investments Plc on Fees

---

24. FEES

As set out in Section 6 of Part 5, the Property Management Company will receive a fee of 1.00% per annum (plus VAT if applicable) based on the gross value of the investment property portfolio at the end of each calendar year, for work undertaken pursuant to the Property Management Agreement for the ten year term of that agreement and until the agreement is terminated. In addition, the Property Management Company will receive an annual investment fee of 1% (plus VAT if applicable) of the gross development value of each development project, payable in the same manner as the fees relating to the investment property portfolio. This is also payable for the ten year term of the agreement and until the agreement is terminated.

As set out in Section 13 of this Part 12, Mr Richard Fitzgerald will receive an annual advisory fee of €30,000 (plus VAT and outlay as applicable) for work undertaken pursuant to the Property Advisory Agreement.

PricewaterhouseCoopers will receive an annual fee for work undertaken as auditor of the Company and the Group.

Computershare will receive on-going fees with regard to registry, transfer agency and related services provided pursuant to the Registry Services Agreement.

Source: Brendan Investments Pan European Property Plc Prospectus, May 2007, p. 55.

These fees are not unusual. However, what led to a substantial amount of media comment[2] regarding Brendan Investments was the existence of 'Founder' shares, which are entitled to preferential rights over all of the other investors (see Figure 7.2).

---

[1] See www.sec.gov/answers/mffees.htm for an example of the different types of fund fees.

[2] For example, see Ross (2007a and 2007b).

Figure 7.2: Extract from Prospectus of Brendan Investments Plc on Founder Shares

---

8. FOUNDER SHARES AND FEES PAYABLE TO THE FOUNDERS

The Founders (Mr Vincent Regan, Mr Hugh O'Neill, Mr Eddie Hobbs and Mr Richard Fitzgerald) are the holders of the Founder Shares. The holders of the Founder Shares, upon the liquidation of the Company (or other form of dissolution, transaction or sale of all or substantially all of the assets) may be entitled to a preferential return of the remaining assets of the Company in priority to any payments to the holders of the Ordinary Shares. Subject to achieving the Milestones (i.e. the expiry of at least 5 years and the Exit Proceeds exceeding the Strike Price (being the investment proceeds compounded at an 8% annual interest rate over a 10 year period – see specific details within the definitions of "Milestones" and "Strike Price" set out in Part 13 of this Document)) the Founders shall receive 20% of the amount by which the Exit Proceeds exceeds the Strike Price as this preferential return.

Other than as described above, the Founder Shares and the Ordinary Shares shall rank pari passu in all respects.

Each of the Founders (save Mr Richard Fitzgerald) are shareholders and directors of the Property Management Company (which will render property management and other services to the Company and the Group) or otherwise involved in the provision of advice to the Company and the Group. The Founders (save Mr Richard Fitzgerald) will be entitled to benefit from fees incurred by the Company and the Group, due to the Property Management Company.

Source: Brendan Investments Pan European Property Plc Prospectus, May 2007, p. 23.

Can you determine the likely return that the founders will receive should the fund perform exceptionally well? For this level of increased return what additional risks have the founders taken? How can this level of fees be justified?

Although there are numerous types of fees there are just four basic methods of determining fees:

1. Based on a percentage of the value of the fund, e.g. investment advisory fees
2. Flat fees, e.g. audit fees
3. A combination of #1 and #2
4. Fees based on achieving a predetermined level of return; often performance fees are determined on this basis

In this chapter we will consider the first three types. The fourth type, performance fees, is beyond the scope of this book. Given the complicated nature of the calculation of performance fees, the accounting for these types of fees on a daily basis is difficult. The 'founder shares' noted above in Brendan Investments Pan European Property is an example of a performance fee.

7.4: Investor Reaction to Fund Expenses

Fund expenses can have a significant impact on the return available to investors. As more expenses are paid out of the fund there is less available for the investors. This has a knock-on effect because of the power of compounding.

The standard measure used by the industry to compare the expense level across different investment funds is the total expense ratio.

$$\textbf{Total Expense Ratio} = \frac{\textbf{Total Fund Expenses}}{\textbf{Total Fund Net Assets}}$$

There is, however, some debate as to what expenses should be included; generally sales loads (front and back end)[3] are not included. Often, broker fees on purchase and sales of investments are not included (these are included as part of the cost of acquisition and disposal of investments). This can result in the total expense ratio being somewhat lower than might otherwise be the case.

The *Financial Times* rates funds based on their expense ratios. Figure 7.3 shows the scale used.

Figure 7.3:   Ratings Scale Used by the *Financial Times* Based on Expense Rations

Total Expense Ratio	Rating
TER up to and including 0.5%	Very Low
Above 0.5% but no greater than 1%	Low
Above 1% but no greater than 1.5%	Medium
Above 1.5% but no greater than 2%	High
Above 2%	Very High

Source: Financial Times, www.ft.com/Markets/Funds/popup_help_gloss.html.

The difference between a very low rating of, say, 0.4 per cent and a very high rating of, say, 2.1 per cent is significant. Consider an investor with €10,000 to invest. Let's assume that the fund generates a 10 per cent annual return before expenses. After fifteen years the €10,000 invested in the low fee fund of 0.4 per cent (net return of 9.6 per cent) will be worth €39,551. If the same €10,000 was invested in the high fee fund with expenses at 2.1 per cent (net return of 7.9 per cent), it would only be worth €31,284, or 20 per cent less than the low expense fund.

Using the above example, it is not difficult to see why investor reaction to fund expenses is so negative. Another reason is because investors often feel that they have little control over the level of fees, although they are provided with the information before investing. Finally, the financial services industry probably does not have

---

[3]   See Section 4.3 for an explanation of these terms.

a great record when it comes to fees and charges, and investors are naturally suspicious.

Apart from knowing the information in the prospectus, investors have little control over fees. In recent years a number of funds have been sold with an expense guarantee. The expenses of the fund will be guaranteed to be less than a specified percentage of the fund's total net assets – if the fees are deemed to be too high then generally the investment manager will be paid less than the full amount due.

Figure 7.4 shows the expenses charged by a sample of funds offered by Vanguard, a fund provider that emphasises its low fee structure. As can be seen, the level of expenses can vary.

Figure 7.4: Expenses Charged by a Sample of Vanguard Funds

Name	Expense Ratio	Purchase Fee	Redemption Fee
500 Index	0.18%	None	None
Asset Allocation	0.29%	None	None
Balanced Index	0.25%	None	None
California Intermediate-Term Tax-Exempt	0.20%	None	None
California Long-Term Tax-Exempt	0.20%	None	None
California Tax-Exempt Money Market	0.17%	None	None
Developed Markets Index	0.22%	None	2% if held < 2 months
Diversified Equity	0.43%	None	None
Dividend Appreciation Index	0.35%	None	None
Dividend Growth	0.32%	None	None
Emerging Markets Stock Index	0.40%	0.50%	0.25%

Source: Vanguard Group, available from: https://personal.vanguard.com/us/funds/vanguard/all?sort=name&sortorder=asc.

The level of fees can vary based on a number of factors:

• The reputation of the investment manager
• Whether the fund is actively managed (more expensive) or passively managed (less expensive)
• The nature of the fund – the more specialist the fund the more expensive the fees. For example, broad–based equity funds have lower fees than specialist emerging markets funds.
• The competition – many funds use their expense level as a means of attracting investors. Thus, when a fund lowers its fees it is likely that its main rivals will do likewise.

Some controversial issues with expenses include:

- Trading costs, fees and commissions (for buying and selling investments) are generally not included in the expenses of a fund; they are subsumed within the investment itself. Thus, a fund that is actively managed has a much higher level of expenses than reported.
- Investment advisory fees are largely determined by the size of the fund; thus, a large fund will attract the highest fees (in monetary terms). For example, a fund with an investment advisory fee of 1 per cent with net assets of €100 million will attract much higher fees than a fund with net assets of €25 million. Notice that the fee is not contingent on the fund-making gains on its investments; this is the issue for investors − when the fund does badly they suffer, but investment advisors suffer to a much lesser extent. Indeed, the real incentive for investment managers is to encourage more investors into the fund as this will increase their fees.
- Distribution fees and service fees (12b-1 fees) − some funds will pay general advertising and marketing costs, costs of printing promotional material, costs of hiring people to deal with potential investor queries, etc. These are contentious as they do not benefit current investors; they really benefit the investment manager, who tends to be paid based on the size of the fund.
- Sales load fees do not tend to be recorded within the fund − these fees can be large (up to 5 per cent of the investment made).

For more information, see the articles 'Stop Paying High Mutual Fund Fees' by Michael Weiss (2007) on www.investopedia.com[4] and 'The 2010 Mutual Fund Survey' by Scott DeCarlo and John Chamberlain (2010) on www.forbes.com.[5]

Do you think that the expense structure of funds encourages fund managers to act in the best interests of the shareholders?

7.5: ACCOUNTING FOR FUND EXPENSE ACCRUAL

- The nature of the daily accrual
- Calculating the daily accrual
- Recording the daily accrual

In accounting, an accrual is where an item of expense (or income) is allocated to the period in which the expense arises as opposed to the period in which the

---

[4] See www.investopedia.com/articles/mutualfund/07/stop_fees.asp for full article.
[5] See www.forbes.com/2010/01/20/mutual-funds-performance-grades-mutual-funds-2010-personal-finance_land.html?boxes=custom for full article.

expense is paid. It has special significance in investment fund accounting as the accounting period can be very short, often daily. As a consequence, expenses need to be allocated (or accounted for) on a daily basis.

7.5.1: The Nature of the Daily Accrual

Investment fund fees are paid periodically, often once a month or once a quarter. However, they may need to be accounted for on a daily basis. The reason for this is because if the fee was recorded when paid then that day's NAV per share would take a disproportionate fall. If someone knew when the fees were being paid they could sell their shares in the fund just before the fees were paid and buy back in again just after the fees were paid and make a small profit; if this ploy was done a number of times across different funds then it would be possible to earn a sizeable profit at relatively low risk.

Take an audit fee, for example. Say the fee is €10,000 and is paid on 28 December 2009 for the year 2009:

- Why would there be an issue with just recording this fee on 28 December?

The NAV per share of 28 December 2009 would bear the full effect of the audit fee, yet the fee probably relates to the accounts for the full year. Depending on the size of the fund this could have a material effect on the fund's pricing.

- How can this be properly accounted for so that no one period (day) bears the brunt of the fee?

As the fee relates to the full year it would probably be best to spread (or allocate) the fee across the full year. Thus, every day should take an expense of €10,000/365, or €27. If this approach is taken every day is allocated a small amount, which will not overly impact on the NAV per share calculation of any individual day. As the year progresses, the daily €27 all add up so that, by the end of the year, the total audit fee equals €10,000, which is the amount that is ultimately paid.

A similar approach is taken with all of the other expenses of the fund: advisory fees, custodian fees, administration fees, etc. The solution described above is known as 'expense accrual' – a small amount is set aside every day so that, when the fee is paid, enough has been 'accrued' to match the payment.

Thus, to summarise:

- To accrue means putting a small amount aside every day; this will have the effect of reducing the NAV per share by a small amount every day rather than a large amount on one individual day. This is more equitable for both current and potential shareholders.

- Under the accrual process a small amount is included in the income statement as an expense (on a daily basis) and a small amount is included on the statement of net assets as a liability (as the amount has not been paid, it is owed to the service provider).

7.5.2 Calculating the Daily Accrual

In the previous section an example regarding audit fees was presented. This was an example of a fixed or flat fee. Calculating the daily accrual is straightforward: divide the expected fee by the number of periods (365 days). However, not all fees are calculated using the same approach. There are four categories of fees:

- Flat fees
- Fees based on a percentage of net assets
- Performance-based fees (these are complex and will not be addressed in detail)
- Combination fees

Flat Fees

Flat fees are where the level of fees is not dependent on the size or performance of the fund. These fees can be agreed in advance, for example, trustees can be paid a flat or fixed fee. The audit fee from earlier is another example of a flat fee.

Calculating the daily accrual for flat fees is not difficult: simply divide the expected fee by the number of periods (days/weeks/months).

Example 7.1

XYZ Fund pays its trustees €15,000 per annum. This was agreed at a recent AGM. Calculate the accrual under the following circumstances:

- The NAV per share of the fund is calculated on a daily basis.
- The NAV per share of the fund is calculated on a weekly basis.

Solution 7.1

- When the NAV per share is calculated on a daily basis – accrual is €15,000/365 = €41
- When the NAV per share is calculated on a weekly basis – accrual is €15,000/52 = €288

In this solution you may have noticed that the accrual was rounded to the nearest euro. This can have the effect of under- or over-accruing the expense by a small amount. For example, 365 multiplied by €41 gives an answer of €14,965. This is €35 less than the full fee of €15,000. Resolving this issue will be considered in Section 7.7.

Fees Based on a Percentage of Net Assets

Some service providers to a fund are paid on the basis of the size of the fund. For example, it can be argued that the larger the fund the more work an investment manger will have to carry out. These fees are generally set out in advance in the fund's prospectus.

Often the size of the fee (the percentage applied) decreases as the fund gets larger. This can reflect the level of work carried out by the service provider. For example, if a fund doubles in size the investment manager's workload does not double. The workload will undoubtedly increase as more investment decisions need to be made (this has a positive effect on workload), but larger amounts can now be invested in each asset. The net effect on the workload of the investment manager is positive but there is not a direct linear relationship between workload and the size of the fund. Thus, the declining fee structure.

The calculation of the accrual is based on the percentages provided. Calculate the fee on an annual basis first, then divide it by the number of periods (days) to arrive at the accrual. Generally the net assets of the previous day are used to calculate the expense for the current day. Consequently, the amount of the fee will fluctuate each day as the net assets of the fund go up or down. By the end of the year, the total fee should approximate the relevant percentage(s) of the average total net assets of the fund for the same period.

Example 7.2

XYZ Fund has net assets (assets less liabilities) of €125,500,000. The investment advisory fee (from the prospectus) is calculated as follows:

- On the first €25,000,000: 0.40 per cent of net assets (Band 1)
- On the next €50,000,000: 0.30 per cent of net assets (Band 2)
- On the balance: 0.25 per cent of net assets (Band 3)

Calculate the accrual under the following circumstances:

- The NAV per share of the fund is calculated on a daily basis.
- The NAV per share of the fund is calculated on a weekly basis.

Solution 7.2

This fund has net assets of €125,500,000, which puts it into Band 3. If the fund remained at this size for the full year the annual investment advisory fee would be:

First €25,000,000 @ 0.40% =	€100,000
Next €50,000,000 @ 0.30% =	€150,000
Balance (€125.5m − €75m = €50.5m) @ 0.25% =	€126,250
Total fee (on annual basis)	€376,250

- When the NAV per share is calculated on a daily basis – accrual is €376,250/365 = €1,031
- When the NAV per share is calculated on a weekly basis – accrual is €376,250/52 = €7,236

Performance-Based Fees

Performance-based fees are generally paid to the investment manager. This is where the investment manager is paid a fee based on the profits of the fund. These types of fees were devised to act as an incentive for investment managers to generate superior investment returns for shareholders. They are very common in the hedge fund sector.

Performance fees are often based on the fund exceeding a preset benchmark; it is not acceptable for a fund to just show a positive return; the fund needs to out-perform a specified metric. The choice of benchmark is important because the softer the benchmark the easier it will be for the investment manager to generate significant fees. Some funds use a benchmark related to the LIBOR rate + a small percentage. LIBOR is the London Interbank Offer Rate and often reflects the cost of money (akin to the deposit rate). It tends to be quite low: on 4 November 2008 (in the middle of the credit crisis) the LIBOR USD rate was 2.86 per cent. An example of a performance fee (taken from the DBS Absolute Return Fund)[6] is shown in Figure 7.5.

Figure 7.5: Performance Fee of the DBS Absolute Return Fund

Performance Fee	10% of the portion of the increase in net asset value (calculated without reduction for the Performance Fee for such fiscal year) of ISF for a fiscal year above a hurdle rate pegged to United States dollars three-month LIBOR rate per annum plus 0.5%.

Source: DBS Absolute Return Fund Prospectus (2008), DBS Asset Management, p. 7, available from www.dbsam.com.

---

[6] Full prospectus is available from www.dbsam.com/resource/funds/prospectus/fund/Pages/Prospectus_Darf.pdf?hasRedirected=true.

Thus, if this fund shows a return of 2.86% + 0.5% = 3.36% then the investment manager will start earning performance fees. This is quite a low benchmark; for any return above this level the investment manager will get 10 per cent of the increase in the value of the fund. So, if the fund was worth $100 million and it increased in value to $120 million (and there were no capital stock transactions in the period) then the investment managers will receive 10 per cent of the gain over $103.36 million, or 10 per cent of $16.64 million, giving the investment manager $1.664 million. This can be in addition to a basic investment advice fee.

There will often be other mechanisms in place to cap the performance fee. These are called high water marks. The high water mark is to protect investors where the fund subsequently suffers a fall in value. In the example above, say the fund fell in value from $120 million to $114 million the following year. No performance fee would be due as the fund lost value (the fee from the previous year is unlikely to be repayable). The following year, the fund increases in value from $114 million to $124 million. The calculation of the performance fee is based on the previous high of the fund (hence the term high water mark). The performance fee will be calculated on the increase from $120 million to $124 million, if indeed any fee will be due.

These types of fees are most commonly found in hedge funds. Their calculation (on a daily basis) is a complex activity and beyond the scope of this book. For further information on the calculation of performance fees, see 'The Ins and Outs of Incentive Fees'.[7]

Combination Fees

Combination fees comprise features of the first two types of fees. For example, an administrator is required to carry out a certain fixed amount of work no matter how big or small the fund. A daily NAV per share will have to be calculated, financial statements will have to be produced, etc. As a fund gets larger then more work will have to be done: a larger fund tends to have more transactions, which means more work for the administrator or accountant. As a result, administration fees tend to have a flat fee element (recognising the fixed amount of work) and a percentage fee element (recognising that as the fund gets bigger the administrator has to do more work).

The calculation of the accrual for a combination fee expense is just an application of the first two types of fees.

Example 7.3

XYZ Fund has net assets (assets less liabilities) of €125,500,000. The custodian of the fund's assets is paid a flat fee of €50,000 per annum and 0.15 per cent of net assets.

---

[7] Stocks (1994); see www.hedgefundnews.com/news_n_info/article_detail.php?id=267 for full article.

Calculate the accrual under the following circumstances:

- The NAV per share of the fund is calculated on a daily basis.
- The NAV per share of the fund is calculated on a weekly basis.

Solution 7.3

Flat fee element	€50,000
Percentage fee element: €125.5m × 0.15%	€188,250
Total fee (on annual basis)	€238,250

- When the NAV per share is calculated on a daily basis – accrual is €238,250/365 = €653
- When the NAV per share is calculated on a weekly basis – accrual is €238,250/52 = €4,582

Now try Question 7.10.1

7.5.3: Recording the Daily Accrual

As with many other aspects of investment fund accounting, calculating the amount is the difficult part; recording the amount is straightforward (and often repetitive). It is no different with investment fund expense accruals.

Once the daily (or weekly, or monthly) expense accrual amount has been calculated then the next task is to record the amount. As the expense has not been paid then a payable account is required. This account keeps track of the amount that is owed to the service providers who are awaiting payment; the account is normally called accrued expenses. As this is a liability account, because the amount is increasing, the appropriate entry is a credit.

The other side of the transaction is the relevant expense account in the statement of operations. These accounts keep track of the total expenses incurred over a period; as the fiscal year progresses this gets larger and larger until the end of the year is reached. These are expense accounts and the amounts in question are increasing; hence the correct entry is a debit to the relevant expense account (debit assets, losses and expenses with increases).

- Dr (or increase) the expense item (e.g. audit fee expense year to date (YTD)) – this is an expense in the statement of operations.
- Cr (or increase) accrued expenses (e.g. audit fee accrual) – this is a liability on the statement of net assets.

Or – for the spreadsheet approach:

- Increase expense item (audit fee expense), an expense (in the statement of operations).
- Increase accrued expenses, a liability (in the statement of net assets).

This transaction gets repeated every day (or week, or month), and the expense and the accrual accounts get larger and larger.

7.6: Accounting for the Payment of Fund Expenses

The fund will pay its expenses on a periodic basis. For example, the management fee may be paid monthly, the trustee fee paid quarterly, the audit fee paid annually, and so on. When an amount is paid it should equal (or close to equal) the amount in the accrual account (see Section 7.7 for what happens when there are under- or over-accruals).

When an expense is paid then the cash account of the fund decreases. Thus, cash, an asset, is decreasing, so the appropriate entry is a credit to the cash account.

The other side of the transaction is that the fund no longer owes the service provider so the liability account should be adjusted, i.e. the accrued expense account. Consequently, accrued expenses, a liability, is decreasing; thus, the correct entry is a debit to the accrued expense account.

Upon payment then:

- Cr (or decrease) bank/cash account in the statement of net assets.
- Dr (or decrease) accrued expenses account in the statement of net assets.

Note that there is no impact on the expense account – the expense has already been accounted for.

Or – for the spreadsheet approach:

- Decrease cash, an asset, in the statement of net assets.
- Decrease accrued expenses, a liability, in the statement of net assets.

Example 7.4

It is 29/03/X and ASD Fund has the following balances from the previous day (28/03/XX):

> In the statement of net assets:
> Bank   €130,000 (dr balance – an asset)
> Trustee fee accrual   €8,600 (cr balance – a liability)
> In the statement of operations:
> Trustee fee expense   €8,600 (dr balance – an expense)

The annual trustee fee is €36,500. On 01/04/XX the fund paid €9,000 of fees to the trustees for the first three months of the year.

Requirements:

1. Calculate the daily accrual.
2. Show the balance on the trustee fee accrual account, the trustee fee expense account and the cash account for every day from 28/03/XX to 01/04/XX inclusive.

Solution 7.4

Daily accrual: €36,500/365 = €100 per day

Table 7.1 shows extracts from ASD Fund's statement of net assets and statement of operations.

Example 7.5

This example considers how the interaction between the expense account and the accrual account operates.

You are the fund accountant for Excel Fund. This fund operates on a monthly basis (the NAV per share is only calculated once a month). You have read the prospectus and have noted that the administration fee for the fund is fixed at €120,000 per annum. The fee is payable every quarter in arrears. Thus, in early April a payment will be made to cover January, February and March, etc.

Show the balances on the administration fee expense account and the administration fee accrual account at the end of each month.

Solution 7.5

Table 7.2 shows the solution to Example 7.2.

Table 7.1:   ASD Fund: Extracts from Statement of Net Assets and Statement of Operations

	28/03/XX	Trans. 1	29/03/XX	Trans. 1	30/03/XX	Trans. 1	31/03/XX	Trans. 1	Trans. 2	01/04/XX
Assets										
Bank A/c	130,000		130,000		130,000		130,000		−9,000	121,000
Liabilities										
Trustee Fee Accrual	8,600	100	8,700	100	8,800	100	8,900	100	−9,000	0
Expenses										
Trustee Fee Expense	8,600	100	8,700	100	8,800	100	8,900	100		9,000

Table 7.2: Balances of the Admin Fee Expense Account and
Admin Fee Accrual Account for Excel Fund

Month	Admin Fee Expense A/c	Admin Fee Accrual A/c	Notes
Jan	€10,000	€10,000	
Feb	€20,000	€20,000	
Mar	€30,000	€30,000	
Apr	€40,000	€10,000	(Note 1)
May	€50,000	€20,000	
June	€60,000	€30,000	
July	€70,000	€10,000	(Note 1)
Aug	€80,000	€20,000	
Sept	€90,000	€30,000	
Oct	€100,000	€10,000	(Note 1)
Nov	€110,000	€20,000	
Dec	€120,000	€30,000	

Note 1:

Opening balance from previous month	€30,000
Additional accrual for current month	€10,000
Payment for previous quarter	(€30,000)
Closing balance for current month	€10,000

Now try Question 7.10.2.

7.7: ACCOUNTING FOR UNDER-ACCRUALS AND OVER-ACCRUALS, UNEXPECTED EXPENSES, CAPS AND WAIVERS

7.7.1: Under-Accruals and Over-Accruals

What happens if, after setting aside, say, €10,000 for audit fees, the final bill is €11,000 and the accrual account is €1,000 too low? This is an example of an under-accrual. An under-accrual is where not enough money has been set aside to meet an expense, whereas an over-accrual is where too much money has been set aside. This can be dealt with in two ways: an immediate write-off or an extended write-off.

Under-/Over-accruals – Method 1 (Write-off Immediately)

If the amount is small then write-off the excess (or shortfall) in the statement of operations in one amount – a small amount will have no real impact on the NAV per share.

In the example given, the following balances exist:

- Audit fee accrual of €10,000
- An audit fee of €11,000 was paid; record the payment. The extra amount is not significant.

This is the normal solution. In fact, this is the normal scenario. It is rare that a fund can predict to the last euro the exact amount of any of its expenses. However, any deviations tend to be small relative to the size of the fund. Hence, the amounts are written off on the day that they become apparent.

The payment of €11,000 can be recorded as follows:

- Cr cash/bank €11,000.
- Dr audit fee accrual €11,000.
  (as normal for a payment of expense)

The under-accrual can be dealt with as follows:

- Cr audit fee accrual €1,000.
- Dr audit fee expense €1,000.

This clears the extra €1,000 out of the audit fee accrual account and transfers the amount to the statement of operations. A failure to make this transaction would result in a debit balance on the audit fee accrual account, which is nonsense for a liability type account.

For the spreadsheet approach the following should be done:

- Decrease cash, an asset, by €11,000 (in the statement of net assets).
- Decrease audit fee accrual, a liability, by €11,000 (in the statement of net assets).
  (as normal for an expense payment)

- Increase audit fee accrual, a liability, by €1,000.
- Increase audit fee expense, an expense, by €1,000 (statement of operations).

Where a fee is overestimated then the opposite is done. Applying the same basic information, the following balances exist:

- Audit fee accrual of €10,000.
- An audit fee of €9,500 was paid; record the payment. The extra amount is not significant.

In this scenario the fund expected (and accrued) for the expense on the basis of €10,000, but the actual outcome was that the fund was charged just €9,500.

The payment of €9,500 can be recorded as follows:

- Cr cash/bank €9,500.
- Dr audit fee accrual €9,500.
  (as normal for a payment of expense)

- Dr audit fee accrual €500.
- Cr audit fee expense €500.

This clears the extra €500 out of the audit fee accrual account and transfers the amount to the statement of operations. The effect of this is to reduce the balance on the audit fee accrual account to zero and to reduce the audit expense by €500 to get it back to its original and correct amount. A failure to make this transaction would result in a credit balance on the audit fee accrual account when no actual amount is payable.

For the spreadsheet approach the following should be done:

- Decrease cash, an asset, by €9,500 (in the statement of net assets).

Decrease audit fee accrual, a liability, by €9,500 (in the statement of net assets) (as normal for an expense).

- Decrease audit fee accrual, a liability, by €500.
- Decrease audit fee expense, an expense, by €500 (in the statement of operations).

Concluding Remarks: In a perfect scenario the expense should be equally apportioned over the period (in this case, one year). However, often it is necessary to estimate the amount of the likely expense. Whenever estimates are involved it is not unusual that differences result between the estimated expense and the actual expense (as was the case with the audit fee above). This would indicate that the daily accrual was incorrect. A possible solution would be to revise the NAV per share of the period concerned. However, it is a recognised accounting principle that errors in estimates do not result in a revision of previously published information (IAS 8), so the approach taken above is acceptable.

Under-/Over-Accruals – Method 2 (Extended Write-off)

If the amount of the over/under–accrual is large (or big enough to impact on the NAV per share) then on very rare occasions it may be appropriate to write–off the excess to the statement of operations over a longer period. It should be stated that this is an extremely unusual occurrence and appropriate legal and regulatory advice may be required.

It is not possible to go back and change the NAV per share of previous days unless there is an extreme situation (fraud or error, for example. However, this is not an error as the amount accrued for was based on an estimate).[8]

If the under-/over-accrual was allocated to the statement of operations of just one day then the effect on the NAV per share could be disproportionate and may impact unfairly on investors.

One solution is to increase the accrual for the next period and spread the under-/over-accrual over a longer time frame. The issue then becomes the length of period over which the under-/over-accrual should be apportioned – this is a matter for judgement. In making this judgement the impact on those investors who bought into and sold out of the fund over the period and the existing investors should be considered.

Using the previous example:

The audit fee was expected to be €10,000 and the final bill was €11,000. Assume that the under-accrual of €1,000 is material to the calculation of the NAV per share (it is unlikely that €1,000 will be material to any fund but we will continue nonetheless).

For the next year the audit fee is expected to be €12,000. The fund could now accrue for €13,000, i.e. €12,000 in respect of the current period + €1,000 shortfall from the previous period. By taking this approach the fund has spread the under-accrual over the next year.

The payment of €11,000 can be recorded as follows:

- Cr cash/bank €11,000.
- Dr audit fee accrual €11,000.
  (as normal for a payment of expense)

Then for every day of the next year the fund should accrue for €13,000/365 days of audit fees. This represents a daily accrual of €36 (as opposed to €33 had €12,000 been used).

- Dr audit fee expense €36.
- Cr audit fee accrual €36.

For the spreadsheet approach the following should be done:

- Decrease cash, an asset, by €11,000 (in the statement of net assets).
- Decrease audit fee accrual, a liability, by €11,000 (in the statement of net assets).
  (as normal for an expense payment)

---

[8] For a general discussion on correction of errors and estimates see International Accounting Standards Board (2008b).

- Increase audit fee accrual, a liability, by €36.
- Increase audit fee expense, an expense, by €36 (in the statement of operations).
  (every day for the next year)

The difficulty with this approach is that the audit fee accrual will become negative. A negative liability is a difficult idea to grasp, i.e. it is an asset. How can an expense item become an asset? In essence the audit fee for the last period has not been fully accounted for in the last period – only €10,000 of it was accounted for in the last period with the remaining €1,000 to be accounted for in the next period. The €1,000 is an expense that is waiting to be accounted for – this is the opposite of an accrual, which is an expense that has been accounted for but is waiting to be paid.

Auditors often have a lot of difficulty in including as an asset items of this nature (the €1,000) as they have no real substance (unlike an investment). Thus, often a compromise solution is to write-off the €1,000 over a shorter period of time, rather than over the next year with next year's audit fee. How short should that period of time be? This depends on the size of the fund and the amount of the over/under-accrual.

Concluding Remarks and Caveat: The events described above should be rare. For most funds, the level of expenses is low, often less then 2 per cent of total net assets. Any single expense item comprises a small element of that total. Thus, an under-/ over-accrual is usually an insignificant percentage of total net assets.

However, should it arise that the under-/over-accrual is significant then, before any write-off is attempted, legal and regulatory advice should be sought. It might also be advisable to enter into a dialogue with the fund's auditors. Any solution (either an immediate write-off or an extended write-off) would have to ensure that investors were treated fairly, in material respects. This will require considerable judgement and experience and is beyond the scope of this book. The rights of all investors will need to be respected, including those who bought into the fund, those who left the fund and those who remained in the fund over the period during which the issue arose and was resolved.

7.7.2: Unexpected Expenses

Unexpected expenses should be very rare. Most of the expenses of a fund are predictable – perhaps not to the last euro but the expense item can be foreseen. Expenses such as investment advice, administration and custody are obvious expenses of any fund. The size of the fees can be determined from the fund's prospectus or other documentation.

However, there can be very few occasions where an expense is truly unexpected. For example, say the trustees of the fund sought legal advice on an issue and the fund will have to pay the legal fees.

This is a once-off, unexpected expense. It is unlikely that the item will be completely unexpected; the fund will probably have some prior notification of the item. Take the case of the cost of unexpected legal advice – from the time that the trustees first sought the advice, then got the advice, then got a bill from the legal advisors and finally paid the bill, many months could have passed. An estimate of the bill can be arrived at when the advice is first sought. This can then be spread over the expected period that the fund will get before actually paying the bill. In circumstances where the final amount differs from the expected amount, this should be treated as an under-/over-accrual (as above).

Where an expense is truly unexpected and the fund is forced to pay an amount at short notice, then consider this in the same manner as an under-/over-accrual:

- If the amount is small, write-off to the income statement immediately.
- If the amount is larger, write-off to the income statement over a number of days, so that no one day will adversely impact on the NAV per share. However, this may present some difficulties; see 'Concluding Remarks and Caveat' in Section 7.7.1.

Example 7.6

Fund XYZ suddenly paid for €15,000 worth of legal fees on 15/05/XX.

Requirements:

1. The amount of the fees is insignificant in the context of the fund. Record the unexpected expenses.
2. The amount of the fees is significant to the fund and should be spread over five days. Record the unexpected expenses.

Solution 7.6

Scenario 1:

- Dr legal expenses by €15,000 (in the statement of operations).
- Cr cash by €15,000 (in the statement of net assets).

Cash, an asset, is decreasing; hence it is a credit. Legal expenses, an expense item, is increasing; hence it is a debit.

For the spreadsheet approach the following should be done:

- Decrease cash, an asset, by €15,000 (in the statement of net assets).
- Increase legal expenses, an expense, by €15,000 (in the statement of operations).

Scenario 2:

- Dr legal fees deferred by €15,000 (in the statement of net assets).
- Cr cash by €15,000 (in the statement of net assets).

'Deferred legal fees' is an asset type account for the legal fees that are waiting to be apportioned to the statement of operations. This 'asset' has no physical substance and does not represent claims on assets (as equities or bonds, for example). As a consequence, the trustees of the fund need to be very clear on the rationale behind the existence of this asset and on its subsequent amortisation. The over-riding principle should be based on the issue of fairness to (both existing and potential) investors in the fund. Proper justification will need to be provided to the fund's auditors where the amount of the expense is material. This area is fraught with difficulty as the potential for conflict is significant; the trustees will need to show that the matter was given due consideration and a proper process was in place. It would be prudent to obtain legal and regulatory advice before embarking on a particular course of action.

- Dr legal expenses by €3,000 (in the statement of operations).
- Cr legal fees deferred by €3,000 (in the statement of net assets).

This is the amortisation of the legal fees deferred – this transaction will be done for the next five days until the €15,000 is fully allocated to the statement of operations. 'Amortisation' is just a technical accounting term; it has a similar meaning to 'accruing', only it relates to assets rather than liabilities.

For the spreadsheet approach the following should be done:

- Decrease cash, an asset, by €15,000 (in the statement of net assets).
- Increase legal fees deferred, an 'asset', by €15,000 (in the statement of net assets).
- Increase legal expenses, an expense, by €3,000 (in the statement of operations).
- Decrease legal fees deferred, an 'asset', by €3,000 (in the statement of net assets).

7.7.3: Expense Caps

An expense cap is where there is a limit on the maximum amount of an expense that can be paid to a service provider. These types of arrangements should be noted in the prospectus. They are often included to protect investors and can be used as a marketing tool.

Example 7.7

In ZXC Fund the investment managers are paid based on 0.5 per cent of net assets but this is subject to a maximum annual limit of €1,000,000 of fees as calculated on a daily basis:

- Scenario A: the fund has net assets of €180,650,000; calculate the daily accrual.
- Scenario B: the fund has net assets of €220,550,000; calculate the daily accrual.

Solution 7.7

Once the daily accrual is calculated, it is recorded in the same way as before.
   Scenario A:

- Annual fee: €180,650,000 × 0.5% = €903,250 (cap not breached)
- Daily accrual: €903,250/365 = €2,475

   Scenario B:

- Annual fee: €220,550,000 × 0.5% = €1,102,750 (cap breached)
- Limit fee to cap: €1,000,000
- Daily accrual: €1,000,000/365 = €2,740

7.7.4: Expense Waivers

An expense waiver is where a service provider (generally the investment advisor) foregoes some of their fees. This may be done in situations where the fund performs badly and the investment advisor wants to show investors that they are prepared to shoulder some of the blame and pain also.

   In situations of poor performance, there is a risk that a lot of investors may try to redeem their shares – an expense waiver is an attempt by the investment manager to try to appease investors and prevent a mass sell-out. The expense waiver may be done on a voluntary basis, after pressure from influential investors, or may (on occasion) be mandated in the prospectus.

Expense waivers (and caps) may also occur in situations where the fund promoters (normally the investment advisors) have given a guarantee as to the maximum amount of fees that a fund can incur. For example, in order to assure investors the promoters may guarantee that the total of all fees of a fund will not exceed, say, 1.5 per cent of net assets. When the fees exceed this amount then the investment advisors will bear the cost in a reduction of the amount that they will receive.

An example is provided in Figure 7.6 from the Growth Fund of America Annual Report for the year ended 31 August 2009.

Figure 7.6: Extract from the Growth Fund of America Annual Report Regarding Fee Waivers

Investment advisory services — The Investment Advisory and Service Agreement with CRMC provides for monthly fees accrued daily. These fees are based on a declining series of annual rates beginning with 0.50% on the first $1 billion of daily net assets and decreasing to 0.233% on such assets in excess of $210 billion. CRMC waived a portion of its investment advisory services fee commencing on September 1, 2004, and terminating on December 31, 2008. During the year ended August 31, 2009, total investment advisory services fees waived by CRMC were $12,213,000. As a result, the fee shown on the accompanying financial statements of $351,152,000, which was equivalent to an annualized rate of 0.278%, was reduced to $338,939,000, or 0.268% of average daily net assets.

Source: Growth Fund of America, Annual Report for the year ended 31 August 2009, p. 24, available from: www.americanfunds.com/pdf/mfgear-905_gfaa.pdf.

CRMC is Capital Research and Management Company, an investment management and advice business. The reason that CRMC gives for waiving part of its fee is because it is committed to providing quality service at modest expense to the funds' shareholders. The more cynical may point out that $351 million to manage an investment fund is not insignificant and the waiver of $12 million is only a token gesture as it represents only a small fraction of the total expense.

Expense waivers tend to be rare (for obvious reasons) and can follow a variety of formats. They can be in a lump sum format — whereby the investment manager hands back, say, half of their recent payment. Or they can be in a periodic format — the investment manager agrees to cut the daily fee for a period of time by a certain percentage, for example, by half. This will impact on how they are accounted for.

The general approach to accounting for expense waivers is to record the full expense as normal. Then record the waived amount as an income. Investment managers tend to prefer this type of recording so that investors can see the amount of fees that are being waived.

Example 7.8

POL Fund has total net assets of €20,000,000. The investment advisors have an agreement for a fee of 0.6 per cent of net assets as calculated on a daily basis. However, the fund has been performing poorly recently and the investment advisors have agreed to waive three-quarters of their fee for the next quarter, when the situation will be reviewed again.

Record the above situation.

Solution 7.8

Calculate the daily accrual:

- Annual fee: €20,000,000 × 0.6% = €120,000
- Daily accrual: €120,000/365 = €329
- Fee waived: €329 × 75% = €247

Record the daily accrual:

- Dr investment management expense by €329.
- Cr investment management accrual by €329.

Record the expense waived:

- Dr investment management accrual by €247.
- Cr investment management expense waived by €247.

In the statement of operations, the investment management expense account and the investment management expense waived account are netted against one another.

For the spreadsheet approach the following should be done:

- Increase investment management expense, an expense, by €329 (in the statement of operations).
- Increase investment management accrual, a liability, by €329 (in the statement of net assets).
- Decrease investment management accrual, a liability, by €247 (in the statement of net assets).
- Increase investment management expense waived, a 'negative' expense, by €247 (in the statement of operations).

Figure 7.7 shows the statement of operations of the Growth Fund of America. Notice how the investment advice fee waiver is treated as a negative expense. It is presented in this format so that investors can be made aware of the 'sacrifices' made by the investment manager.

Figure 7.7: Statement of Operations of the Growth Fund of America Showing Fee Waiver

Statement of operations		
for the year ended August 31, 2009		(dollars in thousands)
Investment income:		
Income:		
Dividend (net of non-U.S. taxes of $46,598; also includes $236,776 from affiliates)	$ 1,972,045	
Interest (also includes $215 from affiliates)	236,711	$ 2,208,756
Fees and expenses:		
Investment advisory services	351,152	
Distribution services	398,313	
Transfer agent services	118,644	
Administrative services	104,709	
Reports to shareholders	14,434	
Registration statement and prospectus	18,295	
Directors' compensation	185	
Auditing and legal	119	
Custodian	3,720	
State and local taxes	1	
Other	7,486	
Total fees and expenses before waiver	1,017,058	
Less investment advisory services waiver	12,213	
Total fees and expenses after waiver		1,004,845
Net investment income		1,203,911

Source: Growth Fund of America Annual Report for the year ended 31 August 2009, p. 20, available from: www.americanfunds.com/pdf/mfgear-905_gfaa.pdf.

7.8: SUMMARY

Key points:

- While expenses are paid periodically, they are accounted for on a daily basis.
- There are three types of expenses:
  o flat fees
  o percentage fees
  o combination fees
- This has an impact on how the fees are calculated and the subsequent daily accrual.

- The accounting treatment of performance fees has not been addressed.
- To account for the daily accrual:
  - o dr the expense item (in the statement of operations)
  - o cr accrued expenses (in the statement of net assets)
- Or – for the spreadsheet approach:
  - o increase expense item, an expense (in the statement of operations)
  - o increase accrued expenses, a liability (in the statement of net assets)
- To account for the payment of expenses:
  - o cr bank/cash account (in the statement of net assets)
  - o dr accrued expenses account (in the statement of net assets)
- Or – for the spreadsheet approach:
  - o decrease cash, an asset (in the statement of net assets)
  - o decrease accrued expenses, a liability (in the statement of net assets)

7.9: Bringing It All Together

Taking into account the previous chapters, it should now be possible to calculate the daily NAV per share of a proper equity fund. This will involve:

- Subscriptions and redemptions of fund shares
- The purchase and sale of equities
- The incurring and payment of expenses
- The preparation of the fund financial statements and the calculation of the NAV per share

Break each transaction into its components and record it on the spreadsheet in Table 7.3a. Accumulate the transactions and draw up the financial statements. Finally, calculate the NAV per share.

7.9.1: Comprehensive Question

Table 7.3a provides the statements for the fund in this comprehensive question, while Table 7.3b lists the holdings of the fund.

You have identified the following fund expenses:

Management Fee

A flat fee of €200,000 per annum plus a percentage of net assets as follows:

- 0.15% p.a. of the first €5,000,000 on a daily basis using the prior day's net assets
- 0.20% p.a. of €5,000,000 to €10,000,000 on a daily basis using the prior day's net assets
- 0.25% p.a. over €10,000,000 on a daily basis using the prior day's net assets

Table 7.3a: Comprehensive Question

Statement of Net Assets

	04/04/X8	Trans. 1	Trans. 2	Trans. 3	05/04/X8	Trans. 1	Trans. 2	Trans. 3	Trans. 4	Trans. 5	Trans. 6	Trans. 7	06/04/X8	Trans. 1	Trans. 2	Trans. 3	Trans. 4	Trans. 5	07/04/X8
Assets																			
Investments at Cost	€25,946,500																		
Unrealised Appreciation/ Depreciation	(€110,250)																		
Investments Sold Receivable	€450,000																		
Fund Shares Sold Receivable	€120,000																		
Cash	€1,400,000																		
Dividends Receivable	€25,000																		
Total Assets	*€27,831,250*																		
Liabilities																			
Investments Purchased Payable	€0																		
Accrued Expenses	€15,000																		
Fund Shares Redeemed Payable	€0																		
Distributions Payable	€0																		
Total Liabilities	*€15,000*																		

(Continued)

Table 7.3a: *(Continued)*

	04/04/X8	Trans. 1	Trans. 2	Trans. 3	05/04/X8	Trans. 1	Trans. 2	Trans. 3	Trans. 4	Trans. 5	06/04/X8	Trans. 1	Trans. 2	Trans. 3	Trans. 4	Trans. 5	Trans. 6	Trans. 7	07/04/X8
Total Net Assets	€27,816,250																		
Investors' Equity	€27,816,250																		
Outstanding Shares	1,000,000																		
NAV per Share	€27.816																		

Statement of Operations for the Period from 01/01/X8 to YY/04/X8

	04/04/X8	Trans. 1	Trans. 2	Trans. 3	05/04/X8	Trans. 1	Trans. 2	Trans. 3	Trans. 4	Trans. 5	06/04/X8	Trans. 1	Trans. 2	Trans. 3	Trans. 4	Trans. 5	Trans. 6	Trans. 7	07/04/X8
Gains/Losses on Investments	€414,186																		
Dividend Income	€2,500																		
Interest Income	€0																		
Total Investment Income	*€416,686*																		
Administration Fee YTD	€16,740																		
Investment Management Fee YTD	€65,671																		
Other Fees YTD	€4,700																		
Auditing Fee YTD	€2,060																		
Total Expenses	*€89,171*																		
Increase/ Decrease in Net Assets from Operations	€327,515																		

(Continued)

Table 7.3a: *(Continued)*

Statement of Changes in Net Assets for the Period from 01/01/X8 to YY/04/X8

	04/04/X8	Trans. 1	Trans. 2	Trans. 3 05/04/X8	Trans. 1	Trans. 2	Trans. 3	Trans. 4	Trans. 5	Trans. 6	Trans. 7 06/04/X8	Trans. 1	Trans. 2	Trans. 3	Trans. 4	Trans. 5	Trans. 07/04/X8
Equity on 01/01/X8	€26,391,542																
Distributions to Investors	(€60,500)																
Capital Transactions																	
Proceeds from the sale of shares	€1,556,221																
Redemption of fund shares	(€398,528)																
Dividend reinvestment	€0																
Total	*€1,157,693*																
Increase/Decrease in Net Assets from Operations	€327,515																
Equity at End	**€27,816,250**																

Table 7.3b: Holdings of the Fund

Security	Date Purchased	Cost Price	Quantity	Commission	04/04/X8 Market Price
Grafton Group	01/01/X1	€8.25	200,000	€2,500	€9.25
Grafton Group	01/01/X2	€8.45	150,000	€3,000	€9.25
Grafton Group	01/01/X3	€8.95	400,000	€3,500	€9.25
Accor	01/01/X1	€55.50	15,000	€2,500	€62.25
Accor	01/01/X2	€57.25	20,000	€3,750	€62.25
Accor	01/01/X3	€59.95	25,000	€4,250	€62.25
Carrefour	01/01/X1	€48.75	80,000	€4,500	€46.00
Carrefour	01/01/X2	€49.65	125,000	€5,500	€46.00
EDF	01/01/X3	€51.25	50,000	€3,000	€53.25
EDF	01/01/X4	€52.45	25,000	€1,000	€53.25
EADS	01/01/X3	€26.25	50,000	€1,600	€23.20
EADS	01/01/X4	€25.75	25,000	€1,400	€23.20

Administration Fees

0.25% p.a. of net assets subject to an annual cap of €100,000 as applied on a daily basis using the prior day's net assets.

Audit Fees

The annual audit is to cost €8,000.

Other Fees and Expenses

All other fees and expenses will amount to €18,250.

For the above expenses assume a 365-day year.
The following transactions occurred on 05/04/X8:

1. The fund purchases 20,000 shares in EADS for €23.00 per share and commission of €3,000, to settle on TD + 3.
2. Record the daily expense accrual.
3. Calculate the daily unrealised appreciation/depreciation and NAV per share.

Current share prices on 05/04/X8:
- Grafton   €9.35
- Accor   €63.00
- Carrefour   €47.50
- EDF   €54.00
- EADS   €22.50

The following transactions occurred on 06/04/X8:

1. The fund sells 25,000 shares in Accor for €63.50 per share and commission of €5,500, to settle on TD + 3.
2. The fund purchases 15,000 shares in LVMH for €86.50 per share and commission of €5,800, to settle on TD + 2.
3. A new shareholder buys 20,000 shares in the fund at yesterday's NAV per share, to settle on TD + 3.
4. The fund settles the investments sold receivable and dividends receivable accounts that were outstanding on 04/04/X8 as of today.
5. The fund declares a distribution to shareholders of €0.50 per share payable on TD + 5 (assume new shareholder will also receive this distribution).
6. Record the daily expense accrual.
7. Calculate the daily unrealised appreciation/depreciation and NAV per share.

Current share prices on 06/04/X8:
- Grafton   €9.35
- Accor   €63.75
- Carrefour   €48.00
- EDF   €54.50
- EADS   €22.75
- LVMH   €87.25

The following transactions occurred on 07/04/X8:

1. Grafton goes ex-div. The amount of the dividend is €0.25 per share, to be paid on 20/04/X8.
2. An existing shareholder wishes to redeem 12,000 shares at yesterday's NAV per share to settle on TD + 3.
3. The fund sells 15,000 shares in Accor for €64.00 per share and commission of €4,500, to settle on TD + 3.
4. Record the daily expense accrual.
5. Calculate the daily unrealised appreciation/depreciation and NAV per share.

Current share prices on 07/04/X8:
- Grafton   €9.45
- Accor   €64.25
- Carrefour   €48.75
- EDF   €54.50
- EADS   €23.00
- LVMH   €87.75

Requirements:

Part A: record the transactions from 05/04/X8 and calculate the daily NAV per share (use the template provided; complete the statement of net assets, statement of operations and the statement of changes in net assets).

Part B: record the transactions from 06/04/X8 and calculate the daily NAV per share (use the template provided; complete the statement of net assets, statement of operations and the statement of changes in net assets).

Part C: record the transactions from 07/04/X8 and calculate the daily NAV per share (use the template provided; complete the statement of net assets, statement of operations and the statement of changes in net assets).

7.9.2: Comprehensive Question – Solution

Part A: Transactions from 05/04/X8

Transaction 1:

1. Calculate cost of EADS share purchase: $20,000 \times €23 + €3,000 = €463,000$

2. Record transaction:

- Increase (dr) investments at cost by €463,000.
- Increase (cr) investments purchased payable by €463,000.

Adjust portfolio – increase the EADS holding by 20,000 shares.

Transaction 2

1. Calculate the fund's expenses for the day – see Table 7.3c.

2. Record the expenses:

- Increase (dr) investment management expense YTD by €718.
- Increase (dr) administration fee YTD by €191.
- Increase (dr) audit fee YTD by €22.
- Increase (dr) other fees YTD by €50.
- Increase (cr) accrued expenses by €981.

Transaction 3 – Daily Unrealised Appreciation/Depreciation

1. Calculate the daily gain/loss in value of the fund's portfolio – see Table 7.3d.

2. Record transaction:

- Increase (dr) unrealised appreciation/deprecation by €418,250.
- Increase (cr) investment gain/loss by €418,250.

Table 7.3c: The Fund's Expenses for 05/04/X8

Fees	Date
Management Fee	**05/04/X8**
First €200,000 flat	€200,000
0.15% of the first €5 million	€7,500
0.2% of the next €5 million	€10,000
The balance, €17,816,250, at 0.25%	€44,541
Total	*€262,041*
Daily Fee (divided by 365 days)	*€718*
Administration Fee	**05/04/X8**
€27,816,250 at 0.25%	€69,541
Daily Fee (divided by 365 days)	*€191*
Audit Fee	**05/04/X8**
Flat fee, €8,000, divided by 365 days	*€22*
Other Fees	**05/04/X8**
Flat fee, €18,250, divided by 365 days	*€50*
Total Daily Expenses	**05/04/X8**
Management Fees	€718
Administration Fee	€191
Audit Fee	€22
Other Fees	€50
Total	*€981*

Table 7.3d: The Daily Gain/Loss in Value of the Fund's Portfolio – 05/04/X8

Step 1: Calculate Market Value of Portfolio

Shares	Quantity	Price	Total	Notes
Grafton	750,000	€9.35	€7,012,500	
Accor	60,000	€63.00	€3,780,000	
Carrefour	205,000	€47.50	€9,737,500	
EDF	75,000	€54.00	€4,050,000	
EADS	95,000	€22.50	€2,137,500	20,000 shares purchased today
	Total		*€26,717,500*	

Step 2: Calculate Total Cost of Portfolio

Investments at Cost from Yesterday (A)	€25,946,500	
+ Purchases during 05/04/X8	€463,000	
− Sales during 05/04/X8	€0	€26,409,500

Step 3: Total Gain on Portfolio	€308,000

(Continued)

Table 7.3d: *(Continued)*

Step 4: Daily Gain/Loss on Portfolio

Gains/Loss from Yesterday		−€110,250
Gains/Losses on Sales	€0	−€110,250
Daily Gain/Loss (Step 3 – Step 4)		**€418,250**[9]

At this point all of the individual transactions have been recorded – the final totals for 05/04/X8 should now be calculated and the daily NAV per share determined (€28.234 per share).

Part B: Transactions from 06/04/X8

Transaction 1

1a. Calculate proceeds of sale of Accor shares: $25,000 \times €63.50 − €5,500 = €1,582,000$

1b. Calculate cost of shares sold (use FIFO):

All of batch 1 sold (15,000 shares)
10,000 out of 20,000 of batch 2 sold
Batch 1: $15,000 \times €55.50 + €2,500 =$ €835,000
Batch 2: $20,000 \times €57.25 + €3,750 = €1,148,750$
   10,000 out of 20,000 sold (50%): $€1,148,750 \times 50\% =$ €574,375
Total cost =   €1,409,375

1c. Calculate the gains sold/realised:

Proceeds (1a)	€1,582,000
Cost (1b)	€1,409,375
Gain Realised	€172,625

2. Record transaction:

- Increase (dr) investments sold receivable by €1,582,000.
- Reduce (cr) investments at cost by €1,409,375.
- Reduce (cr) unrealised appreciation/depreciation by €172,625.

Adjust portfolio – reduce Accor holding by 25,000 shares.

Transaction 2

1. Calculate cost of LVMH share purchase: $15,000 \times €86.50 + €5,800 = €1,303,300$

---

[9] The total of Step 3 is €308,000; the total of Step 4 is −€110,250. Thus, Step 3 − Step 4 is €308,000 − (−€110,250). This is a double minus which gives a positive. Hence, the total gain for the day of €418,250. Perhaps a more logical approach would be that during the day a loss of €110,250 was turned into a gain of €308,000. This represents a total movement (through the zero point) of €418,250.

2. Record transaction:

- Increase (dr) investments at cost by €1,303,300.
- Increase (cr) investments purchased payable by €1,303,300.

Adjust portfolio – increase LMVH holding by 15,000 shares.

Transaction 3

1. Calculate proceeds from the sale of shares in the fund: $20,000 \times €28.234 = €564,680$

2. Record transaction:

- Increase (dr) fund shares sold receivable by €564,680.
- Increase (cr) proceeds from fund shares sold by €564,680 (in the statement of changes in net assets).

Increase number of shares outstanding by 20,000.

Transaction 4

1. Calculate the amount of cash to be settled today:

- Investments sold receivable €450,000.
- Dividends receivable €25,000.
- Total cash received €475,000.

The investments sold receivable and dividends receivable figures are taken from the statement of net assets on 04/04/X8.

2. Record transaction:

- Reduce (cr) investments sold receivable by €450,000.
- Reduce (cr) dividends receivable by €25,000.
- Increase (dr) cash by €475,000.

Transaction 5

1. Calculate total distribution to be given to shareholders:

- Total shares outstanding: 1,020,000 (20,000 new shares today)
- Distribution rate: €0.50 per share
- Total distribution: €510,000

2. Record transaction:

- Increase (dr) distributions to shareholders by €510,000 (in the statement of changes in net assets).
- Increase (cr) distributions payable by €510,000.

Transaction 6

1. Calculate the fund's expenses for the day – see Table 7.3e.

Table 7.3e: The Fund's Expenses for 06/04/X8

Fees	Date
Management Fee	**06/04/X8**
First €200,000 flat	€200,000
0.15% of the first €5 million	€7,500
0.2% of next €5 million	€10,000
The balance, €18,233,519, at 0.25%	€45,584
Total	*€263,084*
Daily Fee (divided by 365 days)	*€721*
Administration Fee	**06/04/X8**
€28,233,519 at 0.25%	€70,584
Daily Fee (divided by 365 days)	*€193*
Audit Fee	**06/04/X8**
Flat fee, €8,000, divided by 365 days	*€22*
Other Fees	**06/04/X8**
Flat fee, €18,250, divided by 365 days	*€50*
Total Daily Expenses	**06/04/X8**
Management Fees	€721
Administration Fee	€193
Audit Fee	€22
Other Fees	€50
Total	*€986*

2. Record expenses:

- Increase (dr) investment management expense YTD by €721.
- Increase (dr) administration fee YTD by €193.
- Increase (dr) audit fee YTD by €22.
- Increase (dr) other fees YTD by €50.
- Increase (cr) accrued expenses by €986.

Transaction 7 – Daily Unrealised Appreciation/Depreciation

1. Calculate the daily gain/loss in value of the fund – see Table 7.3f.

2. Record transaction:

- Increase (dr) unrealised appreciation/depreciation by €202,450.
- Increase (cr) investment gain/loss by €202,450.

Table 7.3f: The Daily Gain/Loss in Value of the Fund's Portfolio – 06/04/X8

Step 1: Calculate Market Value of Portfolio

Shares	Quantity	Price	Total	Notes
Grafton	750,000	€9.35	€7,012,500	
Accor	35,000	€63.75	€2,231,250	25,000 shares sold today
Carrefour	205,000	€48.00	€9,840,000	
EDF	75,000	€54.50	€4,087,500	
EADS	95,000	€22.75	€2,161,250	
LVMH	15,000	€87.25	€1,308,750	15,000 shares bought today
	Total		*€26,641,250*	

Step 2: Calculate Total Cost of Portfolio

Investments at Cost from Yesterday	€26,409,500	
Plus Purchases during 06/04/X8 – LMVH	€1,303,300	
Less Sales during 06/04/X8 – Accor	−€1,409,375	€26,303,425

Step 3: Total Gain on Portfolio €337,825

Step 4: Daily Gain/Loss on Portfolio

Gains/Loss from Yesterday	€308,000	
Gains/Losses on Sales (Accor)	−€172,625	€135,375
Daily Gain/Loss		**€202,450**

At this point all of the individual transactions have been recorded; the final totals for 06/04/X8 should now be calculated and the daily NAV per share determined (€27.931 per share).

Part C: Transactions from 07/04/X8

Transaction 1

1. Calculate amount to be received from the Grafton dividend:

- Number of shares in Grafton: 750,000
- Dividend rate (per share): €0.25
- Total dividend: €187,500

2. Record transaction:

- Increase (dr) dividends receivable by €187,500.
- Increase (cr) dividend income by €187,500 (in the statement of operations).

Transaction 2

1. Calculate amount to be paid to shareholder redeeming shares: $12,000 \times €27.931 =$
   €335,172

2. Record transaction:

   - Increase (cr) fund shares redeemed payable by €335,172.
   - Increase (dr) redemption of fund shares by €335,172.

   Reduce number of shares outstanding by 12,000.

Transaction 3

1. Calculate proceeds and costs for sale of shares in Accor: $15,000 \times €64 - €4,500 =$
   €955,500
   Calculate cost of shares sold (use FIFO):
   > All of batch 1 already sold (previous transaction on 06/04/X8)
   > Remainder of batch 2 sold (10,000 shares left following previous transaction
   > out of 20,000 original shares)
   > 5,000 shares out of batch 3 sold (5,000 out of 25,000)
   > Costs:

   - Batch 2: $20,000 \times €57.25 + €3,750 = €1,148,750$
     - 10,000 out of 20,000 sold (50%) = €574,375
   - Batch 3: $25,000 \times €59.95 + €4,250 = €1,503,000$
     - 5,000 out of 25,000 sold (20%) = €300,600
   - Total cost: $€574,375 + €300,600 =$ €874,975

   Calculate the gains sold/realised:

Proceeds (1)	€955,500
Cost (2)	€874,975
Gain sold	€80,525

2. Record transaction:

   - Increase (dr) investments sold receivable by €955,500.
   - Reduce (cr) investments at cost by €874,975.
   - Reduce (cr) unrealised appreciation/depreciation by €80,525.

   Adjust portfolio – reduce Accor shares by 15,000.

Transaction 4

1. Calculate the fund's expenses for the day – see Table 7.3g.

Table 7.3g: The Fund's Expenses for 07/04/X8

Fees	Date
Management Fee	**07/04/X8**
First €200,000 flat	€200,000
0.15% of the first €5 million	€7,500
0.2% of the next €5 million	€10,000
The balance, €18,489,663, at 0.25%	€46,224
Total	*€263,724*
Daily Fee (divided by 365 days)	*€723*
Administration Fee	**07/04/X8**
€28,489,663 at 0.25%	€71,224
Daily Fee (divided by 365)	*€195*
Audit Fee	**07/04/X8**
Flat fee, €8,000, divided by 365 days	*€22*
Other Fees	**07/04/X8**
Flat fee, €18,250, divided by 365 days	*€50*
Total Daily Expenses	**07/04/X8**
Management Fees	€723
Administration Fee	€195
Audit Fee	€22
Other Fees	€50
Total	*€990*

2. Record expenses:

- Increase (dr) investment management expense YTD by €723.
- Increase (dr) administration fee YTD by €195.
- Increase (dr) audit fee YTD by €22.
- Increase (dr) other fees YTD by €50.
- Increase (cr) accrued expenses by €990.

<u>Transaction 5 – Daily Valuation</u>

1. Calculate the daily gain/loss in the value of the fund – see Table 7.3h.

2. Record transaction:

- Increase (dr) unrealised appreciation/depreciation by €269,250.
- Increase (cr) investment gain/loss by €269,250.

At this point all of the individual transactions have been recorded; the final totals for 07/04/X8 should now be calculated and the daily NAV per share determined (€28.383 per share).

Table 7.3h: The Daily Gain/Loss in Value of the Fund's Portfolio – 07/04/X8

Step 1: Calculate Market Value of Portfolio

Shares	Quantity	Price	Total	Notes
Grafton	750,000	€9.45	€7,087,500	
Accor	20,000	€64.25	€1,285,000	15,000 shares sold today
Carrefour	205,000	€48.75	€9,993,750	
EDF	75,000	€54.50	€4,087,500	
EADS	95,000	€23.00	€2,185,000	
LVMH	15,000	€87.75	€1,316,250	
	Total		€25,955,000	

Step 2: Calculate Total Cost of Portfolio

Investments at Cost from Yesterday	€26,303,425	
+ Purchases during 07/04/X8 – none	€0	
– Sales during 07/04/X8 – Accor	–€874,975	€25,428,450

Step 3: Total Gain on Portfolio €526,550

Step 4: Daily Gain/Loss on Portfolio

Gains/Losses from Yesterday	€337,825	
Gains/Losses on Sales (Accor)	–€80,525	€257,300

Daily Gain/Loss €269,250

7.9.3: Comprehensive Solution

Table 7.3i provides the solution to the comprehensive question.

7.10: ADDITIONAL QUESTIONS

Question 7.10.1: Fund Expenses

You are the fund accountant for The Progressive Fund. You have obtained the following information from the fund's prospectus and other relevant agreements:

- Audit fee – agreed with auditor to be €50,000
- Investment management fee:
  - on the first €10,000,000 – 0.50% of net assets (band 1)
  - on the next €25,000,000 – 0.40% of net assets (band 2)
  - on the balance – 0.25% of net assets (band 3)
  - subject to a maximum annual expense of €250,000

Table 7.3i: Solution to Comprehensive Question

Statement of Net Assets

	04/04/X8	Trans. 1	Trans. 2	Value 05/04/X8	Trans. 1	Trans. 2	Trans. 3	Trans. 4	Trans. 5	Trans. 6	Value 06/04/X8	Trans. 1	Trans. 2	Trans. 3	Trans. 4	Value 07/04/X8
Assets																
Investments at Cost	25,946,500	463,000		26,409,500	−1,409,375	1,303,300					26,303,425			−874,975		25,428,450
Unrealised Appreciation/Depreciation	−110,250		418,250	308,000	−172,625					202,450	337,825			−80,525	269,250	526,550
Investments Sold Unsettled	450,000			450,000	1,582,000			−450,000			1,582,000			955,500		2,537,500
Fund Shares Sold Receivable	120,000			120,000			564,680				684,680					684,680
Cash	1,400,000			1,400,000				475,000			1,875,000					1,875,000
Dividends Receivable	25,000			25,000				−25,000			0	187,500				187,500
Total Assets	*27,831,250*			*28,712,500*							*30,782,930*					*31,239,680*
Liabilities																
Investments Purchased Payable	0	463,000		463,000		1,303,300					1,766,300					1,766,300
Accrued Expenses Payable	15,000		981	15,981						986	16,967				990	17,957
Fund Shares Redeemed Payable	0			0							0		335,172			335,172
Distributions Payable	0								510,000		510,000					510,000
Total Liabilities	*15,000*			*478,981*							*2,293,267*					*2,629,429*
Total Net Assets	**27,816,250**			**28,233,519**							**28,489,663**					**28,610,251**

(Continued)

Table 7.3i: (Continued)

Statement of Net Assets

	04/04/X8	Trans. 1	Trans. 2	Value	05/04/X8	Trans. 1	Trans. 2	Trans. 3	Trans. 4	Trans. 5	Trans. 6	Value	06/04/X8	Trans. 1	Trans. 2	Trans. 3	Trans. 4	Value	07/04/X8
Shareholders' Equity	**27,816,250**				**28,233,519**								**28,489,663**						**28,610,251**
Outstanding Shares	1,000,000				1,000,000			20,000					1,020,000		−12,000				1,008,000
NAV per Share	27.816				28.234								27.931						28.383

Statement of Operations for Period from 01/01/X8 to YY/04/X8

	04/04/X8	Trans. 1	Trans. 2	Value	05/04/X8	Trans. 1	Trans. 2	Trans. 3	Trans. 4	Trans. 5	Trans. 6	Value	06/04/X8	Trans. 1	Trans. 2	Trans. 3	Trans. 4	Value	07/04/X8
Investment Gain/Loss	414,186			418,250	832,436							202,450	1,034,886					269,250	1,304,136
Dividend Income	2,500				2,500								2,500					187,500	190,000
Total Investment Income/Loss	*416,686*				*834,936*								*1,037,386*						*1,494,136*
Administration Fee YTD	16,740			191	16,931							193	17,124					195	17,319
Management Fee YTD	65,671			718	66,389							721	67,110					723	67,833
Other Fees YTD	4,700			50	4,750							50	4,800					50	4,850
Auditing Fee YTD	2,060			22	2,082							22	2,104					22	2,126
Total Fund Expenses	*89,171*				*90,152*								*91,138*						*92,128*
Increase/ Decrease in Net Assets	**327,515**				**744,784**								**946,248**						**1,402,008**

(Continued)

Table 7.3i: *(Continued)*

Statement of Changes in Net Assets for Period from 01/01/X8 to YY/04/X8

	04/04/X8	Trans. 1	Trans. 2	Value 05/04/X8	Trans. 1	Trans. 2	Trans. 3	Trans. 4	Trans. 5	Trans. 6	Value 06/04/X8	Trans. 1	Trans. 2	Trans. 3	Trans. 4	Value 07/04/X8
Shareholders' Equity at 01/01/X8	26,391,514			26,391,514							26,391,514					26,391,514
Distributions to Investors	60,500			60,500					510,000		570,500					570,500
Capital Transactions																
Proceeds from the sale of shares	1,556,221			1,556,221			564,680				2,120,901					2,120,901
Redemption of units	398,500			398,500							398,500		335,172			733,672
Dividend reinvestment	–			–							–					–
Total	*1,157,721*			*1,157,721*							*1,722,401*					*1,387,229*
Increase/Decrease in Net Assets from Operations	327,515			744,784							946,248					1,402,008
Shareholders' Equity	**27,816,250**			**28,233,519**							**28,489,663**					**28,610,251**

- Custodian fees:
  - flat fee of €100,000 per annum
  - plus 0.25% of net assets
- Administration fees:
  - flat fee of €150,000 per annum

The NAV per share for 23/05/08 was €37,500,000 – calculate the daily accrual for each of the above expenses for 24/05/08.

The NAV per share for 24/05/08 was €37,900,000 – calculate the daily accrual for each of the above expenses for 25/05/08.

Note that fees are calculated based on the closing NAV per share of the previous day.

Question 7.10.2: Fund Expenses

You are the fund accountant for the Big Mutual Fund. Table 7.4 provides the balances of the fund on 20/10/X8.

Table 7.4: Fund Account Balances for the Big Mutual Fund on 20/10/X8

Account	Balance
Audit Fee Expense	€30,560
Management Fee Expense	€34,200
Custodian Fee Expense	€188,904
Administration Fee Expense	€45,460
Audit Fee Accrual	€20,400
Management Fee Accrual	€12,900
Custodian Fee Accrual	€43,400
Administration Fee Accrual	€10,800

You have obtained (from the prospectus and other information) the following fee structure:

- Audit fee – agreed with auditor to be €40,000
- Investment management fee:
  - on the first €5,000,000 – 0.75% of net assets (band 1)
  - on the next €5,000,000 – 0.45% of net assets (band 2)
  - on the balance – 0.35% of net assets (band 3)
  - subject to a maximum annual expense of €200,000
- Custodian fees:
  - flat fee of €200,000 per annum
  - plus 0.15% of net assets

- Administration fees:
  - flat fee of €100,000 per annum

Requirements:

Part A: on 19/10/X8 the total net assets of the fund were €9,800,750. During 20/10/X8 the fund made a payment of €9,000 to the administrator and €42,000 to the custodian. Show the balance on the expense and accrual accounts in Table 7.4 at the end of 20/10/X8.

Part B: on 20/10/X8 the total net assets of the fund were €9,950,750. During 21/10/X8 the fund made a payment of €11,000 to the investment manager. Show the balance on the expense and accrual accounts in Table 7.4 at the end of 21/10/X8.

Question 7.10.3: Comprehensive Question

Table 7.5a provides the statements for the Mega Fund, while Table 7.5b lists the holdings of the fund.

You have identified the following fund expenses:

Management Fee

A flat fee of €250,000 per annum plus a percentage of net assets as follows:

- 0.15% p.a. of the first €5,000,000 on a daily basis using the prior day's net assets
- 0.75% p.a. of €5,000,000 to €10,000,000 on a daily basis using the prior day's net assets
- 0.40% p.a. over €10,000,000 on a daily basis using the prior day's net assets

Admin Fees

0.25% p.a. of net assets subject to an annual cap of €50,000, as applied on a daily basis using the prior day's net assets.

Audit Fees

The annual audit is to cost €25,000.

Other Fees and Expenses

All other fees and expenses will amount to €1,460,000.

For the above expenses assume a 365-day year.

Table 7.5a: Comprehensive Question – Statements of the Mega Fund

Statement of Net Assets

	04/04/X9	Trans. 1	Trans. 2	Trans. 3	Trans. 4	Trans. 5	Trans. 6	Trans. 7	Value 05/04/X9	Trans. 1	Trans. 2	Trans. 3	Trans. 4	Trans. 5	Trans. 6	Value 06/04/X9
Assets																
Investments at Cost	€18,229,500															
Unrealised Appreciation/ Depreciation	−€40,350															
Investments Sold Receivable	€2,450,100															
Fund Shares Sold Receivable	€1,200,000															
Cash	€1,815,200															
Dividends Receivable	€45,000															
Total Assets	*€23,699,450*															
Liabilities																
Investments Purchased Payable	€1,400,000															
Accrued Expenses	€108,450															
Fund Shares Redeemed Payable	€600,690															
Distributions Payable	€0															
Total Liabilities	*2,109,140*															
Total Net Assets	**€21,590,310**															
Investors' Equity	**€21,590,310**															
Outstanding Shares	1,050,600															
NAV per Share	**€20.550**															

(Continued)

Table 7.5a: (Continued)

Statement of Operations for the Period from 01/01/X9 to Y/04/X9

	04/04/X9	Trans. 1	Trans. 2	Trans. 3	Trans. 4	Trans. 5	Trans. 6	Trans. 7	Value 05/04/X9	Trans. 1	Trans. 2	Trans. 3	Trans. 4	Trans. 5	Trans. 6	Value 06/04/X9
Gains/Losses on Investments	€250,800															
Dividend Income	€465,120															
Interest Income	€45,690															
Total Investment Income	€761,610															
Administration Fee YTD	€40,200															
Investment Management Fee YTD	€254,870															
Other Fees YTD	€12,500															
Auditing Fee YTD	€8,900															
Total Expenses	€316,470															
Increase/ Decrease in Net Assets from Operations	€445,140															

(Continued)

Table 7.5a *(Continued)*

Statement of Changes in Net Assets for the Period from 01/01/X9 to YY/04/X9

	04/04/X9	Trans. 1	Trans. 2	Trans. 3	Trans. 4	Trans. 5	Trans. 6	Trans. 7	Value 05/04/X9	Trans. 1	Trans. 2	Trans. 3	Trans. 4	Trans. 5	Trans. 6	Value 06/04/XX
Equity on 01/01/X9	€19,071,000															
Distributions to Investors	(€256,400)															
Capital Transactions																
Proceeds from the sale of shares	€4,800,970															
Redemption of fund shares	(€2,568,900)															
Dividend reinvestment	€98,500															
Total	€2,330,570															
Increase/ Decrease in Net Assets from Operations	€445,140															
Equity at End	**€21,590,310**															

Table 7.5b: Holdings of the Mega Fund

Security	Date Purchased	Cost Price	Quantity	Commission	04/04/X9 Market Price
Adidas	10/08/X6	€29.50	34,000	€1,400	€32.10
Adidas	10/09/X7	€31.45	45,000	€1,000	€32.10
Adidas	27/02/X8	€32.95	60,000	€1,200	€32.10
BASF	18/04/X7	€38.25	95,000	€2,200	€39.50
BASF	30/02/X8	€38.45	15,000	€1,500	€39.50
Deutsche Post	23/10/X7	€12.50	90,000	€4,000	€13.25
Henkel	28/01/X7	€28.20	85,000	€2,800	€28.10
MAN	05/09/X7	€51.00	84,000	€1,800	€48.75
MAN	09/02/X7	€51.45	35,000	€1,100	€48.75

The following transactions occurred on 05/04/X9:

1. The investments sold receivable and the fund shares redeemed payable accounts were settled today.
2. Deutsche Post went ex-div today – a dividend of €0.50 per share is due to be paid on 28/04/X9.
3. An existing shareholder wishes to redeem 10,000 shares at yesterday's NAV per share to settle on TD + 3.
4. 40,000 shares in MAN were purchased at €49.75 per share and commission of €2,000 to settle on TD + 3.
5. 100,000 shares in Adidas were sold at €32.75 per share and commission of €3,200 to settle on TD + 3. The fund uses the FIFO method of share identification.
6. BASF announce a share split with an ex-date of today. The split is a 3 for 1 (3 new shares to replace 1 existing share).

The daily expense accrual should be provided for.
Current share prices on 05/04/X9:

- Adidas   €32.50
- BASF   €13.60
- Deutsche Post   €13.50
- Henkel   €29.95
- MAN   €49.50

The following transactions occurred on 06/04/X9:

1. A new shareholder wishes to invest €500,000 in the fund. The investor is charged a front-loaded fee of 2% and will be given shares at yesterday's NAV per share. The transaction will settle on TD + 3.
2. Henkel goes ex-div today – the dividend is €1.00 per share, the fund has opted to receive its dividend in the form of additional shares in Henkel. These shares will be issued at the closing price of 06/04/X9.
3. 25,000 shares in EoN were purchased at €20.75 per share and commission of €2,000 to settle on TD + 3.
4. €20,000 was paid to the investment manager on account (this had been correctly accrued for).
5. The fund declares a distribution to shareholders of €0.60 per share, ex-date today, payable on TD + 5 (the new shareholder will also receive this distribution). Shareholders holding 100,000 shares have elected to reinvest their distribution. It is the fund's policy to account for reinvested distributions at the NAV per share just prior to the ex-date as adjusted for the distribution.

The daily expenses should be provided for.

Current share prices on 06/04/X9:

- Adidas   €32.30
- BASF   €13.60
- Deutsche Post   €13.60
- Henkel   €29.20
- MAN   €49.10
- EoN   €21.25

Requirements:

Part A (50 marks): record the transactions from the 05/04/X9 and calculate the daily NAV per share (use the template provided; complete the statement of net assets, the statement of operations and the statement of changes in net assets).

Part B (50 marks): record the transactions from the 06/04/X9 and calculate the daily NAV per share (use the template provided; complete the statement of net assets, the statement of operations and the statement of changes in net assets).

Chapter 8

Concluding Comments and Reflections

- Introduction
- Looking back
- Key points of each chapter
- Where to from here
- Conclusion

Learning Outcomes

At the end of this chapter you should:

- Be able to reflect on the previous chapters and appreciate the extent of the learning achieved.
- Be able to isolate the key points of each chapter.
- Be able to put the learning to date in a broader context and determine the next stage in your development as a fund accountant.

8.1: Introduction

The first section of this chapter will address the nature and extent of the learning so far. At times the process can be tortuous but, hopefully, it is evident that a lot of knowledge has been gained. In addition, if this is your first time studying investment fund accounting then you will have acquired some important skills. These will form the basis of any further study that you may decide to undertake in this field.

This chapter will also review the main points of the previous chapters. Knowing the detail and the reasoning behind each transaction is important but sometimes it is helpful to have a quick reference point. Furthermore, it has already been noted that many of the transaction types repeat themselves. Thus, a review of this nature should address a large proportion of the total number of transactions that an equity investment fund engages in.

The last section of this chapter will reflect on the future steps that may need to be taken if you are to develop your knowledge and skills. The knowledge learned to date is an important foundation for the acquisition of future knowledge. Equity investment fund accounting would be considered to be at the lower end of the investment fund accounting complexity scale. If you are considering a career in investment fund accounting, you will need to learn more. In particular, you will need to be able to understand and account for more complex transactions. However, the basic principles learned in this book will provide a solid basis to help you in your future professional development.

8.2: LOOKING BACK

When you are halfway up a mountain, it is only human nature to look up and see that there is a long way to go. At times, this can be dispiriting. However, it can be beneficial to turn around and look down to see just how far you have come.

Acquiring knowledge is a similar process to climbing a mountain, particularly in a technical and specialist area such as investment fund accounting. At times, it may have been a tough slog to get to this point in the book, and there is more to go (see Section 8.4). However, now is a good time to reflect on the distance you have travelled. Consider that, when you began this journey, you may have known little about accounting and even less about investment funds.

At this point you should stop reading for five minutes and write down what you know about accounting and investment funds. Hopefully, the list is extensive. Section 8.3 can be used as a reference, in case you need to jog your memory.

Undoubtedly, there will have been sections in this book where you found it heavy going. Learning something new is not a pain-free activity. It takes effort and time but, hopefully, there is a reward in the ability to view the particular issue with a new clarity. Remember previous learning experiences (think about learning to spell, to perform long division, to drive a car); these were hard at the time but now you can look back and wonder why the act of learning these skills was so difficult. It is exactly the same with investment fund accounting. Once you have been working in the field for a while, you will look back and wonder why you found learning the initial concepts so difficult. You are no different to anyone else, learning something new can be challenging. This is particularly the case if you are trying to achieve a deeper understanding of an issue or transaction.

Sometimes, if you are having problems understanding a concept, a strategy often employed is to rote-learn the point that has caused you to reach an impasse. This is a short-term solution. Many of the concepts in this book will act as a foundation for future studies in investment fund accounting. In order to be able to apply the basic principles, a deep understanding is needed so that you can transfer your existing knowledge to the new transactions that you will be trying to account for. In addition, the real work of a fund accountant begins when errors are made in the processing of transactions. In order to correct any errors, you will rely on the basic principles in this book; this is where your understanding will help you to resolve these problems.

To put into context just how much you have learned, the first topic in Section 1.2.1 of this book was 'What is an investment fund?' At this stage you should be more than comfortable with this concept. Not only should you be able to describe the workings of an investment fund, you can also account for the transactions that an investment fund engages in and calculate the daily NAV per share. Along the way, you should have acquired the knowledge and understanding of many corporate and investor transactions. This includes some relatively complex scenarios: stock dividends, rights issues, equity sales, etc.

Be proud of what you have achieved so far and be confident that you can build on your knowledge to develop your skills even further.

8.3: SUMMARY OF THE MAJOR CHAPTERS

This section summarises the main points of each chapter. It does not consider the rationale behind the transactions; you should refer back to the relevant chapter for this. Furthermore, in the interests of brevity, this section does not review the minor aspects of a chapter.

For many issues in investment fund accounting, the detail is important. It is essential that you are comfortable with the context underlying the transactions. This review will not provide you with the detail or context of a transaction.

Each chapter will be considered in turn. It should be evident that many of the transactions repeat themselves. For example, purchasing an equity position is a frequent event for an investment fund. The basic transaction is recorded the same way every time; the figures will change but the principles are similar. This effect is repeated for many other transactions, to the extent that the summary that follows should address a significant proportion of the transactions that an investment fund engages in.

8.3.1: Chapter 1: Introduction

This chapter introduced the notion of an investment fund and how it works. An investment fund is a mechanism where individuals can pool their money to make investments in shares, bonds, commodities or any other asset. The investments are managed by professional investment managers and investment funds are subject to extensive regulation. The regulations are designed to protect investors; however, they are exposed to some risk as the underlying investments may lose value.

The main reasons why individuals choose to invest through an investment fund is to get the benefit of economies of scale. These economies manifest themselves in a number of ways. Firstly, a basic principle of investing is diversification. However, holding a meaningful diversified portfolio is often not realistic for an individual with limited resources; this can be achieved through an investment fund with a vast number of investors. In addition, professional investment management advice is expensive for an individual to obtain but if the cost is spread across a large number of investors (as in an investment fund) then it becomes much cheaper from the perspective of the individual. A similar situation persists with many of the other costs of investing: brokerage fees, audit costs, administration costs, etc. A further benefit of investing through an investment fund is that it is tax efficient. An individual would not achieve the same level of tax efficiency if they were investing on their own behalf. Finally, investors in an investment fund get the benefit of a well-developed framework of regulatory protections which reduces the possibility of loss through fraud, deception or error.

8.3.2: Chapter 2: Review of Double Entry Bookkeeping

The double entry concept was introduced and developed in this chapter. The double entry system is the approach used to record transactions in an investment fund. The approach in Table 8.1 is used to record transactions.

Table 8.1: A Summary of How to Record Transactions

	Double Entry	Spreadsheet
Step 1	Calculate the figures involved	
Step 2	Determine the accounts involved	
Step 3	Decide which accounts to debit and credit	Decide whether the accounts are increasing or decreasing
Step 4	Complete the 'T' accounts	Complete the spreadsheet
	Repeat steps 1 to 4 until all transactions have been recorded	
Step 5	Balance the accounts	Complete the 'closing' column in the spreadsheet
Step 6	Prepare a trial balance	
Step 7	Prepare the balance sheet	

In order to assign the debit and credit to a transaction the method that is presented in Table 8.2 should help.

Table 8.2: Assigning Debits and Credits

Account Type	To Record	Entry	Side of Account
Asset and expense	An increase	Debit	Left-hand side (LHS)
	A decrease	Credit	Right-hand side (RHS)
Liability, capital and income	An increase	Credit	Right-hand side (RHS)
	A decrease	Debit	Left-hand side (LHS)

Chapter 2 also saw the introduction of the spreadsheet approach as a method of recording transactions. This was expanded on significantly as the book progressed. Finally, the individual financial statements were discussed: the statement of net assets, the statement of operations and the statement of changes in net assets.

8.3.3: Chapter 3: Financial Statements of an Investment Fund

The unique nature of the financial statements of an investment fund was explored in this chapter. This was initially done through a live example using the Sprott Canadian Equity Fund and then expanded to a generic format (the template fund). This template fund was then developed further for use within the spreadsheet approach that was employed extensively throughout this text. A glossary of the terminology used was also presented. See Table 3.4 for a detailed explanation of the template fund.

8.3.4: Chapter 4: Fund Shares/Capital Stock

This is the first of the transaction-based chapters, where the accounting implications of transactions with the investors in an investment fund were considered. The most common transactions involving investors are when they invest into the fund (subscriptions), withdraw from the fund (redemptions) or receive an income from the fund (distributions). The accounting entries are reproduced below but, more importantly, try to understand how the debit and credit is assigned to the various accounts.

Accounting for a Subscription

On the trade date:

- Dr fund shares sold receivable.
- Cr proceeds from fund shares sold.
- Increase the number of shares in the fund.

On the settlement date:

- Dr cash.
- Cr fund shares sold receivable.

Accounting for a Redemption

On the trade date:

- Dr redemption of units.
- Cr fund shares redeemed payable.
- Decrease the number of shares in the fund.

On the settlement date:

- Dr fund shares redeemed payable.
- Cr cash.

Accounting for a Distribution

On the ex-date:

- Dr distributions to investors.
- Cr distributions payable.

On the payment date:

- Dr distributions payable.
- Cr cash.

8.3.5: Chapter 5: Accounting for Equities

Investments are the key driver of investment fund value. In this chapter, the accounting for the equity investments of an investment fund was described. To value an investment portfolio that is made up of equities, the fund accountant has to determine the current market price for the shares multiplied by the number of shares held. This is normally a straightforward procedure as most equities can be valued using the official published information from the appropriate stock markets. However, from time to time issues do arise. These tend to be related to circumstances where there is thin trading or some other trading restrictions in the market. Valuation becomes a more difficult exercise in these situations.

Accounting for transactions in equities can be divided into three core areas:

1. Accounting for the purchase of equities.
2. Accounting for the sale of equities.
3. Accounting for the daily valuation/price movements.

Recording the Purchase of Equities

- Calculate the cost (cost of equities + commission).
- Record transaction and settlement as two separate transactions.

On the trade date record the purchase of the equities:

- Dr investments at cost.
- Cr investments purchased payable.

On the settlement date record the payment:

- Dr investments purchased payable.
- Cr cash.

Recording the Sale of Equities

- Calculate the net proceeds (proceeds of sale of equities − commission).
- Identify the shares sold.
- Calculate the cost of the shares sold.
- Calculate the gain/loss on the shares sold.
- Record the transaction and the settlement as two separate transactions.

On the trade date – selling equities where gains are being realised (X (proceeds) = Y (cost) + Z (gain)):

- Dr investments sold receivable   €X
- Cr investments at cost   €Y
- Cr unrealised appreciation/depreciation   €Z

On the trade date – selling equities where losses are being realised (X (proceeds) = Y (cost) − Z (loss)):

- Dr investments sold receivable   €X
- Cr investments at cost   €Y
- Dr unrealised appreciation/depreciation   €Z

On the settlement date record the receipt:

- Dr cash   €X
- Cr investments sold receivable   €X

Recording the Daily Valuation

- Calculate the amount of the movement in the unrealised appreciation/depreciation account using the approach given in Table 8.3.

Table 8.3: Approach for Calculating the Daily Gain/Loss (Unrealised Appreciation/Depreciation)

Market Value of the Portfolio (today) – Step 1		€A
Less Cost of the Portfolio (today) – Step 2		–€B
Total Unrealised Appreciation/Depreciation – Step 2		€C
Less Unrealised Appreciation/Depreciation from Yesterday – Step 3	D	
+/– Movements in Unrealised Appreciation/Depreciation – Step 3	E	–€F
Unrealised Appreciation/Depreciation for today – Step 3		€G

Recording the unrealised appreciation/depreciation:

- If the value of the portfolio is increasing:
  - dr unrealised appreciation/depreciation   €G
  - cr gains/losses on investments   €G
- If the value of the portfolio is decreasing:
  - dr gains/losses on investments   €G
  - cr unrealised appreciation/depreciation   €G

This is a complex calculation. The most effective method of studying this is to practice the examples and questions in Chapter 5 and subsequent chapters. Try to develop an understanding of the rationale behind the calculation as this will also make it easier.

8.3.6: Chapter 6: Accounting for Corporate Actions

Chapter 6 is a direct follow-on from Chapter 5. In this chapter the accounting implications of some of the more complex equity-based transactions are addressed. A corporate action is 'an event in the life of an equity, instigated by the company, which effects the position in that equity.'[1] This definition describes

---

[1]   Simmons and Dalgleish (2006), p. 3.

events such as dividends, share buy backs, bonus issues and rights issues (this is not an exhaustive list).

Dividends are the most common of the corporate actions. The accounting for dividends broadly falls into two categories:

1. The fund takes the dividend in cash.
2. The fund takes the dividend in additional shares in the company.

The Fund Takes the Dividend in Cash

Calculating the dividend: number of shares owned × dividend rate per share
  On the ex-dividend date record the following:

- Dr dividends receivable.
- Cr dividend income.

On the payment date record the following:

- Dr cash.
- Cr dividends receivable.

The Fund Takes the Dividend in Additional Shares in the Company

This can be a complex set of transactions but if it is broken into its components, it is easier to process.

1. The fund receives a dividend (record as if a normal dividend):
   - dr dividends receivable
   - cr dividend income

2. The fund effectively uses the dividend to buy equities (record as if a normal purchase of equities):
   - dr investments at cost
   - cr investments purchased payable

3. The fund receives the equities (offset the receivable with the payable):
   - dr investments purchased payable
   - cr dividends receivable

8.3.7: Chapter 7: Accounting for Fund Expenses

Chapter 7 considered the controversial issue of investment fund expenses. Fortunately, the accounting for these expenses is less contentious. There are four broad categories of fund expenses:

1. Flat fees (where the size of the fee is not related to the performance of the fund)
2. Fees based on a percentage of the net assets of the fund
3. Performance-based fees (where the fees depend on a measure of the performance of the fund)
4. Combination fees (a combination of the previous three types)

The usual procedure in relation to fund expenses is to accrue them on a daily basis (for funds that issue a daily NAV per share). The fees are then paid periodically. Accounting for the daily expense accrual (for funds that issue a daily NAV per share):

- Dr the expense item.
- Cr accrued expenses.

Accounting for the payment of expenses:

- Cr bank/cash account.
- Dr accrued expenses.

8.4: WHERE TO FROM HERE?

This book is an introductory text in equity investment fund accounting. The nature of the word 'introductory' inevitably means that there is more to come. In this regard what to do now can be divided into two categories: applying the knowledge you have learned and acquiring future knowledge.

8.4.1: Applying Knowledge

Your first task will be to take the knowledge that you have acquired in this book and apply it to the processes and systems of your own organisation. [2]

---

[2] If you are still in full-time education, then this stage will have to wait until you go into the workplace. In the interim, you can help your development in a number of ways. You should practice the questions at the end of each chapter. You should consider taking other follow-on modules that are offered as part of your programme of study. If there are no follow-on programmes, then try to select related modules on finance, audit or

Typically, a fund administration company develops its own approach to help it manage the vast quantity of transactions that pass through the investment funds they process. Information technology is employed extensively and many of the systems are propriety.[3] However, behind the technology is the logic and methodology that has been described in this book. At times, it can be difficult to see beyond the input screen but the computer is performing the same tasks, using the same approach. Obtaining an appreciation of how the systems in your organisation operate should be a priority – this text will help by providing the basic principles behind the recording of many of the standard fund transactions. Understanding the system in operation will also prove invaluable when errors, mistakes and misclassifications have to be indentified and corrected.

Some of the transactions in this book have been simplified for illustrative purposes. However, often in the investment fund industry the detail is important. Behind many of the transactions described in this book are vast quantities of information. For example, a rights issue by a company triggers a series of events and information flows. The final outcome will be dependent on a number of factors and decisions taken. To describe the rights issue process in its full detail would result in the basic principles being lost in the fog of detail. Now that you know the basic principles behind many of the investment fund transactions, you should try to apply your understanding to real events as they are processed and tracked in your organisation. This exercise should be made easier by the knowledge that you have already gained.

8.4.2: Acquiring Knowledge

This text considered an equity investment fund. There are a number of other directions that you can now take as part of your continuing development in this discipline. Each of these gives rise to their own idiosyncrasies and accounting implications.

Accounting for Other Investment Products

A logical direction is to consider how other investments purchased by funds are accounted for. The more common investment products are bond instruments

---

financial reporting, for example. Finally, try to follow the financial press to get an appreciation of current events and their impact on the industry. The (London) *Financial Times (FT)* is an excellent source of information, analysis and comment. Some free content is available on www.ft.com. The *FT* also provides special promotional rates for students.

[3] A propriety system is one that has been developed in-house by an organisation, only for the use of that particular organisation.

(both corporate and sovereign), money market instruments and derivatives. This is not an exhaustive list and within each of the categories listed above are numerous subcategories. There are a vast number of different investment products, each with their own unique features that give rise to interesting and complex accounting implications.

Accounting for Different Fund Structures

Without much discussion, this book concentrated on variable capital investment funds. There are a number of other mechanisms that can be used to establish an investment fund. For example, a fixed capital investment fund has a different legal structure and, consequently, this gives rise to some accounting issues. Also, the growth of hedge funds has been a feature of the industry over the past two decades. This method of structuring and operating a fund does give rise to a variety of accounting implications. There are also other structures which can be used to establish a fund; depending on the mechanism used there may be accounting repercussions.

Furthermore, as noted in Section 4.10, many funds offer investors the option of different share classes. The rights of each class can vary depending on the rules of the fund. The accounting for the different share classes will be determined by the rights attached to the shares. This is also an area for future study.

Investment Fund Audit, Control and Governance

Beyond the pure accounting for investment funds, there is the related discipline of the audit and control of investment funds. Ensuring that there are robust systems in place to prevent errors, misstatements and fraud is an ongoing activity. An understanding of audit and control cannot be achieved without considering the governance of investment funds. Effective audit and control is one of the outputs of good governance. The governance of an investment fund articulates how the fund is directed. In view of some of the recent investment fund failures, the governance of investment funds has come under renewed scrutiny.

Investment Fund Reporting

Investment fund reporting describes the formal report that is sent to the investors in the fund. The structure of the report, the frequency of reporting and the information to be included is determined by a variety of regulations. As a consequence there can be variations across different jurisdictions. Often these variations are small but in order to comply with the regulations of a particular country it is important that they are adhered to. This book did not consider this issue.

Investment Fund Regulations

Throughout this text some of the regulations that apply to investment funds were alluded to. These are extensive and come from many different sources. Furthermore, they can differ across countries and tend to change from time to time. Knowledge of the regulatory regime is essential if you are considering a longer-term career in the industry.

Investment Fund Role and Failings

If you would like to broaden your knowledge beyond accounting and related areas then this is an area worth investigating further. It is outside the narrow accounting focus of this book but it does put the industry in context. Issues that can be addressed include the role that investment funds play in the capital markets and an evaluation of the efficiency of that role. This could then be expanded to consider the criticisms of the investment fund industry.

The investment fund industry has undergone significant changes over the past two decades. New fund structures have emerged (hedge funds, for example) and new investment products have been developed (credit default swaps, for example). Added to this mix is the impact of changes in technology (the internet and electronic trading, for example). Finally, there are ongoing regulatory and legal changes that impact on how the industry should conduct itself.

All of these new advances place considerable pressure on those involved in the industry. There is a clear requirement on fund professionals to continue to develop their skill set to ensure that they remain at the forefront of their discipline. This inevitably impacts on the fund accountant. Indeed, the work of the fund accountant today is very different from his or her counterpart of the late twentieth century. Continuing professional development (CPD) should be a personal priority for anyone considering a long-term career in the industry.

Even after many years of experience there will still be a need to develop and change. In the coming decades there will be more changes. You will need to evaluate how these changes will impact on your work and plan your development accordingly.

Acquiring knowledge and learning never ceases.

8.5: CONCLUSION

Reflection was a key theme of this chapter. It began with a look back to consider the knowledge gained. Hopefully, after some thought, you will conclude that significant learning has been achieved. This was followed by a review of the key points of each chapter, which should act as a handy reference point. Finally, your future learning needs were considered and some areas for further development were set out.

Further Reading and References

INVESTMENT FUNDS

If you would like to review the financial statements of an investment fund, then a good place to start is the websites of the various investment fund providers. On these websites you will also get information on fund prices, marketing documentation, fund prospectuses and fee information for all the investment fund types offered. Often the breadth of funds available and the depth of information online can be overwhelming. These websites tend to be straightforward to navigate. Many of these websites were referred to within this book.

www.americanfunds.com – the official website of American Funds
www.irishlife.ie – the website of Irish Life (part of Irish Life and Permanent Plc)
www.jpmorganfunds.com – the website of the investment fund division of JP Morgan
www.legalandgeneral.com – the website of Legal & General
www.sprott.com – the website of Sprott Asset Management; it was one of the Sprott funds (Sprott Canadian Equity) that was used for illustrative purposes within this text.
www.ther.com – the website of The Reserve; The Reserve Primary Fund was one of the high-profile casualties of the credit crunch in September 2008.
www.troweprice.com – the website of T. Rowe Price
www.vanguard.com – the website of the Vanguard Group

FINANCIAL ACCOUNTING REFERENCES

If you are struggling with financial accounting concepts (debits, credits and the double entry system) then the following list of resources should help. Please note that there are numerous introductory financial accounting text books on the market. They are all broadly similar so only a small sample is included here.

Benedict, A. and Elliot, B. (2008), *Financial Accounting: An Introduction*, First Edition, Harlow: FT Prentice Hall.

Thomas, A. and Ward, A. (2009), *An Introduction to Financial Accounting*, Sixth Edition, Maidenhead: McGraw Hill.

Wood, F. and Sangster, R. (2007), *Business Accounting*, Volume 1, Tenth Edition, Harlow: FT Prentice Hall – one of the standard introductory textbooks in accounting.

Wood, F. and Sangster, R. (2007), *Business Accounting*, Volume 2, Tenth Edition, Harlow: FT Prentice Hall – the follow-on book from Volume 1.

TERMINOLOGY AND JARGON

If you are having difficulty understanding the terminology or the investment products within this book then the following websites are excellent places to start.

www.investopedia.com – this website has a huge dictionary facility, even the most obscure financial terms are included. The website also has an extensive library of articles and a bank of tutorials that explain financial terminology and practices in precise detail.

www.wikipedia.org – the usual caveats apply when using Wikipedia as a source for information and knowledge. However, if you are researching something, it is often a good starting point. You should not, however, rely on Wikipedia for your information and you will need to delve deeper in order to get reliable facts and data. See Wikipedia's own disclaimer page for the limitations on the use of Wikipedia, http://en.wikipedia.org/wiki/Wikipedia:General_disclaimer. If you use Wikipedia then it is a good idea to have a look at some of the websites that query the use of Wikipedia. Make up your own mind but Wikipedia is not considered an appropriate source for research by many academics.

REGULATION REFERENCES

If you are interested in regulation, then the following websites and articles may be of assistance.

Deloitte (2008), 'IFRS for Investment Funds: More Than Just Accounting and Reporting', available on www.iasplus.com/usa/0812investmentfunds.pdf, accessed on 10 May 2010 – a Deloitte produced report on the likely changes to investment fund reporting.

International Accounting Standards Board (IASB) (2010), *International Financial Reporting Standards 2010*, London: IASB – for the source material of all the extant accounting standards; special student promotional prices available on www.iasb.org.

www.financialregulator.ie/industry-sectors/funds – this is the area of the Irish Financial Regulator's website that relates to the funds sector in Ireland. Here you will get information on the overall size of the investment fund sector in Ireland along with the regulatory provisions.

www.fsa.gov.uk – this is the website of the UK Financial Services Regulator. Take a look at the FSA Handbook section of the website for the regulations pertaining to fund managers.

www.irishstatuebook.ie – this website gives the source in full of every parliamentary Act and Statutory Instrument (SI) in Irish law. Some Acts and SIs refer specifically to aspects of investment funds, for example, SI 213 of 2003, European Communities (Undertakings for Collective Investment in Transferrable Securities) Regulations 2003, available on www.irishstatutebook.ie/2003/en/si/0211.html, accessed 17 May 2010.

www.ise.ie/index.asp?locID=7&docID=-1 – this is the funds section on the website of the Irish Stock Exchange (ISE). Over 3,300 funds are listed on the Irish Stock Exchange. This website sets out the listing requirements for ISE-listed funds. See Irish Stock Exchange (2010), 'Code of Listing Requirements and Procedures for Investment Funds', available from www.ise.ie/index.asp?locID=85&docID=-1, accessed on 10 May 2010.

www.sec.gov – the website of the US Securities and Exchange Commission, the US regulator.

INVESTING TECHNIQUES AND THEORIES

If you are interested in articles, books or websites on investing techniques and theories then the following may be of some help. This list is not exhaustive as there are numerous books on this topic, but a number of different views are presented.

Chatfeild-Roberts, J. (2006), *Fundology: The Secrets of Successful Fund Investing*, Petersfield: Harriman House.

Fuhr, D. (2001), 'Exchange Traded Funds: A Primer', *Journal of Asset Management*, Vol. 2, No. 3, pp. 260–273.

Ibbotson, R. and Chen, P. (2003), 'Long-Run Stock Returns: Participating in the Real Economy', *Financial Analysts Journal*, Vol. 59, No. 1, pp. 88–98.

Lo, A. and MacKinlay, C. (2002), *A Non-Random Walk Down Wall Street*, Princeton, NJ: Princeton University Press.

Malkiel, B. (1995), 'Returns from Investing in Equity Mutual Funds 1971–1991', *Journal of Finance*, Vol. 50, No. 2, pp. 549–572.

Malkiel, B. (2007), *A Random Walk Down Wall Street*, Ninth Edition, New York, NY; London: W.W. Norton.

Singal, V. (2006), *Beyond the Random Walk*, Oxford: Oxford University Press.

www.socialinvest.org – this is the website of the Social Investment Forum. It contains a lot of research and investment tools on a growing approach to investment. The Social Investment Forum promotes investment using environmental, social and governance criteria.

MISCELLANEOUS

Bhargava, R. and Dubofsky, D. (2001), 'A Note on the Fair Value Pricing of Mutual Funds', *Journal of Banking and Finance*, Feb, Vol. 25, No. 2, pp. 339–354.

Chalmers, J., Edelen, R. and Kadlec, B. (2001), 'On the Perils of Financial Intermediaries Setting Prices: The Mutual Fund Wild Card Option', *Journal of Finance*, Vol. 56, No. 6, pp. 2209–2236.

Gremillion, L. (2005), *Mutual Fund Industry Handbook: A Comprehensive Guide for Investment Professionals*, Hoboken, NJ: John Wiley & Sons.

Simmons, M. and Dalgleish, E. (2006), *Corporate Actions: A Guide to Securities Event Management*, Chichester: John Wiley & Sons – a comprehensive book on the operational processing of corporate actions.

banker.thomsonib.com – Thomson ONE Investment Banking website, commonly referred to as ONE Banker. It is a vast database that has information on companies, historic share prices, financial statements, ownership structures, etc. and is only available on a subscription basis. ONE Banker can also include access to Datastream and other databases, depending on the subscription obtained.

www.adr.com – a JP Morgan website that has a wealth of information on depository receipts (ADRs and GDRs).

www.euronext.com – the official website of NYSE Euronext, a global financial marketplace. NYSE Euronext includes the New York Stock Exchange (NYSE) in America; the Paris, Brussels and Amsterdam Exchanges in Europe and the London International Financial Futures and Options Exchange (LIFFE).

www.ifsl.org.uk – this is the website of International Financial Services London, a body that promotes London as a financial services centre. IFSL produce a number of research reports on the investment fund sector which have useful statistics and activity information.

www.iifa.ca – the website of the International Investment Fund Association; their role is 'to promote the protection of investment fund investors, to facilitate the growth of the investment funds industry internationally, to act as a medium for the advancement of understanding of the investment fund business around the world, and to encourage adherence to high ethical standards by all participants in the industry' (International Investment Fund Association homepage).

www.irishfunds.ie – the website of the Irish Funds Industry Association (IFIA), which is the representative body of the international investment funds community in Ireland, representing the custodian banks, administrators, managers, transfer agents and professional advisory firms involved in the international fund services industry in Ireland.

www.ise.ie – the official website of the Irish Stock Exchange

www.londonstockexchange.com – the official website of the London Stock Exchange

www.marketwatch.com – a useful website for stock prices (there are numerous others)

www.morningstar.com – one of the leading websites giving information on mutual funds; some information is freely available but full access will involve a subscription.

www.quotes-plus.com – a pricing service that includes a vast number of US mutual funds and also includes information on the distribution histories of funds; requires a subscription but a free two-week trial is available.

LIST OF SOURCES REFERENCED IN THE BOOK

3i Group, www.3igroup.com
ADR.com, www.adr.com
American Funds, www.americanfunds.com
Bank of Ireland, www.boi.ie
Berkshire Hathaway, www.berkshirehathaway.com
British Energy, www.british-energy.com
British Land, www.britishland.com
Companies Registration Office, www.cro.ie
Financial Times, www.ft.com
Forbes, www.forbes.com
Goodbody Stockbrokers, www.goodbody.ie/products/costs.html
Honeywell International, www.honeywell.com
Investopedia, www.investopedia.com
Investopedia Financial Dictionary, www.investopedia.com/dictionary/default.asp
Irish Financial Services Regulatory Authority, www.ifsra.ie
Irish Stock Exchange, www.ise.ie
Janus Capital Group, www.janus.com
JP Morgan Funds, www.jpmorganfunds.com
Market Watch, www.marketwatch.com
Microsoft, www.microsoft.com/msft/
MSCI Emerging Markets Index, www.mscibarra.com/products/indices/equity/em.html

OwnaRaceHorse.co.uk, www.ownaracehorse.co.uk

Santander, www.santander.com

Shell, www.shell.com

Social Investment Forum, www.socialinvest.org

Sprott Asset Management, www.sprott.com

T. Rowe Price, www.troweprice.com

UK National Lottery syndicate guidelines, www.national-lottery.co.uk/player/p/help/syndicates.ftl

Vanguard Group, www.vanguard.com

Volkswagen, www.volkswagenag.com

Yahoo Finance, www.yahoofinance.com

3i (2008), 'Annual Report for Year Ended 31 March 2008', available from: www.3i.com, accessed 1 December 2009.

Atkinson, J. (2004), 'The Mutual Fund Industry Scandal and What Is Being Done to Correct It', unpublished article, *Jimmyatkinson.com*, 22 April 2004, available from: www.jimmyatkinson.com/papers/fundscandal.html, accessed 28 June 2010.

Berkshire Hathaway (2009), 'Berkshire Hathaway Inc.: 2008 Annual Report', available from: www.berkshirehathaway.com/2008ar/2008ar.pdf, accessed 28 June 2010.

Bridges Investment Fund (2005), 'Annual Report for the Year Ending 31 December 2004', available from: www.secinfo.com/d14SU9.zz.htm, accessed 28 June 2010.

British Energy (2005), 'British Energy Group Report and Accounts for the Period Ended 31 March 2005: Improvement Through Investment 04–05', available from: http://british–energy.com/documents/BE_annual_report_2005.pdf, accessed 28 June 2010.

British Land (2009), 'The British Land Company PLC – Beyond Buildings: Annual Report and Accounts 2008', available from: www.britishland.com/documents/pdfs/BLND-Annual-Report-2008.pdf, accessed 28 June 2010.

DBS Absolute Return Fund (2008), 'Prospectus, Dated 14 October 2008: DBS Absolute Return Fund', available from: www.dbsam.com/resource/funds/prospectus/fund/Pages/Prospectus_Darf.pdf?hasRedirected=true, accessed 28 June 2010.

DeCarlo, S. and Chamberlain, J. (eds.) (2010), 'The 2010 Mutual Fund Survey', *Forbes*, available from: www.forbes.com/2010/01/20/mutual–funds–performance–grades–mutual–funds–2010–personal–finance_land.html?boxes=custom, accessed on 10 May 2010.

Deloitte (2008), 'IFRS for Investment Funds: More Than Just Accounting and Reporting', available from: www.iasplus.com/usa/0812investmentfunds.pdf, accessed on 10 May 2010.

Dobozs, J. (2005), 'Buybacks versus Dividends: Who's Better?', *Forbes*, 29 April 2005.

Emmett, S. (2009), 'The Spanish Property Could Fall by up to 40%', *The* (London) *Times*, 19 January 2009.

Growth Fund of America (2009a), 'The Growth Fund of America Prospectus, November 1, 2009', available from: www.americanfunds.com/pdf/mfgepr-905_gfap.pdf, accessed 28 June 2010.

Growth Fund of America (2009b), 'The Growth Fund of America: How GFA's Multiple Portfolio Counselor System Fared in a Difficult Market – Annual Report for the Year Ended August 31, 2009', available from: www.americanfunds.com/pdf/mfgear-905_gfaa.pdf, accessed 28 June 2010.

Ibbotson, R. and Chen, P. (2003), 'Long-Run Stock Returns: Participating in the Real Economy', *Financial Analysts Journal*, Vol. 59, No. 1, pp. 88–98.

Income Fund of America (2009a), 'The Income Fund of America Prospectus, October 1, 2009', available from: www.americanfunds.com/pdf/mfgepr-906_ifap.pdf, accessed 28 June 2010.

Income Fund of America (2009b), 'The Income Fund of America: Positioned for the Future – Annual Report for the Year Ended July 31, 2009', available from: www.americanfunds.com/pdf/mfgear-906_ifaa.pdf, accessed 28 June 2010.

International Accounting Standards Board (2001), *Framework for the Preparation and Presentation of Financial Statements*, London: IASB.

International Accounting Standards Board (2008a), *International Accounting Standard 1: Presentation of Financial Statements*, London: IASB.

International Accounting Standards Board (2008b), *International Accounting Standard 8: Accounting Policies, Changes in Accounting Estimates and Errors*, London: IASB.

International Accounting Standards Board (2009a), *International Accounting Standard 32: Financial Instruments – Presentation*, London: IASB.

International Accounting Standards Board (2009b), *International Accounting Standard 1: Presentation of Financial Statements*, London: IASB.

Irish Life (2008), 'Select: Investments to Suit You', April 2008, available from: www.irishlife.ie/uploadedFiles/Investments/select(2).pdf, accessed 28 June 2010.

Irish Stock Exchange (2008), 'Irish Stock Exchange Monthly Report February 2008', available from: www.ise.ie/uploadedfiles/Monthly_Reports/Monthly_Reports_2008/feb08.pdf, accessed 28 June 2010.

Irish Stock Exchange (2009), 'Irish Stock Exchange Monthly Report June 2009', available from: www.ise.ie/index.asp?locID=586&docID=-1, accessed 28 June 2010.

Janus Equity Funds (2009), Prospectuses, available from: https://ww3.janus.com/
Janus/Retail/StaticPage?jsp=jsp/Funds/Prospectus/ProspAnnRpts.jsp&wt.
svl=ProspectusAnnualReports_Top_nav, accessed 28 June 2010.

J.P. Morgan Prime Money Market Fund (2009), 'Annual Report, J.P. Morgan
Money Market Funds: February 28, 2009', available from: www.jpmorgan
funds.com, accessed 1 December 2009.

Legal & General UK Index Trust (2007), 'Annual Managers' Report for the Year
Ended 6 October 2007', available from: www.legalandgeneral.com/investments/
managers-reports/annual-reports/Long/UK_Index_long.pdf, accessed 1 September 2009.

Macquarie Group (2007), 'Macquarie Group Limited, ACN 122 169 279: Summary
of the Dividend Reinvestment Plan for Ordinary Shareholders DRP', available
from: www.macquarie.com.au/au/about_macquarie/acrobat/drp_summary_
Aug07.pdf, accessed 28 June 2010.

Malkiel, B. (1995), 'Returns from Investing in Equity Mutual Funds 1971–1991',
Journal of Finance, Vol. 50, No. 2, pp. 549–572.

Malkiel, B. (2007), *A Random Walk Down Wall Street*, Ninth Edition, New York, NY;
London: W. W. Norton.

Reserve Primary Fund, The (2007), 'Primary Fund of The Reserve Fund, Prospectus,
September 28, 2007', available from: www.ther.com/pdfs/rsvPGTprospectus.
pdf, accessed 28 June 2010.

Reserve Primary Fund, The (2008), 'The Reserve: Annual Report, May 31, 2008',
available from: www.ther.com/pdfs/pgtannual.pdf, accessed 28 June 2010.

Ross, S. (2007a), 'Thumbs Down to Mr Hobbs', *Sunday Independent*, 23 September
2007.

Ross, S. (2007b), 'Eddie Hobbs hits Homer', *Sunday Independent*, 7 October 2007.

Simmons, M. and Dalgleish, E. (2006), *Corporate Actions: A Guide to Securities Event
Management*, Chichester: Wiley & Sons.

Sprott Canadian Equity Fund (2005), 'Sprott Asset Management Inc., Sprott Canadian
Equity Fund: Annual Report 2004', available from: www.sprott.com/docs/
FinancialReports/Reports/Annual/2004_EN.pdf, accessed 28 June 2010.

Sprott Canadian Equity Fund (2008), 'Sprott Canadian Equity Fund: Annual
Management Report of Fund Performance 2007', available from: www.sprott.
com/docs/FinancialReports/Mgmt_Report/2007Dec_CEq_EN.pdf,
accessed 28 June 2010.

Stocks A. (1994), 'The Ins and Outs of Incentive Fees', *Hedge Fund News*, August
1994, available from: www.hedgefundnews.com/news_n_info/article_detail.
php?id=267, accessed on 11 May 2010.

ThisMatter.com, (2005), 'Mutual Fund Fees and Expenses', available from: this
matter.com/money/Mutual-Funds/Mutual-Fund-Fees-Expenses.htm,
accessed 28 June 2010.

T. Rowe Price (2008), 'T. Rowe Price Equity Income Fund Annual Report for Year Ended 31 May 2008', available from: www.troweprice.com, accessed 1 December 2009.

US Securities and Exchange Commission (2007), 'Mutual Fund Fees and Expenses', modified 08 August 2007, available from: www.sec.gov/answers/mffees.htm, accessed 28 June 2010.

Vanguard 500 Index Fund (2008), 'Vanguard 500 Index Fund: Annual Report, December 31, 2007', available from: https://personal.vanguard.com/us/LiteratureRequest?FW_Activity=ViewOnlineActivity&litID=2210024409&FW_Event=start, accessed 1 December 2009.

Vanguard High-Yield Corporate Fund (2009), 'Vanguard Corporate Bond Funds: Annual Report, January 31, 2009', available from www.vanguard.com, accessed 1 December 2009.

Vanguard International Stock Index Funds (2009), 'Vanguard Total International Stock Index Fund Prospectus, February 2009', available from: www.vanguard.com, accessed 1 December 2009.

Weiss, M. (2007), 'Stop Paying High Mutual Fund Fees', *Investopedia*, available from: www.investopedia.com/articles/mutualfund/07/stop_fees.asp, accessed on 11 May 2010.

Index